PANINI:

HIS PLACE IN SANSKRIT LITERATURE

PANINI:

HIS PLACE IN SANSKRIT LITERATURE

AN INVESTIGATION

OF SOME

LITERARY AND CHRONOLOGICAL QUESTIONS

WHICH MAY BE SETTLED BY A STUDY OF HIS WORK.

THEODOR GOLDSTUCKER.

GYAN

Published by

GYAN

Gyan Publishing House
5, Ansari Road
Daryaganj, New Delhi-110002
Phone: 011-47034999, 9811692060
E-mail: books@gyanbooks.com

Distribution Network
gyanbooks.com
India, USA, Canada, UK, Australia, France

ISBN : 978-81-212-9466-9 (PB)
First Published, 1861

2nd Impression 2023

Printed at: Gyan Press, Delhi.

PANINI: HIS PLACE IN SANSKRIT LITERATURE
Author: THEODOR GOLDSTUCKER

PÁNINI:

HIS PLACE IN SANSKRIT LITERATURE.

PÁṆINI:

HIS PLACE IN SANSKRIT LITERATURE

AN INVESTIGATION

OF SOME

LITERARY AND CHRONOLOGICAL QUESTIONS

WHICH MAY BE SETTLED BY A STUDY OF HIS WORK.

A SEPARATE IMPRESSION OF THE PREFACE TO THE FAC-SIMILE OF MS. NO. 17 IN THE LIBRARY OF HER MAJESTY'S HOME GOVERNMENT FOR INDIA, WHICH CONTAINS A PORTION OF THE MÁNAVA-KALPA-SÚTRA WITH THE COMMENTARY OF KUMÁRILA-SWÁMIN.

BY

THEODOR GOLDSTÜCKER.

LONDON:
N. TRÜBNER AND CO., 60, PATERNOSTER ROW.
BERLIN:
A. ASHER AND CO.,
(ALBERT COHN AND DANIEL COLLIN.)

MDCCCLXI.

TO

RUDOLF VIRCHOW,

THE GREAT DISCOVERER AND DEFENDER OF SCIENTIFIC TRUTH

THIS BOOK IS INSCRIBED

AS A TESTIMONY OF RESPECT AND ADMIRATION,

BY HIS AFFECTIONATE FRIEND,

THEODOR GOLDSTÜCKER

The present pages form the Preface to the Fac-simile of the Mánava-Kalpa-Sútra, as mentioned on the title-page. The separate impression has been taken at the suggestion of my publishers and other friends, who thought that it would be desirable to make their contents more easy of access than they are in the original work.

This circumstance will explain the apparent incongruity of presenting them without the Manuscript which they describe.

University College, London,
November 2, 1860.

TABLE OF CONTENTS.

PAGE

The Original Manuscript of the Fac-simile 1

The Fac-simile traced by Miss Amelia Rattenbury 3

Contents of the Manuscript 4

Contents of another Manuscript of the Mánava-Kalpa-Sútra 7

The Commentary of Kumárila 8

Connection between the Kalpa-Sútras of the Taittiriya-Samhitá and the Mímánsá........ 9

Author of the Mánava-Kalpa-Sútra........ 10

Date of this work 12

Literary and Chronological Questions concerning every work of the Vaidik Literature, and therefore bearing on the present Ritual Book 13

Professor Müller holds that the art of writing was not yet known in India when Páṇini lived, or according to him, about 350 B.C.; and that there is not a single word in Páṇini's terminology which presupposes his knowledge of writing........ *ib.*

Refutation of this View .... 15—67

The Civilization of India as depicted in the Ṛigveda 15

Yavanání, probably the cuneiform writing, was known to Páṇini 16

Páṇini mentions the word *lipikara*, "a writer" 17

Paṭala, the name of a division of Sanskrit works, is a further proof that writing was known in ancient India 19

A further proof is derived from the words *káṇḍa* and *pattra*, *sútra* and *grantha* 20

Definition of the word *Sútra* 21

Note.—Objection to the promiscuous use made in Professor Müller's quotations, of the Sútras of Páṇini and the commentaries on them. Objection to his statement concerning the instances to Páṇini's Grammar 22

Probable origin of the Sútra Literature 25

Oscillations of Professor Weber caused by the word *grantha*. Doubts of Professor Müller concerning the occurrence of this word in Páṇini. Meaning of this word 27

Note.—The nursery book *Śiśukrandíya* is considered by Professor Weber to be an epic poem and a forerunner of the Rámáyaṇa 28

Needlessness of the doubts of Professor Müller in reference to the word *grantha*........ 29

Note.—Critical means of ascertaining whether a Sútra of Páṇini be genuine or not. Uncritical assertions made by Dr. Boehtlingk on this subject, in his reprint of the Calcutta edition of Páṇini. Only three or four Sútras out of 3996 do not belong to Páṇini .... *ib.*

PAGE

The meaning of *grantha* in a passage from the Mahábhárata 31

Note.—On the names of the leading characters in this poem, as occurring in the Sútras of, and the commentaries on, Páṇini 32

The phrase *granthato 'rthataścha*, compared with *káṇḍa* and *padártha* 33

Professors Müller and Weber assume that the word *varṇa* does not mean a written letter.—*Refutation of this view* .... 34—43

Varṇa and *kára* mean a letter of the alphabet 35

Use of the two words in the works of Páṇini, Kátyáyana and Patanjali 36

Note—And in the Káśiká, etc. 37

Difference between the two words .... *ib.*

Difference between *varṇa* and *karaṇa* 39

The meaning of *upadeśa* 40

Difference between *varṇa*, *kára*, *karaṇa* and *akshara* 42

The word *udaya* is a further proof that Páṇini was acquainted with writing 44

A further proof results from his technical terms *swaritet* and *anudáttet*, and from the word *swarita* in Páṇini's rule I. 3, 11 45

An unhappy reference of Professor Weber .... *ib.*

Note.—An insight into the character of Dr. Boehtlingk's "*edition*" of Páṇini. An extraordinary explanation given by him, of the Sútra I. 3, 11 46

Kátyáyana, Patanjali and Kaiyyaṭa on Sútra I. 3, 11 47

The commentary of these grammarians proves that Páṇini's manner of defining an *adhikára* would have been impossible without writing 52

Written accents were indispensable for Páṇini's terminology 54

Note.—On the incorrect spelling of the word *uṇádi* .... *ib.*

This results from the Dhátupáṭha 55

Note.—On the pronunciation of the vowel *ă* 57

Even the habit of marking Hindu cattle affords proof of the acquaintance of the Hindus, in the time of Páṇini, with the art of writing 59

The words *lopa* and *dṛiś*, in the Sútras, are a further proof that Páṇini had a knowledge of writing 60

The Vedas were preserved in writing at Páṇini's time 61

Note.—A passage, relating to the mystical powers of the alphabet, from a Chapter of a Dialogue between Śiva and Párvatí .... *ib.*

Note.—A passage from Yájnavalkya, which shows that Manuscripts of the Vedas existed in his time 62

Writing was known before Páṇini.—Ṛishi, a seer of Vaidik hymns 64

Note.—On the title *Ṛishi* 66

Professor Müller holds that there are four distinct periods of Ancient Sanskrit Literature,—the Chhandas, Mantra, Bráhmaṇa and Sútra periods. His distribution of the Ancient Literature over these periods 68

REFUTATION OF HIS VIEWS AND OF HIS DISTRIBUTION OF THE ANCIENT LITERATURE ...68—225

Meaning of the word *mantra* 69

Meaning of the word *chhandas*. Use of both these words in the Sútras of Páṇini 70

Professor Müller assigns dates to his four periods of Ancient Sanskrit Literature. His oldest date is 1200 B.C. 72

But a quotation, by Colebrooke, from the Jyotisha, proves that an arrangement of Vaidik hymns was completed in the 14th century B.C. 74

Professor Weber's slur on Colebrooke's accuracy 75

Professor Weber's silence on Lassen's researches 76

PAGE

Professor Weber as a personal witness of the progress of the Áryas in India up to 1500 B.C. ... 77

Professor Müller holds that the uniform employment of the Anushṭubh Śloka marks a new period, viz., the Classical Period of Sanskrit Literature ... 78

Proof that this view cannot be assented to.—Tittiri and Charaka were authors of Ślokas.—Kátyáyana composed Ślokas, called Bhrája ... 79

Kátyáyana's Karmapradípa is written in Ślokas.—Vyáḍi wrote a work, Sangraha, in 100,000 Ślokas.—All these authors would belong to Professor Müller's Vaidik period ... 80

Professor Müller assigns to Kátyáyana the date 350 B.C., and considers Páṇini to be his contemporary ... 81

Refutation of this view ... 83—213

Dr. Boehtlingk also places Páṇini about 350 B.C. ... 85

Proof that the premises which have led to his conclusion are imaginary ... 86

Note.—An extraordinary view taken by Dr. Boehtlingk of the moral and intellectual condition of ancient India.—The whole of the ancient scientific literature of this country would prove, according to his view, a gigantic swindle and imbecility. 87

Unsatisfactory results concerning the date of Páṇini ... 88

Note.—Páṇini looked upon by the Hindus as a Rishi, in the proper sense of this word *ib.*

An investigation of the position which Páṇini holds in ancient Sanskrit literature is more likely to lead to a solid result, than speculations as to the real date of his life ... *ib.*

On the Chronological relation between Páṇini and Kátyáyana, the author of the Várttikas ... 89—140

The Literature mentioned in the Mahábháshya.—Grammarians prior to Páṇini's Grammar.—Authors of Várttikas later than Kátyáyana ... 90

The Ishṭis of Patanjali ... 91

Note.—An extraordinary syllogism of Dr. Boehtlingk relative to some authors of Várttikas ... 92

Note.—Another extraordinary syllogism of this writer by which *ishṭi* is metamorphosed into *káriká* ... *ib.*

The Kárikás belong to different authors ... 93

Note.—A further insight into the value of the statements of Dr. Boehtlingk ... *ib.*

Various categories of Kárikás ... 94

Authors of the Kárikás not commented upon by Patanjali ... 95

Such Kárikás are later than Kátyáyana's Várttikas.—Authors of the Kárikás commented upon by Patanjali ... 99

The method of Patanjali's Great Commentary ... 100

Repetition of Kárikás ... 101

Instances of works which are written in verse and commented on, in prose, by their own authors ... 103

Note.—A valuable contribution to these instances by Dr. Fitz-Edward Hall ... 104

Authors of the Kárikás with imperfect comment in the Mahábháshya of Patanjali ... 105

Paribháshás.—Definition of the word. Its difference from *sanjná* ... 106

Definition of *paribháshá* as given by the Purushottama-vṛitti-ṭíká and Vaidyanátha ... 107

Vaidyanátha's distinction between Paribháshás founded on *jnápaka*, and Paribháshas founded on *nyáya* ... 108

Note.—On the difficulty which these terms have caused to the native grammarians. Uncritical state of the Calcutta edition of Páṇini on this point ... *ib.*

Paribháshás which are anterior to the Várttikas of Kátyáyana ... 109

None of the Paribháshá collections in existence is the original collection of Paribháshás ... 111

PAGE

Paribháshás composed by Patanjali 111
The oldest Paribháshás are anterior to the Grammar of Pâṇini........ 113
Definition of the term *jnâpaka*........ 115
Relation between *jnâpaka* and *paribhâshâ*........ 117
The character of the Várttikas of Kâtyâyana 119
Note.—A fantastical conjecture of Professor Weber on the Mahâbhâshya, which has not become real by dint of repetition........ *ib.*
The character of the Mahâbhâshya. Its relation to Kâtyâyana and to Pâṇini 120
A summary view of the criticisms of Kâtyâyana 121
Four arguments to prove that Pâṇini must have preceded Kâtyâyana 122
First argument.—There are grammatical forms current in the time of Pâṇini which became obsolete or even incorrect in the time of Kâtyâyana 123
Second argument.—There are meanings of words, in the time of Kâtyâyana, which did not exist in the time of Pâṇini 125
Third argument.—There are words and meanings of words used by Pâṇini which had become obsolete in the time of Kâtyâyana 128
Fourth argument.—There existed a literature in the time of Kâtyâyana which was not known to Pâṇini .... 129—140
Âraṇyakas were not known to Pâṇini, but to Kâtyâyana 129
The Vâjasaneyi-Saṁhitá and the Śatapatha-bráhmaṇa were not known to Pâṇini, but to Kâtyâyana .... 131—140
Professor Weber's first explanation of the Várttika to Sútra IV. 3, 105 133
Professor Weber's second explanation of the same Várttika, which destroys the first 134
An analysis of his critical method 135
Professor Müller's explanation of the same Várttika 136
An analysis of his explanation.—The Várttika made the foundation of chronological results, by both Professors, is misprinted in the Calcutta edition which supplied them with its text 137
The real meaning of this Várttika........ 138
It leads to the conclusion that Pâṇini did not yet know the Śatapatha-bráhmaṇa 139
None of the Bráhmaṇas and Kalpa-works in existence were ancient works from Pâṇini's point of view.—The Kalpa-work of Kâtyâyana was not known to Pâṇini 141
The Upanishads were unknown to Pâṇini........ *ib.*
He was acquainted with the Black Yajur-veda, the Ṛig- and Sáma- veda 142
He did not know the Atharvaveda .... *ib.*
Professor Müller's view of what are the oldest Ṛigveda hymns.—Objections to his view 144
Pâṇini's view of what are the oldest hymns........ 145
Patanjali's theory on the origin of the various versions of the Vaidik hymns 146
Note.—Kaiyyaṭa's and Nágojibhaṭṭa's gloss on Patanjali .... *ib.*
Pâṇini considers the second Maṇḍala of the Ṛigveda, in its present version, to be amongst the less ancient portions of this Veda 149
The six philosophical systems were unknown to Pâṇini.—1. Mímánsá.—2. Vedánta........ 150
3. Sáukhya.—4. Yoga 151
5. Nyáya 152
Note.—A further insight into Dr. Boehtlingk's "*edition*" of Pâṇini .... *ib.*
Gautama's definition of játi (*genus*), ákṛiti (*species*), and vyakti (*individual*) 153
Pâṇini does not make use of the term *âkṛiti*........ 154
His term *jâti* is the same as Gautama's *âkṛiti* .... *ib.*
Note.—Patanjali and Kâtyâyana knew the system of Gautama 155
6. Vaiśeshika was unknown to Pâṇini 157

PAGE

CHRONOLOGICAL RELATION BETWEEN PÁṆINI AND THE UṆṆÁDI-SÚTRAS ... 158—170
Professor Müller's argument that the Uṇṇádi-Sútras are anterior to Páṇini.—Dr. Aufrecht's arguments to the same effect ... 158
Refutation of these arguments ... 159
Note.—New Uṇṇádi-Sútras taken from the Commentary of *Nṛisinha* on the Uṇṇádi-Sútras, this Commentary being a portion of his *Swaramanjari* ... 160
On the critical test by which to judge of the chronological relation of Páṇini to the Uṇṇádi-Sútras and other grammatical works ... 162
Five Sútras of Páṇini, the key-stone of his work ... 163
Note.—A further insight into the character of Dr. Boehtlingk's "*edition*" of Páṇini. *ib.*
Patanjali on the technical terms of Páṇini ... 164
Kaiyyaṭa on Patanjali's gloss in question ... 165
Inferences to be drawn from this gloss as to the originality of certain terms of Páṇini ... 166
Application of the test thus obtained to the Uṇṇádi-Sútras ... 169
These Sútras are consequently later than Páṇini. This is the opinion, also, of Bhaṭṭojidíkshita, Ujjwaladatta and Vimala ... 170

CHRONOLOGICAL RELATION BETWEEN PÁṆINI AND THE UṆṆÁDI-LIST ... 171—182
Nairuktas and Vaiyákaraṇas ... 171
Patanjali must have looked upon Páṇini as belonging to Yáska's "some of the Vaiyákaraṇas". 172
Note.—A further insight into the character Dr. Boehtlingk's "*edition*" of Páṇini... 174
Kátyáyana must have looked upon Páṇini as belonging to the Nairuktas ... *ib.*
Probability that Nágojibhaṭṭa's attributing the Uṇṇádi to Śákaṭáyana is erroneous ... 176
Note.—On the Gaṇaratnamahodadhi of Vardhamána.—Another insight into the character of Dr. Boehtlingk's "*edition*" of Páṇini ... 177
Patanjali's statement that the anubandhas of former grammarians have no anubandha effect in the Grammar of Páṇini ... 181
Páṇini is, consequently, the author of the Uṇṇádi-list ... *ib.*

CHRONOLOGICAL RELATION BETWEEN PÁṆINI AND THE DHÁTUPÁṬHA ... 182
He is the author of the groundwork of the existing Dhátupáṭha ... *ib.*

CHRONOLOGICAL RELATION BETWEEN PÁṆINI AND THE PRÁTIŚÁKHYAS ... 183—213
Professor Müller holds that all the Prátiśákhyas preceded the Grammar of Páṇini ... 184
Professor Roth's view to the same effect. His interesting and graphic account of the rise and progress of Grammar in India ... 185
Unhappily this account is fantastical ... 186
Professor Weber's view of the chronological relation between Páṇini and the Vájasaneyi-Prátiśákhya ... *ib.*
Reasons for giving Professor Weber a full hearing ... 189
The whirlpool. The certain posteriority ... 190
Professor Weber's fantastical story of the letter ă ... 191
Dangerous adverbs ... 192
Professor Müller does not agree with Professor Weber's splitting Kátyáyana into two ... 193
Professor Müller's own theory on the relation of the Vájasaneyi-Prátiśákhya to Páṇini's Grammar ... 194
Refutation of all these theories ... 195—213
Fallacy in the argument that the Prátiśákhyas are anterior to Páṇini. The Prátiśákhyas are no grammars ... 195

PAGE

Vyákaraṇa is a Vedánga, not the Prátiśákhyas. Difference between the character of the Vyákaraṇa and the Prátiśákhyas. An *a-priori* argument for Páṇini's work having preceded the Prátiśákhyas 196

Point of contact between both. How far a comparison between both is admissible. Another *a-priori* argument for the precedence of Páṇini's work 197

The Ṛik-Prátiśákhya is more complete than Páṇini's Grammar, so far as both works can be compared at all. Relation of the Vájasaneyi-Prátiśákhya to Páṇini's work........ 199

Professor Weber schools Kátyáyana for want of practice and skill.—Kátyáyana applies this reproach to Professor Weber by showing him that he did not understand his Prátiśákhya. 200

Kátyáyana sometimes repeats the words of Páṇini merely in order to make his criticisms more prominent .... *ib.*

Further instances of criticisms of his Prátiśákhya on the Grammar of Páṇini. The value of the censure which Professor Weber assiduously passes on Kátyáyana........ 202

Coincidences between the Prátiśákhya, and the Várttikas of, Kátyáyana 204

His Prátiśákhya was written before his Várttikas 205

Further proof for the priority of the Grammar of Páṇini to the Vájasaneyi-Prátiśákhya 206

The historical argument 207

Śaunaka was not the author of the Ṛik-Prátiśákhya 208

Another word on the critical principles of Professor Weber 209

Patanjali calls Vyáḍi, *Dákshdyaṇa* 210

Páṇini is the son of *Dákshí;* he therefore preceded Vyáḍi by at least two generations........ 211

Vyáḍi is quoted in the oldest Prátiśákhya; Páṇini is, therefore, anterior to it. Confirmation of Páṇini's priority to Vyáḍi by the Laghuparibhásháváṛitti and Patanjali 212

Chronological relation between Páṇini and the Phiṭsútras .... 214—219

Professor Müller holds that these Sútras have preceded the Grammar of Páṇini. *Refutation of this view* 214

A doubt as to the ingenuity of Dr. Boehtlingk........ 215

Analogy between the Phiṭsútras and the Prátiśákhyas........ 216

Further analogy between the Phiṭsútras and the Prátiśákhyas. Śántana belongs to the eastern grammarians. Bhaṭṭojidíkshita maintains that the Phiṭsútras are posterior to the Grammar of Páṇini 217

Nágojibhaṭṭa says that "*the Phiṭsútras, when considered in reference to Páṇini, are as if they were made to-day*" 219

Chronological relation between Páṇini and Yáska .... 220—225

Professor Müller holds that Páṇini is anterior to Yáska........ 220

Refutation of this view 221

Yáska is named by Páṇini. Yáska on the Prepositions........ 222

Páṇini on the Prepositions 224

Páṇini is posterior to Yáska 225

Chronological relation between Páṇini and Buddha .... 225—227

Śákyamuni is not mentioned by Páṇini........ 225

Nirváṇa........ 226

Páṇini is anterior to Buddha 227

Date and early History of the Mahábháshya .... 228—238

Professor Müller holds that it is impossible to determine the date of the Mahábháshya; but Patanjali himself states when he did not live and when he did 228

PAGE

Patanjali speaks of the Mauryas as a past dynasty ... 228
Patanjali mentions that Ayodhyá and the Mádhyamikas were besieged by the Yavana, and that these events took place *when he lived* ... 229
Professor Müller holds that Buddha's death took place 477 B.C. ... 231
Objections to his arguments ... 232
Professor Lassen holds that Buddha's death took place 543 B.C. ... 233
The events alluded to by Patanjali must have fallen within the years 140 and 120 B.C.; and this must be therefore the date of the Mahábháshya ... 234
Professor Lassen's view is thus confirmed by the Mahábháshya ... 235
The name of Patanjali's mother is Goṇiká; his birthplace is Gonarda ... *ib.*
He belongs to the East of India, and to the Eastern grammarians ... 236
Bhartṛihari's account of the early History of the Mahábháshya ... 237
Note.—An interesting passage from the Rájataranginí blighted by Dr. Boehtlingk ... 238

BEARING OF THE FOREGOING INVESTIGATION ON THE STUDY OF ANCIENT SANSKRIT LITERATURE ... 239—245
Importance of the Hindu Commentaries. The traditional element in them ... 242
The grammatical element in these Commentaries ... 243
The chronological position of the Grammatical Works is the only critical basis for judging of the correctness of the Commentaries ... 244

THE PRESENT CRITICAL POSITION OF SANSKRIT PHILOLOGY ... 245—258
The Sanskrit Wörterbuch published by the Russian Imperial Academy ... 245
Six Dicta and Critical Principles of Professor Roth ... *ib.*
(1) Professor Roth intimates that Sáyaṇa gives only that sense of the Veda which was current in India some centuries ago. Opinion which must be entertained of this assertion ... 248
(2) Professor Roth believes that he is far more able than Sáyaṇa to give us the correct sense of the Veda. An examination of the foundation on which this assertion rests ... *ib.*
(3) Professor Roth asserts that he can put together some ten or twenty passages for examining the sense of a word, but that Sáyaṇa could not do this. Examination of the foundation on which this assertion rests ... 249
(4) Professor Roth says that the purely etymological proceeding, as it must be followed up by those who endeavour to guess the sense of a word, cannot possibly lead to a correct result. Examination of the foundation on which this assertion rests ... 250
(5) The object of Professor Roth is not to obtain that understanding of the Veda which was current in India a few centuries ago, but to know the meaning which the poets themselves gave to their songs and phrases ... 252
The revelations received by Professor Roth in regard to the Ṛigveda ... *ib.*
The revelations received by him in regard to the Sáma- and Yajur- veda ... 253
(6) Professor Roth is a conscientious European exegete ... 254
The treatment of the scientific and classical literature in the Wörterbuch, by Dr. Boehtlingk. *ib.*
The Wörterbuch cancels authoritatively, and without giving any reason whatever, all the bases in *ṛí*, *ṛi*, *ḷri*, etc. ... 255
The opinion which must be entertained of such a proceeding ... 256
The Sanskrit language under Dr. Boehtlingk's treatment ... 257
Patanjali and the potters ... 258
The Champions of the Wörterbuch and their means of defence.—Professor Kuhn ... 259
A farther glance at the Champions and their means of defence.—Professor Weber ... 261
The climax ... 265
A further glance at the Champions.—The hidden reasons of the "editor" of Páṇini ... 266
Conclusion ... 267

ERRATA.

	FOR	READ
Page 15, line 1 of note 12,	Prâtisákya,	Prâtiśâkhya.
P. 21, l. 13,	*Páráśaryailáślibhyám,*	*Páráśaryaśilálibhyám.*
P. 36, l. 16, before "*da-kára,*" insert "*tha-kára,* P. on VII. 4, 46."		
P. 61, l. 6 of note 62,	क् ।	क्
P. 100, l. 4 of note 114,	(Kár. 1. *a. b.*)	(Kár. 1).
P. 105, l. 14 of note 120,	छन्दस्यमिग्चोरपीति	छन्दस्यमिप्चोरपीति
P. 112, l. 14 of note 130,	°निर्देशो	°निर्देशः
P. 210, l. 11,	Dákshâyana,	Dákshâyaṇa.
P. 227, l. 14,	*avatábhi—*	*avátábhi—*
P. 229, l. 10 of note 266,	याः पूजा	या(ः) पूजा
P. 252, l. 11, 12,	not to understand the Veda such as it was current,	not to obtain that understanding of the Veda which was current.

WHEN collecting materials for a History of the Mímánsá philosophy, I happened to find in the Library of the East India House a Manuscript (No. 17), formerly belonging to the collection of Mr. Colebrooke, which bore on its outer page the remark: "ऋग्वेदकुमारिलभाष्यसं २२००," (*i.e.*, "the number, of 32 syllables, in this commentary of Kumárela on the Ṛigveda is 2,200"), and ended on leaf 120 with these words: "ग्रंथसंख्या ॥ २२०० ॥ क ॥ कुमारिलभाष्यं समाप्तं ॥" (*i.e.*, "the number, of 32 syllables, in the book is 2,200; end of the Commentary of Kumárela"). The remark of the title, which differs in its handwriting from the rest of the book, seems to have been made by a Hindu, who, with much exactness, counted the number of the syllables for the copying of which he had to pay his scribe; but it certainly did not come from one conversant with Sanskrit literature. Nor can a better opinion be entertained of the Shaikh who finished copying this volume—"Samwat 1643 (or 1586 after Christ), when the sun was progressing south of the equator, in the autumn season, during the light fortnight of the month Kárttika (October-November), in the city of Benares, for the perusal of Devayíka (Devakíya?), the son of Jání and Mahídhara"—or of the writer of his Manuscript,—since the Shaikh professes to have copied the latter with the utmost accuracy, faults and all;—for neither were the contents of this volume a commentary on the Ṛigveda, nor would a learned man have mis-spelt several words, and very common ones, too, of his own composition, and, above all, the name of one of the most celebrated authors of India. In short, the Manuscript in question contained no other matter than a portion of the Mánava-Kalpa-Sútras, together with a commentary of Kumárila-Swámin, the great Mímánsá authority.

A discovery of this ritual work, which had thus remained latent under a wrong designation, would at all times have been welcome to those engaged in the study of Vaidik literature; it gained in interest from the facts that a doubt had been raised, I do not know on what grounds, whether a copy of it had survived, and that a commentary of Kumárila on these Sútras, had, so far as my knowledge goes, never yet been spoken of in any European or Sanskrit book.

It was but natural, under these circumstances, that I should think of making the knowledge I had obtained generally available, by editing this manuscript; but, to my utter disappointment, I soon perceived, after having examined it in detail, that it belonged to that class of written books, the contents of which may be partially made out and partially guessed, but which are so hopelessly incorrect that a seeming restoration of their text would require a greater amount of conjecture than could be permitted to an editor, or might be consistent with the respect due to the author of the work itself.

When, therefore, another copy of the Mánava-Kalpa-Sútras with the Commentary of Kumárila was not to be procured, and when I began to surmise that the volume in the possession of the East India House was a unique copy of this rare work, I resolved, with the consent of Professor Wilson, to have a facsimile of it lithographed and printed. This resolution was strengthened by the consideration that even a correct text of these Sútras would be serviceable only to the few scholars who are familiar with this branch of the oldest Sanskrit literature, and that they would be able, by the aid they might get from other existing Sútras on the Vaidik ritual, and the Mímánsá works, to turn to account even this incorrect manuscript, in spite of the many doubts it leaves. It was strengthened, too, by the conviction I entertain, that unique manuscripts, or those which are rarely met with,—every existing copy of which consequently possesses a literary value much exceeding that of ordinary manuscripts,—ought to be saved from possible casualties by mechanical contrivances, the most practical of which, as answering the requirements of the case and entailing the least expense, seems to be that which has been used in the production of the present fac-simile.

I must, however, confess that after several disappointments in trying to secure the necessary aid, I should probably have been compelled to abandon my plan, had I not been able to avail myself of the assistance of a talented young lady, Miss Amelia Rattenbury, who, while devoting herself to the study of Sanskrit, came to my rescue, and, with much patience and skill, accomplished the tracing of the original.

Her work may, indeed, in some parts, be still open to criticism, so far as the exact thickness of the letters on a few pages is concerned, or if some shortcomings, especially those which are noticed in the Errata, be too much insisted upon; but I must in fairness state that several omissions of Anuswáras or strokes, as pointed out in the Errata, are not her fault, but the result of accidents which occurred in transferring the fac-simile to stone; and such defects could not, it would seem, have been wholly avoided, notwithstanding the careful attention which was paid to the work by the lithographic printers, Messrs. Standidge and Co., and, I may add, in spite of the great trouble I took myself in revising the proofs on the stones, and in thus combining the work of a Sanskritist with that of an apprentice in lithography. Several sheets which failed to show distinctly some Anuswáras or parts of the letters themselves, though transferred to the stone and originally visible there, I cancelled at once; but this expeditious process became, by frequent repetition, so little convenient, that I had to submit at last, though reluctantly, to a list of Errata which, however small, seems to be at variance with the notion of a fac-simile.

On the whole, however, and after this censure, the severity of which, I trust, no one will see occasion to increase, I must express my belief, that the text which is laid before the reader is, when amended by the aid of the Errata list, not merely a thoroughly correct representation of the contents of the special manuscript from which it is copied, but, at the same time, a good specimen of a fac-simile of a Sanskrit manuscript.[1]

Of the work itself I have but little to say, for the Sanskrit scholars who will take an interest in it are well acquainted with the general characteristics of those ritual books which bear the name of Kalpa-Sútras, and they know, too, that the Mánava-Kalpa-Sútras teach the ceremonial connected with the old recension of the Yajurveda, the Taittiríya-Samhitá. The portion of these Sútras contained in the present fac-simile comprises the first four books of the whole work: the first or *Yájamána* book, in two chapters (from fol. 1 to 54 *a*, and 54 *a* to 55 *b*); the second on the *Agnyádhána* (from fol. 55 *b* to 84 *b*); the third on the *Agnihotra* (from fol. 84 *b* to 106 *a*); and the fourth on the

---

[1] It is necessary to observe that the original, in its actual bound condition, measures 9¾ inches in length and 3⅝ inches in breadth, with the exception of fol. 62 which is 4 inches broad. The surplus of margin in the fac-simile belongs, therefore, to the latter. The binder, in reducing the leaves of the original to the size stated, has in various instances encroached upon the writing, and cut away either portions of letters or even whole letters; which circumstance will account for the defects in the marginal additions of, especially, fol. 1, 3 *a*, *b*, 5 *b*, 11 *a*, 12 *a*, 13 *a*, 14 *a*, 25 *a*, 26 *a*, 32 *b*, 33 *a*, 34 *a*, 48 *a*, *b*, 50 *b*, 52 *a*, 53 *a*, 54 *a*, 58 *a*, 60 *a*, 61 *a*, 62 *a*, 66 *b*, 68 *a*, 70 *b*, 74 *b*, 80 *b*, 81 *a*, 86 *b*, 89 *b*, 107 *b*, 108 *b*, 113 *a*. Another destructive animal, the white ant, has also added to the work of devastation in the interior of the MS., but much more rarely; on the margin of fol. 16 *a* two strokes (=) indicate the eaten portion. Towards the end of the MS., especially from fol. 90 upwards, the original has the appearance of having been smeared or powdered over; and this carelessness, caused no doubt by putting the leaves together before the writing was dry, has produced in several instances the errors of the fac-simile, especially as it became sometimes difficult or even impossible to tell whether a dot represented an original *anuswára* or a smear. I have to mention, besides, that the leaves of the original are bound so as to read downwards, and that the same arrangement has been preserved in the present work in order not to allow it to deviate from the appearance of its modern prototype. There is good reason, however, to suppose that the ancient Hindus had the leaves of their MSS. arranged so as to read in the reverse or upward direction. For one liberty which has been taken in the fac-simile, I am personally answerable. The remark on the outside page, mentioned above, with its mis-spelling of the name of Kumárila and its literary error, will not be found in this volume; its place is filled by the likeness of the god of literary accuracy who is invoked in the commencement of the work.

Cháturmásya sacrifices, in six chapters (from fol. 106 *a* to 108 *a*, from there to the end of fol. 109 *a*, from 109 *b* to 112 *a*, from there to 113 *a*, from 113 *a* to 115 *a*, and hence to the end).[2] That these books are the *first* portion of the Mánava-Sútra results not merely from the matter treated in them, but also from a fact which accidentally came to my cognizance after the printing of the present volume had been completed.

Professor Müller, who is engaged in writing a history of

---

[2] There occur in the text and commentary of these books the following words for *sacrifices, sacrificial and other acts connected with them*: अंशु, अग्निचयन, अग्निपरिस्तरण, अग्निप्रस्तरण, अग्निमन्थन, अग्नियज्ञ, अग्निष्टोम, अग्निसंस्कार, अग्निहोत्र (दशहोत्राग्निहोत्र, प्रथमाग्निहोत्र), अग्निहोम, अग्न्याधान, अग्न्याधेय (आग्न्याधेयिक), अग्न्याधेयेष्टि, अग्रपाक, अतिरात्र, अधियज्ञ, अधिश्रयण, अनुतापन, अनुमन्त्रण, अनुयाज, अन्वाधान, अन्वारम्भणीया, अभिघार, अभिघारण, अभिनिर्वाप, अभिमर्शन, अभ्यञ्जन, अभ्युक्षण, अभ्यूहन, आग्नेययाग, आग्नेयीष्टि, आग्न्याधेयिक, आग्रायण, आज्यहोम, आज्याहुति, आधान, आमन्त्रण, आरम्भणीया, आवपन, आवसथ्य, आस्तरण, आहुति (यूपा°), आह्वान, इष्टि (ऐष्टिक), उत्पवन, उद्धनन, उद्धाव, उद्धूलन, उद्वासन, उद्वाह (औद्वाहिक), उन्नयन, उपक्लृप्ति, उपचार, उपयमन, उपयाम, उपवपन, उपवसथ, उपसद्, ऐष्टिक, काकहोम, काम्येष्टि, कृष्णलपाक, गोदोह (गोदोहन), चर्विष्टि, चातुर्मास्य, चान्द्रायण, जप, तुषविमोक, तुषावाप, दर्श, दर्शपौर्णमास, दशहोत्राग्निहोत्र, दीक्षा, देवयजन (°नी), दोह (गो°), द्वादशाहिक, नाराशंस, नित्यहोम, नियतभोजन, निर्मन्थ, निर्वपण (निर्वाप), निष्टपन, निष्पावन, पत्नीसंयाज, परिमार्जन, परिवापण, परिषेक, परिस्तरण, परिहरण, पर्यग्निकरण, पर्युक्षण, पशुबन्ध, पशुश्रपण, पाक, पाकयज्ञ, पाणिग्रहण, पिण्डनिधान, पिण्डपितृयज्ञ, पितृकार्य, पितृमेध, पितृयज्ञ, पिष्टपेषण, पिष्टलेप, पूर्णाहुति, पौर्णमास, प्रणयन (अग्नि°), प्रथमाग्निहोत्र, प्रायश्चित्त, प्रैष, प्रोक्षण, प्रोहण, फलीकरण, बर्हिःप्रहरण, बर्हिःस्तरण, बलिहरण, ब्रह्मवरण, भक्तदान, मन्त्रस्तोम, मन्त्रावृत्ति, यज्ञ (यज्ञिय), याग, यूपवेष्टन, यूपसंमार्जन, यूपाहुति, राजसूय, राष्ट्रभृत्, वपन, वरण (ब्रह्म°), वरुणप्रघास, वषट्कार (वषट्कृत), वस्त्रविन्यास, विहार (वैहारिक), वेदिकरण, वेदोपयाम, व्रतविमोक, व्रतोपायन, शुनासीर्य, श्मश्रुवपन, श्रपण, संस्कार, संस्पर्श, सत्त्र, संनहन, संनिवपन, साकमेध (°धिक), सान्तपन (°नीय), सोमपान, सोमाधान, सोमेष्टि, स्तरण, स्वाहाकार, स्विष्टकृत्, होम; for *sacrificial substances, implements, prayers, or objects incidentally mentioned as referring to them*: अग्नि (आहवनीयाग्नि, आहिताग्नि, उद्धताग्नि, गार्हपत्याग्नि, दक्षि-

Vaidik literature, had met among the MSS. of the East India House, which he consulted for his labour, one (No. 599) which bore at its end the intimation of being a part of the Mánava-Sútras; and when he showed me the MS., I saw at once that it was written by the same writer who had copied the original of the present fac-simile, in a similar, though smaller and less elegant, handwriting, and immediately after he had copied the first four books. For he states himself in his closing words

---

णाग्नि, शालाग्नि), अग्निष्ठ, अग्निहोत्रहवणी, अज, अश्व, अश्वत्थ, अष्टाकपाल, आज्य, आनडुह, आमिक्षा, आहवनीयाग्नि, आहिताग्नि, इडा, इध्म, इध्माबर्हिस्, इष्टिपशु, उत्तरवेदि (औत्तरवेदिक), उद्यताग्नि, उपभृत् (औपभृत), उपल, उलूखल, ऊर्णा, एककपाल, ओदन, ओषधि, कपाल (अष्टा°, एक°, दश°, नव°, पञ्च°, षट्°, सप्त°), कर्षू, कांस्य, काष्ठ, कुण्डल, कुम्भी, कृष्णाजिन, क्षौम, खनित्र, खादिर, खलेवाली, गार्हपत्याग्नि, गुग्गुलु, गोक्षीर, गोमय, ग्रावन्, घृत, चमू, चरु, चरुस्थाली, चर्मन्, चात्वाल, जपमन्त्र, जरद्गव, जुहू (जौहव), तण्डुल, तिल, तुष, दक्षिणा, दक्षिणागार, दक्षिणाग्नि, दक्षिणापात्र, दण्ड, दधि, दर्भ, दर्भपिञ्जूल, दर्भरज्जु, दर्वी, दशकपाल, दित्यवाह् (दित्यौही), दृषद्, द्रप्स, धान्य, धिष्ण्य, ध्रुवा (ध्रौव), नवकपाल, नवनीत, पञ्चकपाल, परिधि, पर्णशाखा, पवित्र, पशु, पशुपुरोडाश, पात्र (पात्री), पिञ्जूल (दर्भ°), पिण्ड, पूतीक, पृथुग्रावन्, प्रणीता, प्रस्तर, प्राचीनावीत, बर्हिस्, बलि, ब्रह्मौदन (ब्राह्मौदनिक), भक्त, भद्रस्रुच्, भस्मन्, मधुपर्क, मन्त्र, महाहविस्, मांस, माष, मुञ्ज, मुञ्जर, मुसल, मूल, मृग, मृदङ्ग, मेषी, मौञ्ज, यज्ञायज्ञिय, यज्ञोपवीत (°तिन्), यव, यवागू, याज्यानुवाक्या, यूप, योक्त्र, रज्जु, रथ, लेखा, लेप, लोमन्, वत्स, वस्त्र, वामदेव्य, वारवन्तीय, वेदि (उत्तरवेदि, वेदिश्रोणि), वेहत्, व्रीहि, शकट, शतमान, शतायुध, शमी (शमीशाखा), शर, शराव, शाखा, शाला, शालाग्नि, शुल्क, शूर्प, श्मश्रु, श्यामाक, श्येनी, षट्कपाल, सप्तकपाल, समिष्टयजुस्, संभार, सान्नाय्य, सोम, स्तम्बयजुस्, स्रुच् (स्रौच), स्रुव, स्फ्य, हविर्धान, हविस्, हिरण्य; for *the time of sacrificial acts, asterisms, etc.*: अनुमती, अमावास्या, उपसत्काल, कृत्तिका, चैत्री, दक्षिणाकाल, द्यावापृथिवी, पुनर्वसु, प्रातर्, फाल्गुनी, भुवस्, भू, माध्यन्दिन, मार्गशीर्ष, मृगशिरस्, रात्रि, वर्षाः (वार्षिक), रेवती, रोहिणी, वसन्त, वैशाखी, व्युष्ट, शरद्, शिशिर, शुनासीर, संवत्सर, सद्यःकाल, सायम्, सूर्योदय, स्वर्, स्वर्ग, हेमन्त; for *priests, sacrificer, etc.*: अध्वर्यु (आध्वर्यव), आग्नीध्र, आधानर्त्विज्, उद्गातृ, ऋत्विज्, चमसाध्वर्यु, पत्नी, पुरोहित, प्रतिप्रस्थातृ, ब्रह्मन् (ब्रह्मत्व), यजमान (याजमान), यज्ञपति, यष्टृ, होतृ (हौत्र); for *divinities (and their derivatives)*: अग्नि, अग्निषो-

that he finished copying "the fifth part of the Agnishṭoma book of the Mánava-Sútra, Samwat 1643 (or 1586 after Christ), when the sun was progressing north of the equator, in the winter season, during the light fortnight of the month Pausha (December-January), on the fifteenth lunar day, in the city of Benares"; and the next syllable, immediately succeeded by a blank in the MS., makes it probable that he wrote this portion, too, for the perusal of the son of Mahídhara. His conscience, however, seems to have been more sensitive regarding the accuracy with which he had performed his task, at the end of the Agnishṭoma portion, than it was before, since he makes a very touching appeal to the indulgence of the reader, and is even modest enough to count himself amongst the scribes of limited intellect.[3]

The contents of this latter manuscript, viz., the description of the Agnishṭoma rites in five Adhyáyas,[4] now, too, explain the meaning of the concluding words of our MS. (fol. 120 *b*):

मीय, अग्नीन्द्र (इन्द्राग्नि), अदिति, अपांनप्तृ, अपोनप्तृ (अपोनप्त्रीय), आग्नेन्द्र, आग्नेय, आदित्य, आश्विन, इन्द्र, इन्द्राणी, ऐन्द्र, ऐन्द्राग्न, गन्धर्व, तनूनपाद्, त्र्यम्बक, देव, देवता, पूषन्, बलदेव, बऊदेवत, बृहस्पति, मरुत् (मारुत), महेन्द्र, मैत्रावरुण, मैत्रायण, रक्षस्, रुद्र, वरुण (वारुण), वायु, विश्वदेवाः (वैश्वदेव), विष्णु, वैश्वानर, सूर्य (सौर्य), सोम, सौमपौष्ण, सौर्यवारुण, हिरण्यगर्भ.

[3] I subjoin a literal copy of the last page (37) of this MS. with *all the faults*, which will give some idea of the unhappy fate of these Mánava-Sútras in the hands of their ignorant transcriber: यादृशं पुस्तकं दृष्ट्वा । तादृशं लिषितं मया ॥ यदि शुद्धमशुद्धं वा मम दोषो न दीयते ॥ १ ॥ अदृष्यभावात्मनि विभ्रमाद्वा ॥ यदर्थहीनं लिषितं मयात्र । तत्सर्वमार्यैः परिशोधनीयं कोप न कुर्याखलु लेषकस्य ॥ २ ॥ यासतुल्यो पि यो वक्ता नानाशास्त्रविशारदः । मुह्यते लिषमानो पि किं पुनः स्वल्पबुद्धयः ॥ श्रीं स्वस्ति ॥ संवत् १६४३ वर्षे शाके . . . . . . प्रवर्तमाने उत्तरायने हेमन्त ऋतौ महामांगल्यप्रदः ॥ पौषमासे शुक्लपक्षे १५ मास्यो तिथौ अद्येह काशिवास्तव्यं मोढज्ञातीय ॥ जा . . . . ॥ ॥ लिषितंम् । लेषकपाठकयोः शुभं भवतु ॥ मानवसूत्रस्य अग्निष्टोमाख्यस्य पंचमभागस्य पुस्तकमलेखि । श्रीः ॥ छ ॥ छ ॥ चमसाध्वर्यवः । होता १ ब्रह्म ॥ २ उद्गाता ३ यजमानः । ४ प्रशास्त्रः । ५ ब्राह्मणाछंदसि ६ पोता ॥ ७ नेष्ट । ८ आग्नीध्रः । ९ अछावाकः । १० एते दश चमसाध्वर्यवः; and after this last piece of scholarship is added in a different hand: "स्यपुस्तकं ॥ सौमसूत्रं ॥ अध्याः ५" (!).

[4] Whether the work which is mentioned in the Catalogue of the Sanskrit MSS. at

प्रागसोमभाष्यं संपूर्णं (which ought to be प्राक्सोम॰), for they clearly point to a continuation, treating on the Soma rites, which continuation is given in the MS. 599, so far as the text of the Sútras goes, though this MS. does not contain any further commentary of Kumárila.

The text of the first four books of the Sútras in our MS. is, unhappily, only fragmentary. Sometimes, but rarely, a Sútra is given in full before the gloss of Kumárila; for the most part, however, the copy of the text, as is the case with many manuscripts of Commentaries on Sútras, starts from the assumption that the reader possesses a MS. which contains the words of the Sútra, and refers to them by merely giving the first and the last word of the sentence which is the subject of the commentary. Now and then, it is true, some further words of the Sútra emerge from the gloss of Kumárila, but, though it is possible to understand the purport of his comment, it would be a fruitless task to try to construe from it the full detail of the text, since much of the latter is left unnoticed, as requiring, apparently, no gloss.

The interest connected with the present volume centres, therefore, chiefly in the commentary of Kumárila, and in the fact itself that it is this great Mímánsá writer who composed a commentary on the Mánava-Sútras of the Taittiríya-Samhitá. For, since in Sanskrit literature, commentaries on works which involve scientific convictions or religious belief were, as a rule, written by those alone who shared in these convictions or meant to defend this belief, it is a matter of significance that this celebrated representative of the Mímánsá doctrine, who lived before Śankara, the commentator of the Vedánta-Sútras,[5] should have attached his remarks to a Sútra belonging to the Black-Yajus School.

Benares, p. 118, under the title सोमसूत्रपञ्चविधानम् (No. 2503) be the same as the Agnishṭoma portion of the Mánava-Sútras, I have had no means of ascertaining. The same Catalogue records the existence of the मानवसूत्रम् (p. 78, No. 761), but without naming the Commentary of Kumárila.

[5] Compare the Preface to the first edition of Wilson's Sanskrit Dictionary, p. xviii *seqq.*

That this circumstance cannot be accidental is rendered probable by collateral facts. Kumárila quotes on two occasions (fol. 14 *a* and 85 *b*) the opinion of Śabara-Swámin on passages in the Sútras, and as it is not the commentary of this author on the Jaimini-Sútras to which he refers, his quotation can only imply that Śabara had composed, besides, a gloss either on the Mánava-, or on other Sútras of the same school. Śabara, however, is, like Kumárila whom he preceded, one of the principal authorities of the Mímánsá philosophy.[6] Mádhava also, the commentator on the Vedas, who may be considered as the last writer of eminence on the Mímánsá, composed or indited a commentary on another Sútra work of the Taittiríya-Saṁhitá, the Sútra of Baudháyana. Of commentators on other Sútras of the Black-Yajur-veda I do not speak, since they have not attained a prominent rank among the Mímánsists. But it ought not to be left unnoticed, on the other hand, that neither the Kalpa works connected with the Ṛigveda, nor those belonging to the Sáma-, or White-Yajur-veda, had commentators who, at the same time, wrote Mímánsá works.

It would seem, therefore, and I shall have to advert to this point in detail in a more appropriate place, that the Kalpa-Sútras of the Taittiríya-Saṁhitá represented or countenanced, more than other Kalpa-Sútras, the tenets and decisions of the Mímánsá philosophers.

This intimate connection between the two will enable us, then, not merely to remove all doubt, if any exist, as to the identity

---

[6] I may mention, on this occasion, other quotations made by Kumárila. He speaks several times of other Śákhás, without, however, specifying them (fol. 9 *b*, 17 *a*, 33 *a*, 36 *b*, 41 *b*, etc. etc.), once even of a Krúraśákhá, (fol. 50 *a*); of older teachers (Púrváchāryás, fol. 43 *b*—44 *a*, 85 *a*, Vṛiddhácharya, 119 *a*), of the Varáha Sútras (fol. 75 *a*, 93 *b*, 120 *b*), the Bháshyakára, who is probably the same as Śabara (fol. 115 *a*), the Bráhmaṇabháshyakára (fol. 60 *b*, 63 *a*, 75 *b*), the Gṛihyabháshyakára (fol. 60 *a*), the Háritabháshyakṛit (fol. 75 *b*); he names the Bahvṛichás (20 *a*, 23 *b*); the Yajurveda (fol. 9 *a* and *b*), and Yájurvedika (fol. 12 *b*, 67 *a*), the Káṭhaka (fol. 9 *a*, 98 *b*), the Taittiríyaka (fol. 60 *a*, 61 *b*, 66 *b*), a Bráhmaṇa (fol. 114 *b*); and the Sámaveda (fol. 9 *b*); Manu is usually called by him Sútrakára or Sútrakṛit (*e.g.* fol. 43 *b*, 71 *b*, 75 *b*, etc., 29 *a*, 32 *a*, 35 *b*, etc); other authors of Sútras, Sútrakárás or Sútrakṛitas (fol. 38 *a*, 77 *b*).

of the author of the present commentary with the author of the Várttikas on the Jaimini-Sútras,—even if this identity were not proved by the peculiar style of Kumárila's composition, by his writing alternately in prose and śloka, by his pithy remarks, and his strong expressions; but it will throw light, too, on the nature of the commentary itself.

It is not a commentary in the ordinary sense, merely explaining obsolete or difficult words, and giving the meaning of the sentences; it is often nothing else than a regular discussion and refutation of divergent opinions which were probably expressed in other Kalpa works. And the constant use it makes of current Mímánsá terms, in their Mímánsá sense, such as *apúrva*, *paramápúrva*, *úha*, *bádha*, to which may be added also, *vidhi*, *anuváda*, *arthaváda*, *purushártha*, *kratwartha*, *bheda* (*mantrabheda*, *vákyabheda*), on account of the frequent application these latter words find in the Mímánsá writings,—impresses on the discussions of Kumárila the full stamp of a Mímánsá reasoning.

There is one fact which deserves special mention, though it has only an indirect bearing on the present work. In the Sútras, I. 3, 10-12, Jaimini treats of the question whether the Kalpa works have the same authority as the Veda or not; in other terms, whether they must be ascribed to divine or to human authorship, and decides in favour of the latter alternative. Kumárila, in his Várttikas on this chapter, gives instances of the works of several authors which would fall under this category; he names, in the course of his discussion, the Sútras of Baudháyana, Varáha, Maśaka, Áśwaláyana, Vaijavápa, Dráhyáyaṇa, Láṭyáyana, Kátyáyana, and Ápastamba; but though his "*et cætera*" imply that he did not intend to give a complete list, it is certainly remarkable that he should not have named the Mánava-Sútras, which he has commented upon, more especially as he makes reference to the Dharmaśástra of Manu.

Śabara, also, his predecessor, who mentions, in his Bháshya on the same Sútras of Jaimini, the Máśaka-, Hástika-, and Kauṇḍinya-Kalpa-Sútra, does not speak of the Mánava. And, to conclude, the same omission strikes us in the Jaiminíya-nyáya-málá-vistara of

Mádhava, who names the Baudháyana-, Ápastamba-, Áswaláyana-, and Kátyáyana-Kalpa-Sútras, but makes no allusion to our work.

It may be, and it even is probable, that Kumárila wrote his gloss on the Mánava-Kalpa-Sútra after he had finished his Várttikas on the Sútras of Jaimini. But this circumstance alone cannot account for the omission of this Kalpa work from his Várttikas, nor does it offer any explanation of the general silence in regard to it of the other renowned writers on the Mímánsá philosophy.

I believe that the reason for this silence must be sought for in the decision of Jaimini, and in the legendary character of Manu, the reputed author of our Kalpa work. At the time of Śabara, Manu was no doubt already viewed by his countrymen in the same light in which he appears in the Dharmaśástra that bears his name but professes distinctly not to be the immediate work of Manu himself, and, consequently, could be safely alluded to. This mythical character, however, of Manu results from the legends connected with a personage of this name in the Śatapathabráhmaṇa and the Ṛigveda itself. To prove, therefore, on the one hand, that the Kalpa-Sútras are human work, and to hold before the reader's eye the name of an individual who, if less than a god, was, at all events, believed to be more than a man, would have been a proceeding which might either have shaken the conviction which it was intended to produce, or tinged the doctrine of the propounders with a hue of heresy which certainly neither Śabara, nor Kumárila, nor Mádhava meant to impart to his commentary. Probably, therefore, it appeared safer to evade this awkward illustration of the human character of a Sútrakára, and to be satisfied with instances of a more tangible and less delicate kind.

From our point of view, however, and I conclude from the point of view of the Mímánsists themselves, there is no reason to doubt that *a* Manu, the author of the present Sútras, was as much a real personage as Baudháyana and the other Sútrakáras who were never raised to a superhuman dignity. I can no more see a valid argument for doubting the existence of this Manu, because his name would mean, etymologically, "a thinking being, a man," and because mythology has lent this character to the father of the human race, also called Manu, than there would be for doubting the real existence of the Bráhmaṇa caste, merely because they ascribe their bodily origin to the Creator of the World. And as to the name of Manu (man) itself, it does not seem more striking or even more strange than other proper names in the Vaidik time; than, for instance, the proper names Práṇa, *life*; Eka, *one;* Itará, or Anyatará, *either of two;* Panchan, *five;* Saptan, *seven;* Ashṭan, *eight;* Śiras, *head;* Loman, *hair;* Vindu, *drop*, etc.

To assign a date to the Mánava-Kalpa-Sútras, even approximately, is a task I am incapable of performing; though, judging from the contents of this work, it may seem plausible to assert that they are more recent than the Sútras of Baudháyana and older than those of Ápastamba. But I have not any means of ascertaining when these latter works were composed.

It may not, however, be superfluous to add that they were either younger than Páṇini or, at least, not so much preceding his time as to be ranked by him amongst the old Kalpa works. For in an important Sútra of his grammar he states that the names of old Kalpa works are formed with the affix *in*, and it follows therefore that none of the works cf this kind, which are likely to be still in existence, and amongst them the Mánava-Kalpa-Sútras, are, from Páṇini's point of view, old Kalpa works.[7] And when I express the opinion that there is no tenable ground for assigning to Páṇini so recent a date as that which has been given to him, viz., the middle of the fourth century before Christ, but that there is on the contrary a presumption that he preceded the time of the founder of the Buddhistic creed,—I have advanced as much,

[7] Páṇini, iv. 3, 105. This Sútra is comprised under the head rule iv. 3, 101, which extends as far as 111. In the gloss on some of these Sútras the Káśiká, the Siddh.-k., and the Calcutta Paṇḍits who composed or compiled the printed commentary, have introduced the word अधीयते in addition to प्रोक्तम्, I hold, arbitrarily,—since it is neither indicated by the head rule, nor met with in the Mahábháshya.

or as little, as, I believe, can be safely advanced on the date of the present Kalpa work.

After the foregoing lines were written I received Professor Max Müller's "*History of Ancient Sanskrit Literature, so far as it illustrates the primitive religion of the Brahmans* (1859)." To acknowledge the merits of this work, which shows the great importance of the religious development of India; to acknowledge the light it throws on the obscurest parts of Hindu literature, and the comprehensive learning it has brought to bear on many an intricate topic connected with the rise and progress of Hindu grammar, law, and theology, must be the first and not the least gratifying feeling of every one interested in Sanskrit, and more especially in Vaidik philology. The greater, however, this new claim of the editor of the Ṛigveda to our gratitude, the more does his work impose on us the duty of examining, among the topics of which it treats, those which seem to require additional evidence before they can be considered as having attained a definite settlement. I take advantage of this opportunity, therefore, to re-open the discussion on two points, which seem to me to fall under this predicament, especially as they concern every work of the Vaidik literature, and equally bear on the present ritual book. I mean the question of the introduction of writing into India,[8] and the general question of the chronology of Vaidik works.[9]

Müller's view on the first of these questions is contained in the following words (p. 524): "If writing came in towards the

---

[8] Müller's History, p. 497—524. This chapter is reprinted in the Journal of the Asiatic Society of Bengal (No. ii. 1859), with the following note which became my first inducement to treat the matter on this occasion: "This paper is an extract from a work now in the press on the history of ancient Sanskrit literature. Professor Müller has sent it for the Society's Journal in the hope of eliciting some fresh information from European or native scholars in India on the interesting questions which it discusses."

[9] The same, pp 244, 313, 435, 572.

latter half of the Sûtra period,[10] it would no doubt be applied at the same time to reducing the hymns and Brâhmaṇas to a written form. Previously to that time, however, we are bound to maintain that the collection of the hymns, and the immense mass of the Brâhmaṇa literature, were preserved by means of oral tradition only;" and (p. 507): "But there are stronger arguments than these (viz., the arguments alleged by him, pp. 497-507), to prove that, before the time of Pâṇini, and before the first spreading of Buddhism in India, writing for literary purposes was absolutely unknown. If writing had been known to Pâṇini, some of his grammatical terms would surely point to the graphical appearance of words. I maintain that there is not a single word in Pâṇini's terminology which presupposes the existence of writing etc."

Müller maintains, therefore, that not merely *before* the time of Páṇini, but to Páṇini himself, writing was unknown; and as according to his view, "Pâṇini lived in the middle of the fourth century B.C." (pp. 245, 301 ff.),[11] it would follow that, according to him, India was not yet in possession of the most useful of arts at the time when Plato died and Aristotle flourished.

I must confess that I could not, and cannot, look upon this assertion otherwise than as a splendid paradox, which, it is true, makes up for its want of power of convincing by the ingenuity of the defence with which it is supported, and the interest which may be derived from the extraneous matter it has brought to its aid; and, had I happened to read this chapter before the rest, I should probably have thought that the idea of conceiving India without reed and ink until, or after, Páṇini's death, did not originate with Müller before the close of his learned work, and then only that he might crown, as it were, its merits by some extraordinary feat. But though justice requires me to admit that such is not the case, —that, on the contrary, the same opinion pervades the earlier por-

---

[10] This period extends, according to his views, from 600 to 200 B.C. (p. 244).

[11] This date will be the subject of ulterior remarks.

tions of his book,[12] I must still say that it does not seem to have taken root in his mind with that strong conviction which produces an impression on others, for it appears psychologically doubtful that an author, having that conviction, could even metaphorically speak of the "prayer-*book*" of the Hotṛis (pp. 187, 473), or say that Kátyáyana, whom he defines as "the contemporary of Pâṇini" (p. 138, and elsewhere), "*writes* in the Bhâshya" (p. 138), "*wrote* the Vârttikas" (p. 148), "*writes* in prose" (p. 229), or that he could call the Sútrakáras "*writers* of Sûtras" (p. 215).

No one, I believe, will easily imagine a civilized people who at the time of the Mantras (the period prior to that of the Sútras and Bráhmaṇas), were such as to possess "arts, sciences, institutes, and vices of civilized life, golden ornaments, coats of mail, weapons of offence, the use of precious metals, of musical instruments, the fabrication of cars, and the employment of the needle . . . . . . the knowledge of drugs and antidotes, the practice of medicine, and computation of the divisions of time to a minute extent, including repeated allusions to the seventh season or intercalary month" . . . . and again, "laws of property,"[13] "laws of inheritance, and of simple contract, or buying and selling,"[14]—having a civilization which Professor Wilson characterizes in the preface to his excellent Translation of the Ṛigveda (vol. ii., p. xvii), as "differing little, if at all, from that in which they were found by the Greeks at Alexander's invasion,"—no one, I believe, will easily imagine a people in such a state of civilization unacquainted with the art of writing, though no mention of this art

[12] *E.g.* p. 137, "the rules of the Prâtiśâkyas were not intended for written literature;" p. 200, note, "the question whether the Hindus possessed a knowledge of the art of writing during the Sûtra period, will have to be discussed hereafter;" p. 362, "if we remember that in these old times literary works did not exist in writing" [to 'remember' this on p. 362 is difficult, since the theory is propounded p. 497—524]; p. 311, "in India, where before the time of Pâṇini we have no evidence of any written literature, etc."

[13] See Wilson's Translation of the Ṛigveda, vol. ii. p. xvi.

[14] *Ibid.* vol. iii. p. xvii.

be made in the hymns to the gods. And is it really plausible that even 600 or 700 years later, the greatest grammarian of India composed a most artificial and most scientific system of grammar, utterly ignorant of the simplest tool which might have assisted him in his work? Should it be possible to realize an advanced stage of social development without a knowledge of writing, then it is needless, of course, to refer to the arts, sciences, measures, and coins mentioned in the Sútras of Páṇini; yet I will advert, within the limits of these preliminary remarks, to one fact, at least, which it may be as well not to overlook.

We know from Herodotus that Darius, the son of Hystaspes, subdued the Hindus;[15] and we have inscriptions of this king himself which tell us that amongst the nations subdued by him were the Gadara and Hidhu or the Gandháras, and the peoples living on the banks of the Indus.[16] Could Páṇini, therefore, who was a native of Gandhára, had he lived after Darius, as Müller supposes to be the case, have remained ignorant of the fact that writing was known in Persia? And if not, would he not, in composing his work, have profited by this knowledge, provided, of course, that he was not acquainted previously with this art, independently of his acquaintance with the Persian alphabet? This question is answered, however, I believe, by a word which is the subject of one of his special rules (IV. 1, 49), the word *yavanání*, explained by Kátyáyana and Patanjali as meaning the "*writing* of the Yavanas." Both Weber and Müller mention this word, the former as meaning "the writing of the Greeks or Semites (Ind. St. I. p. 144), or, as he later opines, of the Greeks alone (IV. 89); the latter (p. 521) "a variety of the Semitic alphabet, which, previous to Alexander, and previous to Pâṇini, became the type of the Indian alphabet." It would seem to me, that it denotes the writing of the Persians, and probably the cuneiform writing which was known already, before the time of Darius, and is peculiar enough in its appearance, and different enough from the alphabet of the

---

[15] iv. 44: *μετὰ δὲ τούτους περιπλώσαντας Ἰνδούς τε κατεστρέψατο Δαρεῖος*, etc.

[16] Compare Lassen's Ind. Alterth. i. 422; ii. 112, 113, and the quotations given there.

Hindus, to explain the fact that its name called for the formation of a separate word.

While I intend to address myself now to the special arguments offered by Müller, for the theory that writing was unknown to Páṇini, I find myself, as it were, arrested by his own words; for, after having proposed his reasons in support of this theory (from page 497 to page 520), he makes the following remark on the word *lipikara*, "a writer or engraver," which I quote in full:—"This last word *lipikara* is an important word, for it is the only word in the Sûtras of Pâṇini which can be legitimately adduced to prove that Pâṇini was acquainted with the art of writing. He teaches the formation of this word, iii. 2, 21." Whether it *is* the only word which can be legitimately adduced for such a proof, I shall have to examine. But even on the supposition that it is, I must really question the purport of the whole discussion, if Müller himself admits that Páṇini would have pointed to this word *lipikara* had it been his task to defend himself against the imputation of being ignorant of the art of writing. For it becomes obviously immaterial whether the word *lipikara* occurs once or a hundred times in the Sútras,—whether another similar word be discoverable in his Grammar or not; one word is clearly sufficient to establish the fact, and to remove all doubt. This admission of Müller, which upsets all he has tried to impress upon our minds, is doubtless very creditable to his candour; for it shows his wish to elicit the truth, and fully confirms our faith in what he says at the end of his essay: "It is possible I may have overlooked some words in the Brâhmaṇas and Sûtras, which would prove the existence of written books previous to Pâṇini. If so, it is not from any wish to suppress them." But since he has not even tried to invalidate by a single word the conclusion which necessarily follows from this admission, it would be like carrying owls to Athens if I endeavoured to prove what is sufficiently proved already by himself.

Nevertheless, I will do so; not only out of respect for his labour, but because the observations I am going to make may tend to show that there is much more evidence in Páṇini than this solitary word for the assumption that he was not merely conversant with writing, but that his Grammar could not even have been composed as it is now, without the application to it of written letters and signs.

The chief argument of Müller is a negative one: the absence of words which mean book, ink, paper, and the like. Thus he says of the Vaidik hymns (p. 497): "Where writing is known, it is almost impossible to compose a thousand hymns without bringing in some such words as, writing, reading, paper, or pen. Yet there is not one single allusion in these hymns to anything connected with writing;" or (p. 512) "If we take the ordinary modern words for book, paper, ink, writing, etc., not one of them has yet been discovered in any Sanskrit work of genuine antiquity."[17] I do not think that such an argument, in its generality, can ever be held to be a conclusive proof. It is not the purpose of the Vaidik hymns to tell us that pen and ink were known to the Áryas; it becomes, therefore, entirely a matter of chance whether so prosaic an object be mentioned in them or not,—whether the poets borrow their figures from paper and book, or from the life of the elements. The very instances Müller has adduced from the Psalms will probably leave in every one's mind the impression that these songs might easily have existed, without any damage to their reputation, even if they had not contained the three verses which bespeak the scholarship of their authors; and the book of Job too, if it had not that literary longing which is contained in Müller's *happy quotation:* "Oh that my words were now written! oh, that they were printed in a book!" But what applies to poetical songs, avails with still greater force in a grammatical work. Pâṇini's object is to record such phenomena of the language as are of interest from a *grammatical* point of view. Sometimes the words which belong to his province, will be at the same time also of historical and antiquarian interest; but it does not follow at all, that because a word of the latter category is omitted in his rules, it is absent

---

[17] Not even *lipi?*

from the language also; the extreme conclusion would be that it is a word of no grammatical interest; and this conclusion itself, to be correct, would imply that Páṇini was a perfect author, and did not omit any word or words which ought to have been noticed by him on grammatical grounds.

"There is no word," says Müller, "for book, paper, ink, writing, etc., in any Sanskrit work of genuine antiquity" (p. 512). Of *lip*, "to write," I need say no more, since it is the base of *lipi*. I agree with him that the verbs *adhí* or *vach* (in the caus.) which are used in the sense "to read," contain no proof of their applying to a written work, since the former means literally "to go over mentally, to acquire," and the latter "to cause to speak."[18] I am equally willing to admit that the divisions of literary works which are frequently met with, such as *anuvákas*, *praśnas*, *maṇḍalas*, *-pathas*, *vargas*, *súktas*, etc., cannot be compared with such words as "*volumen*, a volume, *liber*, *i. e.* the inner bark of a tree; or *βίβλος*, *i.e.* *βύβλος*, the inner bark of the papyrus; or *book*, *i e.*, beech-wood" (p. 515). But I cannot admit that there is no word of genuine antiquity meaning book, or division of book, which cannot be compared with those latter words of the cognate languages. One word is indeed supplied by Müller himself, at the end of his essay; it undoes, as it were, all that precedes on this subject, in the same way as *lipikara* undid his arguments against Páṇini's acquaintance with writing.

After the words I have quoted above, "if so, it is not from any wish to suppress them," he continues (523): "I believe, indeed, that the Brâhmaṇas were preserved by oral tradition only, but I should feel inclined to claim an acquaintance with the art of writing for the authors of the Sûtras. And there is one word which seems to strengthen such a supposition. We find that several of the Sûtras are divided into chapters, called *paṭalas*. This is a word never used for the subdivision of the Brâhmaṇas. Its meaning is a covering, the surrounding skin or membrane; it is also used for a tree. If so, it would seem

[18] Thus Páṇini himself says, V. 2, 84, श्रोत्रियँश्छन्दोऽधीते.

to be almost synonymous with *liber* and *βίβλος*, and it would mean *book*, after meaning originally a sheet of paper made of the surrounding bark of trees." But he seems to have entirely overlooked—no doubt on account of its common occurrence—the word *káṇḍa*, which is the name of a division of the Taittiríya-Saṁhitá and -Bráhmaṇas, not to speak of the frequent application it has found at a later period in denoting chapters of ritual books, or ritual books themselves, such as *kámyeshṭi-káṇḍa*, *kámyapaśu-káṇḍa*, *paurodáśika-káṇḍa*, *ágneya-káṇḍa*, *hautra-káṇḍa*, *adhwaryu-káṇḍa*, *yajamána-káṇḍa*, *sattra-káṇḍa*, etc. And *káṇḍa*, before meaning *book*, means "the part of the trunk of a tree whence the branches proceed,—a stalk or stem;"—it is, therefore, a fair representative of our word *book*. But, if such is the original purport of *paṭala*, and of the more frequent *káṇḍa*, I cannot conceive on what grounds Müller founds his doubt (p. 513) of *pattra* meaning the leaf of a book, in works of genuine antiquity, since *pattra* means, originally, the leaf of a tree, and since palm-leaves, even now, bespeak the use which has been made of them for literary purposes. For, though Urvaśí writes her amatory letter on a "birch-leaf,"—which, then, is called, not merely *pattra*, but *bhúrja-pattra*,—it does not follow that ordinary letters of literary works must also have been engraved on what was probably a rarer material than the leaf of a palm-tree or of a lotus.

Besides *káṇḍa* and *paṭala*, there are, however, two other important words, in the sense of work, which could not but attract the attention of Professor Müller—the words *sútra* and *grantha*. The former, which means, literally, "string," has become, according to him (p. 512), the well-known name of an extensive class of works, by assuming the figurative sense, "strings of rules." The latter, he says (p. 522), "is derived from a root *grath*, which means *nectere*, *serere*. *Grantha*, therefore, like the later *sandarbha*, would simply mean a composition. It corresponds etymologically with the Latin *textus*. Thus it is used by the commentator to Nir. i. 20., where he says that former teachers handed down the hymns, *granthato 'rthataścha*,[19] 'according to their text, and according to their meaning.' In the later literature of India, *grantha* was used for a volume, and, in *granthakuṭi*, a library, we see clearly that it has that meaning. But in the early literature *grantha* does not mean *pustaka*, or book; it means simply a composition, as opposed to a traditional work."

That "sûtra" *may* have assumed the sense of "string of rules," before it became the name of a book, is possible; but that it must have gone through *this* metaphorical process, and no other,—as the certainty with which Müller explains the term would imply,—[20] is not corroborated by any proof he has given; nor is it even plausible. Before, however, I give my own opinion on this word, it will be necessary, first, to ascertain whether the word *sútra*,—which is used in the singular both as a name for a whole collection of rules, and as a name for a single *sútra*,—denoted, originally, the latter, and then became the designation of the former, or *vice versâ*. Thus, the Káśikávṛitti calls Páṇini's Sútra, V. 4, 151, *gaṇa-sútram*, and speaks of the *five Sútras*, I. 3, 72—76, *swaritanita iti pañchabhis sútrair átmanepadam, etc. . . . . . . evam panchasútryám udáháryam;* and Patanjali says, in the introduction to Páṇini, *Sútráṇi chápyadhíyána ishyate vaiyákaraṇa iti*, "he who studies the *Sútras* is termed a grammarian." But if we examine the use which Páṇini himself makes of this word, we find that he always uses *sútra* as a term for the whole collection of rules, and not as an expression for a single Sútra: IV. 2, 65, "*Sútrách cha kopadhát;*" IV. 3, 110, "*Páráśaryailáślibhyám bhikshunaṭasútrayoh*" (where the dual shows that the analysis requires *bhikshusútre* and *naṭasútre*). In his Rules, IV. 2, 60, and V. 1. 58, the number of the word is less clear, since it is part of a compound; yet the instances of Patanjali to the Várttikas, and some explanations of the Káśiká (*e. g. Kalpasútram adhíte, Kálpa-*

---

[19] Similarly, *e. g.*, Kullúka on Manu, VII. 43, चिवेदीमर्थतो ग्रन्थतश्चाभ्यसेत्. See also, "Muir's Original Sanskrit Texts," vol. ii. p. 175.

[20] "We meet with *Bráhmaṇas*, the sayings of Brahmans; with *Sútras*, *i. e.*, the strings of rules." (p. 512.)

sútraḥ, and *ashṭáv adhyáyáḥ parimáṇam asya sútrasya ashṭakam páṇiníyam*) leave little doubt that it is likewise to be taken there as a singular. In a similar manner it is used in Patanjali's comment on II. 3, 66, v. 2, "*Śobhaná khalu páṇineḥ sútrasya kṛitiḥ.*"[21] It would seem, therefore, since no higher authority than Páṇini can be quoted, that *sútra*,—when used in the sense of a single rule,—is

---

[21] In the Sútra VIII. 3, 90, and the Gaṇa to V. 4, 29, its sense is the literal one; it is mentioned, too, as a masc. and neuter in the Gaṇa to II. 4, 31.—It is necessary for me to observe, that in the quotations from Páṇini I always distinguish between the text of the Sútras, the Várttikas of Kátyáyana,—and those alone can be held to be Kátyáyana's Várttikas which appear in the Mahábháshya,—Patanjali's Commentary, the Várttikas found in the Káśiká and in the Siddhántakaumudí, and these latter works. The importance of this distinction requires no remark, since all conclusions must become unsafe if the observations or instances of one writer are given as evidence for or against another, especially before it has been decided whether, for instance, Páṇini and Kátyáyana were contemporaries or not. I regret that Professor Müller has paid little attention to this circumstance, for he has frequently confounded the Commentaries, even the latest, with the text of the Sútras of Páṇini; and the very circumstance that he has sometimes pointed out the commentary as distinct from the text, and *vice versâ*, creates still more confusion where he has omitted to do so. Thus, he quotes correctly (p. 44, note 2), "VIII. 3, 95 (*text*)," or, "IV. 1, 176 (*text*)" or, (p. 45, in the same note), "IV. 3, 98 (*text*);" and I admit that an *attentive* reader will conclude that the quotations not marked "*text*" are taken from the commentary; yet, "VI. 3, 75," is not commentary but text. And what does the word "commentary" mean? Patanjali, Káśiká, Siddh.-k., or the Calcutta Paṇḍits? Again, when he says (p. 69, n. 1): "It is remarkable that, in Pâṇini also, the word *śloka* is always used in opposition to Vedic literature," not one of his quotations given to prove this important point, viz., IV. 2, 66; "IV. 3, 102, 1;" IV. 3, 107; "II. 4, 21," belongs to Páṇini, but the two former to Pantajali; and the two latter to the Káśiká. On p. 347, n., the Saulabháni Bráhmaṇáni are attributed by him to Páṇini himself, but Páṇini says nothing about them. The instances to the quotations, of page 361, n. 3, ("IV. 3, 101; IV. 2, 64"), and those to n. 4. (IV. 3, 108), belong to the Káśiká,—none to Páṇini. Nearly all the instances referred to, p. 364, n. 3, belong to Patanjali; and p. 369, nn., where "*com.*" and "*text*" are contradistinguished, "VI. 2, 10" is not Páṇini. P. 370, n. 10, "IV. 3, 104," ought to have been marked "com.," and a similar confusion exists, pp. 362, 371, 521, 522, etc.; while, on the other hand, the *commentary* is correctly quoted in most of the instances of p. 184, 185, 193, 252, 330, 339, 353, 357, though without any mention whether the commentary of Patanjali, or of the Káśiká, etc., be meant. The *text* is marked correctly, pp. 125, n. 2; 340, 368, n. 1 (IV. 3. 128), 5; 369, n. 1, 3; 371, n. 2, 6; 372, n. 2, 8; 373, n. 3; and the *gaṇas* correctly, p. 369, n. 6; 370, n. 7, 8, 9, 10; 372, n. 8; 373, n. 8.—I do not altogether think that this want of accuracy,

pars pro toto, and that its original sense is that of a whole collection of rules.[22] If such be the case the question arises, whether it is

---

in a writer like Professor Müller, is entirely the result of oversight; it seems to me, on the contrary, that the reason for it lies in the words of his note to p. 46:—"It was impossible to teach or to use Pâṇini's Sûtras without examples, which necessarily formed part of the traditional grammatical literature long before the great Commentary was written, and are, therefore, of a much higher historical value than is commonly supposed. The coincidences between the examples used in the Prâtiśâkhyâs and in Pâṇini, show that these examples were by no means selected at random, but that they had long formed part of the traditional teaching." This coincidence, to be of that value which is described in the words quoted, would require first the proof that the Prátiśákhyas, viz. the existing ones of Śaunaka and Kátyáyana, are *older* than Páṇini; otherwise, it ceases to be of any consequence, as regards Páṇini. As to his statement in general, however, I must observe, that it can surely not be received as authoritative in the absence of all proof. I must myself, on the contrary, quite demur to its admissibility. The coincidences, in the first place, between the instances of the existing Prátiśákhyas and those in the Commentaries of Páṇini, considering the great bulk of the latter, are perfectly trifling. Again, as to the other instances, about 2000 Sútras of Páṇini are not criticised by Kátyáyana, nor commented upon by Patanjali; with regard to the instances, therefore, in this considerable number of rules, our oldest authority is nearly always the Káśiká, the infallibility of which Commentary I have had, sometimes, reason to doubt. Scarcely any instances of this category can be traced to the Prátiśákhyas, and, unless it can be proved by Müller that these instances belong to *antiquity*, I do not consider it at all safe to found any conclusions on them, *as regards antiquity*. But on no account can it be consistent with critical research to use even the instances of Patanjali as evidence for or against the Várttikas, and much less for or against the Sútras of Páṇini, since Kátyáyana *never* gives *instances*, but, like Páṇini himself, either lays down a general rule, or specifies the words which are the subject of his rule.

[22] Compare also the following passage of the Mahábháshya (ed. Ballantyne, p. 68). Patanjali: अथ व्याकरणमित्यस्य शब्दस्य कः पदार्थः। सूत्रम् ॥ Kátyáyana: सूत्रे व्याकरणे षष्ठ्यर्थो ऽनुपपन्नः ॥ Patanjali: सूत्रे व्याकरणे षष्ठ्यर्थो नोपपद्यते व्याकरणस्य सूत्रमिति। किं तदन्यत्सूत्राद्व्याकरणम्। यस्यादः सूत्रं स्यात्; Kaiyyaṭa .... षष्ठ्यर्थ इति। द्वाभ्यामपि शब्दाभ्यामष्टाध्याय्याः प्रतिपादनाद्व्यतिरेकाभावः। सामान्यविशेषशब्दतया तु द्वयोः प्रयोगो न विरुध्यते। यदा त्वष्टाध्याय्येकदेशः सूत्रशब्देनोच्यते तदा षष्ठ्यर्थो ऽप्युपपद्यते; Nagojíbh ....: ननु सूत्रसमुदायस्य व्याकरणस्येदं सूत्रमित्युपपद्यते ऽत आह। द्वाभ्यामिति। सूत्रपदेनाप्यष्टाध्याय्येव यदोच्यते तदापीष्यते ऽयं प्रयोगः स न सिध्येदित्यर्थः। ननु किमुच्यते षष्ठ्यर्थो ऽनुपपन्न इति पर्यायतया सहप्रयोगो ऽपि न स्यादत आह। सामान्यविशेषेति। सूत्रं सामान्यं व्याकरणं विशेषः। सूत्रशब्देनाष्टाध्याय्येव। तदेकदेशे तु योगव्यवहार एव योगे योगे उपतिष्ठत इत्यादौ। यदा त्विति। सूत्राणि

the figure implied by Müller's rendering "strings of rules" that has led to the word *sútra* being used in the sense of "book," or not. As, I believe, I am able to show that Páṇini was perfectly well acquainted with the art of writing, and that written books had even existed long before his time, my own opinion is, that the name for book was, as in the case of *paṭala* and *káṇḍa*, borrowed rather from a material fact than from the metaphorical idea of the logical connection of rules. And here I appeal to evidence, and to the admission which will be made to me that there are peculiarities and habits in the life of nations, which may be supposed to have existed at the earliest times such as we see them now. Everyone who has studied Sanskrit MSS. in the libraries of London and Paris, will have found that the oldest specimens of these MSS. are written on palm-leaves, which are pierced in the middle, and kept together by means of a "string." The naturalness of the material of these MSS., and the primitive manner in which they are bound,—if we can use the term "binding," for a parcel of leaves, covered on both sides with oblong pieces of wood, and kept together by a *string* which runs through the middle,—bespeak, in my opinion, the habits of high antiquity, religiously preserved up to a recent date by a nation which, beyond all other nations, is wont to cherish its antiquity, and to defend it, even in practical life, against the intrusions of modern arts. The MSS. I have seen are certainly not more than a few centuries old, as may be easily inferred from the fragility of the material of which they are composed; but I hold them to be genuine specimens of the manner in which books were formed at the earliest periods of the civilization of India. No one, however, ought, I should conceive, to be less surprised at seeing the word "string" becoming the name of "book," than a German who would call his own book "*Band*," translating, as it were, literally, the Sanskrit *sútra*, and having recourse to the same figure of speech.

Since I contrast, in these remarks, opinion with opinion,—not

---

चाप्यधीयान इति भाष्ये वच्यमाणत्वादिति भावः। वस्तुत एकदेशस्य सूत्रत्वे ऽपि तस्यापि साचात्परम्परया वा व्याकरणत्वात्षष्ठ्यर्थानुपपत्तिरेवेति तत्त्वम्.

claiming any greater value for mine than that which may be permitted to the impressions and views of the individual mind,—I will not conceal that I hold the very nature of the works called "Sútra," to have arisen from, and depended on, the material which was kept together by the "string." I cannot consider it plausible that these works,—"written, as they are, in the most artificial, elaborate, and enigmatical form,"—which have been so well defined and described in Müller's work (p. 71, ff.),—in which, to use his words, "shortness is the great object of this style of composition,"—should have been composed merely for the sake of being easily committed to memory. "To introduce and to maintain such a species of literature," argues Müller (p. 74), "was only possible with the Indian system of education, which consisted in little else except implanting these Sûtras and other works into the tender memory of children, and afterwards explaining them by commentaries and glosses." But, though I do not dispute that these Sútras were learnt, and are learnt, by heart up to this day, this circumstance alone does not explain why the matter thus to be inculcated must have been written in such a manner "that an author rejoiceth in the economizing of half a short vowel as much as in the birth of a son;" why, "every doctrine thus propounded, whether grammar, metre, law, or philosophy," must have become "reduced to a mere skeleton." Müller himself says (p. 501),—and I fully concur with him,—that "we can form no opinion of the powers of memory in a state of society so different from ours as the Indian Parishads are from our universities. Feats of memory, such as we hear of now and then, show that our notions of the limits of that faculty are quite arbitrary." And, as he himself produces proof that the three Vedas and their Bráhmaṇas *were* learnt by heart, it does not appear at all likely that the peculiar enigmatic form of this Sútra literature was invented simply to suit the convenience of a memory the capacities of which must have been extraordinary.

The reason which accounts for this form is, in my opinion, of a far more prosaic kind. I hold that it is the awkwardness, the fragility, and, in some parts of India, perhaps the scarcity of proper natural leaves, which imposed upon an author the happy restraint of "economizing half a short vowel;" that the scantiness of the writing material compelled authors to be very concise, and betrayed them, as a consequence, into becoming obscure.

Vaidik hymns and sacrificial Bráhmaṇas stand, clearly, under a different predicament to works on grammar or philosophy. A god cannot be invited with *anubandhas* to partake of the sacrificial meal, nor the religious feelings of a nation be roused with hard and unintelligible phraseology; but the purpose of a grammar may be attained, if there be need to save space, by an artificial method; and a philosophical doctrine may be propounded in riddles, as we can testify in our own days. I draw here, of course, a line between genuine and artificial Sútras,—the former, in my opinion, a creation of material necessity; the latter, a mere imitation when this necessity had ceased. The Sútras of Páṇini, in their dignified brevity, and the Sútras of the Buddhists, in their tedious prolixity, are, probably, the two opposite poles;[23] but it requires, I conceive, no great effort to see that there is a gap, even between Páṇini and the Yoga-Sútras, nay, between him and the Mímánsá- and Vedánta- Sútras as well as the Nyáya-Sútras and the Sánkhya-Pravachana.

Turning now to the second word I have mentioned above, with the word Sútra, I will say at once, that *grantha* likewise appears to me to have become the name of a book, not on account of the connection which exists between the different parts of a literary composition, but on account of the connection of the leaves which form its bulk. Professor Weber, who makes Páṇini live

[23] The lamented Burnouf has given a description of these Sútras, in his invaluable work on the "Buddhisme Indien," p. 36, ff. He particularly points out,—and the fact is important,—that amongst these caricatures of the Bráhmanic Sútras, there are several which have the enigmatic brevity of the latter; he distinguishes, therefore, between Sútras which may be attributed to Śákyamuni, and Sútras which belong to subsequent periods. See "Introduction à l'Histoire du Buddhisme Indien," p. 104, ff.

about 140 years after Christ,[24] but who, nevertheless, is favourable to the view I take of Páṇini's acquaintance with writing, says, in the "Indische Studien," vol. iv. p. 89, that "the word *grantha*, which is several times used by Páṇini, refers, according to its etymology, decidedly to written texts;" yet he informs us (p. 436), that "the word grantha is referred by Böhtlingk-Roth to the *composition*." Whether the latter remark is made "*pújártham*," or whether this author,—according to his habit of leaving the reader to make his own choice amongst a variety of conflicting opinions,—intended to establish a *vibháshá*,[25] or whether he has altered his original view, is more than I can decide, since he has neither supported his first opinion with any explanatory remark, nor expressed adhesion or dissent when he concluded his fourth volume of the "Indische Studien."[26]

That *grantha*, according to its etymology, *may* mean "a literary composition," and that it has been used in that sense, is undeniable; yet I contend that it did not bear this metaphorical sense before it was used in the literal meaning of "a *series* of leaves;" or, in other words, before it designated a written book. Previously to supporting this opinion with other arguments than those which are implied in my remarks on *sútra*, I consider it necessary to remove the suspicion which has been thrown by Müller on this legitimate word. He quotes the four Sútras in Páṇini where it occurs,[27] but remarks in the note of p. 45, "The word *grantha*, used in the Sûtra (IV. 3, 87), is always somewhat suspicious."

---

[24] "Akademische Vorlesungen über Indische Literaturgeschichte," p. 200, 202.

[25] Such is really the case in the "Indische Literaturgeschichte," p. 183, note.

[26] Should I have overlooked any observation of his on this word, it would be quite unintentional, since I have been guided in my quotations by the excellent indices he has appended to his volumes. All I mean to convey is, that the only justification he gives for the sense, "written work," of *grantha*, viz., the etymology of the word, does not appear to be a sufficient one, since Müller is certainly right when he remarks (p. 522), that *granth*, nectere, serere, might be taken also in a figurative sense.

[27] Compare also, IV. 3, 101, v. 2; 105, v. 2; the Káśiká on V. 1, 10, v. 1: पौरुषेयो ग्रन्थः; on IV. 2, 62: ब्राह्मणसदृशो ग्रन्थो ऽनुब्राह्मणम्; on IV. 2, 63: वसन्तसहचरितो

The reason for this sweeping doubt is contained, I suppose, in the words which immediately follow: "That some of the Sûtras which now form part of Pâṇini's Grammar, did not proceed from him, is acknowledged by Kaiyyaṭa (*cf.* IV. 3. 131, 132);" and in the first note of p. 361, where he writes, "Pâṇ., IV. 3, 116, कृते ग्रंथे ॥ Kaiyyaṭa says that this Sûtra does not belong to Pâṇini." That there are *three*, perhaps *four* Sútras in Páṇini's Grammar, which

---

ग्रन्थो वसन्त इत्युच्यते ; on III. 1, 89, v. 1 (a Várttika of the Bháradwájíyas, according to Patanjali): ग्रन्थते ग्रन्थः ; on VII. 3, 4: स्वरमधिकृत्य कृतो ग्रन्थः सौवरो ग्रन्थः.—Of one of the Sútras he quotes, viz. I. 3, 75, Müller observes, (p. 522) that it is used there "so as to apply to the *Veda.*" This remark concerns the commentator, but not Páṇini, who, as he correctly states, a few lines afterwards, uses *grantha* as "opposed to a traditional work." I do not believe that the commentator is absolutely wrong, as will appear from my subsequent remarks; but I think that he might have chosen a better instance. By commentary, however, I do not understand Patanjali's Bháshya, which has no remark on this Sútra, nor the Káśiká, which has the counter-instance, उद्यच्छति चिकित्सां वैद्यः; the first trace of this instance I find in the Siddh.-k. (fol. 167 a.),—uncorrected in the Prauḍhamanoramá,—whence it has crept into more recent books, *e. g.*, the abridged Commentary of Nágoji on Páṇini's Sútras. This instance, one of many, will corroborate my statement in note 21, that the compilation of the Calcutta Paṇḍits,—however meritorious, and superior to its mutilated and unauthorized reprint,—so far from admitting of being identified with Páṇini himself, ought not to be used as evidence for or against Páṇini, without a knowledge of the source whence it has derived its instances.

I feel grieved that I cannot leave this note without destroying one of the most poetical illusions of Professor Weber, connected with this word *grantha.* From the stream of imaginary narrative which meanders through the desert of his "Literaturgeschichte," emerges, *à propos* of the Rámáyaṇa (p. 182), the remark, that this masterpiece of Hindu poetry was probably preceded by some other epic works. To prove that which cannot be proved without a knowledge of the date of the Rámáyaṇa, which we have not,—and without a knowledge of those epic poems, which likewise we have not,—but which is plausible enough without any proof, he quotes Páṇini's Sútra, IV. 3, 88, which treats on the titles of some *granthas.* Among these *granthas* (which are, to his imagination, epic poems), is one called *Śiśukrandíya,* which therefore is, to him, a forerunner of the Rámáyaṇa. The same ingenious conjecture occurs in his "Indische Studien," vol. i. p. 155, where he grows somewhat indignant at Wilson, who, in his Dictionary, renders this term "a work treating of infantine or juvenile grievances," for he adorns Wilson, for this rendering, with a query and note of admiration ("Wilson dict. ? !"). Now, whether *śiśukrandíya* ought to have been, by right, the title of an epic poem (in the same manner as we learn, from another work what the words in the Vedas *ought* to have meant, if they had profited by the last results of Sanskrit

probably did not belong to his work originally, I will concede;[28] but amongst these three or four Sútras out of 3996, there is no Sútra containing the word *grantha;* for I believe Müller was mistaken when he says that Kaiyyaṭa acknowledges that the

---

and comparative philology), I am unable to say. Nevertheless, I believe that Wilson is right; for the *Káśiká* explains this word, शिशूनां क्रन्दनं शिशुक्रन्दनं तमधिकृत्य कृतो ग्रन्थः शिशुक्रन्दीयः, and the *Gaṇaratna-mahodadhi* has even an additional remark: शिशवो बालास्तेषां क्रन्दस्तमधिकृत्य कृतो ग्रन्थः शिशुक्रन्दीयः। बालपुस्तकः. —It is, in other terms, "a book for children, written with reference to their cries,"—a kind of nursery-book for naughty babies.

[28] Dr. Otto Boehtlingk was the first who drew attention to this fact, in the volume which he has annexed to his garbled and unauthorized reprint of the meritorious labour of the Calcutta editors of Páṇini. In a note of p. xx. of his Preface, he enumerates *seven* Sútras, which, according to him, "were originally Várttikas, and only at a later time became embodied into the text of Páṇini;" viz., "IV. 1, 166, 167; IV. 3, 132; V. 1, 36; VI. 1, 62, 100, 136." It certainly raises a strong doubt as to the authenticity of a Sútra, if it occurs also as a Várttika of Kátyáyana; but I hold the indispensable conditions for confirming such a doubt to be—1. that the Várttika must really belong to Kátyáyana; 2. that the wording of the Várttika must be *identical* with that of the doubted Sútra; and 3. that both must have the *same tendency.* In the first place, however, we are entitled to consider as Várttikas of Kátyáyana only such as occur in, and,—what is invariably then the case,—are commented upon by, the Bháshya of Patanjali. Várttikas found in the Káśiká or Siddhántakaumudí, but not in the Bháshya, may be, and *evidently* are in many instances, the critical additions of later times. They afford no basis for doubting the genuineness of a Sútra in Páṇini; nor is a mere remark of Kaiyyaṭa, the commentator of Patanjali, that "some" consider a Sútra as having been a Várttika, sufficient to cancel the Sútra from amongst the original rules. Secondly, if a Várttika is not worded in the same manner as the Sútra,—excepting, of course, the usual addition of Kátyáyana, इति वक्तव्यम्,—the mere similarity of both is no sufficient ground for doubting the originality of the Sútra; for the difference in the wording of the Várttika may have, as it *very frequently* has, the mere object of criticizing the manner in which Páṇini delivered his rule. Lastly, if the Várttika and Sútra are identical in words, but not in tendency, there is not the slightest ground for doubting the authenticity of the Sútra, though Kaiyyaṭa may historically record that "some" have preferred to "throw it among the Várttikas." In applying these tests to the enumeration given by Dr. Boehtlingk, we find, that IV. 1, 166 does *not* occur literally in the Várttika 3 of IV. 1, 163; for, though the Calcutta editors write वृद्धस्य च पूजायाम्, and append their mark, that it occurs in the Siddh.-k. (the printed edition of this work contains on p. 66*a*, line 1, the words वृद्धस्य च पूजायामिति वाच्यम्),—the wording of this Várttika, in the Bháshya is (MS., E.I.H., 330), वृद्धस्य च पूजायां युवसंज्ञा वक्तव्यम् (probably युवसंज्ञेति वक्तव्यम्); but even if the additional words belong, as is possible, not to the Várttika, but to the Bháshya, it is clear

Sútra IV. 3, 116 did not belong to Pánini. I have not been able to discover anywhere, in the Mahábháshya, either by the aid of my memory or my indices, that Kaiyyaṭa expresses any opinion whatever on this Sútra; but even should the mistake be mine, there would be little importance in the mere doubt of Kaiyyaṭa, since Patanjali, when commenting on the Várttikas to IV. 3, 105,

---

that the tendency of the Várttika and that of the Sútra are not identical; for, in the Várttika, the rule is *absolute*, while in the Sútra, IV. 1, 166, it is *optional*, through the *anuvṛitti* of the preceding वा of IV. 1, 165. Therefore, Patanjali comments on the Várttika in question, तत्रभवन्तो गार्ग्यायणाः । तत्रभवन्तो वात्स्यायनाः without the option recorded by the Káśiká on IV. 1, 166, in the instances, तत्रभवान्गार्ग्यायणो गार्ग्यो वा । वात्स्यायनो वात्स्यो वा । दाचायणो दाचिर्वा.—A similar negative conclusion applies to IV. 1, 167. The Várttika mentioned by the Calcutta editors, to IV. 1, 162, does *not* occur in the Bháshya; it is *not* identical, even in the Siddh.-k., with the Sútra, IV. 1, 167; it has *not* the same tendency as the Sútra, the latter being optional, the former absolute. There is no ground, consequently, for doubting that the "some" of Kaiyyaṭa, who maintain the antiquity of the Sútra, are correct.—IV. 3, 132, is suspicious, for it occurs as a Várttika in the Bhásyha to IV. 3, 131, and fulfils the three above-named conditions; equally so V. 1, 36, which is a Várttika to V. 1, 35, and VI. 1, 62, which occurs as a Várttika to VI. 1, 61. On the other hand, VI. 1, 100, need not be rejected absolutely, for its wording is not identical with that of the Várttika of VI. 1. 99; nor is it clear that both coincide in tendency. VI. 1, 99, restricts the rule to the condition of the word इति following a combination like पटत्पटत्; VI. 1, 100, exempts a similar combination, if ending in डाच् from this condition (comp. V. 4, 57): it would seem, therefore, that the Várttika to VI. 1, 99, maintains the condition, but corrects the option वा, by the word नित्यम्. I must admit, however, that Patanjali gives the instance पटपटायति, which would countenance the probability of this Sútra, also, not being an original one. Lastly, the Sútra VI. 1, 136, अडभ्यासव्यवाये ऽपि neither occurs as a Várttika in the Bháshya, nor even as a Várttika in the Káśiká or the Siddh.-k.; nor has its original existence, in fact, been doubted by anybody except Dr. Boehtlingk, who writes in his so-called Commentary (p. 256), "This Sútra has been interpolated at a later time; it owes its origin to the following two Várttikas to the preceding Sútra, अड्व्यवाय उपसंख्यानम् ॥ १ ॥ अभ्यासव्यवाये च ॥ २ ॥ Compare Siddh.-k. p. 144*a*;" where, however, the reader will not find anything relating to the subject, while, on p. 145*a*, he will discover the Sútra, IV. I, 136, such as it is in the Calcutta edition of Páṇini. That both Várttikas are a criticism of Kátyáyana, who clearly disapproved of the condensed wording of the Sútra 136, did not even occur to the mind of Dr. Boehtlingk; but, considering the condition of his knowledge of Páṇini, as displayed in this "Commentary," and even in his very last work, I cannot but express the belief, that his "αὐτὸς ἔφα" to strike out a Sútra of Páṇini, goes for very little indeed,—especially as it touches upon the sphere of reasoning.

distinctly quotes twice the Sútra IV. 3, 116, which is a positive proof that it existed at his time, and was genuine enough.[29]

I will now give an instance from the Mahábhárata, which, in my belief, would be perfectly unintelligible, if *grantha* were taken only in the sense of "composition," and not also in that of "written book," or "volume." I am met here, however, with an objection; viz., that I ought first to show that the Mahábhárata possesses the qualification which Müller has appended to his quoted remark, or, in other words, that it is a work of "the early literature," since he says that "*grantha* does not mean *pustaka*, or book, in 'the early literature,'" while he admits that it has that sense in the later literature. Both Müller and Weber agree that there was *a* Mahábhárata at the time of Áśwaláyana, since they quote a passage from his Gṛihya-Sútra, where the name occurs (Müller, p. 42; Weber, "Literaturgeschichte," p. 56), and neither denies that a work prior to Áśwaláyana would have a claim to be called a work of the earlier literature. Both scholars however question,—and very rightly too,—the claim of the *present* Mahábhárata, to having been *that* Mahábhárata which is quoted by Áśwaláyana. It is, of course, impossible for me to treat here, as it were incidentally, not merely of the question concerning the age of the Mahábhárata, but the relative ages of the various portions of this work, since it must be evident to everyone who has read it, that it is, in its present shape, a collection of literary products belonging to widely distant periods of Hindu literature. To do justice to a subject of this kind, I should have not merely to enter into details which would be here out of place, but to discuss the prior important question, as to how far the printed text in which this colossal

---

[29] There is no Bháshya on IV. 3, 116, and, therefore, no commentary of Kaiyyaṭa on this Sútra. On the Várttika 2, to IV. 3, 105, कृते ग्रन्थे मक्षिकादिभ्यो ऽण् which is a criticism on Páṇini IV. 3, 116, on account of the addition, मक्षिकादिभ्यो ऽण्, and, therefore, a proof that the latter Sútra was originally existing, Patanjali says: कृते ग्रन्थ इत्यत्र (*i.e.*, IV. 3, 116) मक्षिकादिभ्यो ऽण् वक्तव्यः । मक्षिकाभिः कृतं माक्षिकम्; and on a third Várttika योगविभागात्सिद्धं which is not printed in the Calcutta edition, he observes, योगविभागः करिष्यते । कृते ग्रन्थे (IV. 3, 116) ततः संज्ञायां (IV. 3, 117) न कृत इत्येतस्मिन्नर्थे यथाविहितं प्रत्ययो भवति.

epos is generally known to us, may be relied upon; and I should feel all the more bound to do so, as my collations of considerable portions of this text with the best MSS., in this country and abroad, fully convince me that it is neither advisable to make a translation of the Mahábhárata,—a labour which, if done once, should be done once for all,—nor to found a detailed criticism of the several portions of this work, on the printed text, however much I admire the industry, patience, and scholarship, of those who have accomplished the task of laying before us a first edition of this enormous work. Without their labours, it would have been still more difficult than it now is, to perceive the defects of the MSS.; but this tribute, which I gladly pay to their merits, does not dispense with my expressing the conviction, derived from my own labours, that no conclusion founded on special passages of the present text, is safe, before the differences of the MSS.—sometimes great—are thoroughly sifted and discussed with the help of the Commentaries.[30]

In proceeding now to give an instance which I hold to belong to the early (though not the earliest) portions of the Mahá-

---

[30] Weber ("Indische Studien," I. p. 148) and Müller (pp. 44, 45, note) give a valuable synopsis of the leading characters of the Mahábhárata, as they occur in the text and the commentaries of Páṇini. This synopsis, I conceive, must convince even the most sceptic, that Páṇini cannot have ignored the renown of these personages, nor consequently, it is probable, the real or poetical events on which this renown was founded. It forms the subject-matter of the Mahábhárata. Some stress has been laid by both scholars on the circumstance, that the name Páṇḍu or Páṇḍava does not occur in the Grammar of Páṇini (Weber, "Indische Studien," p. 148; Müller, p. 44); but, since both have constructed their list as well from the Gaṇas and commentaries as from the Sútras, it will not be amiss to add, that *Páṇḍava* occurs in Kaiyyaṭa's gloss on Patanjali to IV. 1, 168, v. 4, and in the Káśiká on IV. 1, 171, when the observation of the former implies, what I pointed at in a former remark, that the word Páṇḍu does not occur in the Várttika, as the name of Yudhishṭhira's father, because the word Páṇḍava is too common a derivation to require a grammatical rule; Várttika, पाण्डोर्ड्यण् वक्तव्यः —Patanjali, पाण्ड्यः—Kaiyyaṭa, पाण्डोरिति । बाह्वादिप्रभृतिषु (IV. 1, 96, etc.) येषां दर्शनं लौकिके गोत्रभाव इति (words of Patanjali on a previous Várttika) वचनाद्युधिष्ठिरादिपितुः पाण्डोरग्रहणाद्वाचिनः । पाण्डव इत्येव भवति.—Káśiká on the same Várttika (differently worded; quoted in the Calcutta edition, under the Sútra IV. 1, 168, in the MSS. under IV. 1, 171), पाण्ड्यः । अन्यस्मात्पाण्डव एव. The word पाण्डवेय occurs in the Káśiká on the Gaṇa IV. 1, 123.

bhárata, I must submit, therefore, to having its validity acknowledged or rejected, according to the value the reader may attach to my opinion. Not to be misunderstood, however, I will add that I consider it as posterior to Páṇini. But, as the date I shall assign hereafter to this grammarian will be older than the date originated by Dr. Boehtlingk, the passage in question will still be entitled to rank among the earlier literature. In the *Śántiparvan* of the Mahábhárata we read:[31] "Vasishṭha spoke (to Janaka) 'The doctrines of the Vedas and the (philosophical) Śástras which thou hast uttered, are rightly uttered by thee, but thou understandest them not; for the text (*grantha*) of the Vedas and Śástras is possessed by thee, yet, king, thou dost not know the real sense of the text (*grantha*) according to its truth; for he who is merely bent upon possessing the text (*grantha*) of the Veda and Śástra, but does not understand the real sense of the text, his possession of them is an idle one; he carries *the weight of the book* (*grantha*) who does not know the sense of it; but he who knows the real sense of the text (*grantha*), his is not an idle acquisition of the text." In this instance, *grantha* is used in its double sense, composition or text, and *book*; for there can be no doubt that in the passage, "*Bháraṁ sa vahate tasya granthasya*," "he carries the weight of the *grantha*," the last word can only refer to the material bulk of the book.

I will conclude my observations on this word with a remark on the phrase, "*granthato 'rthataścha*," which must undoubtedly be rendered in the sense proposed by Müller, "according to the text and according to the meaning." An analogous contrast, exactly in the same sense, is that of *káṇḍa* and *padártha*, which is of fre-

[31] V. 11339—11342 (the corrections are founded on the com. and MSS.): यदेतदुक्तं भवता वेदशास्त्रनिदर्शनम् । एवमेतद्यथा चैतन्न गृह्णाति (for चैतन्निगृ°) तथा भवान् ॥ धार्यते हि त्वया ग्रन्थ उभयोर्वेदशास्त्रयोः । न च ग्रन्थस्य तत्त्वज्ञो यथावत्त्वं (for यथा च त्वं) नरेश्वर ॥ यो हि वेदे च शास्त्रे च ग्रन्थधारणतत्परः । न च ग्रन्थार्थतत्त्वज्ञस्तस्य तद्धारणं वृथा ॥ भारं स वहते तस्य ग्रन्थस्यार्थं न वेत्ति यः । यस्तु ग्रन्थार्थतत्त्वज्ञो नास्य ग्रन्थागमो वृथा ॥.

quent occurrence in Mímánsá writers.[32] That, in the latter case, the meaning "text" is a secondary one of *káṇḍa*, no one will dispute, since there is nothing in this word which points to "composition." It must be allowable therefore to conceive, that its synonyme *grantha* may, through the same mental process as *káṇḍa*, have assumed the secondary meaning of "text."

There is another important word which Müller will not admit as evidence of Páṇini's having had a knowledge of writing,—for it is used by this grammarian,—the word *varṇa*. But the only reason he gives for invalidating its testimony is, that this word which, etymologically and otherwise, really means "*colour*,"—when having the sense of letter "does not mean colour in the sense of a painted letter, but the colouring or modulation of the voice" (p. 507). In the absence of any proof for this assertion, he adds, in a note: "Aristotle, Probl. x. 39 : *τὰ δε γράμματα πάθη εστὶ τῆς φωνῆς*." In this respect he coincides, for once, with Weber, not merely in the point at issue, but also in the remarkable brevity of his argument. For all that Weber says on the subject ("Indische Studien," iv. 109) is: "The name *varṇa* is probably (*wohl*) to be understood of the 'colouring,' specializing (*specialisirung*) of the sound; compare *rakta*, which is employed in the Ṛikprátiśákhya in the sense of 'nasalised' (*nasalirt*). With *writing* it has nothing to do." Now, I confess, that I always become somewhat suspicious when I meet with a definition which prefers the language of similes to plain prose. How, I must ask, for instance, does the figure of colouring apply to the notion of specialising? It is striking, moreover, that Weber, who starts with a *probability*, in two lines reaches a positive certainty, founded only on the analogy of *rakta*. And, in turning again to Müller's words, I must, in the first place, ask, what does an analogy taken from Aristotle prove for the Sanskrit word? But, supposing it could prove anything, would it not be more plausible to make use of it in favour of the contrary conclusion to that which Müller

[32] *E.g.* in Mádhava's Jaiminíya-nyáya-málá-vistara, where काण्डानुसमय is contrasted with पदार्थानुसमय, for instance, V. 2, 1, 2, 3, 4, 5, 6, 7, etc. etc.

has drawn? Aristotle speaks of *γράμματα*, which word applies originally to none but *written* signs; and if *he* may apply *γράμμα* to the voice, might not the same liberty be claimed for a Sanskrit word meaning a written letter? Again, the notion of "colouring," itself supposes necessarily a condition which may be called indifferent or colourless: green, blue, red, are colours, because there is an indifferent condition, called white. A coloured sound is not intelligible, except on the supposition that there is also an indifferent, or uncoloured sound. Hence we speak, for instance, in modern terminology, of *i*, *u*, *ṛ*, *e*, *o*, etc., as coloured vowels, because we contrast them with the fundamental uncoloured vowel *a*. But I shall show that *varṇa* is applied indifferently to all vowels, inclusive of *a*.

I do not dispute that *varṇa* is used like *γράμμα*, "letter," *also* for the spoken letter,[33] but I hold that there is strong evidence to prove that its *original* sense is that of *written* letter, as arising naturally from its primitive sense "colour," and that the appearance of this word in Páṇini or other authors, may serve as one of many arguments that they practised the art of writing. To make good this statement I must advert to another word which may also mean letter, and in this sense is always the latter part of a compound, the former of which is the letter itself designated by it, viz., the word *kára*; *e. g.* *a-kára*, the letter *a*; *i-kára*, the letter *i*, etc. It corresponds with *varṇa*, in the synonymous expressions, *a-varṇa*, *i-varṇa*, etc. Kátyáyana looks upon it in the light of an affix, probably on account of its being always compounded with the letter itself; and Kaiyyaṭa enlarges upon the expression *varṇa*, in saying that this word means, in the Várttika quoted, "that which expresses a *varṇa* or adequately realizes a *varṇa* (*i.e.*, is the adequate value of a *varṇa*)." He, therefore, like Kátyáyana, contrasts the purport of *kára* and *varṇa*, though *a-kára* and *a-varṇa*, *i-kára* and *i-varṇa*, may appear to be,—and we shall see

[33] Thus Nagojibhaṭṭa explains, in the commencement of the Vivaraṇa, नादो वर्णः; or Kaiyyaṭa says: घोषवन्तो ये वर्णाः etc.

from what reason,—convertible terms.[34] To understand, however, this contrast, and the use of two other terms which I shall have to name, I will first give instances from Páṇini, the Várttikas of Kátyáyana, and the Bháshya, which will illustrate the manner in which these grammarians have used both terms.

We find: *a-kára*, Śivas. 1, v. 1 (omitted in the Calcutta edition of Páṇini); II. 4, 30, v. 4,; IV. 4, 128, v. 2; III. 3, 108, v. 3, P.;—*á-kára*, Śivas. 1, v. 1 (om. Calc. ed.); I. 1, v. 4; I. 1, 56, v. 11; III. 1, 8, P.; VI. 1, 87, kár. 2. P.;—*i-kára*, III. 3, 108, v. 3, P.; IV. 4, 128, v. 2;—*í-kára*, VII. 1, 39, v. 3; VIII. 2, 15, v. 1. P.;—*u-kára*, VI. 1, 185, par. 1. P.;—*ṛi-kára*, P. on Śivas. 2 and Vártt. (om. in the Calc. ed.); I. 1, 9, v. 2; VI. 1, 101, v. I. P.; VIII. 4, 1, v. 1; *ṛí-kára*, VI. 1, 87, v. 1 (om. Calc. ed.);—*ḷṛi-kára*, P. on Śivas. 2; Śivas. 4, v. 5, (om. Calc. ed.); I. 1, 9, v. 2; VI. 1, 101, v. 2, P.;—*e-kára*, P. on a Vártt. to Śivas. 3 (om. Calc. ed.), IV. 3, 23, v. 6;—*o-kára*, P. on a Vártt. to Śivas. 3 (om. Calc. ed.); V. 3, 72, v. 1; VII. 2, 1. v. 1, 2, 3; VIII. 3, 20, v. 1;—*au-kára*, VIII. 2, 89, P.;—*ka-kára*, P. on a Vártt. to Śivas. 4, 5 (om. Calc. ed.); VII. 3, 44, v. 1. P.;—*ńga-kára*, I. 3, 12, v. 1 P.;—*cha-kára*, P. on III. 1, 8;—*jha-kara* and *ña-kára*, P. on a Vártt. to Śivas. 8 (om. Calc. ed.);—*ṇa-kára*, P. on a Vártt. to Śivas. 6 (om. Calc. ed.); VI. 1, 1, v. 10; VI. 4, 120, v. 1; VIII. 3, 55, v. 1. P.—*ta-kára*, P. on a Vártt. to Śivas. 4 (om. Calc. ed.); VII. 2, 48, v. 1;—*da-kára* and *pa-kára*, P. on a Vártt. to Śivas. 4;—*dha-kára*, VIII. 3, 78, v. 1, P. and v. 3;—*na-kára*, P. on a Vártt. to Śivas. 2; —*bha-kára*, P. on a Vártt. to Śivas. 8 (om. Calc. ed.); V. 3. 72, v. 1;

---

[34] Várttika 3, III. 3, 108: वर्णात्कारः; Patanjali—वर्णात्कारप्रत्ययो वक्तव्यः। अकार इकारः; Kaiyyaṭa—वर्णादिति वर्णवाचिनो वर्णानुकरणादित्यर्थः। बहुलग्रहणात्क्वचिन्न भवति। अस्य च्वाविति (VII. 4, 32) यथा तथा क्वचिद्वर्णसमुदयानुकरणादपि एवकार इति. To remove the apparent strangeness of the manner in which I have rendered अनुकरण which usually means "imitating, doing in conformity with," I subjoin two other instances from Kaiyyaṭa, where the same word is also used by him in the sense of "adequate, or real value." Kátyáyana having given this derivation of अक्षर, "अश्नोतेर्वा सरो ऽक्षरम्," and Patanjali having added अश्नोतेर्वा पुनरयमौणादिकः सरन्प्रत्ययः, Kaiyyaṭa observes अश्नोतेर्वेति। सरन्प्रत्ययस्यानुबन्धलोपे कृते ऽनुकरणं सर इति etc.; or सर्वेषामकाराणां यत्सामान्यं तदनुकरणमचाकारः.

—*ma-kara*, P. on a Vártt. to Śivas. 7 ;—*ya-kára*, P. on a Vártt. to Śivas. 6 ;—*la-kára*, I. 3, 3, v. 2 ;—*va-kára*, P. on a Vártt. to Śivas. 5 ;—*śa-kára*, P. on a Vártt. to Śivas. 5 ;—*sha-kara*, VI. 1, 1, v. 10 ;—*sa-kára*, V. 3, 72, v. 1 ;—*ha-kára*, P. on a Vártt. to Śivas. 5 (all these Vártt. to the Śivas. om. in the Calc. ed.).

On the other hand: *a-varṇa*, P. on a Vártt. to Śivas. 1 (om. Calc. ed.); IV. 1, 1, v. 3 ; VI. 3, 97, v. (not of K., but mentioned in P.); VIII. 3, 64, v. 3 ; VII. 1, 82, v. 2 ; and in the *Sútras*: VI. 1, 182 ; VI. 2, 90 ; VI. 3, 112 ;—*i-varṇa*, P. on a Vártt. to the Śivas. 1 and 3 (om. Calc. ed.); VII. 2, 10. P. ; VIII. 2, 106, v. 1. P. ; Sútra VII. 4, 53 ; *u-varṇa*, P. on a Vártt. to Śivas. 1. (om. Calc. ed.); V. 3. 83, v. 5, and Kár. 1 ; VII. 2, 10. P. ; VIII. 2, 106, v. 1. P. ;—*varṇa y* (or *y-varṇa*) Sútra VII. 4, 53.[35]

The foregoing combinations of a letter of the alphabet with *kára* and *varṇa* are, I believe, all that occur in the grammarians named, and they show at once that *kára* enters into composition with all vowels and all consonants, provided the latter are *followed by the letter a*—(for it may be assumed without risk that the absence of some combinations, such as *kha-kára*, *gha-kára*, etc.,

---

[35] The instances quoted are restricted, as I have stated, to the Sútras of Páṇini, the Várttikas of Kátyáyana, as they occur in the Bháshya of Patanjali, and to the latter, (marked P.) Some of the above-named Várttikas are marked in the Calcutta edition, "Káś.," or "Siddh.-k.," but they occur, too, in the Bháshya. These instances might have been multiplied, and had it been necessary to add quotations from the Káśiká, Siddh.-k., or the words of the Calcutta editors: f. i. by *ṛi-kára*, VI. 1, 91, Káśiká ; Kaiyyaṭa on Śivas. 5 ;—*ṭha-kára*, VIII. 3, 7, Káśiká ; VIII. 3, 34, Káśiká ; VIII. 4, 54, Káśiká ; —*ḍha-kára*, VIII. 3. 55, Káśiká ;—*tha-kára*, I. 2, 23, Káśiká ; VIII. 3, 7, Káśiká ; VIII. 3, 34, Káśiká ;—*na-kára*, VIII. 2, 16, Káśiká ;—*pha-kára*, I. 2, 23, Káśiká ; VIII. 4, 54, Káśiká ;—*śa-kara*, I. 3, 8, Káśiká ;—or *ṛi-varṇa*, I. 1, 9, v. 1, Siddh.-k. ; V. 3, 83, v. 5, Káśiká (thus quoted in the Calcutta edition, but not met with in the MS. 2441 of the E.I.H.); VIII. 4, 1, v. 1, Káśiká and Siddh.-k. ;—*ḷṛi-varṇa*, I. 1, 9. v. 1, Siddh.-k. The very unusual *ra-kára* in the Commentary to VIII. 2, 15 (it occurs chiefly in mystical, not in grammatical, works ; *e.g.* in the dialogue between Umá and Śiva of the Rudrayámalatantra), I must leave to the responsibility of the Calcutta editors ; for the Bháshya on the Várttika does not speak of the letter *ra*, and the Káśiká and Siddh.-k. have, instead of *rakárántát*, the usual *rephántát*. I have omitted, of course, to quote passages of the Sútras, etc., where *varṇa* or *kára* have other meanings than "letter."

is merely a matter of chance, not of necessity; compare the additional instances of the note 35)—while *varṇa* is joined merely to vowels and to such consonants as are *without a vowel sound*[36] (*cf.* Sútra, VII. 4, 53).

This circumstance is significant, but at once intelligible, if we draw a distinction between a spoken sound and a written letter. To sound a consonant (*k*, *t*, *p*, etc.) we must combine it with a vowel; in writing, we may omit that vowel, and should omit it, unless it have its own peculiar value: the spoken *k* has a different value to the written *ka*, which means *k* and *a*. Unless, therefore, Páṇini intended, for instance, to give a rule on *y* and *a*, he could not employ a term *ya*, which merely refers to the spoken sound *y*; or, if he did so, he would have had to give a special rule to the effect that the sound *a* in this combination is mute or insignificant, as he has given various rules to a similar effect when he employs for his technical purposes *anubandhas* or letters without significance. Now, such a rule on the suppression of vowels which appear in his grammar, but are not to be sounded when the word with which they are combined becomes a spoken word, is given by him (I. 3, 2), but for a distinct and *special* purpose, and not with the intent of *general* application; a vowel, such as it is treated in this rule, is (and ought to have been always edited with the appropriate sign) *anunásika*. Therefore, when Páṇini gives a rule in which the vowel *a* is appended to a consonant, but valueless,—though the absence of its value would not follow from the rule quoted (I. 3, 2) or otherwise,—the commentators notice such an exceptional case as worthy of a special remark, and defend it in their fashion if they deem it advisable.[37] In other words, expressions like *a-kára*, *i-kára*, *u-kára*, etc., and *a-varṇa*, *i-varṇa*, *u-varṇa*, etc., are

---

[36] Páṇini never uses *varṇa* of a consonant followed by the vowel *a*; but the late Káśiká writes झभ इत्येतौवर्णौ, or घढध इत्येतान्वर्णान्, or जबगडद इत्येतान्वर्णान्, if the MSS. are to be trusted.

[37] The Káśiká, *e.g.*, observes on the Śivasútra लण्,—हकारादिष्वकार उच्चारणार्थो नानुबन्धः। लकारे त्वकारो ऽनुनासिक इत्संज्ञः प्रतिज्ञायते; or the Sútra VII. 1, 25 अद्डु॰ where the first अ is mute, is excused by Kátyáyana in this way: सिद्धं त्वनुनासिकोपधात्.

equivalent, because the value of a *spoken vowel* coincides with that of the *written vowel-sign;* they admit of a doubt whether *kára* or *varṇa*, or both or neither, apply to a written sign; but when we see that *sa-kára*, *bha-kára*, *ṇa-kára*, *sha-kára*, *ta-kára*, etc., are portions of rules, in which not *sa*, *bha*, *ṇa*, *sha*, *ta*, etc., but *s*, *bh*, *ṇ*, *sh*, *t*, etc., are meant, we perceive at once that *kára* must apply to the uttered sound. On the other hand, when Páṇini speaks (VII. 4, 53) of two *varṇas*, *yí*, *i.e.* of a *varṇa y* and of a *varṇa í*, we must conclude that *varṇa* did not apply to the spoken sound, but to the written sign, since the value *y* without a vowel would be unpronounceable.

I will give some additional proof for this conclusion on the meaning of both these words. In the foregoing remarks I rendered *kára* in combination with *í*, *u*, *sa*, etc. "letter," since we use this word in its double acceptation, uttered sound and written sign. If *kára*, however, is the uttered sound, it will be a synonyme of *śabda*, and we find it therefore, *e.g.* in the comment of the Káśiká, used as a convertible term with *śabda*.[38] *This is never the case with varṇa.*

Since an uttered sound may comprise more than *one* letter, we find *kára*, as Kaiyyaṭa already remarks (compare note 34), equally applied to complicated sounds, *e.g.* *eva-kára* (III. 4, 67, v. 3 and 6; I. 4, 8, Káś.; VI. 2, 80 P.); and Páṇini, who never uses it for expressing a simple letter-sound (because his terms are such as apply to a written book), applies it to the sound *vashaṭ* in *vashaṭ-kára* (I. 2. 35). *Varṇa is never used in a similar manner.*

In this respect *kára* coincides with the term *karaṇa*, which occurs in combinations quite analogous, *e.g*, *iti-karaṇa*, I. 1, 44, v. 1, P.; IV. 2, 21, v. 2, P.; *duk-karaṇa*, VII. 1, 25, v. 3; *ḍit-karaṇa*, VII. 1, 25, v. 4; 3, 118, v. 6; *chit-karaṇa*, III. 1, 8, v. 4, P; or even combined with *kára*, as *evakára-karaṇa*, VI. 2, 80, Kás., etc. *Varṇa*, on the contrary, is used by Kátyáyana and Pa-

---

[38] Páṇini (VIII. 2, 37) uses the expression स्ध्वोः, which is rendered by the Káśiká सकारे ध्वशब्दे च. The word शब्द is used in a similar manner, *e.g.*, in these combinations: तिशब्द, VI. 2, 81, Káśiká (ति being there the last syllable of शिति); तुशब्द, VI. 2, 50, Káśiká (तु being affix); अच्छब्द, VII. 1, 25, v. 4, P. (अद्‌ being the ending of pronouns in the neuter); भ्यम्शब्द VII. 1, 30, v. 1, P. (भ्यम्‌ being the declension ending).

tanjali in the same manner as in Páṇini's Sútra which speaks of the *varṇa y*, viz., of *unutterable consonantal sounds*, which therefore must have been written signs. Thus, a discussion is raised by Kátyáyana on the Sútra VI. 4, 49, which treats of the elision of *ya*, in reference to the question whether *ya* is to be dropped or merely *y*; and on this occasion, he calls the former *sangháta*, "combination," (viz., of *y* and *a*), and the latter *varṇa*. In a Várttika to VII. 3, 50, a similar discussion is started on *ṭha*; again, *ṭha* is called there *sangháta*, and the unpronounceable *ṭh*, *varṇa*. The same term *sangháta* is applied to *ka* in a Várttika to VII. 3, 44, and *varṇa* to the vowelless *k*.

The same sense of *varṇa* is conveyed by a definition of Patanjali concerning the term *upadeśa*, which literally means demonstration, and then assumes the special sense of grammatical mode of denotating, or of grammatical appearance, and of the book in which such grammatical denotations occur:[39] it means, for instance, the grammatical appearance of the radicals in the Dhátupáṭha, or the Dhátupáṭha itself; and, in like manner, the grammatical appearance of the letters in the Śivasútras, "the root of Páṇini's Gram-

---

[39] Patanjali on the Sútra I. 3, 2: किं पुनरुपदेशनम्। शास्त्रम्. A Várttika on I. 3, 3: सिद्धं तु व्यवसितांत्यत्वात्; on which Patanjali comments: सिद्धमेतत्। कथम्। व्यवसितान्त्यत्वात्। व्यवसितान्त्यो हलित्संज्ञो भवतीति वक्तव्यम् (Kátyáyana, says Patanjali, ought rather to have said व्यव° . . . . भवति; these latter words of Patanjali have been mistaken by the Calcutta editors for the Várttika itself; and they of course again make their appearance in the reprint of Dr. Boehtlingk, who besides, and for the sake of greater clearness, adds: "Ein Várttika:", and prints °न्त्य, as if he had looked into the Mahábháshya and amended the "Várttika" from the original work.—Patanjali then continues:) के पुनर्व्यवसिताः। धातुप्रातिपदिकप्रत्ययनिपातागमादेशाः.—On account of the double sense of *upadeśa*, "book, etc." and "grammatical appearance," Patanjali raises this question when speaking of the Sútra VI. 1, 45: कथमिदं विज्ञायते। एज्य उपदेश इति। आहोस्विदेजन्तं यदुपदेश इति, when Kaiyyaṭa is still more explicit: कथमिति। यदोपदेशशब्देन करणसाधनेन शास्त्रमुच्यते तदा विशेष्यस्यानुपादानादेव नास्ति तदन्तविधिरित्ययं पक्षो भवति एज्य उपदेश इति। यदा तु कर्मसाधन उपदेशशब्द उपदिश्यमानार्थवाची षष्ठ्यर्थे च सप्तमी तदोपदेशस्यैवाविशेषणात्तदन्तविधावित्ययं पक्षो भवति एजन्तं यदुपदेश इति.—A similar question of Patanjali occurs in his com. on VI. 1, 186: अदुपदेशादिति कथमिदं विज्ञायते। अकारो य उपदेश इति। आहोस्विदकारान्तं यदुपदेश इति.

mar," as Nagojibhaṭṭa calls them. For when Kátyáyana, in several introductory Várttikas, enlarges on the purpose of the letters, as they occur in the Śivasútras, Patanjali asks:[40] "Now, what is *upadeśa*, or technical denotation? Pronunciation. How is that? The radical *diś*, 'to show,' (whence *upa-deśa* is derived) implies the act of pronouncing; for, after having pronounced the *varṇas*, one may say, 'these *varṇas* are *upadishṭa*, or technically denoted.'" Patanjali distinguishes, therefore, between *varṇas* and *upadishṭa-varṇas*; only the latter are, according to him, the pronounceable *varṇas*; and it would have been useless for him to draw this distinction, if *varṇa* itself originally signified the spoken letter.

What the *simple* consonantal sound is to the pronounceable consonant, the *simple* vowel is, in some measure, to the diphthong or combined vowel sound. It is, perhaps, on this ground that, while we find a general name for vowel-letters, viz., *swara-varṇa* (IV. 1, 3, v. 7), the compounds *e-varṇa*, *o-varṇa*, *ai-varṇa*, *au-varṇa*, neither occur in Páṇini nor Kátyáyana, for *e* is *a* and *i*, *o* = *a* and *u*, *ai* = *a* and *e*, *au* = *a* and *o*. Their general name is, in "older grammars," *sandhy-akshara*; and in Kátyáyana and Patanjali, for *e* and *o*, *praślishṭa-varṇa*, for *ai* and *au*, *samáhára-varṇa*.[41] The Káśiká, it is true, speaks of these vowels simply as *varṇas*;[42] but, in the first place, it does not form a compound *e-varṇa*, etc., like *i-varṇa*, etc.; and, secondly, however great the value of this commentary, it cannot always be considered as fulfilling the conditions of critical accuracy, and cannot therefore be quoted as evidence against Páṇini or Kátyáyana. But even if there were in Páṇini's Grammar such compounds as *e-varṇa*, *o-varṇa*, their occurrence

---

[40] Patanjali on the Introduction: अथ क उपदेशः। उच्चारणम्। कुत एतत्। दिशिरुच्चारणक्रियः। उच्चार्य हि वर्णानाह। उपदिष्टा इमे वर्णा इति.

[41] Kaiyyaṭa to Patanjali on Śivas. 3 and 4: संध्यक्षराणीत्यन्वर्था पूर्वाचार्यसंज्ञा. Whether this term "older teachers" applies to the present Prátiśákhyas where the same term occurs, or not, will be included in the subsequent discussion on the relation of these works to Páṇini's grammar.—Patanjali on the same Śivas.: इमावैचौ समाहारवर्णौ the same on I. 1, 9: (ए ओ) प्रश्लिष्टवर्णावेतौ.

[42] Káśiká on the Śivas. 3: ए ओ इत्येतौ वर्णौ; on Śivas. 4: ऐ औ इत्येतौ वर्णौ.

would not invalidate the conclusion that *varṇa* represents the written sign, since it is the combination of *varṇa* with a consonant that alone can enable us to decide the question at issue. And that there are other values in Páṇini which could not have been spoken, though they are an essential portion of his Grammar, will be seen afterwards.

How far *varṇa* coincides, and is synonymous with *akshara*, "syllable," or not, is obvious: it coincides with the latter term when it means vowel, otherwise not.[43] The distinction between these terms may therefore be comprised in the following definition: *kára* denotes the pronounceable sound, which *must* always be one syllable, but may also consist of more than one syllable; if denoting one syllable, it may mean a simple vowel (*a, á, i, í, u, ú, ṛi, ṛí, ḷri,*), or a complex vowel (*e, o, ai, au*), or a simple consonant made pronounceable by a vowel (usually the vowel *a*); *karana* denotes more especially the pronounceable sound represented either by more than one syllable or by one syllable containing more than one consonant. *Varṇa*, on the contrary, implies merely the simple letter,—among vowels, especially the simple vowel; among consonants, merely the ***single consonant, not accompanied with a vowel sign.*** Lastly, *akshara* means "syllable" in our sense of the word, and may sometimes therefore coincide in value with *kára*, or *varṇa*, in the same way that *kára* and *varṇa* are apparently convertible terms when they are the latter parts of compounds, the former of which are *a, á, i, í, u, ú, ṛi, ṛí, ḷri.*

I have, in the foregoing observations, purposely abstained from alluding to the use which has been made of these terms in the existing Prátiśákhyas of Śaunaka and Kátyáyana; in the first place, because it was my object to show their meaning in Páṇini's work, as well as in those old Commentaries which have strictly adhered to his terminology, and because it would have been an uncritical proceeding to confound the meaning or bearing of these terms in works belonging to a different class of Hindu litera-

---

[43] Kaiyyaṭa on VIII. 2, 89: अक्षरमच्; the same on the Introduction to the Śivas.: अक्षरं व्यञ्जनसहितोऽच्; Nagojíbh.: यथा ये यजामह इति पञ्चाक्षरमिति.

ture;[44] secondly, because the date of these works, themselves,—or, at least, their relative position towards Páṇini,—will have to be ascertained, before any conclusion can be drawn from a difference which may have existed between them in the use of these terms. Though I shall recur to this point, I may now state my belief, that even if grammatical works older than Páṇini had used *varṇa* in the general sense of *akshara*, such a circumstance would not disprove the fact that *varṇa* might have meant a written sign even before Páṇini's time. There is, for instance, an introductory Várttika of Kátyáyana which countenances the assumption that *varṇa* had such a sense in some older grammarian; but the very manner in which it is brought before the reader shows that Kátyáyana contrasts the use of this word in Páṇini with that in his predecessor, and confirms, therefore, the definition I have given before. At the same time, it leaves the question undecided whether *varṇa* was, or was not, a written letter in this older work. The Várttika I am alluding to occurs at the end of the general introduction, and refers to the following Vaidik passage mentioned in the beginning of the introduction: "Whoever establishes this speech according to its words, its accent, and its syllables, he is fit to institute or to perform sacrificial work; and that it is a duty to study grammar, follows from the words 'let us be fit to institute, or to perform sacrificial work.'"[45] The Várttika then says: "*akshara*, you must

---

[44] This confusion, unhappily, does not seldom occur in the definition of words, as found in our dictionaries; thus, अभ्यस्त is used by Yáska in the general sense "reduplicated," and as applied to a *dhátu*, or radical portion of the verb (Nir. IV. 23: एरिर इतीर्तिरुपसृष्टो ऽभ्यस्तः; or IV. 25: ररिवान्रातिरभ्यस्तः); in Páṇini, however, it means the first two syllables of a reduplicated *anga* or base (VI. 1, 5); अभ्यास means *reduplication*, in the *Nirukta* (V. 12), on the form बभ्राम, आदिनाभ्यासेनोपहितेनोपधामादत्ते बभस्तिरत्तकर्मा; in *Páṇini* it means the first *syllable* of reduplication (VI. 1, 4). To philosophical terms this remark applies in a still stronger sense; they have been generally dealt with as if the same term, *e.g.*, मनस्, आत्मन्, बुद्धि, etc., had the same sense in all the philosophical systems, which is not the case.

[45] Patanjali: यो वा इमां पदशः स्वरशो ऽक्षरशो वाचं विदधाति स आर्त्विजीनो भवति। आर्त्विजीनाः स्यामेत्यध्येयं व्याकरणम्; Kaiyyaṭa: ऋत्विजमर्हतीत्यार्त्विजीनो यजमानः (Páṇini, V. 1, 71)। ऋत्विक्कर्मार्हतीति याजको ऽप्यार्त्विजीनः (*ib.* Várttika).

know, means *na kshara, i. e.*, not perishable," and continues, "or *akshara* comes from *aś*, 'to pervade,' with the affix *sara* (*Kaiyyaṭa*: 'because it pervades the sense');" and concludes, "or they call *varṇa* so in the Sútra of a former (grammarian)" [*Patanjali: i. e.* "or in the Sútra of a former (grammarian) *varṇa* has the name *akshara.*" *Kaiyyaṭa:* "For it is said in another grammar, that the *varṇas* are *aksharas.*" *Nagojibhaṭṭa:* "In a similar manner the term *aksharasamámnáya* means a multitude of *varṇas*, as seen in the Vedas].[46]

Before I proceed to give other evidence as to Páṇini's knowledge of writing, I will draw attention to two words which have here a claim to notice; and first to the word *úrdhwa.* It is used adverbially in the sense of "after;" for instance, in Manu, ix. 77, *úrdhwam saṁvatsarát*, "after a year," or, Chhándogya-Upanishad: *tata úrdhwam vakshyámi*, "after that I shall say." But *úrdhwa* means, originally, "upwards, above, high, or (in combination with an ablative) higher." It is possible to conceive progress as an act of rising, when the sense "after" would follow from this latter acceptation. But it is more probable that the metaphorical sense of the word was first applied to passages in books,—where it is frequently used in this way,—before it became a more general one; and, if so, the figure would naturally follow from the description I have given of a Hindu book; for the beginning of a Sanskrit MS., —as may still be seen in some of the oldest specimens,—was at the bottom of the pile of leaves which constitute its bulk. What is "above," in a Hindu book, is, therefore, "after;" while, with us, the term "above" denotes the opposite sense, from the circumstance of the progress of our books being a descending one. And this assumption is corroborated by a second synonymous word, viz.: *udaya*, which also means, originally, "going upwards," and

---

[46] Kátyáyana: अक्षरं न क्षरं विद्यात् ॥ अश्नोतेर्वा सरो ऽक्षरम् ॥ वर्णे वाहुः पूर्वसूत्रे. Patanjali (on the latter): अथवा पूर्वसूत्रे वर्णस्याक्षरमिति संज्ञा क्रियते; Kaiyyaṭa: ..... पूर्वसूत्र इति । व्याकरणान्तरे वर्णा अक्षराणीति वचनात्.....; Nagojibhaṭṭa .... पूर्वसूत्रशब्दे षष्ठीतत्पुरुष इति भावः । एवं चाक्षरसमाम्नाय इत्यस्य श्रुतिरूपो वर्णसंघात इत्यत्र तात्पर्यम्.

then, "after, following," and which, moreover, is never used in this sense, except of passages in books. It occurs frequently thus in the Prátiśákhyas; but, for the reasons stated before, I content myself with quoting, for its occurrence in Páṇini, the Sútra VIII. 4, 67.[47]

"If writing," says Müller, "had been known to Pâṇini, some of his grammatical terms would surely point to the graphical appearance of words. I maintain that there is not a single word in Pâṇini's terminology which presupposes the existence of writing" (p. 507).

As Weber, in his "Indische Studien" (vol. iv. p. 89), had already mentioned two grammatical terms of "Pâṇini," viz., *swaritet* and *udáttet*, which he considers as "founded on graphical appearance," I cannot suppose that Müller has overlooked the remark of this scholar, but must assume that he has silently rejected it, either on account of its incorrectness or its inconclusiveness. It is true, that the latter term does not occur at all in the Sútras of Páṇini, nor the former, such as it is given by Weber; but, in the first place, there can be no doubt that, in the Sútra I. 3, 72, *swaritañitas* must be analysed *swaritetas* and *ñitas* (comp. the commentaries), and on the other hand, Müller can neither have ignored that Páṇini's expression, *anudáttangitas* (I. 3, 12), is equivalent to *anudáttetas* and *ṅgitas*, nor that the term *anudáttet* distinctly occurs in the rules III. 2, 149 and VI. 1, 186. His absolute silence on this point was probably, therefore, not caused by Weber's partial inaccuracy, but by the reference the latter gives when naming these terms,—the reference to Dr. Boehtlingk's "Comment" on the Sútra I. 3, 11. For it must be readily admitted that the gloss of this writer is quite enough to raise the strongest apprehensions as to the sanity of Páṇini, provided that it does not induce the reader to arrive at a peculiar view of the

[47] For the same reasons I do not avail myself of the word अधिक "above," though it occurs in the same sense, "after," *e.g.*, in Kátyáyana's Prátiśákhya, I. 33. (The word अधस्तन is used in the sense "before," *e.g.*, in Uvaṭa's com. on this Prátiśákhya, I. 85; उपरिष्टात्, in the sense "after," *e.g.*, in the introduction of the Jaiminíya-nyáya-málá-vistara).

fitness of Páṇini's "*editor*" himself to compose a comment on this great grammarian.[48]

I must, therefore, while rejecting Weber's reference, defend first his quotation of the Sútra with the assistance of Kátyá-

---

[48] I subjoin a literal copy of this gloss, which but poorly illustrates the character of the second volume of Dr. Boehtlingk's "*edition*" of Páṇini. It runs thus:—"Wo der Circumflex gestanden hat, will ich nicht entscheiden; wenn zu *Pâṇinî's* Zeiten die Accente in der gewöhnlichen Schrift nicht gebraucht wurden, konnte der Circumflex über einen beliebigen Buchstaben des *adhikâra* gesetzt werden, ohne Verwirrung hervorzubringen. Die Handschriften unseres Grammatikers, die ich verglichen habe, sind alle aus der neusten Zeit und bezeichnen diesen Accent ebenso wenig wie die nasalen Vocale im *upadeça*. Wenn ich 2 *vârtikas* zu unserer Regel recht verstehe, so wurde bei einem *adhikâra* ein Buchstabe angefügt (der vielleicht der Träger des Circumflex war) und zwar so oft als der *adhikâra* in der Folge ergänzt werden musste; konnte er nicht so weit ergänzt werden, dann musste man ihn die fehlenden Male bei den vorhergehenden (?) Regeln ergänzen. Hier die beiden *vârtika's* selbst: यावतिथो ऽलनुबध्यते तावतो योगानधिकारो ऽनुवर्तेत इति वक्तव्यं ॥ १ ॥ भूयसि प्रागसुत इति वक्तव्यं ॥ २ ॥." Translation: "Where the circumflex [*sic.*, this rendering of *swarita* shows that the writer has no idea of the nature of this accent] was placed, *I will not decide* (*sic.!*); if, at the time of Páṇini, accents were not used in common writing, the circumflex could be put over any letter of an *adhikára* without causing confusion. The MSS. of our grammarian which I have compared (*sic*) are all of the most recent date, and mark this accent as little as the nasal vowels in the *upadeśa*. If I understand rightly two *Várttikas* to our rule, a letter (which, perhaps, was the bearer of the circumflex) was added to an *adhikára*: that is to say, as often as the *adhikára* had to be supplied in the sequel; if it could not be supplied so often, one had to supply it when wanted, at the preceding (?) [this query belongs to Dr. B.] rules. Here are the two Várttikas themselves: [then follow the Sanskrit words as given above].—The latter words ("if it could not," etc.) are beyond my comprehension; for, what reasons could prevent an *adhikára* from being supplied, and if there was such an obstructed *adhikára*, how could it be supplied at a preceding rule? I doubt, however, whether this sentence, which is intended to represent the meaning of the second Várttika as quoted above, was understood by its own author. But the very words of this "Várttika" revenge themselves on the person who has ill-used them so much: they betray the character of the work which has commented on them. For, however intelligible they are in themselves, it must be observed that the Calcutta Paṇḍits have made a mistake in the wording of this Várttika. Dr. Boehtlingk, therefore, in giving himself the appearance of having quoted a rule laboriously examined in an original work, is simply detected in reprinting, without any examination whatever, the error of the Calcutta editors. *And this, I may add, is generally the case* in his "comment." The fact, in short, is this:—the Káśiká and Siddh.-k. have no Várttikas on this Sútra, and in the Mahábháshya the words given belong to two dis-

yana and Patanjali. Páṇini says (I. 3, 11): "An *adhikára*, or heading rule (will be recognized in my Grammar) by the accent *swarita*."[49] Upon this *Patanjali* remarks: "Why does he say that?"—*Várttika*: "An adhikára ...... to every rule belonging to it; its object is to avoid a (repeated) designation."—*Patanjali*: "'An adhikára (says Kátyáyana) is made (so as to

---

tinct passages, which have been erroneously contracted by the Paṇḍits into one; viz., to a passage of a Várttika, भूयसि प्राग्वचनम्, and to a passage from the commentary of Patanjali: भूयसि प्राग्वचनं कर्तव्यम् । प्रागमुत इति वक्तव्यम् ("Kátyáyana ought to have said—instead of प्राक्, प्राक् with a word following in the ablative"). The second of these passages is therefore merely a correction, by Patanjali, of the vague expression of Kátyáyana, and the इति वक्तव्यम् which conveys the correction, becomes purposeless, or assumes a different bearing, in the version of the Calcutta edition. And I may add, that the Paṇḍits have erred, too, in publishing what is their first Várttika, for they mistook the comment of, and a quotation made by, Patanjali, for the text of a Várttika. The reprint has been, of course, as conscientious in the latter case as in the former. Compare for both Várttikas the following note with its translation. But to show in its proper light the astounding explanation of Dr. Boehtlingk on this second Várttika, I shall illustrate his ingenuity by taking some instances of the Káśiká, as quoted in its comment on this Sútra, and apply to them his comment on the first Várttika. According to the Káśiká, the Sútras VI. 4, 129; III. 1, 91; VI. 4, 1; IV. 1, 1; III. 1, 1, are among those marked with a *swarita*, to indicate that they are *adhikáras*; the first of these *adhikáras* extends over 47, the second over 541, the third over 613, the fourth over 1190, and the fifth over 1821 Sútras. If we credit, therefore, the explanation of Dr. Boehtlingk, a letter of the alphabet (he does not say which; probably, therefore, any one) was added, perhaps, as he says in the parenthesis, as the bearer of this swarita, "that is to say, as often as the *adhikára* had to be supplied in the sequel." In other words, in the five instances quoted such a letter was added to the Sútra VI. 4, 129, 47 times, and so on to the other Sútras severally 541, 613, 1190, and 1821 times! And this method, he conceives, had been devised in a kind of literature, where shortness is the chief object, and where "an author rejoiceth in the economizing of half a short vowel as much as in the birth of a son." Surely, it requires neither knowledge nor scholarship, but merely something else, to deter a rational writer from eliciting such a sense from a sane book.

[49] Páṇini I. 3, 11: स्वरितेनाधिकारः—Patanjali: किमर्थमिदमुच्यते.—Várttika omitted in the Calc. ed. at this Sútra, but mentioned VI. 1, 158, where it occurs as a quotation) अधिकारः प्रतियोगं तस्यानिर्देशार्थः—Patanjali: अधिकारः क्रियते प्रतियोगं तस्यानिर्देशार्थ इति । किमिदं प्रतियोगमिति। योगं योगं प्रति प्रतियोगं योगे योगे तस्य ग्रहणं माभार्षमिति—Kaiyyaṭa: स्वरितेनेतीत्थंभूतलक्षणे तृतीया । स्वरितेनाधिकारो लक्ष्यत इत्यर्थः । स्वरितत्वं सूत्रस्थानां केवलमधिकारज्ञानार्थं प्रतिज्ञायते न तु

apply) to every rule belonging to it; its object is to avoid a (repeated) designation.' What does that mean, 'to every rule belonging to it?' 'To every rule belonging to it,' means in reference to each such rule; and he wants to imply that I must not make special mention (of the adhikára) in each such rule."—*Kaiyyaṭa*: "The words, 'by the accent swarita' [in Sanskrit it is only one word], are the third case in the sense of 'such and such a mark' (as ruled by Páṇini, II. 3, 21); *i.e.* an adhikára is *marked* with the accent swarita. The plan to mark *words which are in the Sútra* with the swarita, is merely devised in order that the adhikára may become recognizable, *but it has nothing to do with practical application* [*i.e.* the swarita is not pronounced]. The word adhikára either expresses a condition or it expresses an act; in common language, adhikára is the same as *viniyoga*, or appointment to an office; and *this* is understood here. Patanjali asks: 'Why does Páṇini say that?' This question means: Will there be (in his grammar) as in common language, a connection of the matter treated under the same head, because the subjects refer necessarily to one another, and the like?" .... [Then follows in the Bháshya a discussion of Patanjali, the purport of which is to show that the word *adhikára*, which literally means *superintendence*, *government*, has, in grammar, an analogous sense to that which it has in common life].—*Várttika*: "But (there is) no knowing how far an adhikára goes."—*Patanjali* (repeats these words in the manner we

---

प्रयोगसमवायि। अधिकारशब्दो भावसाधनः कर्मसाधनो वा। विनियोगो लोके ऽधिकार उच्यते स एवेह गृह्यते। किमर्थमिति। आकाङ्क्षादिवशात्प्रकृतस्य संबन्धो लोक इव भविष्यतीति प्रश्नः।—.................... Várttika (omitted in the Calc. ed.) अधिकारपरिमाणाज्ञानं तु—Patanjali: अधिकारपरिमाणाज्ञानं तु भवति। न ज्ञायेत कियन्तमवधिमधिकारो ऽनुवर्तत इति।—Várttika (omitted in the Calc. ed.) अधिकारपरिमाणज्ञानार्थं तु—Patanjali: अधिकारपरिमाणज्ञानार्थमेव तर्ह्ययं योगो वक्तव्यः। अधिकारपरिमाणं ज्ञास्यामीति। कथं पुनः स्वरितेनाधिकार इत्यनेनाधिकारपरिमाणं शक्यं विज्ञातुम्। एवं वक्ष्यामि स्वरितेनाधिकार इति—Kaiyyaṭa: अधिकारपरिमाणाज्ञानं त्विति। यथा धातोरिति किं प्राग्लादेशेभ्यः। अथाध्यायपरिसमाप्तेः। अङ्गाधिकारः प्रागभ्यासविकारेभ्यः। अथा सप्तमपरिसमाप्तेरिति—

have seen before, adding the ellipsis 'there is,' as he usually repeats the words of a Várttika which he explains, in order to ensure its proper text, and then continues): "These words mean: It might not be known to what limit an adhikára is applicable." —*Várttika*: "However, that the extent of an adhikára might be known."—*Patanjali*: "Just that the extent of an adhikára might be known, on that account this rule (I. 3, 11) had to be uttered; in other words, that I may know how far an adhikára goes. But again, how can the extent of an adhikára be known through the Sútra, which says 'an adhikára (will be recognized in my grammar) by the accent swarita,' so that I could say: 'the adhikára (is recognized) by the accent swarita?'"—*Kaiyyaṭa*: "'But, there is no knowing how far an adhikára goes,' says the Várttika; for instance, does adhikára III. 1, 91, stop before the Sútra III. 4, 78, or does it go to the end of the (third) book? Does the adhikára VI. 4, 1, stop before the Sútra VI. 4, 73, or does it go to the end of the seventh book?"—*Patanjali*: "Since, as soon as (another) swarita is *seen*, there is an end of the adhikára (indicated by the previous swarita); by what means, then, can there be now an adhikára? Adhikára is (as we have seen) a term of common life. Now, if you say there is no such adhikára (meant in this grammar), why was it said before [in a previous discussion], 'that a new injunction stopping (the applicability of the adhikára), a paribháshá (had to be given).' Therefore on account of an adhikára this rule had to be uttered."—*Kaiyyaṭa*: "(When Patanjali says), 'As soon as (another) swarita

---

Patanjali: स्वरित दृष्टाधिकारो न भवतीति केनेदानीमधिकारो भविष्यति। लौकिको ऽधिकारः। नाधिकार इति चेदुक्तम्। किमुक्तम्। अन्यनिर्देशस्तु निवर्तकस्तस्मात्परिभाषेति। अधिकारार्थमेव तर्ह्ययं योगो वक्तव्यः—Kaiyyaṭa: स्वरितं दृष्टेति। प्रकृतस्याधिकारनिवृत्तये शब्दान्तरस्य स्वरितत्वं प्रतिज्ञायते। तेन विंशतिकात्त्व इत्यत्र स्वरितत्वदर्शनात्। द्विचिपूर्वादित्यस्य निवृत्तिरनुमीयते —Patanjali: ननु चोक्तम्। अधिकारपरिमाणाज्ञानं त्विति। —Várttika: यावतिथो ऽलनुबन्धस्तावतो योगानिति वचनात्सिद्धम्—Patanjali: यावतिथो ऽलनुबध्यते तावतो योगानधिकारो ऽनुवर्तत इति वक्तव्यम्—Kaiyyaṭa: यावतिथ इति।

is *seen*,' etc., (his words mean): to stop the (applicability of an) adhikára on a subject-matter, the plan is devised to mark another word with the swarita; thus, because the swarita mark is seen in the Sútra V. 1, 32, it must be inferred that the applicability of the adhikára, V. 1, 30 (which also was marked with the swarita) has ceased."—*Patanjali*: "Now, has not Kátyáyana said, 'But there is no knowing how far an adhikára goes?'" (Quite so; hence the) *Várttika* (continues): "This results from what is said elsewhere: '*whatever the numerical value of the letter which is joined (to an adhikára-rule)*, to as many rules ....'"—*Patanjali:* "These words would have been better quoted thus: 'With whatever numerical value a letter is joined (as anubandha to an adhikára-rule), to as many (following) rules *the adhikára applies*.'"—*Kaiyyaṭa*: "For instance: to the Sútra V. I, 30, the mute letter *i* (the *second* in the Śivasútras) is to be joined; therefore it applies to *two* subsequent rules; and similarly in other adhikára rules."—*Patanjali*: "Now, what is to be done when an adhikára applies to more rules, while there are fewer letters of the alphabet?"—*Kaiyyaṭa*: "(When Patanjali says) 'Fewer (and more),' is this comparative (literally, is the affix of the higher degree, *i.e.* the affix of the comparative), used in reference to different species (of the same class)? (No;) it is used in an absolute sense. (For he means): If you think the rules belonging to the same adhikára are *few*, then (you would have to take his words as implying that) the letters of the alphabet may be (still) *fewer*; on the other hand, if

---

द्विचिपूर्वान्निष्कादित्यचेकारो ऽनुबन्धः कर्तव्यः । तेन द्वयोर्योगयोरनुवृत्तिर्भवति । एवमन्यत्रापि वेदितव्यम् — Patanjali : अथेदानीं यत्राल्पीयांसो ऽलः भूयसश्च योगानधिकारो ऽनुवर्तते कथं तत्र कर्तव्यम् —Kaiyyaṭa : अल्पीयांस इति । कथं पुनर्भिन्नजातीयापेक्षया प्रकर्षप्रत्ययः । परमतापेक्षया । अल्पे योगा इति चेन्मन्यसे तत्राल्पीयांसो ऽलः । तथा बहवो ऽल इति चेद्भूयांसो योगाः—Várttika : भूयसि प्राग्वचनम् — Patanjali : भूयसि प्राग्वचनं कर्तव्यम् । प्रागमुत इति वक्तव्यम् । तत्तर्हि वक्तव्यम् । न वक्तव्यम् । संदेहमात्रमेतद्भवति । सर्वसंदेहेषु चेदमुपतिष्ठते व्याख्यानतो विशेषप्रतिपत्तिर्न हि संदेहादलक्षणमिति—Kaiyyaṭa : भूयसीति । अङ्गस्य

you think the letters are *many*, then (his words would imply that) there may be still *more* rules belonging to the same adhikára."—*Várttika*: "If there are more (rules for the same adhikára than letters), the expression *prák*, 'before,' . . . . . ."—*Patanjali*: "If there are more (rules for the same adhikára than letters), Páṇini (says the Várttika) ought always to have made use of the expression *prák*, 'before;' or the Várttika ought to have rather said '*before, with a word following in the ablative.*'" [The Várttika means that the adhikára then should have been always indicated in the Sútra by the expression that such and such an adhikára is valid "before," *i.e.* goes no further than, such and such a rule or word; as is the case, *e.g.* I. 4, 56; II. 1, 3; IV. 4, 1 and 75; V. 1, 1 and 18; 3, 1 and 70, etc.] Ought Páṇini indeed (in such a case) to have expressed himself thus? No, he ought not. This is a mere question of a doubtful case, and in all such cases there avails the Paribh//áshá which says that 'the solution of the special (difficulty) results from explanation,[50] for it does not follow that because there is a doubt there is no criterion (to solve it).'"—*Kaiyyaṭa*: "The foregoing words, 'if there are more, etc.' mean that Páṇini (instead of giving, *e.g.* his rule, VI. 4, 1, as he does in the word *angasya*, *i.e.* 'this is the adhikára on base'), ought to have said, '*angasya prág dveḥ*,' *i.e.* 'this is the *adhikára* on *base* which avails before (*i.e.* does not go further than) VIII. 1, 1 (exclusively).' The words of Patanjali, 'ought Páṇini, indeed, etc.,' mean: ought Páṇini to have given the contents of the two preceding Várttikas?"

प्राग्द्वेरित्यादि वक्तव्यम । तत्तर्हीति । यावतिथो ऽलिति भूयसि प्राग्वचनं चेत्यर्थः —Patanjali: . . . . किं प्रयोजनम्—Várttika (omitted in the Calc. ed.) स्वरितेनाधिकारगतिर्यथा विज्ञायेत—Patanjali: अधिकारगतिः। अधिकः कारः। अधिकं कार्यम्। गोस्त्रियोरुपसर्जनस्येत्यत्र गोटाङ्ग्रहणं चोदितं न कर्तव्यं भवति। स्त्रीग्रहणं स्वरयिष्यते। स्वरितेनाधिकारगतिर्भविष्यतीति स्त्रियामित्येवं प्रकृत्य ये विहितास्तेषां ग्रहणं विज्ञास्यते तत्र स्वरितेनाधिकारगतिर्भवतीति न दोषो भवति etc.

[50] "व्याख्यानतः." The word व्याख्यान "explanation" is defined in the Introduction of Patanjali: उदाहरणं प्रत्युदाहरणं वाक्याध्याहार इत्येतत्समुदितं व्याख्यानं भवति; "explanation is giving an instance, giving a counter-instance, and supplying the elliptical expression of a sentence: all these three together."

[Then follows, in the Bháshya, an observation of *Patanjali* on a doubtful passage, which is the subject of his comment in its appropriate place. He continues]: "What is the purpose of the Sútra?"—*Várttika*: "That the proper way of applying an adhikára might be known by means of the swarita."—*Patanjali*: "'Proper way of applying an adhikára.' (Just so). (*Adhi-kára* means) an agent placed over, or an act to be done, placed over. Now, at the Sútra I.2, 48, the expression *goṭáñg* (used in the Várttika to this rule) must not be considered as the subject of the adhikára; for the expression *strí* will have the swarita. Therefore, according to the words of the Várttika ('that the proper way,' etc.) those affixes alone will have to be understood in that Sútra (I. 2, 48) which fall under the head *strí*, and, according to the Várttika's own words, there is no defect in the Sútra I. 2, 48." [To understand this latter illustration of our rule, it is necessary to know that *Kátyáyana*, in giving the Várttika *goṭáñgrahaṇam kṛinnivṛittyartham*, to the Sútra I. 2, 48, intends to point out an omission in the rule of Páṇini. Patanjali, however, shows that the swarita over *strí* in this rule obviates the punctiliousness of the Várttika, and he therefore taunts Kátyáyana, as well on this occasion as when he comments on I. 2, 48, for not having understood 'the proper way of applying the adhikára,' by repeating to him his own criticisms on the Sútra of the present discussion. Then follow other illustrations of Patanjali as to the proper way of applying an adhikára, which it is not necessary for our immediate purpose to add to the foregoing translation].

The passage I have given here from the "Great Commentary" on Páṇini,—and which may serve too as a specimen of the manner in which the two grammatical saints, Kátyáyana and Patanjali, scrutinized every doubtful word of the Sútras,—will have shown that the rule of Páṇini, which teaches the manner of defining an *adhikára*, or heading rule, is interpreted by them as being based on *the application of writing* to his terminology. There are three modes, as we learn from them (and the fact is, of course, fully borne out by the Sútras themselves), by which Páṇini indicates a heading-rule in his Grammar. The one consists in his using the word *prák*, "before," with a word following in the ablative, by which expression he implies that the heading continues up to that word, which will occur in a later Sútra. Another mode of his is merely to indicate the heading, the extent of which is then, as the Bháshya says, matter of "explanation." His third and last mode consists in putting the sign of a swarita,—*which was not intended for pronunciation*,—not over any word of the Sútra, arbitrarily, as Dr. Boehtlingk imagines, but, as common sense would suggest, over that word which is the heading, as over the word *strí*, in the Sútra I. 2, 48. Kátyáyana, moreover, indicates (by the expression *bhúyasí*), and Patanjali expressly states, that in those cases in which the number of Sútras comprised under an adhikára did not exceed the number of the letters of the alphabet, a letter representing a numerical value (without, of course, being "the bearer of a swarita"), was added to indicate the extent of the adhikára; and from the example given by Kaiyyaṭa we must infer that the numerical value of the letter was determined by the position it has in the Śivasútras, since *i* is to him an equivalent of the figure 2. And this representation of figures by letters of the alphabet derives an additional interest from the circumstance that it is quite different from the method we meet with at a later period of Hindu progress in mathematics and astronomy.[51] In short, we see that Patanjali and Kátyáyana not merely presuppose a knowledge of writing in Páṇini, but consider the use he has made of writing as one of the *chief means by which he has built up the technical structure of his work.*

I will obviate, at once, an objection which may be raised,—though it could scarcely be raised by those who treat Kátyáyana as a contemporary of Páṇini, or use the Commentaries as direct evidence for or against Páṇini,—I mean the objection that the comments of Kátyáyana and Patanjali would only testify to their own knowledge and use of written accents; but that neither necessitate the conclusion that Páṇini knew and employed, as they suppose him

---

[51] Compare the system of Áryabhaṭṭa, who uses vowels and nasals = 0; *ka, ṭa, pa, ja* = 1; *kha, ṭha, pha, ra* = 2; *ga, ḍa, ba, la* = 3, etc. See Lassen's Zeitschrift, II. 423 ff., "Journal Asiatique" (1835), vol. XVI., p. 116, etc.

to have done, written accents, nor that he was acquainted with the use of written letters for the purpose of denoting numerical values. And should there be any who attach more faith to Kaiyyaṭa, the late commentator on Patanjali, than to Patanjali himself and Kátyáyana, they might, perhaps, adduce an observation of this grammarian, "that the Sútras of Páṇini were read in one breath, (without any regard to accent)," in order to infer that the swarita might have been *sounded* over the word which it intended to mark as adhikára.[52] Such a conclusion, however, would be invalidated, not only by the natural sense of the passage quoted, but by the remark of the same grammarian, which is contained in the translation I have given before, and which states that the swarita was not intended, in our present case, for "practical application." It remains, therefore, to be seen whether this remark of Kaiyyaṭa is confirmed by analogous facts in Páṇini's Grammar.

Páṇini frequently refers, in his Sútras, not only to grammarians who have preceded him, but to lists of affixes, and to arrangements of the verbal roots, which must have coincided with his own terminology. The personal relation of Páṇini to these collections or books will be the subject of future remark; it will suffice, at present, to show that Páṇini's work, and these works, were based on the same grammatical system. Páṇini refers, for instance, to a list of affixes which begin with *uṇ*;[53] where the mute letter *ṇ*—which has exactly the same technical value in the affix *uṇ* as it would have in

---

[52] *Kaiyyaṭa* towards the end of the Introduction: एकश्रुत्या सूत्राणां पाठात्सर्वेषामुदात्तादीनामुपदेशः.—Another discussion on *adhikára* occurs incidentally in Patanjali's comment on I. 1, 49.

[53] उण्णादि; compare Páṇini, III. 3, 1; 4, 75.—This word is sometimes written उणादि; but wrongly, for the Sandhi rules apply not only to real words, but equally to the technical language of the Sútras. Since उण्, in उण्णादि, is a pada (púrvapada), it has to follow the Sandhi rule given, VIII. 3, 32. Real padas ending in ण्, it is true, are rare, and perhaps still rarer as first parts of a compound; but a word वृषणश्व becomes on that very ground the subject of an exceptional rule; its first part is said to be not पद but भ (I. 4, 18, v. 3). As the phonetic rules of the grammarians bespeak the necessities and predilections of the Hindu organ of speech, technical names could not but follow the general rules of pronunciation, and there is no cause, therefore, to establish an exception for the term उण्णादि.

Páṇini's affixes *aṇ*, *ṇa*, or in other terms containing this anubandha —proves that these affixes rested on the terminology which governs the Sútras of Páṇini. He speaks of *bhuvádi*, *adádi*, *tudádi*,—in short, of the ten classes of radicals, just as they are given in *the* Dhátupáṭha, and even of subdivisions of this work, *e.g.*, *dyutádi*, *pushádi*, *bhidádi*, *muchádi*, *yajádi*, *radhádi*, etc.;[54] and if there existed a doubt that the expressions quoted, which contain the first word of a list, necessarily imply the whole list, and in the order in which the words of such a list appear in this work,[55] the doubter would have at least to admit that the anubandhas or technical letters which accompany each radical in the Dhátupáṭha, possess the grammatical value which is expressly defined as inhering in them by special rules of Páṇini.[56] He refers to the Upadeśa, which is, according to Patanjali, a list, not only of the radicals, but of nominal bases, affixes, particles, increases of the base and grammatical substitutes, all of which are "settled," as Kátyáyana says.[57]

Now, if we consult the Sútras which treat of the verbal roots, we find, for instance, that, as a rule, a root is *udátta* on the last

---

[54] Compare *e.g.* Páṇini I. 3, 1; II. 4, 72 and 75; III. 1, 69, 73, 77, 78, 79, 81, 25; III. 1, 55; 3, 104; VII. 1, 59; VI. 1, 15; VII. 2, 45, and other instances which are quoted in the excellent *Radices Linguæ Sanscritæ* of *Westergaard.*

[55] It is barely possible, however, to admit such a doubt; for Páṇini does not restrict himself to generally mentioning radicals by giving the first word of the order, such as *bhuvádi*, *adádi*, etc.; he refers, also, to distinct numbers. Thus, VII. 2, 59, he speaks of *the four* radicals beginning with वृत्, and the rule he gives applies to no other four radicals than वृत् and the three radicals which follow it in the Dhátup. (§ 18, 19—22); he speaks, VII. 2, 75, of *the five* radicals beginning with कॄ, and his rule avails only for कॄ and the four radicals which follow it in the Dhátup. (§ 28, 116—120); or, VII. 3, 98, of *the five* radicals beginning with रुद् (= Dhátup. § 24, 59—63); or, VI. 1, 6, of *the six* radicals beginning with जक्ष् (= Dhátup. § 24, 63—69); or, VI. 4, 125, of *the seven* radicals beginning with फण् (Dhátup. § 19, 73—79), etc. In all these instances, therefore, the order of the radicals in the Dhátupáṭha, as referred to by Páṇini, is the absolute condition of his rule.

[56] Compare the quotations in Westergaard's Radices, p. 342, 343.

[57] Compare Páṇini I. 3, 2; VI. 1, 45, 186; 4, 37; VIII. 4, 14, 18; (the term occurs frequently, too, in the Várttikas and Kárikás,) and see note 39.

syllable (VI. 1, 162). Yet (VII. 2, 10) Páṇini states that a radical has not the connecting vowel *i*, if in the Upadeśa it is a *monosyllable* and *anudátta*. As the former rule concerns a radical, which is part of, and embodied in, a real word, while the latter describes the theoretical existence of the radical in the Dhátupáṭha, we may imagine, it is true, that for the purpose of grammatical teaching a pronunciation of the radical was devised in the Upadeśa different to that which it has in real language. But, even on the supposition that a radical could be pronounced *anudátta*, is it probable that Páṇini or the authors of the Dhátupáṭha could have recourse to so clumsy a method for conveying the rule implied by the term *anudátta*? Would they, gratuitously, have created the confusion that must necessarily arise from a twofold pronunciation of the same radical, when any other technical *anubandha* would have enabled them to attain the same end? Let us suppose, on the contrary, that *anudátta*, in the Upadeśa, does not mean the spoken, but the *written* accent, and the difficulty is solved without the necessity of impugning the ability or the common sense of the grammarians.

This inference is strengthened, moreover, by another analogous fact, which may be recalled before I give further proof from a synopsis of Páṇini's rules and the appearance of the radicals in the Upadeśa. This fact is contained in the last Sútra of Páṇini's grammar, where he teaches that the short vowel *a*, which in his rules is treated as *vivṛita*, or pronounced with the expansion of the throat, is, in reality, *samvṛita*, or pronounced with the contraction of the throat. This Sútra did certainly not intend to impose upon the pupil the task of pronouncing, during his grammar lessons, the short vowel *a* in such a manner as no Hindu can pronounce it, or of sounding, when learning the properties of this vowel, instead of it, some nondescript deputy vowel-sound: it can only mean that, for the sake of technical purposes defined by the commentators, Páṇini made a fiction in his grammar, which, of course, he had to remove when terminating his book. This fiction, however, being based on a *phonetic impossibility*, would be a very awkward one if it applied to oral teaching only; it becomes quite unobjectionable if it is supported by a *written* text.[58]

If a radical in the Upadeśa, says Páṇini (I. 3, 12) has the *anudátta* (or *ṅg*) as anubandha, it is, in general, inflected in the *átmanepada*; if its anubandha is the *swarita* (or *ñ*) it is, under certain conditions, inflected in the *átmanepada*; under others, in the *parasmaipada* (I. 3, 72); if it has neither of these *anubandhas* (nor is subject to any of the rules I. 3, 12—77), it is inflected in the *parasmaipada* only (I. 3, 78). Again, from the Dhátupáṭha we learn that, for instance, the radicals *jyá*, *ri*, *lí*, *vri*, *bhri*, *kshi(sh)*, *jñá*, are *anudátta* (*i.e.*, do not assume the connecting vowel *i*), but have neither the *anudátta* nor the *swarita* as *anubandha*.[59] The latter term implies that the sign which bears this denomination is added *after* the significant element. Since, however, the roots named are monosyllables *in the Upadeśa*, and since it is impossible to pronounce an accent without a vowel-sound supporting it, the assumption that the *anudátta* and other accent-*anubandhas* were spoken sounds, would lead to the conclusion that the same verbal root was simultaneously *anudátta* and *not anudátta*.[60]

---

[58] I call it a *phonetic impossibility*, since अ, if it were pronounced विवृत, would assume the properties of आ; but as Páṇini does not allow such an अ to occupy the same portion of time which is required for the pronunciation of आ, a *short* अ pronounced with the expansion of the throat, becomes, to a Hindu organ of speech and from Páṇini's point of view, impossible. For this reason, Patanjali, too, who on a previous occasion had defined the letters which occur in the Upadeśa, *i.e.*, the *upadishṭa-varṇas*, as *pronounced* or pronounceable letters [see note 40], looks upon this last Sútra of Páṇini as merely given to counteract the effect of the Upadeśa; he thus implies that this is the only case in which an *upadishṭa-varṇa* was not pronounceable: अ अ (VIII. 4, 68) ॥ किमर्थमिदमुच्यते । अकारो ऽयमक्षरसमाम्नाये विवृत उपदिष्टस्तस्य संवृतताप्रत्यापत्तिः क्रियते.—Kaiyyaṭa: किमर्थमिति । अकारस्याकारवचने प्रयोजनाभावात्प्रश्नः । अकारो ऽयमिति । सवर्णार्थमिह शास्त्रे विवृतदोषयुक्तो ऽकार उपदिष्टः । तस्य प्रयोगे संवृतस्यैवोच्चारणार्थमिदं प्रत्यापत्तिवचनम् । अक्षरसमाम्नायग्रहणं सकलशास्त्रोपलक्षणम्.

[59] Westergaard's Radices, § 31, 29—36.

[60] Other instances may be gathered from Westergaard's Radices. I must exclude, however, some which are not countenanced by the best MSS. I have consulted; those,

If I had adhered to the terminology of the Dhátupáṭha, as it is met with in the best MSS. of Mádhava's commentary, the foregoing illustration would have become still more striking; for, according to them, the roots *jyá*, *rí*, etc., are *anudátta*, and have the *udátta* as their anubandha. In general, it may be observed, that the Sútra I. 3, 78 is apparently understood by Mádhava and other commentators as referring to roots which have *udátta* as anubandha: for a root which is neither *anudáttet* nor *swaritet*, is described by them as *udáttet*. There is some reason, however, to doubt whether the latter term really occurred in the Upadeśa referred to by Páṇini; and as the solution of this doubt, in an affirmative sense, would add another fact to those already obtained, it will not be superfluous to advert to it here.

The misgiving I entertain is based on Páṇini's own terminology. He speaks of roots which, in the Upadeśa, are *udátta* (VII. 3, 34) and *anudátta* (VI. 4, 37; VII. 2, 10), which are *anudáttet* and *swaritet* (see the preceding quotations, p. 45); but there is no trace in his grammar of radicals which are *udáttet*. And this omission is the more striking, as the number of roots which are marked *udáttet* in the present MSS. of the Dhátupáṭha is considerable. Nor is it satisfactorily explained by the negative tenor of the Sútra I. 3, 78, since there is no other instance in Páṇini's

---

especially, which are met with in the Radices under the term स्वरितेत्. For when we read in the latter work (*e.g.* § 22 and § 31, 1, etc.) that भृञ्, हृञ्, धृञ्, etc., डुक्रीञ्, प्रीञ्, श्रीञ्, etc., are अनुदात्ताः and स्वरितेतः, or (§ 31, 10, etc.) that क्नूञ्, द्रूञ्, पूञ्, etc. are उदात्ताः and स्वरितेतः, I could not adduce these and similar instances in support of my conclusions; since Mádhava is certainly right in giving, instead of the term स्वरितेतः, the word उभयपदिनः or उभयतोभाषाः, as the anubandha ञ् would become meaningless, if these roots had, besides, the anubandha स्वरित. The term स्वरितेत् is correctly indicated by Westergaard and the MSS., for instance, of the roots हिक्क, अन्चु, etc. (§ 21); णिजिर्, विजिर्, विष्लृ (§ 25); मृष, इरुचिर्, णह, रञ्ज, etc. (§ 26); तुद, णुद, etc. (§ 28); रुधिर्, भिदिर्, etc. (§ 29), etc., for all these radicals have not the anubandha ञ्. A proof of the accuracy of the commentators in this respect, is afforded by the instance of the root चच् (§ 24, 7) which is described in the Dhátupáṭha as अनुदात्तेत्, and represented at the same time as चक्षिङ्, for they explain on this occasion that the anubandha ङ् does not indicate the átmanepada-inflection, marked by the term अनुदात्तेत्, but refers to the effect of the Sútra III. 2, 149.

work of a technical and important term being given vaguely and inferentially.

If, however, we apply to the present case the conclusions we have been already compelled to draw as to Páṇini's having used accents as written signs, we may surmise the reason why *udáttet* is not amongst the terms employed by this grammarian. Of the three accents, *udátta*, *swarita*, and *anudátta*, the two latter only are marked in the principal Vaidik writings, the *swarita* being indicated by a perpendicular line over the syllable, the *anudátta* by a horizontal line under it. The syllable not marked is *udátta*. It is possible, therefore, to say that a radical or syllable which is not marked is *udátta*, and that one with a horizontal stroke under it is *anudátta*; it is possible, too, to speak of a line *added* under or over the last letter of the radical; but it is surely impossible to call that 'addition' (*anubandha*) which, not being visible, could not be added at all. This explanation of the absence of the term *udáttet* is founded, of course, on the supposition that the system of marking the accents was the same at Páṇini's time, as it occurs in our MSS. of the principal Veda-Sanhitás; but it can hardly be doubted that this system is as deeply rooted in Hindu tradition as everything else connected with the preservation of the sacred books. If, then, it becomes certain that Páṇini knew written accent signs, which were not pronounced, it will not be hazardous to put faith in the statement of Kaiyyaṭa, that the swarita, which was intended as a mark of an adhikára, was also a written sign, a perpendicular stroke, "but had nothing to do with practical application."

That Páṇini, as Patanjali tells us, and Kátyáyana gives us to understand, used letters in his adhikára rules for the notation of numeral values, does not follow, we must admit, from his own words in the quoted Sútra (I. 3, 11), but there is a rule of his (VI. 3, 115) in which he informs us that the owners of cattle were, at his time, in the habit of marking their beasts on the ears, in order to make them recognizable. Such signs, he says, were, for instance, a swastika, a ladle, a pearl, etc.; yet he mentions besides, *eight* and *five*. Now, either the graziers used letters of the alphabet to denote these numerals, or they employed special figures, as we do. In either case it is obvious that they must have been acquainted with writing; in the latter, moreover, that the age to which they belonged had already overcome the primitive mode of denoting numerals by letters, and that writing must have been, therefore, already a matter of the commonest kind. At all events, and whichever alternative be taken—if even the Hindu cattle paraded the acquaintance of the Hindus with the art of writing and of marking numerals,—one may surely believe that Páṇini was as proficient in writing as the cowherds of his time, and that, like them, he resorted to the marking of numerals whenever it was convenient to him to do so.

The absence of a letter or grammatical element, or even of a word, the presence of which would have been required by a previous rule, is called by Páṇini *lopa.* The literal sense of this word, which is derived from *lup*, "to cut off," is "cutting off." It will be conceded that it is not possible to "cut off" any but a visible sign, and that a metaphorical expression of this kind could not have arisen, unless the reality existed. Indeed, the very definition which Páṇini gives of this term must remove every doubt, if there existed any. He says: "*lopa* ('cutting off') is the not being *seen*" (*scil.*, of a letter, etc.)[61] For, whatever scope may be given to the figurative meaning of the radical "to see," it is plainly impossible that an author could speak of a thing visible, literally or metaphorically, unless it were referable to his sense of sight. A letter or word, which is no more *seen*, or has undergone the effect of *lopa*, must, therefore, previously to its *lopa*, have been a visible or written letter to him. And the same remark applies to an expression which occurs several times in the Sútras; for Páṇini speaks more than once of affixes which are *seen*, or of a vowel which is *seen* in words.[62]

---

[61] I. 1, 60: अदर्शनं लोपः.

[62] अन्येभ्यो ऽपि दृश्यते III. 2, 178; 3, 130.—अन्येभ्यो ऽपि दृश्यन्ते III. 2, 75.—अन्येषामपि दृश्यते VI. 3, 137.—अन्येष्वपि दृश्यते III. 2, 101.—इतराभ्यो ऽपि दृश्यन्ते V. 3, 14. —Though in the foregoing observations no conclusion of mine is founded on statements of the later grammarians alone, it may not be without some interest to mention now that these grammarians do not seem to have conceived as much as the idea of Páṇini's

If it becomes evident from the foregoing arguments that Páṇini not only *wrote*, but that *writing* was a main element in the *technical* arrangement of his rules, it may not be superfluous to ask, whether the sacred texts had been committed to writing at the time at which he lived, or whether they were preserved then by memory only? That the mere fact of learning the Veda does not disprove the possibility of its having been preserved by written letters also, is clear enough, and is indirectly acknowledged by Müller himself.[63]

---

grammar ever having existed except in writing. For Kaiyyaṭa, amongst others, refers to a written text of this grammar, even when there is no necessity whatever of making allusion to such a circumstance. We must infer, therefore, that it was a matter of course to him to look upon Páṇini's rules as having been at all times written rules. Thus, in commenting on the vowel ऋ of the *pratyáhára* ऋक्, and in adverting to its last letter, he might have simply spoken of a letter क्, but he speaks of a *letter-sign* क्।, "अत्र हि ककारेण चिह्नेन प्रत्याहारस्थो विवृतो निर्दिष्टः etc."—And when Professor Müller, as we shall presently see, avails himself of so late an authority as the *Mímánsá-Várttikas* of *Kumárila* to prove or to make plausible facts concerning the highest antiquity, I will quote, as a counterpart, another late work which introduces to us the god Śiva himself as recommending the *writing* and wearing of grammatical texts as a means for the attainment of boons and the prevention of evils. I need not add that I look upon neither work as a sufficient authority to settle the points of the present discussion. The passage alluded to occurs in the chapter of a mystical dialogue between Śiva and his wife, called *Jnánakáṇḍaśesharáhasya*, where Śiva, after having explained to Párvatí the letters of the alphabet, concludes his instruction with the following words: एतद्व्याकरणं देवि लिखित्वा भूर्जपत्रके। गोरोचनाकुङ्कुमेन तथा शल्लचञ्चुना। कण्ठे वा यदि वा बाहौ मस्तके वा वरानने। सर्वव्याधिविनिर्मुक्तो दिनानां त्रितये भवेत्। संतानार्थे पठेद्विद्वान्धारयित्वा समाहितः। अवश्यं लभते पुत्रं बन्ध्यायां मम तुल्यकम्। रणे राजकुले घोरे अपि व्याघ्रभयादिके। स्मरणादेव नश्यन्ति किमन्यत्कथयामि ते *i.e.*, "if a man *writes* this grammatical explanation on a birch-leaf, with a mixture of the yellow pigment Gorochaná and saffron, or if he has it written by a scribe with the quill of a porcupine on his neck or his arm or his head, he becomes after three days free from all disease; and if a wise man, wishing for progeny, reads and retains it attentively, he is sure to obtain a son, who will be like me, from his (previously) barren wife. If a battle (rages), or the royal family spreads terror, or if a tiger causes alarm, or on similar occasions, all danger vanishes in merely remembering (this grammatical explanation). What further shall I tell thee?" etc.

[63] History, etc., p. 246: "The ancient literature of India was continually learnt by heart; and even at the present day, when MSS. have become so common, some of its more sacred portions must still be acquired by the pupil from the mouth of a teacher, and not from MSS."

He quotes, it is true, a passage from the Mahábhárata, and one from Kumárila's Várttikas, which condemn, the one the writing of the Veda, and the other the learning it from a written text;[64] but I hold that neither quotation proves anything against the practice of writing the Veda at or before Páṇini's time. Both passages might, on the contrary, be alleged to confirm the fact that the offence of writing the Vedas had already been committed when these verses were composed. They betray, it is true, as we should expect, the apprehension of their authors lest oral teaching might become superfluous, and the services of the Bráhmaṇa caste be altogether dispensed with; but they convey nothing else—not even the prohibition that the teacher or Guru himself might not have recourse to a written text of the Veda if he wanted to refresh his memory or to support his meditation. Nay, we may go further, and assert that by an authority certainly much older than both the authors of this passage of the Mahábhárata and the Mímánsá-Várttikas, all the first *three castes* were distinctly recommended to possess written Vaidik texts. For, let us hear what the lawgiver Yájnavalkya says: "All the religious orders must certainly have the desire of knowing the Veda: therefore the first three classes—the twice-born—should *see* it, think on it, and hear it." But how could Yájnavalkya order them to see the Veda, unless it could be obtained in writing?[65] And that Páṇini, too,

---

[64] p. 502: "In the Mahâbhârata, we read: 'Those who sell the Vedas and even those who write them, those also who defile them, they shall go to hell.' Kumârila says: 'that knowledge of the truth is worthless which has been acquired from the Veda, if the Veda has not been rightly comprehended, if it has been learnt from writing, or been received from a Śûdra.'"—The passage of the Mahábhárata quoted by Müller, occurs in the *Anuśásanap.* verse 1645. I doubt, however, whether his rendering of वेदानां चैव दूषकाः "those also who defile the Vedas," is quite correct. It seems to me that it means "those who corrupt the text of the Vedas," and that it is synonymous with the expression वेदविस्रावकाः which occurs in the second act of the *Prabodha-chandrodaya* (ed. Brockhaus, p. 20, l. 14; ed. Calc. p. 12*a*, l. 5). The expression समयानां च दूषकाः which precedes by a few verses (*Anuśásanap.* v. 1630) *i.e.*, "those who vitiate agreements" is analogous. There is, unhappily, no comment of *Nílakantha* on either of these passages.

[65] Yájnav. III. 191: स ह्याश्रमैर्विजिज्ञास्यः समस्तैरेवमेव तु । द्रष्टव्यस्त्वथ मन्तव्यः

must have seen written Vaidik texts follows clearly, in my opinion, from two Sútras, in which he says: "(the augment *á*) is *seen* also in the Veda (viz., in other instances than those mentioned in a former rule)," and (the ádeśa *an*) is *seen* also in the Veda (viz., in other cases of *asthi*, *dadhi*, etc., than those mentioned previously).[66] It is on this ground that—while disapproving the loose manner in which the Siddhánta-kaumudí imparts to the word *grantha* in Páṇini's Sútra, I. 3, 75, the meaning *Veda*,—I cannot altogether reject the identity which is established by this commentary between the two words, though it would have been better, in a gloss on Páṇini, to have retained the distinction which he himself established for facilitating a clearer understanding of those Sútras which refer to revealed books, and of others which speak of unrevealed ones.[67]

श्रोतव्यश्च द्विजातिभिः. Vijnáneśwara, the modern commentator of Yájnavalkya, who, like Kumárila, is evidently not pleased with the recommendation of "seeing" the Veda, twists the construction of the latter passage into the following sense: "the twice-born should first hear (the expounding of) the Veda, then reflect on it and thus (by reflection) keep it present (to their mind)." In order to impart to the word "to see" the figurative sense, he reverses the entire, and, it would seem, natural order of the injunction, which recommends the twice-born first to look into the Veda, then to reflect on it, and ultimately to ask the teacher to give his own explanation of it; the latter becoming, of course, more effectual, if the pupil is already somewhat familiar with his subject.—This is the comment of the *Mitákshará*: यस्मान्नित्यतयात्मप्रमाणभूतो वेदस्तस्मादसावुक्तमार्गेण सकलाश्रमिभिर्नानाप्रकारं जिज्ञासितव्यस्तमेव प्रकारं दर्शयति। द्विजातिभिर्द्रष्टव्यो ऽपरोक्षीकर्तव्यस्तत्रोपायं दर्शयति। श्रोतव्यो मन्तव्य इति। प्रथमतो वेदान्तश्रवणेन निर्णेतव्यस्तदनन्तरं मन्तव्यो युक्तिभिर्विचारयितव्यस्ततो ऽसौ ध्यानेनापरोक्षीभवति.

[66] VI. 4, 73, and VII. 1. 76: छन्दस्यपि दृश्यते.

[67] Compare note 27. I alluded above to the analogy which exists between the contrasted words *grantha-artha* and *káṇḍa-padártha*. After having shown that the Veda was a written book at Páṇini's time, I may now quote a passage from the Pariśishṭa of the Nirukta (I. 12): अयं मन्त्रार्थचिन्ताभ्यूहो ऽभ्यूढो ऽपि श्रुतितो ऽपि तर्कतो न तु पृथक्त्वेन मन्त्रा निर्वक्तव्याः प्रकरणश एव तु निर्वक्तव्याः, which is thus rendered by Mr. Muir, in his valuable work, "Original Sanskrit Texts" (vol. II., p. 188): "This reflective deduction of the sense of the hymns is effected by the help of oral tradition and reasoning. The hymns are not to be interpreted as isolated texts, but according to their context." In this passage the words श्रुतितो ऽपि तर्कतः are equivalent of ग्रन्थतो ऽर्थतश्च.

There is but one other question which can be raised in connection with the present inquiry: Was writing known *before* Páṇini?

One word, of frequent occurrence in the Vaidik hymns, or rather the sense which is imparted to it, may enable us, perhaps. to form an opinion on this difficult problem. I mean the word *Ṛishi*. It is explained by old and modern commentators as "a seer of hymns," a saint to whom those Vaidik hymns referred to his authorship, were revealed by a divinity. Thus it is said in the Śatapatha-Bráhmaṇa that the *Ṛishi* Vámadeva obtained *seeing* the Ṛigveda-hymn, IV. 26, 1; or in the Aitareya-Bráhmaṇa that the Ṛishi *seeing* the hymn II. 41, 2, spoke it.[68] For reasons which will appear from the statement I shall have to make on the chronological relation of these works to Páṇini, I cannot appeal to these Bráhmaṇas as evidence for the present purpose; it is safer to quote Páṇini himself, who also speaks of hymns which are *seen* (IV. 2, 7), and who must therefore be supposed to record an impression current at, and very probably anterior to, his time. This probability, however, becomes a certainty when we consider the distinct evidence of Yáska, who says that "the Ṛishis see the hymns with all kinds of intentions," and who makes mention of a predecessor of his, a son or descendant of Upamanyu, who defined the word "*Ṛishi as coming from seeing; for he saw the hymns.*"[69]

There were authorities, consequently, before Páṇini's time, who

---

[68] *Śatap.* XIV. 4, 2, 22: तद्धैतत्पश्यन्नृषिर्वामदेवः प्रतिपेदे। अहं मनुरभवं सूर्यश्चेति. —*Aitar. Br.* 9, 1: तदेतदृषिः पश्यन्नभ्यनूवाच नियुत्वाँ इन्द्रसारथिरिति. Compare also Müller's "Ancient History," p. 237: शौनको...... द्वितीयं मण्डलं दृष्टा, etc.; or *Uvata* on the first verse of the Ṛik-prátiśákya (in the valuable edition of Mr. Regnier, "Journal Asiatique," tome VII. 1856, p. 181) ऋषयो मन्त्रद्रष्टारः; or *Nágojíbhaṭṭa* on Páṇini, I. 1, 1: यज्ञकाण्डद्रष्टार ऋषयः; or the same on IV. 1, 79: ऋषिशब्देनात्र मन्त्रद्रष्टारः etc.

[69] *Nirukta*, 7, 3: एवमुच्चावचैरभिप्रायैरृषीणां मन्त्रदृष्टयो भवन्ति; and 2, 11: ऋषिर्दर्शनात्। स्तोमान्ददर्शेत्यौपमन्यवः. Hence Ṛishi becomes a synonyme of a Vaidik hymn. Compare *Páṇini*, IV. 4, 96, or *Sáyaṇa* on Ṛig-v. I. 189, 8: ऋषिभिरतीन्द्रियार्थप्रकाशकैर्मन्त्रैः.

maintained the doctrine that the hymns were revealed—not to the sense of hearing, but to the sense of sight. That the act of *seeing* may be applied metaphorically to the faculty of thinking or imagining, and the term *seen* to what is imagined or thought, is no matter of dispute. But when we read numerous hymns of the Ṛigveda which neither express a truth, nor depict nature or events of life, but which simply manifest the desire of a pious mind;—when we read, for instance, such sentences as, "may this oblation, Agni, be most acceptable to thee;" or "may afflictions fall upon him who does not propitiate the gods;" or "we address our pious prayers to thee, Agni," etc., what *metaphorical* meaning could connect such words with the notion of seeing?

And we know, too, that it is not merely the general idea conveyed by a hymn, the ethical truth, or the picture of the elementary life, or the display of sacrificial rites, or the praise of the gods, or the imprecation against foes, which is looked to by the worshipper as having been revealed to a Ṛishi by a divinity,—but that the very words of the hymn, and the very order in which they stand, were deemed equally a gift from above. The various methods devised by the learned to preserve the words in their integrity and to prevent their order from being disturbed, prove that they did not view these hymns in the light of mere revelations of truths, but in that of revelations of words and of sentences held sacred in the very order and form in which they appear. Nor does the fact that there were various Śákhás with various recensions of several hymns or passages of hymns, invalidate this argument; for each Śákhá claimed its text as the original one, as *the* revealed text; and its belief was, therefore, based on the same ground which was common to all.

If, then, such is the case, the word *seer* loses altogether the power of metaphorical expression; it then applies only to the material fact of seeing material words, such as the divinity holds before the seer's material eye. The inference to be drawn from these premises is obvious. It seems to derive some corroboration from a collateral fact. The Vaidik writings from immemorial times being communicated by the teacher to his pupil orally, and the pupil being bound to receive them in this and in no other way, their name, as we find it at the time of the Bráhmaṇas and Kalpa-Sútras, is *śruti*, "hearing," or the sacred text received by the sense of hearing. Though Páṇini does not use this term, we may fairly admit, on account of his using the word *śrotriya*,[70] that he was acquainted with it, and that the same mode of studying the Vedas was already usual in his time. Now the contrast is marked between "seeing" the Veda and "hearing" it. In metaphorical language both terms would be equivalent; they would express comprehension of the revealed truth. But there is no metaphor in the term "*śruti*." "Hearing" the Veda rests on a material fact. Why should "seeing" the hymns be considered to rest on a less solid ground?[71]

To extend this view from Yáska and the predecessors he quotes, to the authors of the hymns themselves, would, no doubt, be very hazardous. For even on the supposition that the etymology

---

[70] II. 1, 65, and V. 2, 84. Compare also the Gaṇas to V. 1, 130, 133, श्रुत in the Gaṇa to V. 2, 88, and श्रौति in the Gaṇa to IV. 2, 138.

[71] The title of Ṛishi was, at a later period, given to renowned authors, though they were not considered as inspired by a divinity. The Kalpa works, for instance, are admitted on all hands to be human and uninspired compositions; yet Kumárila writes in one of his Várttikas (I. 3, 10): न तावदनृषिः कश्चित्स्मर्यते कल्पसूत्रकृत् । कर्तृत्वं यदृषीणां तु तत्सर्वं मन्त्रकृत्समम् .... and again: आर्षेयवचनं नित्यपर्यायत्वेन गम्यते । आर्षेयत्वप्रसिद्धिश्च कल्पसूत्रेष्ववस्थिता । .... and आचार्यवचनानां च प्रामाण्यं श्रूयते श्रुतौ । अङ्गानां च प्रणेतार आचार्या ऋषयो मताः, *i.e.*, "No mention occurs of an author of a Kalpa work who was not a Ṛishi; but all that Ṛishis compose is like that which the authors of Mantras compose ..... The word *ársheya* is a synonym of eternal, and the quality of *ársheya* is vested in the Kalpa-Sútras ....; moreover, the Veda says that the words of *Áchâryas* have authority, and the *Áchâryas* who have composed the Vedángas are deemed Ṛishis." And though these words of his make part of a Púrvapaksha, and the proposition that the Kalpa works have the same claim to divine origin as the Mantras, is refuted by him in the Siddhánta, his refutation merely concerns this latter part of the discussion, but does not invalidate the title of Ṛishi given by him to the authors of the Kalpas. For, as he said on a previous occasion: न ह्यत्यन्तानृतं वक्तुं शक्यते पूर्वपक्षिणा, 'the propounder even of a Púrvapaksha should not say that which is too much at variance with truth (if his Púrvapaksha is to be worthy of being part of a discussion).' The title Ṛishi had, therefore, already lost its primitive worth in the days of Kumárila, and had undergone the same fate which is common to titles in general.

proposed by the son of Upamanyu is correct,[72] no proof exists that Ṛishi is conceived in the hymns as implying the seer of *words* or *sentences.* He may be there the real representative of the Roeh who sees the general idea of his prayer or praise, but fashions it with his own—uninspired—words. There are, we may add in proof of this assertion, various instances in the poetry of the Ṛigveda, where the poet is spoken of as having "composed" (literally *fabricated* or *generated*), not as having "seen," a hymn; and they belong undoubtedly to real antiquity, as they show greater common sense. Thus it is said in the Ṛigveda (I. 171, 2) "this praise accompanied with offerings, Maruts, is made (lit. *fabricated*) for you by the heart;" or (VI. 16, 47): "we offer to thee, Agni, the clarified butter in the shape of a hymn made (lit. *fabricated*) by the heart;" or (I. 109, 1, 2): ". . . . . my clear understanding has been given to me by no one else than by you, Indra and Agni; with it I have made (lit. *fabricated*) to you this hymn, the product of intelligence, which intimates my desire for sustenance. For I have heard that you are more munificent givers than an unworthy bridegroom or the brother of a bride; therefore, in offering you the Soma, I produce (lit. *generate*) for you a new hymn;" or (VII. 7, 6): "these men who have cleverly made (lit. *fabricated*) the hymn, have increased the prosperity of all (living beings) with food."[73] And when the poet says in a Válakhilya hymn: "Indra and Varuṇa, I have seen through devotion that which, after it was heard in the beginning, you gave to the poets—wisdom, understanding of speech;" *seeing* is obviously used by him in none but a metaphorical sense.[74]

---

[72] That in दृश्, the दृ may be a prefix, is countenanced by the following analogies: दृह् (= दृध्) and ऋध्, दृप् and ऋप्, दृ (दृणोति) and ऋ (ऋणोति), दृत (respected) and ऋत (respected), दह् and अह् (whence अहन्) दिव् (to be glad) and इव्, दृश् and ऋश्.

[73] Compare, for other instances, Muir's "Original Sanskrit Texts," vol. II. p. 208, note 163, and p. 220.

[74] Compare *ibid.* p. 220: इन्द्रवरुणा यदृषिभ्यो मनीषां वाचो मतिं श्रुतमदत्तमग्रे । . . . . . . तपसाभ्यपश्यम्. In the same sense *Yáska* says (I. 20): साक्षात्कृतधर्माण

There are in the Vaidik age, says Professor Müller (p. 70), "four distinct periods which can be established with sufficient evidence. They may be called the *Chhandas period*, *Mantra period*, *Brâhmaṇa period*, and *Sûtra period*, according to the general form of the literary productions which give to each of them its peculiar historical character." In the continuation of his work he then defines the Chhandas period as embracing the earliest hymns of the Ṛigveda, such as he conceives them to be according to the instances he has selected from the bulk of this Veda (p. 525 *ff.*). The Mantra period is, in his opinion, represented by the remaining part of the Ṛigveda (p. 456 *ff.*); and the Bráhmaṇa period by the Sáma-veda-saṁhitá, "or the prayer-book of the Udgâtṛi priests," which is entirely collected from the Ṛigveda,[75] the Saṁhitás of the Yajurveda (p. 457), the Bráhmaṇa portion of the Vedas, properly so called, and "on the frontier between the Brâhmaṇa and Sûtra literature," the oldest theological treatises or Áraṇyakas and Upanishads (p. 313 *ff.*). Lastly, the Sútra period contains, according to him (p. 71 *ff.*), the Vaidik words written in the Sútra style, viz.: the six Vedángas or the works on "Sikshâ (*pronunciation*), Chhandas (*metre*), Vyâkaraṇa (*grammar*), Nirukta (*explanation of words*), Jyotisha (*astronomy*), and Kalpa (*ceremonial*)" (p. 113 *ff.*).

An author has, in general, the right of choosing his terms; nor should I consider it necessary to add a remark on the names by which Müller designates these four periods of his Ancient History, were it not to obviate a misunderstanding which he has not guarded against, though it may be of consequence to do so. Two terms which have served him for the marking of two periods of

---

ऋषयो बभूवुः, 'the Ṛishis had an intuitive insight into duty' (Muir, vol. II. p. 174); and Sáyaṇa, *e.g.* in his gloss on Ṛigv. I. 162, 7: ऋषयो ऽतीन्द्रियद्रष्टारः, or on IV. 36, 6: ऋषिरतीन्द्रियज्ञानी.

[75] Professor Benfey has pointed out, in his valuable edition of this Veda, the few verses which cannot be found in the Ṛigveda (Pref. p. xix). This redundance, which is apparently at variance with the general doctrine of the Hindu commentators, that the Sámaveda is extracted from the Ṛigveda, proves, in reality, that there must have been, at one time, another recension of the Ṛigveda than that which we possess now; a fact clearly proved also by Müller's "Ancient History."

the ancient literature, viz., *Sútra* and *Bráhmaṇa*, have been used by him nearly in the same sense in which they occur in the ancient writers; and if he embraces more works under these heads than those writers would have comprised, it may be fairly admitted that no misconception will result from this enlargement of the original acceptation of the words Sútra and Bráhmaṇa. But if he designates the two first epochs by the names of *Chhandas* and *Mantra*, with the explicit remark that he has made this division of four periods "*according to the general form of the literary productions which give to each of them its peculiar historical character*" (p. 70), it may be inferred that, as in the case of Sútra and Bráhmaṇa, he has chosen those names in conformity with the bearing they have in the ancient literature itself; that the Hindus, when using the words Chhandas and Mantra, meant by them the older and the more recent hymns of the Ṛigveda. Such, however, is not the case.

Mantra means, as Colebrooke has already defined the word—in conformity with the Mímánsá writers—"a prayer, invocation, or declaration. It is expressed in the first person or is addressed in the second; it declares the purpose of a pious act, or lauds or invokes the object; it asks a question or returns an answer; directs, inquires, or deliberates; blesses or imprecates; exults or laments; counts or narrates," etc. "Mantras are distinguished under three designations. Those which are in metre are termed *ṛich*, those chanted are *sáman*, and the rest are *yajus*, sacrificial prayers in prose," etc.[76]

---

[76] "Transactions of the Royal Asiatic Society," I. p. 448, 449.—Compare also Jaiminíya-nyáyamálá-vistara, I. 4, 1 (*púrvapaksha*): तथा चोक्तम् । उत्तमामन्त्रणाख्यन्तत्वान्तरूपाद्यभावतः । मन्त्रप्रसिद्ध्यभावाच्च मन्त्रतैषां न युज्यत इति । अग्मये जुष्टं निर्वपामीत्युत्तमपुरुषः । अग्ने यशस्विन्यशसे समर्पयेत्यामन्त्रणम् । उर्वी चासि वस्वी चासीत्यस्यन्तरूपम् । इषे त्वोर्जे त्वेति त्वान्तरूपम् । आदिशब्देनाशीर्देवताप्रतिपादनादयः etc. —II. 1, 7: तच्च समाख्यानमनुष्ठानस्मारकादीनां मन्त्रत्वं गमयति । उरु प्रथस्वेत्यादयोऽनुष्ठानस्मारकाः । अग्निमीळे पुरोहितमित्यादयः स्तुतिरूपाः । इषे त्वेत्यादयस्त्वान्ताः । अग्न आ याहि वीतय इत्यादय आमन्त्रणोपेताः । अग्नीदग्नीन्विहरेत्यादयः प्रैषरूपाः । अधःस्विदासीदुपरिस्विदासीदित्यादयो विचाररूपाः । अम्बे अम्बिके ऽम्बालिके न मा नयति कश्चनेत्यादयः परिदेवनरूपाः । पृच्छामि त्वा परमन्तं पृथिव्या इत्यादयः

The first meaning of *Chhandas*, in the ancient writers, is metre; the second is *verse* in general, and in this sense it is contrasted with the prosaic passages of the Yajurveda. Thus the *Purusha-súkta* of the Ṛigveda—the late origin of which hymn is proved by its contents—says:[77] "From this sacrifice which was offered to the universal spirit sprang the Ṛichas (Ṛig-verses), the Sámans (Sámaveda-verses), *the* metrical passages (Chhandas) and the Yajus;" which latter words seem to be referable only to the two characteristic portions of the Yajurveda, since Yajus in general designates its prosaic part. In a verse of the Atharvaveda it is contrasted, in a similar manner, with the Yajurveda, and seems to imply there the verses of the Atharvaveda: "From the remainder of the sacrifice sprang the Ṛichas, Sámans, the verses (*Chhandas*), the old legendary lore, together with the Yajus."[78] In the Sútras of Páṇini the word *Chhandas* occurs, in rules which concern Vaidik words, one hundred and ten times, and its sense extends over two hundred and thirty-three Sútras; in rules of this category it means Veda in general, comprising thus the Mantra- as well as the Bráhmaṇa- portion of the Veda. Whenever, therefore, such a general rule concerning a Vaidik word is restricted or modified in the Mantra portion, Chhandas then becomes contrasted with Mantra, and thus assumes the sense of Bráhmaṇa; or whenever such a general rule is restricted or modified in the Bráhmaṇa portion,

---

प्रश्नरूपाः । वेदिमाहुः परमन्तं पृथिव्या इत्यादय उत्तररूपाः । एवमन्यदप्युदाहार्यम् etc.—II. I, 10—12: पादबन्धेनार्थबन्धेन चोपेता वृत्तबद्धा मन्त्रा ऋचः । गीतिरूपा मन्त्राः सामानि । वृत्तगीतिवर्जितत्वेन प्रश्लिष्टपठिता मन्त्रा यजूंषीत्युक्ते न क्वापि संकरः —II. I, 13: . . . . ततो मन्त्राणां त्रैविध्यं सुस्थितम्.

[77] Ṛigveda (X. 90, 9): तस्माद्यज्ञात्सर्वहुत ऋचः सामानि जज्ञिरे । छन्दांसि जज्ञिरे तस्माद्यजुस्तस्मादजायत. Sáyaṇa, it is true, renders छन्दांसि with गायत्र्यादीनि, when the word would simply mean "metre;" but it does not seem natural that the enumeration of the three Vedas should be interrupted by a word meaning "metre," while on the other hand the word Yajus alone might have left a doubt as to whether the metrical contents of this Veda are included in it or not.

[78] Atharv. XI. 7, 24: ऋचः सामानि छन्दांसि पुराणं यजुषा सह । उच्छिष्टाज्जज्ञिरे etc.—In this sentence *Chhandas* is separated from the word *Yajus* by the word *Puráṇa*, which here probably implies the legends of the Bráhmaṇas.

Chhandas then becomes contrasted with Bráhmaṇa, and therefore assumes the sense of Mantra.[79]

From no passage, however, in the ancient literature, can we infer that *Mantra* conveyed or implied the idea of a later portion, and *Chhandas* that of an earlier portion of the Ṛigveda hymns.

Some very questionable points in the detail of this distribution of the Vaidik literature will be noticed by me hereafter as touching the ground on which I have raised this inquiry into the chronological results of Professor Müller's work. There is, however, one general question which must be dealt with previously. If Müller had contented himself with simply arranging his subject-matter as he has done, we could readily assent to the logical or esthetical point of view which, we might have inferred, had guided him in

---

[79] Thus it is used by Páṇini in the general sense of *Veda*: I. 2, 61; 4, 9. 20. 81; II. 3, 3; 4, 28. 39. 73. 76; III. 1, 42. 50. 59. 84. 123; 2, 63. 88. 105. 137. 170; 3, 129; 4, 6. 88. 117; IV. 1, 29. 46. 59; 3, 19. 150; 4, 106, 110, etc. It is contrasted with *Mantra*, for instance, I. 2, 36 (comp. 34. 35. 37); III. 2, 73 (comp. 71. 72); with *Bráhmaṇa*, for instance, IV. 2, 66; IV. 3, 106 (comp. 105).—The meaning "desire" of the word *chhandas* has not been mentioned above, as being irrelevant for the present purpose; nor was it necessary to give passages from Páṇini where the word has the general sense "metre," such as III. 3, 34, etc., or as base becomes the subject of rules respecting its derivatives.—Professor Weber has adverted in his "Indische Studien" (vol. i. p. 29 note) to the manner in which Páṇini has used *chhandas*; he defines it, however, as meaning first, "desire;" then "a prayer of desire, prayer, *mantra*, contrasted with *bráhmaṇa*, IV. 2, 66; then in a more extended sense, even *bráhmaṇártham*, III. 2, 73" [or shall this mean, asks he, *bráhmaṇanirdsárthaṃ*? Certainly not, for the word is contrasted in III. 2, 73 with the word *mantra* of III. 2, 71 (72), and implies therefore in this Sútra the sense *bráhmaṇa*]; and then "in the widest sense, generally, *veda*, as contrasted with *loke*, *bháshâyám* and its ślokas (IV. 3, 102 *n*)." [The latter instance is not happy, since it belongs to a Várttika of the Káśiká, and since there are more than a hundred Sútras of Páṇini which might have been referred to for the corroboration of the sense *Veda*]. Lastly he says, it means "metre."—But this reversal of the meanings of *chhandas* is not only objectionable etymologically; it prevents our understanding how *chhandas* could mean both a poetical and a prosaic passage of the Vedas. Hence, the incidental question of Weber and his conjecture,—which could not have arisen if he had started from the general sense *Veda*, which *if contrasted* (but only then) with *mantra*, would imply the sense *Bráhmaṇa*, and *vice versâ*. It seems, moreover, that the sense "desire" marks the last stage of its development; in short, that *chhandas* means: 1. metre; 2. a verse; 3*a*. a verse as prayer; *b*. Veda in general, which may become modified to Mantra or Bráhmaṇa; 4. desire.

planning his work. But he does not allow us to take this view, when he assigns dates to these periods severally. The "Chhandas period," he says, comprises the space of time from 1200 to 1000 B.C. (p. 572), the "Mantra period" from 1000 to 800 B.C. (pp. 497, 572), the Bráhmaṇa period" from 800 to 600 B.C. (p. 435), and the "Sútra period" from 600 to 200 B.C. (pp. 249, 313). In other words, his arrangement is meant to be an historical one. He does not classify ancient Sanskrit literature into a scientific, a ritual, a theological, and poetical literature, each of which might have had *its coeval representatives*, but he implies by these dates that when the poetical epoch, his Chhandas- and Mantra- epoch, had terminated its verses, the theological time, that of the Bráhmaṇas and Upanishads etc., set to work; and when this had done with theology, the ritual and scientific period displayed its activity, until it paused about 200 B.C. I need scarcely observe that such an assumption is highly improbable, unless we suppose that India which, from the time of Herodotus, has always enjoyed the privilege of being deemed the land of supernatural facts, has also in this matter set at defiance the ordinary law of human development. But this doubt seems to derive some support from Müller's own arguments. In the course of his researches he has confirmed the general opinion, that a Sútra work presupposes, of necessity, the existence of a Bráhmaṇa, and that a Bráhmaṇa cannot be conceived without a collection of hymns, the Saṁhitá. Thus the ritual Sútras of Áśwaláyana would have been impossible unless a Bráhmaṇa of the Ṛigveda—for instance, the Aitareya-Bráhmaṇa, —had been known to him; for he founds his precepts on it; and such a Bráhmaṇa, in quoting the hymns of the Ṛigveda, implies, as a matter of course, a previous collection of hymns, a Ṛigveda itself. Yet, though this argument is unexceptionable, and may be used, perhaps—not without objections of some weight—so as to presuppose in Áśwaláyana a knowledge of, and therefore as prior to him, a Sámaveda and a Taittiríya-Saṁhitá—where is the logical necessity that the Vájasaneyi-Saṁhitá and the Śatapatha-Bráhmaṇa (belonging to Müller's third period, 800—600 B.C.) existed before Áśwaláyana who lived, according to him, between 600 and 200 before Christ? His Sútras would be perfectly intelligible if neither of the two last-named works had been composed at all. And, again, where is the logical necessity that the Upanishads should have been written before the authors of the Kalpa Sútras, the Grammar, etc., since all these works are quite independent in spirit and in substance from the theosophy of Upanishads or Áraṇyakas. On what ground does Professor Müller separate Páṇini from these latter writings by at least 250 years, when there is no trace of any description in his Sútras, either that he knew this kind of literature or that his Grammar would not have been exactly the same as it is now if he had lived much before the time of these theological works? I shall recur to this latter question; but I cannot conclude the expression of my misgivings as to this historical division without questioning, too, the usefulness of these dates in general. They are not founded, as Müller himself repeatedly admits, on any basis whatever.[80] Neither is there a single reason to account for his allotting 200 years to the three first of his periods, nor for his doubling this amount of time in the case of the Sútra period. He records, it is true, his personal impression alone in speaking of 1200, 1000 years, and so on; but the expediency of giving vent to feelings which deal with hundreds and thousands of years, as if such abstract calculations were suitable

---

[80] "Ancient Sanskrit Literature," p. 244: "It will readily be seen, how entirely hypothetical all these arguments are . . . . . As an experiment, therefore, though as no more than an experiment, we propose to fix the years 600 and 200 B.C. as the limits of that age during which the Brahmanic literature was carried on in the strange style of Sûtras." p. 435: "Considering, therefore, that the Brâhmaṇa period must comprehend the first establishment of the threefold ceremonial, the composition of separate Brâhmaṇas, the formation of Brâhmaṇa-charaṇas and the schism between old and new Charaṇas, and their various collections, it would seem impossible to bring the whole within a shorter space than 200 years. Of course this is merely conjectural, but it would require a greater stretch of imagination to account for the production in a smaller number of years of that mass of Brâhmaṇic literature which still exists, or is known to have existed." P. 497: "I therefore fix the probable chronological limits of the Mantra period between 800 and 1000 B.C." [Where is the least probability of this date?] P. 572: "The chronological limits assigned to the Sûtra and Brâhmaṇa periods will seem to most Sanskrit scholars too narrow rather than too wide, and if we assign but 200 years to

to the conditions of human life, appears very doubtful, if we consider that there are many who will not read his learned work with the special interest and criticism which it inspires in a Sanskrit philologer, but will attach a much higher import to his feelings than he himself does. One omission, moreover, I cannot leave unnoticed in these general dates, since it has a bearing, not merely on the intervals of his periods, but on their starting points.

Colebrooke, in his essay on the Vedas, speaks of the Jyotisha, the ancient Vaidik calendar; and after having quoted a "remarkable" passage of this Vedánga, in which the then place of the colures is stated, continues (M.E. vol. i. p. 109, or As. Res. viii. p. 493): "Hence it is clear that Dhanishṭhá and Áśleshá are the constellations meant; and that when this Hindu calendar was regulated, the solstitial points were reckoned to be at the beginning of the one, and in the middle of the other: and such was the situation of those cardinal points, in the *fourteenth century before the Christian era.* I formerly (As. Res. vii. p. 283, or Essays, i. p. 201) had occasion to show from another passage of the Vedas, that the correspondence of seasons with months, as there stated, and as also suggested in the passage now quoted from the Jyotish, agrees with such a situation of the cardinal points."

We have evidence, therefore, from this passage of the Jyotisha, that an arrangement of Vaidik hymns must have been completed in the fourteenth century before Christ; and as such an arrangement cannot have preceded the origin of the hymns comprised by it, we have evidence that these hymns do not belong to a more recent date. Nor is there any ground for doubting the genuineness of this calendar, or for assuming that the Hindu astronomers, when it was written, had knowledge enough to forge a combination, or if they had, that, in the habit of dealing with millions of years, they would have

---

the Mantra period, from 800 to 1000 B.C., and an equal number to the Chhandas period, from 1000 to 1200 B.C., we can do so only under the supposition that during the early periods of history the growth of the human mind was more luxuriant than in later times, and that the layers of thought were formed less slowly in the primary than in the tertiary ages of the world."—But is 1200 B.C. a primary age of the world, except in biblical geology?

used this knowledge for the sake of forging an antiquity of a few hundred years. Yet the oldest hymns of the Ṛigveda are, according to Müller's opinion, not older than 1200 before Christ.

He has not only not invalidated the passage I have quoted, but he has not even made mention of it. Yet a scholar like Colebrooke, laid, as I have shown, great stress on it: it is he who calls it "remarkable;" and scholars like Wilson and Lassen have based their conclusions on Colebrooke's words.[81] Should we, therefore, be satisfied with the absolute silence of Müller on the statements and opinions of these distinguished scholars, or account for it by the words of his preface?[82]

No one, indeed, to the best of my knowledge, has ever doubted the accuracy of Colebrooke's calculation, but Professor Weber, who, in his "Indische Studien," vol. i. p. 85, thus expresses himself:—"I avail myself of this opportunity to observe that before Colebrooke's astronomical calculation (M. E. i. p. 110, 201) has been examined once more, astronomically, and found correct, I cannot make up my mind, to assign to the present Jyotiḥ-çâstras, the composition of which betrays—in language and style—a very recent period, any historical importance whatever for the fixing of the time when the Vedas were composed." Thus it seems that Professor Weber would make up his mind to that effect if some one would comply with his desire, and confirm the result of Colebrooke's calculation. But, we must ask, on what ground rests this desire, which, in other words, is nothing but a very off-hand slur aimed at Colebrooke's scholarship or accuracy? Is Colebrooke a third-rate writer, to deserve this supercilious treatment? Has he, in his editions or translations of texts, taken such liberties as to forfeit our confidence? Has he falsified antiquity by substituting

[81] See Lassen's "Indische Alterthumskunde," I. p. 747. Wilson's Introduction to his Translation of the Ṛigveda, vol. I. p. xlviii.

[82] Page vi.: "Believing, as I do, that literary controversy is more apt to impede than to advance the cause of truth, I have throughout carefully abstained from it. Where it seemed necessary to controvert unfounded statements or hasty conclusions, I have endeavoured to do so by stating the true facts of the case, and the legitimate conclusions that may be drawn from these facts."

for its traditions his own foregone conclusions or ignorance? Has he appropriated to himself the labour of others, or meddled with subjects he did not thoroughly understand? His writings, one would think, prove that he is a type of accuracy and conscientiousness,—an author in whom even unguarded expressions are of the rarest kind, much more so errors or hasty conclusions drawn from erroneous facts. But Colebrooke was not only a distinguished Sanskritist, he was an excellent astronomer. Lassen calls him the profoundest judge in matters of Hindu astronomy;[83] and he is looked upon as such by common consent. Yet, to invalidate the testimony of a scholar of his learning and character, Professor Weber, simply because a certain date does not suit his taste, and because his feelings, unsupported by any evidence, make him suppose that the Jyotisha "betrays in language and style a very recent period," has nothing to say but that he "will not make up his mind" to take that date for any good until somebody shall have examined that which Colebrooke had already examined, and, by referring to it, had relied upon as an established fact!

It is but just to add, that three or seven years after he had administered this singular lesson to Colebrooke, Weber once more is haunted by the asterisms Dhanishṭhá and Áśleshá, and once more rejects their evidence as to Hindu antiquity.[84] This time, however, it is no longer the accuracy of Colebrooke's statement which inspires his doubt—he passes it over in silence altogether—but the origin of the arrangement of the Hindu Nakshatras. "Since," he says, "the latter was not made by the Hindus themselves, but borrowed from the Chaldeans, it is obvious that no conclusion whatever can be drawn from it respecting Hindu antiquity."[85] But he does not mention that Lassen, whose opinion

---

[83] "Indische Alterth." vol. I. p. 824: "Ueber die Fortschritte der Inder in der Astronomie in der ältesten Zeit drückt sich *der gründlichste Kenner des Gegenstandes* (Colebrooke, a. a. O. II. p. 447) auf folgende Weise aus, etc."

[84] In an essay on "Die Verbindungen Indiens mit den Ländern im Westen," written in April, 1853, and printed in the "Indische Skizzen," 1857.

[85] "Indische Skizzen," p. 73, note.

will have, I assume, as much claim to notice as his own, had adduced weighty reasons for assigning the Hindu Nakshatras to Chinese origin; and had likewise, referring to the Veda-calendar, observed:—"As it is certain now that there existed in ancient times an intercourse, not thought of hitherto, between the Hindus and the Chinese, and that, with the latter, the use of the *sieu* ascends to a far higher antiquity, no objection can be founded on the Chinese origin of the Nakshatras, against their having been used by the Hindus at a time which is adverted to in their oldest astronomical observations on record. These observations belong to the fourteenth century B.C., and it results from them that the Hindus at that period dwelt in the northern part of India." [86]

But, strange to remark, a year after having expressed his repeated doubt, Professor Weber records his poetical views on the earliest period of Hindu civilisation in the following manner:—"From the Kabul river to the Sadánírá, from the remotest point of the western to that of the eastern border of India, there are twenty degrees, three hundred geographical miles, which had to be conquered (by the Áryas) one after the other. Thus we are able to claim, without any further remark, 1000 years as a minimum time for the period of occupying, subjecting to complete cultivation, and brahmanizing this immense tract of land; and thus we are brought back to about 1500 B.C. as the time when the Indian Áryas still dwelt on the Kabul, and after which they commenced to extend themselves over India." [87]

In short, with fantastical certainty he scruples about astronomical facts, and presents fantastical facts with astronomical certainty. I doubt whether this critical method will strengthen the faith of the general public in certain results of Sanskrit philology.

"If we succeed," says Professor Müller (p. 215), "in fixing

---

[86] "Indische Alterthumskunde," vol. I. p. 747.

[87] "Die nenern Forschungen über das alte Indien. Ein Vortrag, im berliner wissenschaftlichen Verein gehalten am 4. März, 1854;" printed in the "Indische Skizzen," 1857, p. 14.

the relative age of any one of these Sûtrakâras, or writers of Sûtras, we shall have fixed the age of a period of literature which forms a transition between the Vedic and the classical literature of India." This inference does not seem conclusive; for neither can the age of one individual author be held sufficient to fix the extent of a period which, according to Müller's own views, may embrace, at least, 400 years, and probably more; nor has Müller shown that the older portions of the Mahábhárata and, perhaps, the Rámáyaṇa, might not have co-existed with some, at least, of the authors of his Sútra period. He says, it is true, in the commencement of his work (p. 68):—"Now it seems that the regular and continuous Anusṭhubh-śloka is a metre unknown during the Vedic age, and every work written in it may at once be put down as post-Vedic. It is no valid objection that this epic Śloka occurs also in Vedic hymns, that Anushṭubh verses are frequently quoted in the Brâhmaṇas, and that, in some of the Sûtras, the Anushṭubh-śloka occurs intermixed with Trishṭubhs, and is used for the purpose of recapitulating what had been explained before in prose. For it is only the *uniform* employment of that metre which constitutes the characteristic mark of a new period of literature." But this very important assertion, even with its last restriction, is left by him without any proof. For, when he adds, in a note (p. 69), "It is remarkable that in Pâṇini also, the word *śloka* is always used in opposition to Vedic literature (Pâṇ. IV. 2, 66; IV. 3, 102, v. 1; IV. 3, 107)," I must observe, in the first place, that in none of these quotations does the word *Śloka* belong to Páṇini.[88] The first of these instances, where *Śloka* occurs, cannot be traced to a higher antiquity than that of Patanjali; the second, which coincides with it, occurs in the commentary of the late Káśiká on a Várttika, the

[88] The quotations of Müller's note to his p. 69 are IV. 1, 66, instead of IV. 2, 66, and IV. 3, 103, 1, instead of IV. 3, 102, v. 1; but as the word *śloka* neither occurs in the Sútra, nor in the Várttika nor in the commentaries on the former quotations, I was probably right in assuming that they were errors of the press, and in substituting for them the figures given, which are the nearest approach to them. There is indeed one Sútra of Páṇini where *śloka* and *mantra* are mentioned together, viz., the Sútra III. 2, 23, but I am not aware that any conclusion similar to that mentioned above could be drawn from it.

antiquity of which rests on the authority of this work; and, in the last quoted rule, the word *Śloka* likewise belongs to no other authority than that of the same late commentary. But, in the second place, it seems to me that these very instances may be used to prove exactly the reverse of Müller's views.

I should quite admit the expediency of his observation if its object had been to lay down a criterion by which a class of works might become recognisable. There is, however, clearly, a vast difference between an external mark, concerning the *contents* of certain writings, and the making of such a mark a basis for computing *periods* of literature. For, when Patanjali or the Káśiká, in illustrating the rules IV. 2, 66, or IV. 3, 102, says that a Vaidik composition of *Tittiri* is called *Taittiríya*, but that such a derivative would not apply to the Ślokas composed by Tittiri; they distinctly contrast the two kinds of composition, but they as distinctly state that the same personage was the author of both. And the same author, of course, cannot belong to two different *periods* of literature, separated, as Müller suggests, from one another by at least several centuries. The same remark applies to the instance by which the Káśiká exemplifies the import of the rule IV. 3, 107; it contrasts here the Vaidik work with the Ślokas of the same author, *Charaka.*

But I will give some other instances, which, in my opinion, corroborate the doubt I have expressed as to the chronological bearing of this word. Kátyáyana, who is assigned by Müller to the Sútra period, and rightly so, so far as the character of some of his works is concerned, is the author of *Ślokas* which are called *Bhrája*, "the Splendid." This fact is drawn from Patanjali's commentary on Páṇini and Kaiyyaṭa's gloss on Patanjali (p. 23 and 24 of Dr. Ballantyne's valuable edition.)[89] Now, the word Śloka, if used in

[89] Patanjali (p. 23): क्व पुनरिदं पठितम्। भ्राजा नाम श्लोकाः.—Kaiyyaṭa (p. 24): कात्यायनोपनिबद्धभ्राजाख्यश्लोकमध्यपठितस्य तस्य श्रुतिरनुग्राहिकास्ति। एकः शब्दः सुज्ञातः सुप्रयुक्तः स्वर्गे लोके कामधुग्भवतीति.—Nágojibhaṭṭa (p. 23): भ्राजा नाम कात्यायनप्रणीताः श्लोका इत्याहुः

reference to whole works, always implies the Anushṭubh-śloka: thus Müller himself properly calls the laws of Manu, Yájnavalkya, and Paráśara, "Śloka-works." (p. 86). It would seem, therefore, that the *Bhrája-ślokas* of Kátyáyana were such a work in *continuous* Anushṭubhs. A second instance is the *Karmapradípa*, which is a work of the same Kátyáyana, and is mentioned as such by Müller himself (p. 235) on the authority of Shadguruśishya; it is written in the "regular and continuous Anushṭubh-śloka," as every one may ascertain from the existing MS. copies of this work. *Vyáḍi*, or *Vyáḷi*, who is an earlier authority than Kátyáyana (see Müller's History, p. 241), composed a work called *Sangraha*, or "Compendium" in one hundred thousand Ślokas; and there can be little doubt that this information, which is given by Nágojibhaṭṭa, applies to a work in the *continuous* Anushṭubh verse.[90] And this very *Vyáḍi*, I may here state, will hereafter become of peculiar interest to us on account of his near relationship to Páṇini. It is evident, therefore, that the "uniform employment of that metre" is not a criterion necessitating the relegation of a work written in it to a period more recent than 200 before Christ.

The "writer of a Sútra" which, in Müller's opinion, may help us to fix the whole period of the Sútra literature, is KÁTYÁYANA; and, if I do not mistake his meaning, PÁṆINI too. For Müller arrives at the conclusion that Kátyáyana lived about 350 B.C., and, if I am right, that Páṇini was his contemporary.[91]

---

[90] Patanjali (ed. Ballantyne, p. 43): संग्रह एतत्प्राधान्येन परीक्षितम्.—Kaiyyaṭa: संग्रह इति । ग्रन्थविशेषे.—Nágojibhaṭṭa: संग्रहो व्याडिकृतो लक्षश्लोकसंख्यो ग्रन्थ इति प्रसिद्धिः.—This remark concerns the use which is made of the word Śloka in reference to whole, especially extensive, works. *Single verses*, not of the Anushṭubh class, are sometimes also called Ślokas; thus Kaiyyaṭa calls so the *Áryá* verse of the Káriká to II. 4, 85, or IV. 4, 9, etc., or the *Dodhaka* verses of the Kárikás to VI. 4, 12, or VIII. 2, 108; and Nágojibhaṭṭa gives the name of Śloka to the *Indravajra* and *Upendravajra* of the Káriká to I. 1, 38; but I know of no instance in which a whole work written in such verses is simply spoken of as having been written in Ślokas.

[91] I regret that I am not able to refer with greater certainty to Müller's views on their contemporaneousness. In page 138 he writes: "Kâtyâyana, the contemporary and critic of Pâṇini;" p. 245: "Now, if Pâṇini lived in the middle of the fourth century

The reason for assigning this date to Kátyáyana is contained in the following passage of the "Ancient Sanskrit Literature:"— "Let us consider," says Müller, after having established the identity of Kátyáyana and Kátyáyana Vararuchi (p. 240 ff.), "the information which we receive about Kâtyâyana Vararuchi from Brahmanic sources. Somadevabhaṭṭa of Kashmir collected the popular stories current in his time, and published them towards the beginning of the twelfth century under the title of Kathâ-sarit-sâgara, the Ocean of the Rivers of Stories. Here we read that Kâtyâyana Vararuchi, being cursed by the wife of Śiva, was born at Kauśambî, the capital of Vatsa. He was a boy of great talent, and extraordinary powers of memory. He was able to repeat to his mother an entire play, after hearing it once at the

B.C., etc." [this is the date which Müller assigns to Kátyáyana]; p. 303: "the old Kâtyâyana Vararuchi, the contemporary of Pâṇini;" but at p. 184 he says: "at the time of Kâtyâyana, if not at the time of Pâṇini"—which clearly implies that he here considers Páṇini's time as prior to Kátyáyana's, since Kátyáyana wrote a critical work on Páṇini, the Várttikas; and on p. 44, 45 he observes: "if, then, Âśvalâyana can be shown to have been a contemporary, or at least an immediate successor of Pâṇini, etc.;" but p. 239: "we should have to admit at least five generations of teachers and pupils: first, Śaunaka; after him, Âśvalâyana, in whose favour Śaunaka is said to have destroyed one of his works; thirdly, Kâtyâyana, who studied the works both of Saunaka and Âśvalâyana; fourthly, Patanjali, who wrote a commentary on one of Kâtyâyana's works; and lastly, Vyâsa, who commented on a work of Patanjali. It does not follow that Kâtyâyana was a pupil of Âśvalâyana, or that Patanjali lived immediately after Kâtyâyana, but the smallest interval which we can admit between every two of these names is that between teacher and pupil, an interval as large as that between father and son, or rather larger." Now, if according to the first alternative of p. 45, Áśwaláyana was a contemporary of Páṇini, the latter becomes a doubtful contemporary of Kátyáyana, according to the quotation from p. 239; and if, according to the other alternative of p. 45, Áśwaláyana was a successor of Páṇini, there is, according to p. 239, still a greater probability that Páṇini and Kátyáyana were not contemporaries. Again, at p. 230, he says: "from all these indications we should naturally be led to expect that the relation between Śaunaka and Kâtyâyana was very intimate, that both belonged to the same Śâkhâ, and that Śaunaka was anterior to Kâtyâyana." But if Áśwaláyana is an *immediate* successor of Páṇini (p. 45), and an *immediate* successor of Śaunaka (p. 239), Páṇini and Śaunaka must be contemporaries; and if Śaunaka is anterior to Kátyáyana (p. 230, and comp. p. 242), Páṇini, too, must have preceded Kátyáyana. Acting, therefore, on the rule of

theatre; and before he was even initiated he was able to repeat the Prâtiśâkhya which he had heard from Vyâḍi. He was afterwards the pupil of Varsha, became proficient in all sacred knowledge, and actually defeated Pâṇini in a grammatical controversy. By the interference of Śiva, however, the final victory fell to Pâṇini. Kâtyâyana had to appease the anger of Śiva, became himself a student of Pâṇini's Grammar, and completed and corrected it. He afterwards is said to have become minister of King Nanda and his mysterious successor Yogananda at Pâṭaliputra.

"We know that Kâtyâyana completed and corrected Pâṇini's Grammar, such as we now possess it.[92] His Vârttikas are supplementary rules, which show a more extensive and accurate knowledge of Sanskrit than even the work of Pâṇini. The story of the contest between them was most likely intended as a mythical way of explaining this fact. Again, we know that Kâtyâyana was himself the author of one of the Prâtiśâkhyas, and Vyâḍi is quoted by the authors of the Prâtiśâkhyas as an earlier authority on the same subject. So far the story of Somadeva agrees with the account of Shaḍguruśishya and with the facts as we still find them in the works of Kâtyâyana. It would be wrong to expect in a work like that of Somadeva historical and chronological facts in the strict sense of the word; yet the mention of King Nanda, who is an historical personage, in connection with our grammarian,

---

probabilities, and perceiving that Müller three times distinctly calls Páṇini a contemporary of Kátyáyana, and allows by inference only this date to be subverted two-and-a-half times, it is fair to assume that he believed rather in the contemporaneousness of both, than otherwise. The correctness of this belief I shall have to make the subject of further discussion; but when I find myself compelled to infer from Müller's expressions that Páṇini is, to him, a contemporary of Śaunaka, I must, in passing, observe that Páṇini himself repudiates this conclusion, for in the Sútra IV. 3, 106, which is intimately connected with IV. 3, 105, Páṇini speaks of Śaunaka as of an *ancient* authority.

[92] Note of Müller: "The same question with regard to the probable age of Pâṇini, has been discussed by Prof. Böhtlingk in his edition of Pâṇini. Objections to Prof. Böhtlingk's arguments have been raised by Prof. Weber in his Indische Studien. See also Ṛig-veda, Leipzig, 1857, Introduction."

may, if properly interpreted, help to fix approximately the date of Kâtyâyana and his predecessors, Śaunaka and Âśvalâyana. If Somadeva followed the same chronological system as his contemporary and countryman Kalhaṇa Paṇḍita, the author of the Râja-taranginî or History of Kashmir, he would, in calling Pâṇini and Kâtyâyana the contemporaries of Nanda and Chandragupta, have placed them long before the times which we are wont to call historical. But the name of Chandragupta fortunately enables us to check the extravagant systems of Indian chronology. Chandragupta, of Pâṭaliputra, the successor of the Nandas, is Sandrocottus, of Palibothra, to whom Megasthenes was sent as ambassador from Seleucus Nicator; and, if our classical chronology is right, he must have been king at the turning point of the fourth and third centuries B.C. We shall have to examine hereafter the different accounts which the Buddhists and Brahmans give of Chandragupta and his relation to the preceding dynasty of the Nandas. Suffice it for the present that, if Chandragupta was king in 315, Kâtyâyana may be placed, according to our interpretation of Somadeva's story, in the second half of the fourth century B.C. We may disregard the story of Somadeva, which actually makes Kâtyâyana himself minister of Nanda, and thus would make him an old man at the time of Chandragupta's accession to the throne. This is, according to its own showing, a mere episode in a ghost story,[93] and had to be inserted in order to connect Kâtyâyana's story with other fables of the Kathâ-sarit-sâgara. But there still remains this one fact, however slender it may appear, that, as late as the twelfth century A.D., the popular tradition of the Brahmans connected the famous grammarians Kâtyâyana and Pâṇini with that period of their history which immediately preceded the rise of Chandragupta and his Śûdra dynasty; and this, from an European point of view, we must place in the second half of the fourth century B.C."

Thus, the whole foundation of Müller's date rests on the

[93] Note of Müller: "According to the southern Buddhists it was Chandragupta, and not Nanda, whose corpse was reanimated. As. Res. xx. p. 167."

authority of Somadeva, the author of "an Ocean of [or rather, *for*] the Rivers of Stories," who narrated his tales in the twelfth century after Christ. Somadeva, I am satisfied, would not be a little surprised to learn that "a European point of view" raises a "ghost story" of his to the dignity of an historical document. Müller himself, as we see, says that it would be "wrong" to expect in a work of this kind "historical or chronological facts;" he is doubtful as to the date which might have been in Somadeva's mind when he speaks of King Nanda; he will "disregard" the fact that Kátyáyana becomes, in the tale quoted, a minister of Nanda; he admits that a story current in the middle of the 12th century about Kátyáyana and Páṇini is but a "slender" fact;—in short, he pulls down every stone of this historical fabric; and yet, because Nanda is mentioned in this amusing tale, he "*must*" place Kátyáyana's life about 350 B.C.

I have but one word to add: however correct the criticisms of Müller on the value of this tale may be, the strength of his conclusion would have become still more apparent than it is now, if instead of the abstract of the story, which he has given, a literal translation of it had preceded his premises; for the very form of the tale, and its incidental absurdities, would have illustrated, much better than his sober account of it, its value as a source of chronology. I subjoin, therefore, a portion of it, from the fourth chapter of this work. Kátyáyana, the grammatical saint and author of the Kalpa-sútras, after having told Káṇabhúti how once upon a time he became enamoured of a beautiful damsel, by what feelings he was moved, and that he at last married the fair Upakośá, continues as follows: "Some time after, Varsha (who in another tale is said to have lived at Páṭaliputra during the reign of Nanda) had a great number of pupils. One of them was a *great blockhead, by the name of Páṇini*; he, tired of the service, was sent away by the wife of Varsha. To do penance, he went, grieved yet desirous of knowledge, to the Himálaya; there he obtained from Śiva, who was pleased with his fierce austerities, a new grammar which was the introduction to all science. Now he came back and challenged me to a disputation; and seven days passed on while our disputation proceeded. When on the eighth day, however, he was defeated by me, instantly Śiva (appeared) in a cloud (and) raised a tremendous uproar. Thus my grammar, which had been given to me by Indra, was destroyed on earth; and we all, vanquished by Páṇini, became fools again."

It is almost needless for me to state, that the *profound* researches of Dr. Otto Boehtlingk in his "*commentary*" on Páṇini, are based on the same interesting "Ocean for the Rivers of Stories," and have duly advocated the same date of Páṇini's life. But as we have become already acquainted with the *reasoning* of the "*editor*" of Páṇini, it will not appear devoid of interest to recall his arguments, which differ in several respects from those of Professor Müller. In the Rájataranginí, the Chronicle of Kashmir, he says (p. xv.), we read that Abhimanyu ordered Chandra and other grammarians to introduce the great commentary of Patanjali into Kashmir. Now, continues he (p. xvii), "the age of King Abhimanyu, under whose reign Chandra lived, can be ascertained by various ways, which all lead to the same result," viz., to the date 100 B.C.; and (p. xviii) "since we have found that Patanjali's Mahábháshya came into general use in Kashmir through Chandra, about 100 B.C., we are probably justified in pushing the composition of this great commentary to the Sútras of Páṇini, into the year 150. Between Patanjali and Páṇini there are still three grammarians known to us, as we have observed before (p. xiv; viz., Kátyáyana, the author of the Paribháshás, and the author of the Kárikás), who made contributions to the Grammar of Páṇini. We need therefore only make a space of fifty years between each couple of them, in order to arrive at the year 350, into the neighbourhood of which date our grammarian is to be placed, according to the Kathá-sarit-ságara."

"Every way," says the French proverb, "leads to Rome,"—but not every way leads to truth, even in chronology. There is one way for instance, and it was the proper way, which led Professor Lassen[94] to the correct result that Abhimanyu did not live about

---

[94] "Indische Alterthumskunde," vol. II. p. 413.

100 B.C., but between 40 and 65 after Christ. As to the triad of grammarians which is "known" to Dr. Boehtlingk between Páṇini and Patanjali, and represented to his mind by Kátyáyana, and what he calls *the* author of the Paribháshás and *the* author of the Kárikás, I must refer to my subsequent statements, which will show the worth of this specious enumeration. But, when Dr. Boehtlingk required 200 years between Patanjali and Páṇini, simply to square his account with the "Ocean for the Rivers of Stories," it would be wrong to deny that he has rightly divided 200 by 4; nor should I doubt that he would have managed with less ability the more difficult task of dividing 2000 or 20000 years by 4, if such an arithmetical feat had been required of him by that source of historical chronology, the Kathá-sarit-ságara.

Professor Müller must have had some misgivings like my own as to the critical acumen and accuracy of Dr. Boehtlingk's investigations. For, in the first instance, he does not start from the Kathá-sarit-ságara in order to arrive at the conclusion that Kátyáyana lived fifty years after Páṇini; on the contrary, he makes, as we have seen, both grammarians contemporaries; judging, no doubt, that two men who enjoyed a very substantial fight cannot have lived at different times, even in a story book. Then he adverts likewise (p. 243) to the little mistake of Dr. Boehtlingk concerning Abhimanyu's date; in short, he denies the validity of all the arguments alleged by Dr. Boehtlingk, save those which are founded on the Kathá-sarit-ságara. When therefore he, nevertheless, says (p. 301) that the researches of Professor Boehtlingk "with regard to the age of Pâṇini deserve the highest credit," I am at a loss to understand this handsome compliment, even though it strengthen his assurance (p. 310) "that Kâtyâyana's date is as safe as any date is likely to be in ancient Oriental chronology."[95]

That Sanskrit philology should not yet possess the means of ascertaining the date of Páṇini's life, is, no doubt, a serious

---

[95] In reply to this compliment, Dr. Boehtlingk makes the following bow: "Alles was zur Entscheidung dieser Frage beitragen könnte, finden wir auf das sorgfältigste

impediment to any research concerning the chronology of ancient Hindu works. For Páṇini's Grammar is the centre of a vast and important branch of the ancient literature. No work has struck deeper roots than his in the soil of the scientific development of

---

zusammengestellt und erwogen in einem so eben erchienenen Werke von Max Müller, einem Werke, in welchem überraschende Belesenheit, Scharfsinn und geistreiche Behandlung des Stoffes den Leser in beständiger Spannung erhalten;" *i.e.*, "All that can contribute to the solution of this question—(viz., that of the introduction of writing into India) we find put together and examined in the most careful manner, in a work by Max Müller, just published, a work in which surprising acquaintance with the literature, acuteness and ingenious treatment of the subject-matter, never suffer the reader's attention to flag." The testimonial he thus gratuitously gives to his own knowledge of "all that can contribute to the solution of that question," reached me too late to be noticed in the previous pages, as they were already in the press; it is contained in a paper of his, having the title "Ein Paar Worte zur Frage über das Alter der Schrift in Indien." These "few words" do not contain, indeed, a particle of fact bearing on the question, but much *reasoning*, of which the following concluding passage is the summary: "Nach meinem Dafürhalten also wurde die Schrift zur *Verbreitung* der Literatur in den älteren Zeiten nicht verwandt, wohl aber wurde sie zum *Schaffen* neuer Werke zu Hülfe genommen. Der Verfasser schrieb sein Werk nieder, lernte es aber dann auswendig oder liess es durch Andere memoriren. Niedergeschriebene Werke wurden in der älteren Zeit wohl selten von Neuem abgeschrieben, mögen aber im Original in der Familie als Heiligthümer aufbewahrt und geheim gehalten worden sein. Möglicher Weise vernichtete aber auch der Autor sein Schriftwerk, sobald er dasselbe memorirt hatte, um nicht durch sein Beispiel Andere zu verleiten, um sich nicht des Vorwurfes einer Verrätherei an der Priesterkaste schuldig zu machen, vielleicht auch um nicht als gewöhnlicher Autor, dem das Werk allmählich unter den Händen entsteht, zu erscheinen, sondern als ein inspirirter Seher, der, ohne alle Mühe und Anstrengung von seiner Seite beim Schaffen, ein Werk in abgeschlossener Gestalt im Geiste erschaut und als ein solcher von den Göttern Bevorzugter weiter verkündet;" *i.e.*, "In my opinion, therefore, writing was not used in the olden times for the *propagation* of literature, but was resorted to for the *production* of new works. The author wrote down his work, but then learnt it by heart, or made others commit it to memory. Probably, works once written down, were not copied anew in the olden time, with rare exceptions; but the original manuscripts were perhaps preserved as sacred relics in the family, and kept secret. But it is possible, too, that the author destroyed his written work, after he had committed it to memory, in order not to seduce others by his example, nor to make himself guilty of the reproach of treason towards the caste of priests; perhaps, too, not to appear as an ordinary author, whose work grew gradually under his hands, but as an inspired seer who, without any labour and exertion in producing, had seen in his mind a work in a finished form, and, as a person thus favoured by the gods, had proclaimed it abroad."—This *reasoning* will not surprise

India. It is the standard of accuracy in speech,—the grammatical basis of the Vaidik commentaries. It is appealed to by every scientific writer whenever he meets with a linguistic difficulty. Besides the inspired seers of the works which are the root of Hindu belief, Páṇini is the only one, among those authors of scientific works who may be looked upon as real personages, who is a Ṛishi in the proper sense of the word,—an author supposed to have had the foundation of his work revealed to him by a divinity.[96] Yet, however we may regret the necessity

---

us in the author of a "commentary on Páṇini" (compare note 48, etc.). Yet I must ask, whence he derived his information that it was treason towards the Bráhmaṇa caste to write or to produce a manuscript? or whence he has learnt that an author could, in olden times, pass himself off as an inspired seer who was favoured by the gods, without, of course, being chastised by his countrymen, as an impostor? *Manu* XI. 55, treats *false boasting*—अनृतं समुत्कर्षे—as a crime equal to that of killing a Bráhmaṇa; and *Yájnavalkya*, III. 229, places it on the same level with the drinking of spirituous liquors, which crime is expiated only after the sinner has drunk either boiling spirits, or boiling butter, cow's urine, or milk, until he dies (III. 253). Veracity, moreover, is known to be one of the principal features of the character of the ancient Hindus, as, in the epic legends, a word spoken, or a promise made, is always deemed irrevocable and binding. It is notorious that the Hindu authorities did not look upon any one as an inspired seer, except the author of a Mantra, and, probably, at a more recent period, of a Bráhmaṇa. The Kalpa works were never considered to be anything but human productions, and I know only of one instance, viz., that of Páṇini, where the author of a scientific work was supposed to have received it from a divinity.—In other words, to the mind of Dr. Boehtlingk the whole of the ancient scientific literature of India presents a picture of a gigantic swindle and imbecility; on the one side are the charlatans who write works, learn them by heart, and burn the manuscripts, in order to appear in direct communication with a divinity; on the other, is the idiotic nation which believes that the learned quacks are inspired seers favoured by the gods! It is not a little characteristic, but at the same time very intelligible, that this should be the view of the "*editor*" of Páṇini.

[96] Patanjali frequently, therefore, makes use of the expression, "Páṇini *sees*," when an ordinary author is quoted by him as "saying" or the like; *e.g.* p. 145 (in Dr. Ballantyne's edition): पश्यति त्वाचार्यो नाकारस्यस्यातो लोपो भवतीति; or p. 246, पश्यति त्वाचार्यो न व्यञ्जनस्य गुणो भवतीति; p. 281, पश्यति त्वाचार्यो न सिच्यन्तरङ्गं भवतीति; p. 615, पश्यति त्वाचार्यः स्थानिवदादेशो भवतीति; p. 787, पश्यति त्वाचार्यस्तदेकदेशभूतं तद्ग्रहणेन गृह्यत इति etc.; but p. 658, वक्ष्यति ह्याचार्यः (viz. Kátyáyana, in his Várttikas to VI. 4, 104) । चिणो लुकि तग्रहणानर्थक्यं संघातस्याप्रत्ययत्वात्तलोपस्य चासिद्धत्वादिति etc.—For the same reason, when Kaiyyaṭa, for instance, speaks of "the author of the Sútras," viz. Páṇini, Nágojibhaṭṭa explains this

of leaving this important personage in the chaos which envelopes the historical existence of all ancient Hindu celebrities, it is better to acknowledge this necessity than attach faith to a date devoid of real substance and resting on no trustworthy testimony. For, in doing so, we may feel induced to direct our efforts towards an investigation more likely to lead to a solid result, — I mean the investigation of the *internal evidence* afforded by the ancient literature—as to the position of Páṇini relatively to the works which are its chief representatives. If we could succeed in establishing this position, or, at least, in determining the critical means by which this end could be obtained, future research into the chronology of Sanskrit literature would have, at least, some ground to build upon, as well as a test by which to recognise the place that may be allotted to many important works within the structure raised.

In making an attempt in this direction, we feel our immediate interest naturally engaged by the question whether Páṇini and Kátyáyana (the author of the Várttikas), were in reality contemporaries or not, whatever be the age at which they lived. As a substantial record of these Várttikas is met with in no other work than the "Great Commentary" of Patanjali, it will first be necessary for us to examine the literature embodied or alluded to, in the Mahábháshya, so far as it bears on this inquiry, in order to ascertain what portion of this literature is anterior to Kátyáyana, and what portion belongs to his own authorship. We may consult for this purpose, Kaiyyaṭa, the principal commentator on Patanjali; but we need not descend to the recent period of the Káśiká, the Siddhánta-kaumudí, the commentaries of Nágeśa, Purushottama, or other Vṛittis and Ṭíkás, for all these works are at too great a distance from the period of Patanjali to assist us in the solution of our problem.

---

expression with "*Śiva*," who revealed to Páṇini the first fourteen Sútras; *e.g.* p. 86, सूत्रकारो महेश्वरः । वेदपुरुषो वा; or when Kaiyyaṭa calls Páṇini, Ácharya, Nágojibhaṭṭa says (p. 120) शिवो वेदपुरुषो वाचाचार्यः; or p. 197, आचार्यः शिवः. Of the first fourteen, or the Śivasútras, Nágojibhaṭṭa says that they existed from eternity, while Páṇini made the rest: (p. 763 ed. Ballantyne) तेषामनादित्वादेषां पाणिनिकृतत्वात् etc.

Of the grammatical writers named by the author of the Mahábháshya, we pass over those which are quoted by Páṇini himself, as by his testimony we are enabled at once to assign to them an existence prior to his Grammar.[97] We may pass over, too, those authorities to whom Patanjali adverts when he speaks of a "Sútra of the former" grammarians[98]; for such an expression on his part invariably refers to Páṇini's Sútras; and the substance of the opinions or rules of these "former" grammarians must equally, therefore, have preceded Páṇini's work, and, consequently, the Várttikas of Kátyáyana.

The first category of writings deserving our notice here will therefore be those Várttikas and grammatical dicta which are quoted by Patanjali in relation to Kátyáyana's own Várttikas. As authors of such writings we meet, for instance, with the grammarians of the school of the *Bháradwájíyas* and *Saunágas*, with *Kuṇaravádava*, *Váḍava*, who is perhaps the same as this grammarian, with *Sauryabhagavat*, with *Kuṇi*, who is spoken of by Kaiyyaṭa as a predecessor of Patanjali, and an indefinite number of grammarians who are introduced to us under the general designation of "some" or "others."[99] Whether the latter term com-

---

[97] These authors are Ápiśali, Káśyapa, Gárgya, Gálava, Chákravarmaṇa, Bháradwája, Śákaṭáyana, Śákalya, Senaka, Sphoṭáyana, and those designated by the collective appellation of eastern and northern grammarians. These names have been correctly mentioned by Dr. Boehtlingk, vol. II. p. iii—v.

[98] Kaiyyaṭa calls them पूर्वाचार्याः or the "former teachers;" *e.g.* in his comment on the third Śivasútra; on I. 1, 4; V. 2, 39; VI. 1, 6, etc. The word पूर्वसूत्र which in the sense given is a Tatpurusha, the former part of which is to be understood in the sense of a genitive, occurs *e.g.* in the Bháshya to VII. 1, 18; compare also note 46.—And the authorities quoted by Patanjali, under the name of आचार्याः, are probably also meant as "older grammarians;" *e.g.* in his gloss on the fifth Śivasútra, on I. 1, 1 and 2, 18, etc.

[99] The *Bháradwájíyas* are quoted several times in the Bháshya; and in the Calc. ed. *four* times, viz. III. 1, 89, v. 1; IV. 1, 79, v. 1; VI. 4, 47, v. 1, and 155, v. 1.—The *Saunágas* are mentioned there to II. 2, 18, v. 1—4; VI. 3, 44, v. 1; and VII. 2, 17; the latter quotation, however, does not occur in the Bháshya.—*Kuṇaraváḍava* is mentioned in the Bháshya to VII. 3, 1, v. 6; *Váḍava* and *Sauryabhagavat* to VIII. 2, 106. v. 3.; *Kuṇi* in Kaiyyaṭa's gloss on I. 1, 75, where he says that Patanjali follows, in the words referred to, the opinion of *Kuṇi* (Kaiyyaṭa: कुणिना प्राग्ग्रहणमाचार्यनिर्देशार्थम्। .... भाष्यकारस्तु कुणिदर्शनमशिश्रियत्.) Some of these quotations are given by Dr. Boehtlingk, vol. II. pp. iv. li. The phrase "अपर आह" is of frequent occurrence in

prise the grammarians just named, or other authorities, we cannot infer from the words of Patanjali; probably, however, we are justified in deciding for the latter alternative, since Patanjali is a writer who chooses his words deliberately, and would scarcely have quoted his authority at one time by name, and at another by a general term which does not imply that great respect entertained for a high authority. But, whatever view we take of the matter,—setting aside those grammarians quoted by Patanjali, who will require some additional remark before we can establish their relation to Kátyáyana—we may see that all that are named must have lived before Patanjali, and after Kátyáyana, since all their Várttikas or remarks, recorded by Patanjali are criticisms on, and emendations of, the Várttikas of Kátyáyana.[100] Of Patanjali's *Ishṭis* or "desiderata," which

---

the Bháshya, *e.g.* to the second Śivasútra, to I. 1, 10; 2, 50. 51; II. 2, 24; 3, 66; III. 1, 27. 112. 123; 2, 109. 123, etc.; or कश्चिद्वैयाकरण आह *e.g.* II. 4, 56; अन्ये वैयाकरणाः *e.g.* I. 1, 27; केचित् *e.g.*, VIII. 2, 80 (केचित् . . . . . एके); अपरे *e.g.* I. 1, 1 and 2; III. 2, 123; and four sets of grammarians are contrasted by Patanjali in his comment on III. 2, 115: कथंजातीयकं पुनः परोक्षं नाम। केचित्तावदाहुः। वर्षशतवृत्तं परोक्षमिति। अपर आहुः। वर्षसहस्रवृत्तं परोक्षमिति। अपर आहुः। कुड्यकटान्तरितं परोक्षमिति। अपर आहुः। द्व्यहवृत्तं त्र्यहवृत्तं वेति.

[100] A few instances will bear out this conclusion. Kátyáyana's third Várttika to II. 2, 18 runs thus: सिद्धं तु क्त्वाङ्स्वतिदुर्गतिवचनात्; and his fourth: प्रादयः क्तार्थे (omitted in the Calc. ed.). After having explained both, Patanjali adds: एतदेव च सौनागैर्विस्तरतरकेण पठितम् and quotes the four Várttikas of the Saunágas as given in the Calc. edition; Kaiyyaṭa is even more explicit on this occasion, for he says: एतदेवेति। कात्यायनाभिप्रायमेव प्रदर्शयितुं सौनागैरतिविस्तरेण पठितमित्यर्थः.—The Várttika of Kátyáyana to I. 1, 20 reads: घुसंज्ञायां प्रकृतिग्रहणं शिदर्थम्; but, says Patanjali, the Bháradwájíyas read it otherwise: भारद्वाजीयाः पठन्ति। घुसंज्ञायां प्रकृतिग्रहणं शिद्विकृतार्थम्, which last compound contains an important improvement on the rule of Kátyáyana.—The latter enlarges Páṇini's rule III. 1, 89, by this Várttika: यक्चिणोः प्रतिषेधे हेतुमण्णिच्श्रिब्रूञामुपसंख्यानम्; but, says Patanjali after his explanation of it, भारद्वाजीयाः पठन्ति। यक्चिणोः प्रतिषेधे णिश्रन्थिग्रन्थिब्रूञामात्मनेपदाकर्मकाणामुपसंख्यानम् which version of the Bháradwájíyas is a distinct criticism on Kátyáyana.—His two Várttikas on VI. 4, 155 are the following: णाविष्ठवत्प्रातिपदिकस्य and पुंवद्भावरभावटिलोपयणादिपरार्थम्, but the Bháradwájíyas improved them in this way: (Patanjali: भारद्वाजीयाः पठन्ति।) णाविष्ठवत्प्रातिपदिकस्य पुंवद्भावरभावटिलोपयणादिपरप्रादिविन्मतोर्लुक्कन्विध्यर्थम्. The same Bháradwájiyas have criticised Páṇini also, independently of Kátyáyana, for Patanjali mentions at the Sútra

are his own additions to Kátyáyana's Várttikas, I need not speak, since they are an essential portion of his own Great Commentary.[101]

VI. 4, 47: भ्रस्जोरोपधयो रमन्यतरस्याम्, their Várttika: भ्रस्जोरोपधयोर्लोप आगमो रम्विधीयते. The mere comparison of their Várttikas and the passages quoted, will clearly show that these grammarians not only lived after Páṇini, but also after Kátyáyana; and that they were engaged on the same task which was the object of Kátyáyana, viz., that of criticising Páṇini. Dr. Boehtlingk, however, (vol. II. p. iv.)—when speaking of the Várttikas of the Bháradwájíyas and one Várttika of the Ápiśalas, which improves Páṇini's Sútra VII. 3, 95, तुरुस्तुशम्यमः सार्वधातुके in this manner: तुरुस्तुशम्यमः सार्वधातुके छन्दसि (quoted by the Káśiká, not by Patanjali),—draws from them the twofold conclusion, "first, that the grammatical terminology of both predecessors of our grammarian (Páṇini) was the same, partly at least (*dass die grammatische Terminologie bei den beiden Vorgängern unseres Grammatikers, zum Theil wenigstens, dieselbe gewesen ist*), and then, that their original works, in time, received similar emendations and additions as the grammar of Páṇini." I know not by what logical process either of these conclusions could be extracted from these Várttikas. The passages quoted are obvious criticisms on Páṇini and Kátyáyana,—and so are the other Várttikas of the Bháradwájíyas named by Patanjali. There is not the slightest evidence afforded by these Várttikas that they are in any connection whatever with works of Bháradwája and Ápiśali, and any *reasoning* concerning the latter becomes therefore without foundation. Or do we find that in India all pupils and descendants are compelled to confine their writings or remarks to the works of their teachers and ancestors? and will their criticisms on these latter works turn out, by some marvellous process, to fit exactly the productions of other authors also?

[101] It will probably be thought desirable that an editor should at least understand the title-page of the work which he is committing to the press, even when editing is merely tantamount to reprinting the labours of others, faults and all; but I fear that this much cannot be said of Dr. Boehtlingk's *edition* of Páṇini; for, in translating the title-page of the Calcutta edition, he renders इष्टि "*káriká*" and justifies this version in the following note (vol. II. p. xxxvii): "I take परिभाषेष्टिभिः as a dwandwa, and इष्टि as synonymous with *káriká*, because I should not like to miss these (the Kárikás) on the title." Thus, because the Calcutta Pandits, rightly or wrongly, did not say on the title-page of their edition that their compilation will comprise the *Kárikás*, but merely stated that it will give Várttikas, Gaṇas, Paribháshás and Ishṭis, Dr. Boehtlingk *reasons*, that "since *he* does not like the omission of the Kárikás," *Ishṭi* is the same as *Káriká*. There is, indeed, nothing strange in this *reasoning* of Dr. Boehtlingk; we have seen already some specimens of it, and if any one would take upon himself the ungrateful task of reviewing the second volume which he has annexed to his "*edition*" of Páṇini, he would have to add a good many more of the same quality. But if Dr. Boehtlingk had chosen to consult, by letter or otherwise, the editors of his edition of Páṇini, they would in all probability have told him that *ishṭi* means a "desideratum," and that *ishṭis*, emphatically

Another category of literary compositions, which are either entirely or partly embodied in the Mahábháshya, are the *Kárikás*.[102] To assign these verses to one author, would be as erroneous as to speak of one author of the Várttikas.[103] For, even the Calcutta edition of Pánini enables us to see, *at first*

---

so called, and not qualified otherwise (as Ishṭis of the Kásiká, etc.), designate the *Várttikas of Patanjali*. They might, too, have referred him to the *Padachandrikávṛitti*, which in the introduction plainly says: इष्टयो भाष्यकारस्य; or to Nágojibhaṭṭa, who when referring to the word इष्टि applied by Kaiyyaṭa to the *Várttika* (of Patanjali to I. 1, 1, omitted in the edition) छन्दोवत्सूत्राणि भवन्ति comments: इष्टिरिति। तथा च भाष्यकारीयातिदेशात्सूत्रेषु छन्दःकार्यप्रवृत्तिरिति भावः. But, for aught I know, they might have simply requested him to read their own edition, before sending it to the printer, since they have themselves written the word भाष्यकारेष्टिः, for instance, after a Várttika to I. 1, 9, or भाष्येष्टिः after a Várttika to I. 1, 68; or the words इष्टिर्भाष्यकृतः after a Várttika to II. 2, 28; and it is clear enough that in none of these instances can इष्टि be synonymous with कारिका.

[102] It is almost superfluous to state that I merely speak of the *Kárikás* which are recorded by Patanjali. Those belonging to Bhartṛihari, who wrote a gloss on Patanjali (comp. *e.g. Gaṇaratnamahodadhi*: भर्तृहरिर्वाक्यपदीयकर्ता महाभाष्यव्याख्याता च, and my subsequent observations on the *Vákyapadíya*), as well as the Kárikás met with exclusively in the Kásiká or Siddhánta-kaumudí, can have no bearing on the present investigation.

[103] These assertions have nevertheless been made by Dr Boehtlingk, vol. II. p. xiv., where he states that "between Páṇini and Amara-Sinha there are still *four* grammarians: Kátyáyana, *the* author of the Paribháshás, *the* author of the Kárikás, and Patanjali;" and p. xviii. xix., where he states that each couple of these grammarians may be separated from one another by a space of fifty years, he repeats, "as we have observed above (p. xiv), there are between Patanjali and Páṇini still three grammarians *known to us*, who made contributions to the grammar of Páṇini." On page xlix, it is true, he says, "no doubt the Kárikás do not all belong to the same author, since the same subject is treated sometimes in two different Kárikás in a perfectly different manner;" but as he observed before that the Kárikás are "scattered in various grammars (*sic*), viz. in the Mahábháshya, the Kásiká, the Padamanjarí and the Kaumudí," and as two quotations which he adds in corroboration of his statement, viz. VI. 3, 109, and VII. 2, 10, have reference to the Kásiká and Siddhánta-kaumudí only, we should be in fairness bound to conclude that, in his opinion, it was the literary period *after* Patanjali which produced this variety of authors of the Kárikás. Yet when he presents us with a third quotation, viz. "Calc. ed. p. 274," which clearly points to the fact that there were different authors of Kárikás *at or before Patanjali's time*, it would be curious to learn how he reconciles this latter quotation with his previous statements at pages xiv and xix, according to which there is but *one* author of the Kárikás between Páṇini and

sight, in four instances, that they cannot be the work of the same author; and, besides these, two other instances of the same kind may be found in the "Great Commentary."[104] But, to define the relation of these verses to Kátyáyana, it will not be sufficient simply to state that some of them embody the rules of Kátyáyana, while others deviate from them, and others again enlarge and criticise the Várttikas:[105] it will be necessary to describe the characteristic features of these Káriká́s such as we find them in Patanjali's work.

An external, but very important mark, is afforded by the circumstance that one portion of the Káriká́s is left by Patanjali entirely without comment, while he comments on another portion in the same manner as he does on the Várttikas; and we may add, too, that there are a few Várttikas which are not altogether without a gloss, but the gloss on which is so scanty

---

Patanjali, and a personage, too, who lived 50 years after the author of the Paribháshás and 50 years before Patanjali! Compare also the following note.

[104] The Káriká́s not met with in the Bháshya are, usually, correctly marked in the Calcutta edition with the name of the work whence they have been taken; those not marked, are therefore, nearly always, recognizable in this edition as belonging to the Mahábháshya. That such Káriká́s of the latter kind, to the same Sútra of Páṇini, belong to different authors, is indicated in the Calc. ed. at I. 4, 51; III. 2, 123 (*p.* 274); IV. 1, 44 and 63. From the Bháshya we learn it, *at first sight*, besides, in the two instances, I. 2, 50,—where the words गोण्या इत्वं etc. are preceded by अपर आह—and VIII. 2, 58, where the latter words precede the Káriká वेत्तेस्तु etc. Compare the notes 107, 108, 111.

[105] Three striking instances of the latter kind are the Káriká́s to IV. 2, 60; VIII. 1, 69; and III. 2, 118. The first occurs at the end of Patanjali's commentary on the Várttikas of this Sútra, is without comment, and contains, for the greater part, new matter, which is given in the shape of Várttikas in the Siddhánta-kaumudí. It is omitted in the Calc. ed. and runs thus: अनुसूर्लक्ष्यलक्षणे सर्वसादेर्द्विगोश्च लः । इकन्पदोत्तरपदाच्छतषष्टेः षिकन्पथः. The Káriká to VIII. 1, 69 embodies the Várttikas 1, 2, 3 to the same Sútra and Várttika 2 to VIII. 1, 67, but in the latter Kátyáyana says मलोपवचनं च, and the Káriká enlarges this rule to मकारलोपो ऽतिङि (Nágojibhaṭṭa: मलोपश्चेति वार्तिकोक्तो मलोपस्तिङन्तेनेष्टः). The Káriká to III. 2, 118 is thus introduced by Patanjali: किं चातः स्मादि°° । न स्म पुराद्यतन इति (second Várttika) ब्रुवता कात्यायनेनेह स्मादि°°; and by Kaiyyaṭa: एकतरस्मिन्वार्त्तिके स्मपुराशब्दावुपलक्षणत्वेनाश्रयणीयौ । तत्र पूर्वस्मिन्परस्मिन्वा विशेषमपश्यन्पृच्छति । इतरो वार्त्तिकप्रत्याख्यानाय मया विकल्पितमेतदित्याह । स्मादि°°.

and so different from the kind of comment bestowed on the Várttikas, that they might seem to constitute a third category of Kárikás.[106]

If we first examine *the Kárikás without comment*, we meet twice with the remark of Patanjali that "*another*," or "others," have composed the verse in question, when the Káriká is contrasted by him with the preceding *Várttika*; and the same remark occurs four times, when the Káriká thus introduced to our notice is contrasted with a preceding *Káriká*.[107] More definite statements, I believe, are not volunteered by Patanjali; but Kaiyyaṭa once tells us, that such an uncommented Káriká was composed by the *Śloka-várttika-kára*, or the "author of the versified Várttikas;" and though this information is not more distinct or more satisfactory than that of Patanjali, it has, at least, the merit of having on another occasion elicited the remark of Nágoji, that this author is *not* Kátyáyana.[108]

---

106 *Without any comment* of Patanjali we find the Kárikás to I. 1, 0. 14. 20. 38. 70; 2, 64; 4, 51 (Kár. 5-7).—II. 1, 10. 60; 4, 36. 85.—III. 1, 7 (= V. 2, 94. Kár. 1). 22. 27. 79. 122. 127; 2, 3. 123 (Kár. 1, 2. 4. 5. 6); 3, 1. (Kár. 3.) 156 (= VII. 4, 41); 4, 79.—IV. 1, 44. 63. 161; 2, 9. 60. (comp. the preceding note); 4, 9.—V. 1, 115; 2, 48; 3, 55.—VI. 1, 1. 77 (Kár. 2). 87; 2, 199; 4, 114.—VII. 1, 18. 73 (Kár. 2); 4, 46 (Kár. 2). 92.—VIII. 1, 70; 2. 58. (Kár. 3). 59. 62. 80. 108; 3, 43.—There are Kárikás *commented upon* by Patanjali, in his usual manner, to I. 1, 19. 57; 2, 9. 17. 18. 50. 51; 4, 21 (= III. 3, 161). 51 (Kár. 1. 2. 1-4).—III. 1, 112; 2, 57. 109. 115. 139; 3. 1 (Kár. 1. 2).—IV. 1, 3. 10. 18. 32. 54. 78. 92. 93. 120. 165; 2, 8. 45; 3, 60. 84. 134.—V. 1, 19; 2, 39. 45. 94 (Kár. 2); 3, 83.—VI. 1, 77 (Kár. 1) 103. 158; 2, 1; 3, 46; 4, 3. 12. 22. 46. 62. 74. 128.—VII. 1, 9. 21. 40. 73 (Kár. 1). 96; 2, 102. 107; 3, 3. 86; 4, 46 (Kár. 1).—VIII. 1, 69 (comp. the preceding note); 2, 25. 55. 58 (Kár. 1. 2); 3, 88; 4, 68.—To the *third category* belong the Kárikás to I. 1, 38 (om. Calc. ed.).—III. 1, 123; 2, 118. 123 (Kár. 3).—IV. 2, 13.—VI. 4, 120. 149.—VIII. 3, 45.—Other Kárikás quoted in the Calcutta edition do not occur in the Bháshya.

107 Patanjali to III. 1, 27: अपर आह । धातु°° (contrasted with the preceding Várttika); III. 2, 123, Kár. 1: अपर आहुः। नास्ति वर्तमानः काल इति। अपि चात्र श्लोकानुदाहरन्ति। न वर्तते°° ..... सो ऽप्यनन्ध इति (contrasted with the preceding Várttika), etc.; but the last Káriká, which is introduced by the words अपर आह । अस्ति वर्तमान काल इति । आदित्यगतिवन्नोपलभ्यते । अपि चात्र श्लोकानुदाहरन्ति । विसस्य°°, is contrasted with the preceding Kárikás; at IV. I. 44, after गुणः he says, अपर आह । उपेत्य etc.; at IV. 1, 63, after °चरणैः सह, he adds, अपर आह । प्रादुर्भाव°°; at VIII. 2, 58, after °दृष्यते, his words are, अपर आह। वेत्तेस्तु etc.

108 Patanjali on IV. 4, 9: अत्र किं न्याय्यम्। परिगणनं कर्तव्यम्। आकर्षात्पर्पादेः

Being here merely concerned with the question of the relation of these Kárikás to Kátyáyana, we should not feel under the necessity of examining the contents of the six verses just mentioned, even if they differed in character from the rest—which is not the case,—for the statements alleged enable us, as it is, to conclude that they are *later* than his Várttikas. Still, as the remaining portion of these uncommented Kárikás does not admit of a similar inference without an inquiry into the evidence which they yield, it will be necessary to observe that they fall into two distinct divisions.

One class of them merely records the substance of the preceding Várttikas. These, for the most part, stand at the end of Patanjali's commentary on the Sútra to which they belong; but some of them are also met with in the midst of the discussion of the Bháshya, but only when they comprise the contents of a portion, not of the whole, of the Várttikas to the Sútra of Páṇini.[109]

---

etc.—Kaiyyaṭa: श्लोकवार्त्तिककारः संदिग्धानसंदिग्धांश्च भ्रान्तिनिरासाय पर्यजीगणत्.—Kaiyyaṭa on the Kárikás to VI. 4, 22: वार्त्तिककारोक्तेषु प्रयोजनेषु प्राख्यातेषु श्लोकवार्त्तिककारोक्तप्रयोजनापक्षेपः.—Nágojibhaṭṭa: वार्त्तिककारः कात्यायनः। श्लोकवार्त्तिककारस्त्वन्य एवेति भावः. See also page 99.

[109] Such uncommented Kárikás standing *at the end* of the commentary occur at the Sútras II. 1. 10; 4. 85 (Kár. 2. 3).—III. 1, 79; 2, 3.—V. 2, 48.; 3, 55 (Kár. 3-5).—VI. 1, 77 (Kár. 2). 87.—VII. 1, 73 (Kár. 2),—VIII. 2, 62. 108; 3, 43.—*In the middle* of the discussion they occur at the Sútras II. 1, 60, before the fourth Várttika, and summing up the Várttikas 1, 2, 3; II. 4, 85 (Kár. 1, being a summary of the Várttikas preceding the third Várttika in the Calc. ed.).—The summary character of these Kárikás is sometimes expressly adverted to by the commentators. Thus at II. 1. 60, Kaiyyaṭa observes: अवधारणं नञा चेदिति पूर्व एवार्थ आर्यया संगृहीतः; II. 4, 85 (Kár. 1), एष एवार्थ (of what precedes) आर्यया दर्शितः; II. 4, 85 (Kár. 2. 3), पूर्वोक्त एवार्थः श्लोकेन संगृहीतः; III. 2, 3, उक्तार्थसंग्रहाय श्लोकाः। नित्यं प्रसारणमिति; V. 2, 48, प्रकृत्यर्थादिति पूर्वोक्तार्थसंग्रहश्लोकाः, etc. etc. I may here observe that the word इति, which is usually added by authors after quotations they make from other authors, is scarcely ever met with after the last word of these or any other Kárikás. There is the following instance which clearly proves that no inference can be drawn from the presence or absence of this word इति after the Kárikás; viz. the Káriká to III. 1, 7 is identical with the first Káriká to V. 2, 94; इति occurs after the former, not after the latter. Only one of the Kárikás introduced by अपर आहुः—a clear

The second class has not the character of summaries of the Várttikas. It is an *essential part of the discussion of the Bháshya itself*, now introducing the point at issue with some general remark, then connecting or strengthening the links of the debate by an important definition or a new argument, then again summing up the substance of the discussion itself, and throwing, as it were, some additional light on it.[110]

---

instance of a quotation—is followed by this word, viz.: III. 2, 123 (Kár. 1); none of the uncommented Kárikás except the one mentioned (III. 1, 7) has this word after it; and among the Kárikás with comment, it occurs only at III. 2, 139. It is not necessary, on the present occasion, to make any further statement concerning the use of इति in Patanjali's commentary; but compare also note 130.—The Calcutta editors, who, unfortunately, have considered themselves justified in giving us "Extracts" from the Várttikas of Kátyáyana, do not enable their readers fully to recognize the summary character of these Kárikás; and, in placing the Kárikás either at the end or at the beginning, they have, in this class of the Kárikás, and still more so in the following classes, entirely destroyed all possibility of perceiving how these Kárikás are sometimes summaries of a portion only of Várttikas, sometimes the summary of Patanjali's discussion, and sometimes an essential portion of his arguments. When, in the MSS. of the Bháshya, to judge from the one at my command, a Kárika, which occurs in the middle of the discussion, is sometimes—not always,—*repeated* at the end, such a device on the part of Patanjali, or, as it seems more probable, on the part of the copyists, is intelligible, and deserves approval, as it is calculated to draw our attention to the occurrence, in the middle of the discussion, of such a verse, which usually contains important information. But when such a verse is always taken from its original and proper place, and always put either at the beginning or at the end, for no other reason than that it is a verse, such a method, in a book, moreover, of that equivocal class which gives dribbled extracts of an important literature, makes the same impression, on my mind at all events, as if an editor of a garbled Shakspeare were to present us first with all the prosaic and then with all the poetical parts of the play, or *vice versâ.*

[110] Uncommented verses of this kind are met with in the Bháshya *at* or *near the beginning of the discussion* on IV. 1, 44 (वोतो गुण° । गुणवचनादित्युच्यते । को गुणो नाम । सत्वे निवेशते etc., when he contrasts the following Káriká—अपर आह । उपैत्य° —with the preceding words); IV. 1, 63 (जातेरस्त्री° । जातेरित्युच्यते का जातिर्नाम । आकृतिग्रहण°°, which words are contrasted with the Káriká of "another:" अपर आह । प्रादुर्भाव°°); IV. 1, 161 (मनोर्जातावञ्य° । अपत्ये कुत्सिते etc.); V. 1, 115 (तेन तुल्यं° । इदमयुक्तं वर्तते । किमत्रायुक्तम् । यत्तत्तृतीयासमर्थं क्रिया चेत्सा भवतीत्युच्यते । कथं च तृतीयासमर्थं नाम क्रिया स्यात् । नैतदयुक्तं वर्तते । सर्व एव ते शब्दा गुणसमुदायेषु वर्तन्ते ब्राह्मणः क्षत्रियो वैश्यः शूद्र इति । तपः श्रुतं°°); VI, 2, 199 (परादिश्छन्दसि बहुलम् । अत्यल्पमिदमुच्यते । परादिश्च परान्तश्च°°); VII. 4, 46, Kár. 2, (दो दद्° ।

A comparison of these two classes of *uncommented* Kárikás shows, therefore, that while the former might have been omitted in the Great Commentary, without any detriment to the contents of this work, the latter was indispensable to it. We may look upon the summary Kárikás as memorial verses, adapted for forming a separate collection for the convenience of teachers and pupils; but the independent existence of the commentatorial Kárikás is quite unintelligible, and would be altogether purposeless. In short, though there might be a doubt whether Patanjali, or some other grammarian, poetically inclined, had versified the Várttikas, it seems impossible to assume that the second class of those Kárikás was composed by any one but Patanjali. It is very probable, however, that the author of the Mahábháshya was not the author of the summary or memorial Kárikás. For since there *was* an "author of versified Kárikás," as we learn from Kaiyyaṭa and Nágojibhaṭṭa, and as we shall see that a considerable number of the commented Kárikás do not belong to his authorship, the literary activity of this personage would become restricted to,

---

अवदत्तं विदत्तं च etc.).—The foregoing quotations, which begin with the Sútra itself, will show the introductory character of these Kárikás.—*In the middle of the discussion* of the Bháshya we find such Kárikás at I. 1, 0 (ed. Ballantyne, p. 201, 202, towards the end of the Introduction); I. 1, 20 (preceding the fourth Várttika of the Calc. ed.); I. 1, 38 (the first Káriká of the Calc. ed.; it stands after the Várttikas of this ed., and is followed by a Káriká of the third category—see note 106,—which is omitted in the Calc. ed.); I. 2, 64 (preceding the eighteenth Várttika of the ed.); III. 1, 22 (after the Várttika of the ed., but before other Várttikas omitted there); V. 3, 55 (Kár. 1. 2; preceding the ninth Várttika of the Calc. ed.; Patanjali speaks in the first person); VI. 4, 114 (before the third Várttika of the ed.); VIII. 2, 80 (before the second Várttika of the ed.)—Uncommented Kárikás occur *at the end of the discussion* of the Bháshya at I. 1, 14, 38 (the last Káriká of the ed.; the Calc. editors add that this Káriká is originally a Vaidik passage referring to ब्रह्म. Kaiyyaṭa and Nágojibhaṭṭa have no remark to this effect; but even if the editors be right, they ought to have proved first that the "Vaidik" passage in question—a very vague definition—is older than Patanjali's Bháshya, and not taken from it); on I. 1, 70; 4, 51 (Kár. 5—7); II. 4, 36; III. 1, 7 (which occurs once more in the middle of the discussion on V. 2, 94 as Kár. 1); III. 1, 122. 127; 3, 1. Kár. 3 (see note 113). 156 (= VII. 4, 41); 4, 79; IV. 2, 9, 60 (omitted in the Calc. ed.; see note 105, अनुसूर्ल००); V. 3, 55 (Kár. 3—5); VI. 1, 1; VII. 1, 18; 4, 92 (where Patanjali speaks in the first person); VIII. 1, 70; 2, 59.

and his fame would have been founded on, less than half-a-dozen lines, if we did not ascribe to him more Káriká́s than those expressly attributed to him by these commentators, or if we fathered these summary Kárikás on Patanjali. Whether the "*other*" mentioned in the first six instances be the same, or not, as the "author of the versified Kárikás," I have no means of deciding; but, at all events, it becomes certain, after this brief explanation, that *all the uncommented Kárikás are later than the Várttikas of Kátyáyana.*

The Kárikás *commented upon* by Patanjali are in one respect similar to the foregoing class, but in another wholly different from it. As regards an external mark, we again meet here with "another," who has twice composed a Káriká which is contrasted by Patanjali with a preceding Várttika, and twice a Káriká which he contrasts with a preceding Káriká, the authorship of which is left without a remark.[111] Another such Káriká, too, is distinctly ascribed by Kaiyyaṭa to the "author of the versified Kárikás."[112] And when we examine the contents of this second class of Kárikás, we again find many which form an essential part of the arguments in the discussion of Patanjali.[113] Here, however, the analogy stops; for the remainder have in no way the nature of summaries; they are to all intents and purposes identical in character with the Várttikas of Kátyáyana; and even Patanjali's commentary

---

[111] III. 1, 112, Patanjali says, अपर आह । संज्ञायां पुंसि etc., when he contrasts the Káriká with the preceding Várttika; III. 2, 109, अपर आह । नोपेयिवान् etc. contrasted with preceding Várttikas omitted in the Calc. ed.; I. 2, 50 (Kár. 2), अपर आह । गोण्या ह्रस्वं etc. contrasted with the preceding Káriká; I. 4, 51, अपर आह । प्रधानकर्मण्याख्येये etc. (commented on up to कवयो विदुः Kár. I-4) contrasted with the preceding Káriká.

[112] VI. 4. 22. Compare note 108.

[113] Such Kárikás are met with at or *near the beginning* of the Bháshya on I. 4, 51 (the two first Kár. of the Calc. ed.); III. 3. 1. (Kár. 1. 2.; the last Káriká is left without comment); IV. 1, 3. 54. 78. (the first four Kárikás stand at the beginning, before the first Várttika; the following nine after the second Várttika of the Calcutta edition, which, in the Bháshya, however, is the fourth); 92. 165; V. 2, 45; VI. 1, 103. *In the middle* of the discussion on I. 1, 57; IV. 1, 93; V. 1, 19; 2, 94, Kár. 2 (before the seventh Várttika of the Calc. ed.); VII. 4, 46 (Kár. 1).

on them follows the same method that he observes in his comment on the Várttikas.[114]

This method is analogous to that which has become familiar through the classical commentaries of Śankara on the Upanishads, of Medhátithi and Kullúka on Manu, of Sáyaṇa on the Vedas, of Vijnáneśwara on Yájnavalkya, and so on. Its character chiefly consists in establishing, usually by repetition, the correct reading of the text, in explaining every important or doubtful word, in showing the connection of the principal parts of the sentence, and in adding such observations as may be required for a better understanding of the author. Patanjali even excels, in the latter respect, the commentaries instanced, for he frequently attaches his own critical remarks to the emendations of Kátyáyana, often in support of the views of the latter, but not seldom, too, in order to refute his criticisms and to defend Páṇini; while, again, at other times, he completes the statement of one of them by his own additional rules.

Now this method Patanjali strictly follows in his comment on the Kárikás I am alluding to. As they nearly always constitute a whole verse, and as such a verse is generally too complicated an assemblage of words to be thoroughly intelligible without being interrupted by some explanatory remark, it seldom happens that the comment of Patanjali does not begin till he has given the whole verse in its uninterrupted order. Nor is it often that so many words of the Káriká as constitute half a verse remain together in the Bháshya, though it is obvious that half a verse is

---

[114] Kárikás of this description occur in the Bháshya *at* or *near the beginning* of the commentary on I, 1, 19; 2, 9. 17. 18. 50 (Kár. 1); III. 2, 115; IV. 1, 10 (the Várttika of the Calc. ed. on this Sútra is no Várttika but Bháshya); 3, 60, 84. 134; V. 3. 83; VI. 1, 77 (Kár. 1 *a. b.*). 158; 2, 1; 3, 46; 4, 3. 46. 128; VII. 1, 21. 40. 73 (Kár. 1). 96; 2, 107; 3, 3 (Kár. 1). 86; VIII. 1, 69 (?); 2, 25. 55. 58 (Kár. 1. 2); 3, 88; 4, 68.—*In the middle*, at I. 2, 51; 4, 21 (= III. 3, 161); III. 2, 57. 139; IV. 1, 18. 32 (the second Várttika of the Calc. ed. is no Várttika but Bháshya on the last part of the Káriká); 2, 8 (the second Várttika of the Calc. ed. is misedited; it runs thus: दृष्टे सामनि जाते वाप्यण्डिद्द्विर्वा विधीयते). 45; V. 2, 39; VI. 4, 12. 62. 74; VII. 1, 9; 2, 102; 3, 3 (Kár. 2 and 3).—*Towards the end*, at IV. 1, 120.—In several of these instances there are no other Várttikas to the Sútra besides the Káriká, which is then the subject of the whole commentary, *e.g.* at IV. 3, 60. 84; VI. 4, 46, 128; VII. 1, 21; 3, 86.

more likely to afford undivided matter for comment than a whole one. The rule, therefore, is, that small portions of the Káriká, for the most part of the extent of an ordinary Várttika, are, like so many Várttikas, separately commented upon by Patanjali, and that in all such instances we have to gather the scattered parts of the Káriká from amongst the commentatorial interruptions of Patanjali, in order to see that, put together, they form a verse,—a Śloka, an Indravajra, a Dodhaka, an Áryá, or the like.[115] This trouble we are frequently saved, either by the author of the Great Commentary himself, or by the attentive copyists of his work, as he or they usually repeat, at the end of the gloss on the Várttikas,

---

[115] The text of the *whole* verse of Kárikás of this class is given before the comment of Patanjali, at I. 2, 51; V. 2, 94. Kár. 2; VI. 4, 46; VIII. 4, 68. There occur *half* verses of the Kárikás, without commentatorial interruptions, *e.g.* at I. 4, 21 (= III. 3, 161). 51; III. 2, 57. 115; IV. 1, 3. 10. 32. 93. 165; 2, 8. 45; V. 2, 39; VI. 4, 3. 12. 62. 128; VII. 1, 9. 96; 2, 102. 107; 3, 3. 86.—Both modes are combined at VIII. 3, 45 (a Kár. of the *third category*) where Patanjali first comments on the text of the first Káriká, which is given without any interruption; then on the first half of the second Káriká; then on the second half of the second and the first half of the third Káriká, both given together; then on the second half of the third; and lastly, on the first half of the fourth Káriká. The comment on the second half of the fourth Káriká follows first after the words सिद्धं च मे समासे, and then after the words प्रतिषेधार्थस्तु यत्नो ऽयम्.—The manner in which the great majority of *these* Kárikás is interrupted in the Mahábháshya may be guessed from a very few instances which have escaped the garbling process of the Calcutta editors; from IV. 1, 120, where the four Várttikas are the literal text of the Káriká; and from V. 3, 83, where the first five Várttikas constitute the Káriká. The injudiciousness of giving these Kárikás on all other occasions, without indicating the manner in which they have arisen from a number of short Várttikas, requires no remark after the foregoing explanation; but this proceeding becomes still more subject to censure, when some portions of the Káriká *are* given as Várttikas and others are omitted, or ascribed to other works than the Bháshya, while the Káriká, nevertheless, is printed as belonging to the latter work. For it becomes evident that, in all such cases, there was not even a principle which guided the so-called selection or quotation of the works whence the Várttikas are taken. Thus at IV. 1, 32 the Calcutta edition gives the Káriká, but only the last portion of it as Várttika—mistaking, moreover, the words of the commentary वा छन्दसि नुग्वक्तव्यः for the Káriká-Várttika, which runs thus: वा छन्दसि नुग्भवेत्—. A similar mis-edition of the second Várttika to IV. 2, 8, and the attributing to the Káśiká of the fifth Várttika, make it impossible to see that the Várttikas 2—5 form, in the Mahábháshya, the text of the printed Káriká.—In ascribing the third and the fifth Várttika of V. 3, 83 to the Siddhánta-kaumudí, the

the whole Káriká in its metrical integrity. Sometimes, however, they omitted to do this; and if I may judge from the copy of the Mahábháshya in the possession of the Library of the Home Government for India, the Calcutta Pandits, who published an edition of Páṇini, have, in some instances, supplied the apparent defect of this manuscript.[116]

The foregoing remarks sufficiently express my views on these *commented Kárikás.* Where the authorship of "another," or of the *Śloka-várttika-kára*, is distinctly mentioned by Patanjali or Kaiyyaṭa, I see no reason to doubt that the Kárikás to which this remark applies are neither Patanjali's nor Kátyáyana's. When the Kárikás are part of the arguments of the Bháshya itself, it seems certain, as in the case of the analogous Kárikás without comment, that their author is Patanjali; but when they have entirely

---

editors obscure the origin of the Káriká to this Sútra, which repeats the text of the first five Várttikas, such as they occur in the Bháshya.—At VIII. 2, 25 the same edition does not allow us to perceive more than the first stop of the first Káriká, while it gives the three Kárikás in full.—I may mention, too, that there is no such Káriká in the Bháshya as that printed at VI. 4, 19. It certainly was very tempting to roll up into a Śloka the words of Patanjali, तुकप्रसज्येत, which explain the second Várttika तुकप्रसङ्गश्च, together with the three other Várttikas which belong to Kátyáyana; but there is no evidence to show that Patanjali made this verse; nor does it occur in the Káśiká or the Siddháṇta-kaumudí.—For one Káriká Patanjali seems, indeed, to be himself answerable, for the Várttikas to VIII. 1, 69 merely contain the material for the first fourth and the second half of the Káriká, which occurs at the end of his Bháshya on this Sútra. It is possible, however, under the circumstances, that this Káriká may be one of the summary class. See note 105.

[116] Dr. Ballantyne's edition of the first Páda of the first Adhyáya of the Mahábháshya, and the MS. of the E. I. H., which have the four Várttikas to I. 1, 57, नित्यः परस्यसादेशः (MS. परस्यसादेशो नित्यः। comm. . . . . .। परस्वासौ व्यवस्थया। comm. . . . . .। युगपत्संभवो नास्ति। comm. . . . . .। वहिरङ्गेन सिध्यति। comm. ।, do not repeat these words without interruptions in order to show their Káriká nature; and the same remark applies to the MS. with regard to the *commented* Kárikás I. 2, 51; 4, 21. 51; IV. 1, 3. 32. 78. 92. 93. 120. 165; 2, 45; 3, 60. 134; V. 1, 19; 2, 39. 45. 94 (Kár. 2); 3, 83; VI. 1, 158; 4, 46. 62. 74. 128; VII. 1, 96; 4, 46 (Kár. 1); VIII. 2, 25. 55. 58 (Kár. 1, 2); 3, 45; 4, 68. The repetition of some of these Káriká-Várttikas has no doubt been omitted, because the commentary of Patanjali allowed the whole verse or half a verse of this text to remain uninterrupted (see note 115). In the Calcutta edition all these Kárikás are given in their metrical integrity.

the character of Várttikas—which will later be defined—they are undoubtedly the composition of Kátyáyana; and such, I hold, is the view of Kaiyyaṭa and Nágojibhaṭṭa also. For though it is no part of their task to specify the authorship of the Kárikás, except when such a remark is essential to their gloss, they, nevertheless, have done so occasionally; and when thus we find that they plainly ascribe some of these commented Kárikás either to the author of the Várttikas or the author of the Great Commentary, as the case may be, we must be allowed to infer that they entertained a similar opinion on other Kárikás which would fall under either of the heads I have mentioned above.[117] Nor need we hesitate at the idea of a poetical author of Várttikas. Not only were whole grammatical works, ancient and modern, written in verse,[118] but it is a common occurrence with scientific commentators in India, that they cannot resist the temptation of running into verse, even at the risk of endangering their prosaic task. We need only remember another celebrated author of Várttikas, Kumárila, who writes alternately in Śloka and prose. It might seem more remarkable that Patanjali should write in verse and comment upon this himself; but *Mádhava* affords an analogous instance in his Jaiminíya-nyáya-málá-vistara; *Viśwanátha-Panchánana*

---

[117] Thus, on the first four Kárikás to IV. 1, 78, *Nágojibhaṭṭa* observes: एते श्लोका भाष्यकृत एव न वार्त्तिककृतः—which words, moreover, plainly intimate that there exist Kárikás composed by Kátyáyana; or in the latter part of Kaiyyaṭa's comment on the Káriká to VI. 1, 103 we read: . . . . . इत्यादिना विशिष्टमेव लिङ्गलक्षणं भाष्यकारेणाश्रितम्.—In his comment on the Káriká to IV. 3, 60, Nágojibhaṭṭa, in referring to the remark of Patanjali, मुखपार्श्व इत्येताभ्यां तसन्ताभ्यामीयप्रत्ययो वक्तव्यः (which words explain the beginning of the second Káriká) observes: भाष्ये तसन्ताभ्यामिति वार्त्तिके आर्षत्वात्समासः; and on a further remark of Kaiyyaṭa: प्रकृतवार्त्तिकप्रयोजनमाह. On the affix तवै in the second Káriká to VI. 1,158, Nágojibhaṭṭa remarks: वार्त्तिके तवैग्रहणं सूत्रोपलक्षणम्; on the first Káriká to VI. 2, 1: . . . . इति नियमोऽसिद्ध इति वार्त्तिकार्थः; on Kaiyyaṭa to the first Káriká to VI. 3, 46: अन्यप्रकृतिरिति वार्त्तिकस्थमन्यशब्दं व्याचष्टे; on Kaiyyaṭa to the second fourth of Káriká 1. to VI. 4, 12: वार्त्तिके सुटीति, etc.; on a various reading in the second Káriká to VII. 3, 86: वार्त्तिके ऽनल्लोप इति पाठे, etc.—In his gloss on the Káriká to VIII. 4, 68, Kaiyyaṭa says: तस्य विवृतोपदेशादन्यत्रापि विवृतोपदेशः सवर्णग्रहणार्थ इति वार्त्तिककृता पूर्वमेव प्रतिपादितम्.

[118] For instance, the Páṇiníya-Śikshá and the Ṛik-Prátiśákhya.

wrote a commentary in prose, the Siddhántamuktávalí, on his metrical exposition of the Vaiśeshika Philosophy, the Bháshá-parichchheda; *Daivajnaráma* explained in prose his versified Muhúrtachintámani; *Vardhamána* did the same with his Gaṇa-ratnamahodadhi; and many more instances could be adduced to show that there is nothing striking, or even remarkable, in the assumption that Patanjali composed grammatical verses and commented on them in prose.[119]

After the foregoing observations, the authorship of those Kárikás, which, apparently, form a third category, can create no difficulty so far as Kátyáyana is concerned. They were neither written by him, nor before his time. The manner in which Patanjali comments on them, and their very contents, show that they cannot be assimilated to Kátyáyana's Kárikás, which, as I mentioned before, are dealt with by him in the same manner as the Várttikas in prose. There is either scarcely any comment on

---

[119] I owe to the kindness of Dr. Fitz-Edward Hall an extract from his "*Contribution towards an Index to the Bibliography of the Indian Philosophical Systems*," which mentions besides Viśwanátha-Panchánana, eleven authors who wrote twelve works in verse and commented on them in prose. As this extract is, on other grounds, of considerable interest, I will, with Dr. Hall's permission, forestall the arrival in Europe of his important work, and here subjoin the substance of his communication. He names in it, besides the author of the Bháshá-parichchheda — 1. *Jívarája-Díkshita*, who wrote the Tarka-káśiká (on the Vaiśeshika) in verse, and a commentary on it in prose, the Tarka-manjarí; 2. *Vidyáraṇyácharya*, the author of the Vedántádhikaraṇa-málá (in verse) and a prose exposition interspersed; 3. *Prakáśánanda* or *Anantánanda-krishṇa* (?), the author of the Siddhántamuktávalí; 4. *Vasudeva-Brahma-Prasáda*, the author of the Sachchidánandánubhavapradípiká; 5. *Lakshmadhara-Kavi*, who wrote the Adwaita-makaraṇḍa; 6. *Śankaráchárya*, to whom the Átmabodha is ascribed, and likewise a comment on it, entitled Ajnánabodhiní; 7. *Śankaránanda*, the author of the Átmapuráṇa and a comment on it, the Átmapuráṇa-dípiká; 8. *Appayya-Díkshita*, the author of the Brahmatarkastava and the Brahmatarkastáva-vivaraṇa; 9. 10. *Vallabháchárya*, the author of the Pushṭipraváhamaryádábheda and a Vivaraṇa on it, and likewise of the Antaḥkaraṇaprabodha and a Vivṛiti on it; 11. *Gangádharasaraswatí*, the author of the Siddhántasúktimanjarí (an abridgement of the Siddhántaleśa) and a Prakáśa of it; and 12. *Govindaśástrin*, who wrote the Atharvaṇa-ráhasya and a commentary on it.—All these works (except the first) treat on the Vedánta; their text is in verse and their commentary in prose.

the Kárikás of this class, or his comment assumes more the nature of a general exposition, which is intended to work out the sense of the Káriká, but not to give, at the same time, a gloss, in the usual sense of this word.[120] In short, a comparison of these Kárikás with those of the two other classes, must lead to the conclusion that, in reality, they are no separate class, but belong either to one or the other. They are partly Patanjali's own arguments expressed in verse and amplified in prose, or the composition of that "other" grammarian whom we have encountered before. There are, indeed, two of these Kárikás which are distinctly ascribed by

---

[120] Thus the two half verses of a Káriká to I. 1, 38 (omitted in the Calc. ed.), are interrupted and accompanied by a brief remark, as will appear from the following quotation (ed. Ballantyne, p. 492): कृत्तद्धितानां ग्रहणं तु कार्यं संख्याविशेषं ह्यभिनिश्रिता ये (first half verse) ‖ तेषां प्रतिषेधो भवतीति वक्तव्यम् । द्वहा मा भूत् । एको द्वौ बहव इति ‖ तस्मात्स्वरादिग्रहणं च कार्यं कृत्तद्धितानां ग्रहणं च पाठे (second half verse) ‖ पाठेनैयमव्ययसंज्ञा क्रियते सेह न प्राप्नोति । परमोच्चैः परमनीचैरिति.—The Bháshya on the first two half verses of the Káriká to III. 1, 123 (which are left uninterrupted), merely consists of the words: निष्टर्क्यं चिन्वीत पशुकामः; on the following portion, ण्यादेकस्माच्चतुर्भ्यः क्यप्, of the instances: देवहूयः । प्रणीयः । उन्नीयः । उच्छिष्यः ।; on चतुर्भ्यश्च यतो विधिः, of the instances मर्यः । स्तर्याध्वर्यः । खन्यः, and the like on the last half verse.—The comment on the Káriká to IV. 2, 13 runs thus: अथवा कुमार्यां भवः कौमारः । यद्येवं कौमारी भार्येति न सिध्यति पुंयोगादभिधानं भविष्यति । कौमारस्य भार्या कौमारी.—The whole Bháshya on the Kárikás to VI. 4, 120, is the following; on the first half verse: छन्दस्यमिपचोरपीति वक्तव्यम् । किं प्रयोजनम् । अनेश°°; and on the rest, which is given without any interruption: अनित्यो ऽयं विधिरिति.—The Káriká to VI. 4, 149, which also is given entire—up to तथा, which is preceded only by the word अन्तिषद्—is followed by these words: आन्तिये च दूरके सूर्या.—The Bháshya on the whole continuous first Káriká to VIII. 3, 45, consists of these words: व्यपेक्षासामर्थ्ये पूर्वयोगः । न चात्र व्यपेक्षासामर्थ्यं । किं पुनः कारणम् । पूर्वस्मिन्योगे व्यपेक्षासामर्थ्यमाश्रीयते न पुनरेकार्थीभावो यथान्यत्र; on the first half of the second, the Bháshya runs: ऐकार्थ्ये सति वाक्ये षत्वं न स्यात् । सर्पिष्करोति । सर्पिः करोतीति; on the uninterrupted second half and first half of the third Káriká; यदि क्षदन्तमेतत्ततो ऽधिकस्य षत्वं न प्राप्नोति । किं कारणं । प्रत्ययग्रहणे यस्मात्स तदादेर्ग्रहणं भवतीति वाक्ये ऽपि तर्हि न प्राप्नोति । परमसर्पिष्करोति; on the second half of the third Káriká: यदयमनुत्तरपदस्थस्येति प्रतिषेधं शास्ति तज्ज्ञापयत्याचार्यः । भवति वाक्ये विभाषेति; fourth Káriká, etc.

Patanjali to this grammarian, and a third which quotes Kátyáyana, and cannot therefore belong to this author of the Várttikas.[121]

Another and very important class of grammatical writings frequently adverted to in the Máhabháshya is familiar to Hindu grammarians under the name of *Paribháshás.* They do not amend and criticize, but teach the proper application of, the rules of Páṇini. While the *Sanjná-rules* explain the technical terms of his work, the *Paribháshás* explain the general principles, according to which the Sútras are to be applied. Thus, when Páṇini or other grammarians teach the meaning of the terms *Guṇa*, *Vṛiddhi*, *Upasarga*, *Gati*, *Dwandwa*, etc., the rules devoted to this purpose are *Sanjná-rules;* but when Páṇini says, "If a grammatical element in the Sútras has the mute letter *m*, this anubandha indicates that such an element has to be added after the last vowel of the radical or base with which it is to be joined;" or if he states, "The sixth case in a Sútra means that, instead of that which is expressed by this case, something else, enjoined by the Sútra, is to be substituted,"—such rules are *Paribháshá-rules.*[122]

---

[121] The Kárikás to I. 1, 38; VI. 4, 149; and VIII. 3, 45, belong, in all probability, to Patanjali, and those to III. 1, 123; 2, 118. 123 (Kár. 3); IV. 2, 13; and VI. 4, 120, to the "other" grammarians. The Káriká to III. 1, 123, is distinctly introduced by Patanjali with the words अपर आह.—The third Káriká to III. 2, 123, which has no other comment than the words हिमवानपि गच्छति, is thus introduced by him, together with the two preceding and the two following verses: अपर आह: । नास्ति वर्तमानः काल इति । अपि चात्र श्लोकानुदाहरन्ति । न वर्तते, etc. Compare note 107.—The first Káriká to III. 2, 118, explicitly refers to Kátyáyana, in quoting his second Várttika to this Sútra.

[122] Compare I. 1, 1. 2. etc., and other Sútras marked in the edition संज्ञाप्रदेशः; and I. 1, 47. 49. and other Sútras marked there परिभाषासूत्रम्. But the Calcutta editors have failed in accuracy, also, in this respect. Thus the rule I. 1, 21, आद्यन्तवदेकस्मिन्, is marked by them as an अतिदेशः, but Patanjali calls it distinctly परिभाषा; or I. 1, 69, अणुदित्सवर्णस्य चाप्रत्ययः, has their mark सञ्ज्ञाप्रदेशः, but is called by Kátyáyana himself a Paribháshá (ed. Ballantyne, p. 763); or I. 1. 72, येन विधिस्तदन्तस्य is marked by them संज्ञाप्रदेशः, but Patanjali likewise calls it a Paribháshá (ed. Ballantyne, p. 372): द्वयोः परिभाषयोः सावकाशयोः समवस्थितयोराद्यन्तवदेकस्मिन्येन विधिस्तदन्तस्येति च । इयमिह परिभाषा भविष्यति आद्यन्तवदेकस्मिन्निति । इयं च न भविष्यति येन विधिस्तदन्तस्येति, etc.

A *Paribháshá* contains either a special mark, which enables the reader to recognise at once the Sútra to which it refers, or it is delivered without such a criterion. In the latter case, it is matter of discrimination to see whether it applies unconditionally or conditionally to a given Sútra. In explaining, for instance (I. 1, 3), that "whenever *Guṇa* or *Vṛiddhi* is the subject of a rule, these terms are used in reference to the vowels *i*, *í*, *u*, *ú*, *ṛi*, *ṛí*, and *ḷṛi* only," Páṇini, by these technical terms, gives us the power of distinguishing at first sight, as it were, the Sútras affected by this *Paribháshá*. But when he says (I. 1, 54), "If a rule is given in reference to something which follows, it concerns merely the beginning of such a following element," it is for the reader to judge whether this *Paribháshá* prevails unconditionally at, and is an essential part of, for instance, rule VII. 2, 83, or not. Again, when a *Paribháshá* (I. 4, 2) teaches that "If two rules connected with one another, but of a different purport, apparently apply to the same case, the later rule only is valid," it is left to his judgment to decide whether it may be applicable or not to rule VII. 3, 103, for instance.[123]

The Paribháshás, however, which are to be the subject of the following remarks, are not those given by Páṇini himself: they are the Paribháshás met with in the Great Commentary of Patanjali, and have been defined by *Vaidyanátha*, surnamed *Páyaguṇḍa*, in his gloss on the *Paribháshenduśekhara* of *Nágo-*

---

[123] *Purushottama-vṛitti-ṭiká* on Páṇini, I. 1, 3: परि सर्वशास्त्र उपयुक्ता वाणी भाषा सा परिभाषा सा च लिङ्गवती विध्यङ्गशेषभूता च। या लिङ्गद्वाराभावे (MS. E.I.H. No. 224, °भावो) नोपयुज्यते सा लिङ्गवती। या सर्वैव विधिवाक्य उपयुज्यते सापरा। सापि काचिद्विधेरङ्गभूता यां विना विधिर्वाक्यान्नैव प्रवर्तते। यथा। आदेः परस्येति (I. 1, 54)। न (MS. म) हि तद्विना ईदास इति (VII. 2, 83) प्रवर्तते। काचिच्च विधिशेषभूता। विप्रतिषेधे परमिति (I. 4, 2) अविरोधे वृद्धोष्वित्यादौ झल्येत्त्वमव्याहतमेव (comp. VII. 3, 103)। विरोधविषये तु एत्त्वात्परं (MS. णत्वापरं) कारयतीति. The explanation of the Káśiká—which in general is much more lucid, and on the whole not more extensive than the compiled gloss of the Calcutta edition—runs thus on the word विप्रतिषेध (I. 4, 2): विरोधो विप्रतिषेधः। यत्र द्वौ प्रसङ्गावन्यार्थावेकस्मिन्युगपत्प्राप्नुतः स विप्रतिषेधः। तुल्यबलविरोधो विप्रतिषेधः.

jibhaṭṭa, surnamed the *Upádhyáya*, as "axioms (the existence and authority of) which are established by certain Sútras of Páṇini, and axioms (the existence and authority of) which are established by the method that governs other works, but is applicable to Páṇini also." Each of these categories has been taught, as they state, by "older grammarians, in the shape of Sútras;" the former however, Vaidyanátha observes, prevail in number and authority over the latter. In other words, these Paribháshás are, according to the grammarians quoted, special axioms referring to Páṇini exclusively, and general axioms which avail for *his* Grammar as well as for *other* works. The "certain" Sútras of Páṇini which indicate that such Paribháshás are in existence and are required for a proper application of the rules, are called *Jnápaka*, and the method of other authors which indicates that those Paribháshás are applicable as well to them as to Páṇini, bear the name of *Nyáya*.[124] We shall see, however, that this definition, to be correct, will have to be modified; and I may mention, besides, that older commentators, Kaiyyaṭa, for instance, merely speak of Paribháshás and Nyáyas, not of Paribháshás founded on Nyáyas; while the author of the Paribháshenduśekhara himself frequently gives the name of Nyáya to those Paribháshás which, according to his introductory words, are such as are founded on Nyáya.[125]

---

[124] *Paribháshenduśekhara*, in the introduction: प्राचीनवैयाकरणतन्त्रे वाचनिकान्यत्र पाणिनीये तन्त्रे ज्ञापकन्यायसिद्धानि भाष्यवार्त्तिकयोर्निबद्धानि यानि परिभाषारूपाणि तानि व्याख्यायन्ते. *Paribháshenduśekhara-Kaśiká* of Vaidyanátha on these words: प्राचीनेति । इन्द्रादीत्यर्थः । वाचनिकानि । सूत्ररूपेण पठितानि । अत्र । अस्मिन् । एवमग्रे ऽपि ज्ञापकेत्यस्य प्रायेणेत्यादिः । तथा च वाचनिकानामपि तत्सहचरितानां संग्रहः । न्यायसिद्धाज्ज्ञापकसिद्धस्य (MS. E.I.H. No. 490: न्यायसिद्धा ऽज्ञा°) प्राबल्येनाभ्यर्हितत्वाज्ज्ञापकशब्दस्य द्वन्द्वे पूर्वनिपातः (comp. II. 2, 34, v. 3) । तच्चैतच्छास्त्रीयलिङ्गं ज्ञापकम् । एतच्छास्त्रलोकतन्त्रान्तरप्रसिद्धयुक्तिर्न्यायः । सूत्रपाठस्थपरिभाषाणामत्राव्याख्यानाय प्राचीनोक्तानां कासांचिदप्रामाण्याय चाह भाष्येति etc.

[125] The *Laghuparibháshávṛitti* is therefore divided into a gloss on what we may call the Paribháshás proper and a gloss on the न्यायमूलाः परिभाषाः which comprise twenty-eight axioms. This distinction is somewhat obscured in the

In now adverting to the chronological relation in which these axioms stand to Páṇini and Kátyáyana, we are, in the first place, enabled to decide that Paribháshás of this kind must have existed before the Várttikas of Kátyáyana, for the latter quotes such Paribháshás in his Várttikas.[126] Another question, how-

---

Paribháshenduśekhara, where both categories are mentioned in the introduction (comp. the preceding note), but afterwards treated promiscuously. The Calcutta edition has, in most instances, correctly appended the Paribháshá to the Sútra which is its *Jnápaka*: thus the P. निर्दिश्यमानस्यादेशा भवन्ति which is required for the proper application of, *e.g.* the Sútra VI. 4, 130; VII. 2, 101, etc., is correctly appended in this edition to the *Jnápaka-Sútra* I. 1, 49; the P. नानुबन्धकृतमनेकाल्त्वम् which applies *e.g.* to VI. 4, 127, to the *Jnápaka* I. 1, 55; the P. सकृद्गतौ विप्रतिषेधे यद्बाधितं तद्बाधितमेव which applies *e.g.* to VI. 4, 105 combined with VII. 1, 35, to the *Jnápaka* I. 4, 2, and so on. Sometimes, however, the editors have appended the Paribáshá to the Sútra for the interpretation of which it is required, but not to the *Jnápaka* rule where it ought to have been placed; *e.g.* the P. विकरणेभ्यो नियमो बलीयान् applies to I. 3, 12, but its *Jnápaka* is I. 3, 43; or the P. नानुबन्धकृतमनेजन्तत्वम् is required for the proper interpretation of I. 1, 20; VI. 1, 45, etc., but its *Jnápaka* is III. 4, 19, etc. In some instances the authorities named differ as to the *Jnápaka* of a Paribháshá; thus the P. अर्थवद्ग्रहणेनानर्थकस्य ग्रहणम् is indicated according to the *Paribháshenduśekhara* which invokes the authority of Patanjali, by the *Jnápaka* I. 1, 72; according to the *Laghu-paribháshávṛitti*, by the *Jnápaka* I. 1, 34; the Calc. editors have placed it under I. 1, 68. —The P. प्रकृतिवदनुकरणं भवति is indicated, according to the first named work, by the *Jnápaka* VI. 4, 59, according to the second, by the *Jnápaka* I. 3, 18; the editors have appended it to VIII. 2, 46, which Sútra, however, merely illustrates its applicability. Many other instances of this kind might be alleged in order to show that the matter is one of great difficulty to the Hindu grammarians themselves, and that in this respect, also, much scope is left for a future conscientious editor of Páṇini. That the Paribháshás are not met with at the end of Patanjali's Bháshya to a Sútra, requires no further observation after the statement of note 109; for they are an essential portion of the arguments of his discussion.—The term न्याय is applied six times to Paribháshás by the Calcutta editors (viz. at the Sútras I. 1, 23. 42. 47; twice II. 1, 1; III. 1, 12); but if they followed the Paribháshá collections quoted, they ought to have marked in a similar manner several axioms which are given by them simply as Paribháshás. At all events, they ought not to have called the same axiom नञिवयुक्तम्°° *Nyáya*, at III. 1, 12, and *Paribháshá*, at VI. 1, 71; and since they repeated it in order to show its application, they might have mentioned it also at VI. 1. 135, where it likewise occurs in the commentary of Patanjali.

[126] A Várttika to I. 1, 65, which has disappeared in the Calcutta edition, says: अन्त्यविज्ञानात्सिद्धमिति चेन्नानर्थके ऽलो ऽन्त्यविधिरनभ्यासविकारे; its last words नानर्थके, etc., are a Paribháshá, as results from the Bháshya on this Várttika:

ever, is, whether those Paribháshás which existed before Kátyáyana existed also before Páṇini, and whether we should be justified in looking upon the Paribháshas collected in the Paribháshendusekhara, the Paribháshásangraha, and similar works, as the original Paribháshás to the Sútras of Páṇini. If we believed Vaidyanátha's definition of the two categories of Paribháshás, and of the distinction he establishes between *Jnápaka* and *Nyáya*, as just mentioned, it would become very probable that the Paribháshás were composed *after* the Grammar of Páṇini, and by another grammarian than Páṇini, since there is no evidence to show that he wrote other Paribháshás than those which are embodied in his own Sútras; and if we assumed that the collections of Paribháshás made and commented upon by Nágojibhaṭṭa, Śíradeva, and others, are the original collections, there would be a certainty that the "older grammarians," whom the former quotes as his authority, did not precede Páṇini, for one, or perhaps two, of these axioms, *mentioned in each of these collections*, distinctly refer to him.[127]

There are, however, reasons which must induce us to doubt the originality of the Paribháshás contained in these collections, and to doubt too the strict correctness of Vaidyanátha's definition. In the first place, because these collections, each of which appears to be entitled to equal authority, differ in the number, and even in the wording, of the Paribháshás which they contain, though they coincide in giving all those Paribháshás which espe-

---

अन्त्यविज्ञात्सिद्धमिति चेत्। तन्न। किं कारणम्। नानर्थके ऽलो ऽन्त्यस्यविधिरनभ्यासविकारे। अनर्थके ऽलो ऽन्त्यस्य विधिर्नेत्येषा परिभाषा कर्तव्या। किमविशेषेण। नेत्याह। अनभ्यासविकारे. Compare also a similar instance, in note 137.

[127] The Paribháshá to IV. 1, 82: अकृतव्यूहाः पाणिनीयाः; and the P. to VIII. I. 1: पूर्वत्रासिद्धीयमद्विर्वचने, which is, *perhaps*, founded on the Sútra VIII. 2, 1; but as the expression पूर्वत्रासिद्धं need not be a quotation from Páṇini, it would not be safe to found a conclusion on it with the same certainty as on the word पाणिनीयाः. For this reason I do not lay stress on another Paribháshá which occurs in the *Paribháshárthasangrahavyákhyáchandriká* and the *Laghuparibháshávṛitti*, and is founded on VII. 4, 2: पूर्वत्रासिद्धे न स्थानिवत् (its wording in the *Laghup.* पूर्वत्रासिद्धीये न स्थानिवत् is erroneous. Compare note 132).

cially concern us here.[128] It is not probable, therefore, that the original collection of Paribháshás was any of those now preserved in manuscript. But there is more ground to confirm this doubt. The *Paribháshenduśekhara* states, in its introduction, that it is going to explain "the axioms explicitly mentioned by the older grammarians . . . . *and recorded in the Bháshya and the Várttikas;*"—whereupon Vaidyanátha comments: "'The older grammarians' are Indra and so on; 'explicitly mentioned' means read in the shape of Sútras; . . . . . . 'in the Bháshya' says the author of the Paribháshenduśekhara, because it is not his intention to explain the Paribháshás which are embodied in Páṇini's Sútras, and because some of those mentioned by the older grammarians carry no authority with them." [129]

Now, if we compare the Paribháshás collected in the last-named work, and in the other works devoted to the same purpose, with the Great Commentary itself, we find that they frequently call that a Paribháshá which is not a quotation made by Patanjali from authorities which preceded him, but simply a portion of his own argument. No doubt, when this great critic considered himself justified in laying down general principles, according to which certain Sútras are to be interpreted or applied, such axioms of his are to all intents and purposes Paribháshás, but they are Paribháshás of his, not of the authorities who preceded him.[130] And this dis-

---

[128] The number of Paribháshás in the *Paribháshenduśekhara* is 108; it may, however, be given as 112, as several P. are contracted into one; in the *Paribháshávṛitti* of *Śíradeva* it is 130; in the *Laghuparibháshávṛitti* and the *Paribháshárthasangrahavyákhyáchandriká* there are 108 Paribháshás proper and 28 *nyáyamúláḥ* P., some of the latter being included in the 108 of the first named work. Another collection, which does not mention the name of the compiler, but bears the title of *Páṇinimatánugáminí Paribháshá*, has 123 Paribháshás. Each of these collections has some Paribháshás which are not named in several of the others.

[129] See note 124.

[130] I mentioned in note 109 that the absence or presence in the Bháshya of the quotational word इति affords no criterion in the case of the *metrical Káriká*s. It is necessary to state now that this word is always met with when a Paribháshá is quoted by Patanjali, and its absence is therefore a safe mark that a general axiom which occurs in his commentary is one of his own creation. A few instances chosen from the first

tinction we must draw in order to judge whether Patanjali originated an axiom merely for the purpose of defending Páṇini, or whether the Sútra in question is *boná fide* entitled to the benefit of such a general rule, since it is certain that several of these axioms were invented at later periods, either to palliate the shortcomings of Páṇini, or to make his rules so conveniently elastic as to extend

---

chapters of the Mahábháshya will make good this assertion. We read in the Bháshya on I. 1, 20 (p. 395, ed. Ballantyne): दोष एवैतस्याः परिभाषायाः । लक्षणप्रतिपदोक्तयोः प्रतिपदोक्तस्यैवेति । गामादाग्रहणेष्वविशेष इति (the former of these P. is omitted in the Calc. ed.); or at I. 1, 49 (p. 565) निर्दिश्यमानस्यादेशा भवन्तीत्येषा परिभाषा etc.; or at I. 1, 55 (p. 608) अस्त्वेषा परिभाषा । नानुबन्धकृतमनेकाल्त्वं भवतीति; or at I. 1, 15 (p. 377) एवं तर्हि गौणमुख्ययोर्मुख्ये कार्यसंप्रत्यय इति; or at I. 2, 63 तज्ज्ञापयत्याचार्यः सर्वो द्वन्द्वो विभाषयैकवद्भवतीति (not विभावैक° as in the Calc. ed.); or at I. 4, 2 विप्रतिषेधे परमेव भवतीति तदेतदुपपन्नं भवति । सकृद्गतौ विप्रतिषेधे यद्बाधितं तद्बाधितमेवेति; when in the latter three instances the word इति *indicates* that the preceding words are a Paribháshá, while in the first three instances the term itself is added, and इति afterwards. On the other hand, when we read at I. 1, 27 (p. 442): .... नैष दोषः । भवति हि बहुव्रीहौ तद्गुणसंविज्ञानमपि । तद्यथा । चित्रवाससमानय etc.; or in the Bháshya on the same Sútra (p. 448): कर्तव्योऽत्र यत्नः । बाधकान्येव हि निपातनानि भवन्ति, the words बहुव्रीहौ ° ° मपि and बाधकान्येव° are undoubtedly Patanjali's own; and it may, in passing, be observed that the Paribháshenduśekhara and the Calc. ed. have omitted the word हि in giving these words as Paribháshás. Or when the Bháshya on the Várttika शतृशानचोश्च निमित्तभावात्तिङो ऽभावस्तयोरपवादत्वात् (omitted in the Calc. ed.), to II. 3, 46, says: ... शतृशानचौ तिङोऽपवादौ तौ चात्र बाधकौ । न चापवादविषयमुत्सर्गो ऽभिनिविशते । पूर्वं ह्यपवादा अभिनिविशन्ते पश्चादुत्सर्गाः । प्रकल्प्य वापवादविषयं तत उत्सर्गो ऽभिनिविशते । न तावदत्र कदाचित्तिङादेशो भवति etc., the words पूर्वं ° ° ऽभिनिविशते are clearly a portion of Patanjali's general argument, and do not contain Paribháshás of older grammarians.—These instances will illustrate the uncritical condition of the actual collections of Paribháshás. Some of these Paribháshás, moreover, are nothing else than Várttikas of Kátyáyana forming part of the discussion of the latter; they, too, are therefore not the oldest Paribháshás, since, as we have seen above (note 126) Kátyáyana quotes a Paribháshá which must have preceded his Várttikas. Such Paribháshá-Várttikas, which are commented upon by Patanjali in the same manner as the Várttikas—while he *generally* contents himself with merely quoting a Paribháshá rule—are, for instance, the P. to I, 1, 66: उभयनिर्देशे विप्रतिषेधात्पञ्चमीनिर्देशो; or to I. 1, 72: व्यपदेशिवद्भावो ऽप्रातिपदिकेन; or *ib.* पदाङ्गाधिकारे तस्य च तदुत्तरपदस्य च; or प्रत्ययग्रहणं चापञ्चम्याः, etc. Other Paribháshás of the Paribháshenduśekhara, etc., do not even represent the words of Patanjali, but merely the meaning of his general argu-

from the time at which he lived down to a period of linguistic development, which could not but find them defective in many respects.[131]

There is a material difference, therefore, between the Paribháshás contained in these collections, *when taken as a whole*, and the Paribháshás quoted by Patanjali; and no conclusion becomes safe until we know which Paribháshás are quotations made by Kátyáyana and Patanjali, and which belong to their authorship, or even to other and later works. It suffices for our present purpose to add, that neither the first Paribháshá already mentioned, which distinctly refers to Páṇini, nor the second, is a Paribháshá quoted by Patanjali or Kátyáyana.[132]

We are left, then, free to judge of the relative age of these axioms entirely from their contents, and to weigh the probabilities which decide whether they could all have been written after Páṇini or not. These probabilities strongly tend in favour of the latter alternative. For, however many of these *old* Paribháshás may have been additions made after Páṇini's,

---

ments; *e.g.*, the P. given at I. 2, 9, पर्जन्यवल्लक्षणप्रवृत्तिः, is the representative of the following words of the Bháshya: छतकारि खल्वपि शास्त्रं पर्जन्यवत् । तद्यथा । पर्जन्यो यावदूनं पूर्णं च सर्वमभिवर्षति, etc.; and other Paribháshás, again, so far as I was able to ascertain, do not occur at all in the Bháshya; *e.g.*, the P. at I. 1, 62. 63; II. 3, 46 (par. 2), etc.

[131] Such Paribháshás are, *e.g.*, समासान्तविधिरनित्यः, at VI. 2, 197, and the nine P. mentioned at III. 1, 79, by the Calcutta editors.

[132] The Paribháshá अकृतव्यूहाः पाणिनीयाः is mentioned in Kaiyyaṭa's gloss on the Bháshya to IV. 1, 82, but not by Patanjali. The P. पूर्वत्रासिद्धीयमद्विर्वचने is, in my opinion, a portion of Patanjali's own argument, when commenting on the 10th Várttika (of the Calcutta edition), to VIII. 1, 1, as results from the following quotation: . . . . पौनःपुन्यं पौनःपुनिक इति । अप्रातिपदिकत्वात्तद्धितोत्पत्तिर्न स्यात् । यदि तर्हि स्थाने द्विर्वचनं राजा वाकवाकपदस्येति (?) नलोपादीनि न सिध्यन्ति । इदमिह संप्रधार्यं द्विर्वचनं क्रियतां नलोपादीनीति । किमत्र कर्तव्यम् । परत्वान्नलोपादीनि पूर्वत्रासिद्धे नलोपादीनि सिद्धासिद्धयोश्च नास्ति संप्रधारणा । एवं तर्हि पूर्वत्रासिद्धीयमद्विर्वचन इति वक्ष्यामि etc. The same remark applies to the third Paribháshá mentioned in note 127; for the passage of the Bháshya to VII. 4, 2, whence this Paribháshá is taken, runs thus: तज्ज्ञापयत्याचार्यः । इत उत्तरं स्थानिवद्भावो न भवतीति । किमेतस्य ज्ञापने प्रयोजनं पूर्वत्रासिद्धे न स्थानिवदित्युक्तम । तन्न वक्तव्यं भवति etc.

though before Patanjali's, time, we still shall have to admit that without a *great number* of them, a *proper* application of his rules is absolutely impossible. Without them, many rules would become open to equivocations and doubts, nay, to such serious objections, that it is hardly possible to conceive a grammarian of the mould of Páṇini handing his work to his contemporaries in a condition so needlessly precarious, and so little creditable to his skill.[133] Nevertheless, if he had delivered his grammar entirely without any Paribhásha, we might still be free to assume, without inconsistency, that in doing so, he meant to leave to the acumen of

---

[133] Two instances will suffice to illustrate this character of what I consider to be the oldest Paribháshás. In the rule III. 1, 94, Páṇini teaches that if, in his chapter on kṛit-affixes, a subsequent rule supersedes a preceding rule, either of the kind of affixes enjoined by such rules may be at will employed in the formation of a kṛit-derivative, except when the affix enjoined is used exclusively in the feminine gender, and when the affixes in the preceding and subsequent rules are of *the same form*. Thus the Sútra III. I, 133, teaches that nouns denoting the agent are formed with the affixes *ṇwul* (= *aka*) and *tṛich* (= *tṛi*). Again, Sútra III. 1, 135, says that from *kship* and other radicals there named, such derivatives are formed with the affix *ka* (= *a*); hence, according to the Paribháshá-rule III. I, 94, the nouns of agent formed of *kship* may be *kshipa*, or *kshepa* or *ksheptṛi*, since none of these affixes is used exclusively in the feminine gender, and none has the same form as the two remaining ones. But when Páṇini rules, in III. 2, 3, that from *dá* a derivative may be formed *-da* (as latter part of compounds like *go-da*, etc.), and, in III. 3, 12, a derivative *-dáya* (as latter part of such compounds as *go-dáya*, etc.) it would become doubtful whether there be an option also in these instances, since the technical affix of the form *-da* is *ka*, and of the form *-dáya*, *aṇ*, and since it is not clear whether *ka* and *aṇ* could be considered as affixes of a different form, or—on account of their representing the real affix *a*, though with a different influence on the radical—as affixes of the same form. This doubt is not solved by Páṇini himself, but by a Paribháshá quoted by Patanjali, which says: नानुबन्धकृतमसारूप्यम्, "dissimilarity (of the affixes) is not produced by the mute *anubandhas*." And Páṇini must have supposed that his readers were acquainted with this Paribháshá; for otherwise, as an accurate writer, he could not—in the Sútra III. 1, 139—have treated, without any further explanation, the affixes *śa* (= *a*) and *ṇa* (= *a*) as similar affixes, and exempted them as such from the influence of the rule III. 1, 94.—Or when, in the Sútra VI. I, 48 (and VII. 3, 36), he says that the radical *i*, before the affix of the causal, becomes *áp*, his rule (VI. 4, 57) on *áp* would be equivocal, since the form *áp* may represent a simple radical, too,—unless he relied on the familiarity of his reader with the Paribháshá, which states: लक्षणप्रतिपदोक्तयोः प्रतिपदोक्तस्य, "(if there is a doubt) whether a secondary or a primitive form (be meant), the primitive form (has the precedence)."

his commentators the task of eliciting these general principles from his grammatical rules. But we know that such is not the case; his work bears evidence that he *has* given Paribháshá-rules,—axioms which are in no way more important than many of those which are met with in the Mahábháshya, but not in his work;—axioms which admit of the same arguments for or against their desirability or their indispensableness in a book of this kind. The omission of these rules, then, would not be one made on principle; it would assume the nature of a serious defect, unless we discovered a motive which would reconcile it with the accuracy that characterizes this great grammarian.

We have proof—and some will be afforded in the sequel—that Páṇini was not the *inventor* of the grammatical system preserved in his work, though he improved the system of his predecessors, and made his own additions to it. We shall see, moreover, that he availed himself of the technical means of the older grammarians, and, in such a case, never gave any explanation of those technicalities which must have been known to his contemporaries, and, therefore, required no remark. If, then, we supposed that he followed the same course with regard to the Paribháshá-rules—and there is no reason why he should not—our inference would, of necessity, be that he was compelled to give such Paribháshás as did not occur in the works of his predecessors, and were required as special axioms for his own work; but that, without exposing himself to the reproach of carelessness, he could omit all those Paribháshás which were already in existence, and were available, as well for the grammar of his predecessors as for his own.

And this conclusion is confirmed by the sense in which the term *Jnápaka* is used in the older commentaries, especially in the Mahabháshya itself, where by this name are called such rules of Páṇini as "indicate" or point to other rules which show how the former rules are to be applied properly. In commenting, for instance, on a Várttika to the Sútra I. 1, 23, which defines the technical term *sankhyá*, Patanjali asks, "how will there be in rules on *sankhyá* a correct understanding of this term?" and answers this question in the following manner: "(This understanding) results from the *Jnápaka*-rule. What is such a *Jnápaka*-rule? When Páṇini, in his Sútra V. 1, 23, teaches that bases formed with the affix *vat*, have an additional vowel *i* before the affix *ka* enjoined in the preceding rule for *sankhyás*,—is this Sútra V. 1, 23, the *Jnápaka*-rule of *sankhyá?* (*i.e.* does this Sútra indicate that bases formed with *vat* are comprised under the technical name *sankhyá?*) No. For the term *Jnápaka* concerns the application of a rule (*i.e.* this term is not used of a Sútra when its application is prohibited; the Sútras V. 2, 51 and 52, for instance, as Kaiyyaṭa observes, are *Jnápakas* of the Sútra on *sankhyá).*[134]

Hence, though a rule may stand in relation to another rule, it is not its *Jnápaka* unless it indicate its real purpose;[135]

---

[134] Várttika to I. 1, 23 (om. in the Calc. ed.; p. 432 ed. Ballantyne): वह्लादीनामग्रहणम्. *Patanjali:* बह्लादीनां ग्रहणं शक्यमकर्तुम्। केनेदानीं संख्याप्रदेशेषु संख्यासंप्रत्ययो भविष्यति। ज्ञापकात्सिद्धम्। ज्ञापकं किम्। यदयं वतोरिड्वेति (V. 1, 23) संख्याया विहितस्य कनो (comp. V. 1, 22) वत्वन्तादिटं शास्ति। वतोरेव तज्ज्ञापकं स्यात्। नेत्याह। योगापेक्षं ज्ञापकम्.—*Kaiyyaṭa:* ज्ञापकात्सिद्धमिति। एकादिवन्नियतसंख्यावाचित्वं बह्लादीनां नास्तीति ज्ञापकाश्रयः। योगापेक्षमिति। अस्य योगस्य प्रत्याख्यानादेतद्योगापेक्षमिति न बोद्धव्यम्। किं तु योगानपेक्षत इति योगापेक्षम्। यदयं बहुपूगगणसंघस्य तिथुक् (V. 2, 52) षड्कतीति (V. 2, 51) डतिपरत आगमं शास्ति तज्ज्ञापयति भवति संख्याकार्यमिति. Nágojibhaṭṭa explains: . . , . . योगापेक्षमिति। प्रयोगापेक्षमित्यर्थः.—This instance will suffice to illustrate the use of the word *jnápaka*, which is of constant occurrence in the Bháshya, and is always employed in a similar manner. In order to obviate an objection which might be raised by those not familiar with the Mahábháshya against my rendering वतोरेव तज्ज्ञापकं स्यात् "is this Sútra V. 1, 23," etc.,—I have to observe that Patanjali when quoting a Sútra, often merely mentions its principal word, instead of repeating the words of the Sútra and adding after them the quotational word इति. The word वतोः taken from the Sútra वतोरिड्वा is therefore here an equivalent of वतोरिड्वेति. Analogous instances will be found in note 136.

[135] Patanjali observes, for instance, in his comment on the first Śivasútra (p. 87 ed. Ballantyne): कथं ज्ञायते यदयम अ (VIII. 4, 68) इत्यकारस्य विवृतस्य संवृतताप्रत्यापत्तिं शास्ति। नैतदस्ति ज्ञापकम्। अस्ति ह्यन्यदेतस्य प्रयोजनम् etc.; or on the Várttika to I. 1, 56, आहिभुवोरीट्प्रतिषेधः, he observes (p. 633, ed. Ballantyne): आहिभुवोरीट्प्रतिषेधो वक्तव्यः। आत्थ। अभूत्। अस्ति ब्रूग्रहणेन ग्रहणादीट् प्राप्नोति। आहेस्ता-

and as Patanjali expressly and repeatedly states, a rule has the character of a Jnápaka only when it is given in reference to a rule already previously established, and when its sense becomes completed by it. Thus the Sútra III. 2, 97, says Patanjali, is no *Jnápaka* of the Guṇa-rule I. 1, 3, since the former rule does not become completed through the contents of the latter. Or, the Sútra VII. 2, 103 is not a *Jnápaka* of the rule VII. 2, 102, since its object would not be accomplished by the contents of this latter rule, though the words concerned by both rules are comprised under the term *sarvanáman.*[136] In consequence, a *Jnápaka* rule cannot precede, but must come after the rule which is indicated by it.

In now considering the relation which exists between the Jnápakas and the Paribháshá-Sútras,[137] we cannot but perceive that it nowise differs from the relation which exists between rules instanced before and ordinary rules indicated by these Jnápakas. In the same manner as there are Jnápaka-rules which indicate the purpose of other rules, there are Jnápaka-rules which indicate the purpose of Paribháshás, and all the Paribháshás given by Páṇini

---

वन्न वक्तव्यः। आचार्यप्रवृत्तिर्ज्ञापयति। नाहेरीड् भवतीति। यदयमाहस्थ इति (VIII. 2, 35) झलादिप्रकरणे षत्वं शास्ति। नैतदस्ति ज्ञापकम्। अस्ति ह्यन्यदेतस्य वचने प्रयोजनम्। किम्। भूतपूर्वगतिर्यथा विज्ञायेत। झलादिर्यो भूतपूर्व इति। यद्येवं षवचनमनर्थकं स्यात् etc.; and the like in other instances.

[136] Patanjali *e.g.* in his gloss on the Várttikas to *I.* 1. 3 (ed. Ballantyne, p. 248): . . . . यदप्युच्यते जनेर्डवचनं (III. 2, 97) ज्ञापकं न व्यञ्जनस्य गुणो भवतीति सिद्धे विधिरारभ्यमाणो ज्ञापकार्थो भवति। न च जनेर्गुणेन सिध्यति; on the last words of the third Káriká to VII. 2, 102: एवं तर्ह्याचार्यप्रवृत्तिर्ज्ञापयति न सर्वेषां त्यदादीनामत्वं भवतीति। यदयं किमः क इति (VII. 2, 103) कादेशं शास्ति। इतरथा हि किमो ऽद्भवतीत्येव ब्रूयात्। सिद्धे विधिरारभ्यमाणो ज्ञापकार्थो भवति। न च किमो ऽत्वेन सिध्यति.

[137] A Paribháshá is, on account of this relation, also called ज्ञाप्य. In his comment, for instance, to *I.* 4, 14, Patanjali says: अन्तग्रहणं किमर्थम्। न सुप्तिङन्तं पदमित्येवोच्यते केनेदानीं तदन्तानां भविष्यति। तदन्तविधिना। अत उत्तरं पठति.—Várttika: पदसंज्ञायामन्तवचनमन्यत्र संज्ञाविधौ प्रत्ययग्रहणे तदन्तविधिप्रतिषेधार्थं.—Patanjali. पदसंज्ञायामन्तग्रहणं क्रियते। किं ज्ञाप्यम्। एतज्ज्ञापयत्याचार्यः। अन्यत्र संज्ञाविधौ प्रत्ययग्रहणे तदन्तविधिर्न भवतीति etc. Compare note 126.

himself, therefore, precede their Jnápaka-rules. If, then, as we learn from Kátyáyana and Patanjali, there existed Paribháshás which are not contained in Páṇini's grammar, but which nevertheless are indicated by Jnápakas, which are Sútras of Páṇini, such Paribháshás must, at least in Patanjali's opinion, have existed before Páṇini's work; for otherwise the definition given by the Mahábháshya of the term *Jnápaka* would become inconsistent with itself. And since Paribháshás or principles of interpretation cannot be conceived without matter to be interpreted according to them, such Paribháshás must not only have preceded Páṇini, but they must have been taught in one or more other grammatical works; and Vaidyanátha, therefore, as I suggested above, cannot be correct in basing his distinction between *Nyáya* and *Jnápaka* on the circumstance that the latter refers to Páṇini exclusively, while the former applies also to other works. In all probability the difference is this: that *Jnápaka* is used especially of grammatical rules, while *Nyáya* is a synonyme of Paribháshá, but applies to writings which are not grammatical.

In now summing up the result we have obtained from the previous investigation, so far as it bears on our immediate problem, we find that the oldest author on record who wrote on Páṇini was Kátyáyana, and that he was not merely the author of the Várttikas, properly so called, but also of a certain number of Kárikás, which, in reality, however, are nothing else than an assemblage of single Várttikas, forming, combined, a stanza or a verse. We have seen, too, that Várttikas, which form an essential part of the Mahábháshya itself, are of Patanjali's authorship.

What, then, is the relation of Kátyáyana to Páṇini, and of Patanjali to Páṇini and to Kátyáyana? Is it that of commentators, or is it to be defined otherwise?

Professor Müller confers upon Kátyáyana the title of "editor" of Páṇini, and says that "the Great Commentary of Patanjali embraces both the Vârttikas of Kâtyâyana and the Sûtras of Pâṇini."[138] Professor Weber, on the contrary—who, even in some

[138] Ancient Sanskrit Literature, pp. 353 and 243.

of his latest writings, candidly confesses that he has never read the Mahábháshya, but nevertheless, or perhaps for this reason, abounds in conjectures on this work, which not only is in existence but within reach,—goes so far as to throw doubt on the genuineness of those Sútras which are not explained, *because* they are not explained, in the Great Commentary.[139] I fear that neither scholar will find adherents for his opinion amongst the pupils of Patanjali and Kátyáyana. The mutual relation of these latter grammarians and their relation to Páṇini is, indeed, implied by the word *Várttika*.

"The characteristic feature of a Várttika," says Nágojibhaṭṭa, "is criticism in regard to that which is omitted or imperfectly expressed in a Sútra."[140] A Várttika of Kátyáyana is therefore not a commentary which explains, but an animadversion which completes. In proposing to himself to write Várttikas on Páṇini, Kátyáyana did not mean to justify and to defend the rules of Páṇini, but to find fault with them; and whoever has gone through his work must avow that he has done so to his heart's content. He will even have to admit that Kátyáyana has frequently failed in justice to Páṇini, by twisting the words of the Sútras into a sense which they need not have, or by upbraiding Páṇini with

---

[139] For instance, in the *Indische Studien*, vol. IV., p. 78: "Die Plâxâs kommen in dem Schol. zu Pâṇini (IV. 1, 95; 2, 112) vor (ob aus dem Mahâbhâshya?);" or in a note to the same vol., p. 168, when referring to the Sútra VI. 2, 142 of Páṇini, he observes: "Allerdings: *bhâshye tu na vyâkhyâtam*, also unsicher, ob ihm gehörig." ["*Also*" —, on what basis does this conclusion rest? "*Unsicher*" —, for whom?] The same confession and the same conjecture occur, indeed, so often in Professor Weber's multifarious writings, that it becomes a matter of psychological curiosity to see how an author, apparently much concerned about a certain subject, instead of acquiring the necessary information—which in the present case could not have caused any great difficulty,—or of consulting at least some one who might have allayed his disquietude, constantly displays before the public his feelings and theories, whereas, by dint of a stereotyped repetition of the same words, he must convey to a confiding reader the impression that there may be some foundation, at least, for his would-be critical surmise.

[140] Nágojibhaṭṭa on Kaiyyaṭa to the first Várttika (of the Calc. ed.) of I. 1, 1 (ed. Ballantyne, p. 213): वार्त्तिकमिति । सूत्रे ऽनुक्तादुरुक्तचिन्ताकरत्वं वार्त्तिकत्वम्.

failings he was not guilty of. On this score he is not unfrequently rebuked by Patanjali, who on such occasions severely rates him for his ungenerous treatment of Páṇini, and, as we have seen in an instance above (p. 52), proves to him that he himself is wanting in proficiency, not Páṇini. Kátyáyana, in short, does not leave the impression of an admirer or friend of Páṇini, but that of an antagonist,—often, too, of an unfair antagonist. In consequence, his remarks are attached to those Sútras alone which are open to the censure of abstruseness or ambiguity, and the contents of which were liable to being completed or modified : he is silent on those which do not admit of criticism or rebuke.

The position of Patanjali is analogous, though not identical. Far from being a commentator on Páṇini, he also could more properly be called an author of Várttikas. But as he has two predecessors to deal with, instead of one,—and two predecessors, too, one of whom is an adversary of the other,—his Great Commentary undergoes, of necessity, the influence of the double task he has to perform, now of criticising Páṇini and then of animadverting upon Kátyáyana. Therefore, in order to show where he coincided with, or where he differed from, the criticisms of Kátyáyana, he had to write a comment on the Várttikas of this latter grammarian ; and thus the Mahábháshya became not only a commentary in the ordinary sense of the word, but also, as the case might be, a critical discussion, *on the Várttikas of Kátyáyana* ; while its *Ishṭis*, on the other hand, are original Várttikas on such Sútras of Páṇini as called for his own remarks.

I have already mentioned that Patanjali often refutes the strictures of Kátyáyana and takes the part of Páṇini ; I may now add that, in my opinion, and as a few instances hereafter will show, he sometimes overdoes his defence of Páṇini, and becomes unjust to Kátyáyana. It is easy, however, to understand the cause of this tendency in Patanjali. The spirit of independent thought, combined with the great acumen and consummate scholarship which pervade the work of this admirable grammarian—to whom, as far as my knowledge goes, only one author of the later literature bears a comparison, I mean the Mímánsá philosopher, Kumárila—

could not allow him to become a mere paraphraser of another's words. An author like Patanjali can only comment on the condition that, in doing so, he developes his own mind, be it as adherent or as antagonist. And since Kátyáyana had left but little chance for a successor to discover many more blemishes in the Grammar of Páṇini than he had pointed out, an active and critical mind like that of Patanjali would find more scope and more satisfaction in contending with Kátyáyana than in completing Páṇini; and thus, I hold, we may explain his proneness to weaken even those censures of Kátyáyana which we should see reason to approve, did we not discover in favour of Páṇini arguments which will appear hereafter, but which were foreign to Patanjali.

As little, therefore, as it entered into the purpose of Kátyáyana to advert to every Sútra of Páṇini, did it come within the aim of Patanjali to write a commentary on Páṇini, and, according to the requirements of such a commentary, to explain every rule of this grammarian. His object being, like that of Kátyáyana, merely a critical one, Patanjali comments upon the Várttikas of Kátyáyana, because such a comment of his implies, of necessity, criticisms, either on Páṇini or on Kátyáyana; and, in consequence, no Várttika could be left unnoticed by him. Again, independently of Kátyáyana, he writes his own Várttikas to Sútras not sufficiently or not at all animadverted upon by the latter grammarian, because they, too, are criticisms, viz., on Páṇini. And, like Kátyáyana, therefore, he passes over altogether all those Sútras which are unexceptionable to his mind. It is obvious, therefore, that no doubt whatever concerning the genuineness of a Sútra of Páṇini can be justified on the ground alone that it has no Bháshya of Patanjali; and the unsoundness of such a doubt becomes still more obvious when we consider that a great many Sútras of Páṇini, which have no Várttikas and no Bháshya of Patanjali, nevertheless make their appearance as quotations and as part of Patanjali's argument in his Commentary on other Sútras criticized by Kátyáyana.

Now, if we take a summary view of the labours of Kátyáyana, we find that of the 3993 or 3992 Sútras of Páṇini, more than 1500 offered him the opportunity of showing his superior skill; that his criticisms called forth more than 4000 Várttikas, which, at the lowest estimate, contain 10,000 special cases comprised in his remarks.

Having arrived at this point, let us ask—How could India resound with the fame of a work which was so imperfect as to contain at least 10,000 inaccuracies, omissions, and mistakes? Suppose that there existed in our days a work of 4000 paragraphs, every second or third of which not merely called for an emendation, an addition, and corrections, in formal respects, but which, on the whole, compelled us to draw the conclusion that there were twice and a half times as many blunders in it as it contained matter to be relied upon,—is it possible to assume that such a work could create a reputation for its author except one which no sensible man would be desirous of? If we assumed such a possibility, it could only be on the supposition that such an author originated the subject he brought before the public, and, as an inventor, had a special claim to indulgence and fame; or, on the supposition of public ignorance and individual immorality.

But there is evidence to show that Páṇini was not the first Hindu grammarian who wrote, nor even the inventor of the technical system which has caused so much uneasiness to would-be philologers. It is certain, too, that grammar was not, in ancient India, the esoteric study of the few; and there is no proof of any kind that Páṇini had influenced or hired a number of scribes to puff his Grammar and his fame. We must needs, therefore, resort to another explanation, if we want to reconcile the fact of the Várttikas with the fact of Páṇini's reputation, which was so great that supernatural agency was considered as having assisted him in his work.

This explanation, I hold, can only be derived from the circumstance that *Páṇini and Kátyáyana belonged to different periods of Hindu antiquity*,—periods separated by such a space of time as was sufficient to allow—

1. *Grammatical forms which were current in the time of Páṇini to become obsolete or even incorrect;*

2. *Words to assume meanings which they did not possess at the period when he lived;*

3. *Words and meanings of words used by him to become antiquated; and*

4. *A literature unknown to him to arise.*

It is on this supposition alone that it seems possible to realise Páṇini's influence and celebrity; of course, on the supposition, too, that in his time he gave so accurate, so complete, and so learned a record of the language he spoke, that his contemporaries, and the next ages which succeeded him, could look with admiration on the rules he uttered, as if they were founded on revelations from above. If he had bungled along, as he must appear to have done, had he been a contemporary of Kátyáyana,—not he, but the author of the Várttikas, would have been the inspired Ṛishi and the reputed father of the Vyákaraṇa. It is not necessary to exaggerate this view by assuming that Páṇini was an infallible author, who committed no mistakes, omitted no linguistic fact, and gave complete perfection to a system already in use: we need take no other view of the causes of his great success than we should take of those which produce the fame of a living man. His work may or may not have been looked upon by his contemporaries as having attained the summit of excellency, but, at all events, it must have ascended far beyond mediocrity. At its own period it cannot have failed so signally, and in so many respects, as it would have done if Páṇini and Kátyáyana had been contemporaries.

In order fully to substantiate this view, I should have to submit a considerable portion of Páṇini's Grammar and the Várttikas connected with it, to an investigation which would exceed by far the limits prescribed by the present inquiry; and such an investigation might, moreover, appear to be superfluous on the present occasion, since I shall adduce hereafter arguments of another kind, which will add materially to the force of these deductions. Yet the importance of this question is so great that I will indicate, at least by a few instances, the direction in which, I believe, the facts may be found that lead to the conclusions named.

1. Páṇini says (I. 2, 6) that the radical *indh* is *kit* in *liṭ*, which words mean that, according to rule VI. 4, 24, the preterit of *indh* is

ídhe. This radical he treats together with *bhú;* and he does not observe—as he always does if such be the case—that his rule concerns the Vaidik use of the preterit of *indh.* Yet Kátyáyana corrects the injunction of the Sútra by adding this restriction; and, for reasons connected with the latter, goes so far as to declare this Sútra of Páṇini to be superfluous.[141]

In rule VII. 1, 25, Páṇini states that the *sarvanámáni* (which word is usually but inaccurately rendered "pronouns") which are formed with the affixes *ḍatara*, and *ḍatama*,—moreover, *itara*, *anya*, and *anyatara* (Gaṇa to I. 1, 27) form their neuters not in *m*, but in *d*, e.g. *katarad*, *katamad*, *anyad*, etc.; but he says in a following special rule, that, in the Veda, *itara* has *itaram* for its neuter. It is obvious, therefore, that he intended to exhaust his subject by these rules; yet Kátyáyana has to state that "*ekatara* forms *ekataram* in the Veda as well as in the language of common life."[142]

The letters *k*, *t*, *ṭ*, *p*, at the end of a Pada, says Páṇini (VIII. 4, 45) may become *g*, *d*, *ḍ*, *b*, before a following nasal, or be changed into the nasal of their class. Kátyáyana adds: "If, however, the following nasal is part of an affix, these letters *must always* become the nasal of their class, *in the language of common life.*"[143]

Now I have chosen these instances from the sphere of conjugation, declension, and phonetic laws, simply because they at once suggest the question whether Páṇini knew as much grammar as

---

[141] I. 2, 6: इन्धिभवतिभ्यां च.—Várttika: इन्धेश्छन्दोविषयत्वाद्भुवो वुको नित्यत्वात्ताभ्यां किद्वचनानर्थक्यम्.—Bháshya: इन्धेश्छन्दोविषयो लिट्। न ह्यन्तरेण च्छन्द इन्धेरनन्तरो लिड् लभ्यः। आमा भाषायां भवितव्यम्। भुवो वुको नित्यत्वाद्भवतेरपि नित्यो वुक्कृते गुणे प्राप्नोति। अकृते ऽपि प्राप्नोति। ताभ्यां किद्वचनानर्थक्यम्। ताभ्यामिन्धिभवतिभ्यां किद्वचनमनर्थकम्. (The Calcutta editors have on this occasion mistaken Kátyáyana's Várttika for Patanjali's Bháshya).

[142] VII. 1, 26: नेतराच्छन्दसि.—Várttika: इतराच्छन्दसि प्रतिषेध एकतरात्सर्वत्र.

[143] VIII. 4, 45: यरो ऽनुनासिके ऽनुनासिको वा.—Várttika: यरो ऽनुनासिके प्रत्यये भाषायां नित्यवचनम्.—Bháshya: यरो ऽनुनासिके प्रत्यये भाषायां नित्यमिति वक्तव्यम्। वाङ्मयं त्वङ्मयम्.

we should fairly expect from a beginner, who had studied Sanskrit for a few months. Is it probable or not, that he was proficient enough to form the preterite of the common radical *indh*, "to kindle," the nominative of the neuter of *ekatara*, "one of two,"—a word which, moreover, is the subject of one of his special rules (V. 3, 94)? and was he really so ignorant as not to be able to combine *vák* or *twak*, with the common affix *maya* into *váṅgmaya* or *twangmaya*, though a phonetic influence of the affix *maya* on the base *hiraṇya* is adverted to in his rule VI. 4, 174? Or is it more plausible to assume that *ídhe* and *ekatarad* were forms current in his time, though no longer current and correct when Kátyáyana wrote; and that when Páṇini lived, *vágmaya* or *twagmaya* were as legitimate as *váṅgmaya* or *twaṅgmaya*? That Kátyáyana's stricture may be as much open to censure as the rule of Páṇini, unless we, in fairness, gave it the benefit of a similar argument, is proved by the words *kakudmat*, *kakudmin*, and *garutmat*, which "in the (classical) language of common life" are quite correct, but would have been incorrect according to the Várttika, if they had been used in such language at the time when it was composed.[144]

2. Páṇini says (VI. 1, 150), "the bird (*nominative*) may be *vishkira* or *vikira*" (either of which means any eatable bird but a cock). This rule is thus modified by Kátyáyana: "the form may be *vishkira* or *vikira* if the sense of the word is 'bird'" (*locative*). Patanjali, it is true, sides with Páṇini. The Várttika, he says, is irrelevant, since it teaches that either form *vishkira* or *vikira*, is correct, if the word means "bird," but that *vishkira* would be the only legitimate form, if the word has any other sense. Páṇini, however, he adds, did not mean to affect the sense "bird" by his optional "or," but the irregular form of the derivative.[145]

---

[144] It is not permitted to adduce also वाग्मिन्, for this word ought to be written—as, for instance, the commentators of the Amarakosha do write it—वाग्ग्मिन्, since its affix is not मिन् ,but ग्मिन्, according to Páṇini, V. 2, 124: वाचो ग्मिनिः. That in ग्मिनि the letter ग् is not an *anubandha*, results from I. 3, 8.

[145] VI. 1, 150: विष्किरः शकुनिर्विकिरो वा.—Várttika: विष्किरः शकुनौ विकिरो वेति वक्तव्यम्.—Bháshya: शकुनौ वेत्युच्यमाने शकुनौ या (वा?) स्यादन्यत्रापि नित्यम्।

Nevertheless, it appears to me that both grammarians are right, and that Patanjali's decision is open to doubt. Whenever Páṇini binds the application of a rule to the condition of a special sense, he expresses the latter by a word either in the locative or nominative. If he gives the meaning of the word in the locative it does not necessarily follow, though it usually happens to be the case, that such a word has other meanings, too, which are then excluded from the influence of the rule; but if he expresses the sense of the word in the nominative, he seems always to indicate that the word has this sense, and this sense only,—that both sense and word, being expressed in the same case, are, as it were, congruous.[146] His present rule would therefore imply that each form, *vishkira* or *vikira*, has no other sense than that of "bird;" but Kátyáyana's corrections would mean that both forms are optional in the sense of "bird," while in any other sense both forms represent separate words. This fact is borne out by the meanings given in Wilson's Dictionary under each form.

The word *áścharya* is rendered by Páṇini *anitya* (VI. 1, 147), *i.e.* "not permanent, rare." Kátyáyana corrects this meaning, in substituting for it *adbhuta*, *i.e.* "that which has not existed before, miraculous, wonderful." On this occasion, too, Patanjali defends Páṇini, by observing that this remark might have been spared, for the sense, "wonderful, miraculous," is implied by the sense "rare;" and he gives instances to confirm this view, viz., "the height of (this) tree is something 'rare' (or wonderful); the blueness of the sky is something 'rare' (or wonderful);" but I very much doubt whether logicians will assent to this view of Patanjali; for, though all that is wonderful is rare, not all that is rare need be wonderful. And he himself seems to break down under his third instance, which runs thus: "That the stars which are not fastened in the

---

तत्तर्हि वक्तव्यम्। न वक्तव्यम्। न वाvचनेन शकुनिरभिसंबध्यते किं तर्हि निपातनमभिसंबध्यते विष्किर इत्येतन्निपातनं शकुनौ वा निपात्यत इति.

[146] Compare *e.g.* III. 3, 80. 81. 87; V. 2, 15; VI. I, 149 (the meanings 2 and 3 of अपस्कर, in my Dictionary, are of later origin); VI. 1, 155. 156, etc.

atmosphere do not fall down, is"—surely not rare, but wonderful.[147] In other terms, the meaning of *áścharya*, given by Paṇini, seems to have been only "rare;" and if so, it preceded that which became more usual at a later time, and is mentioned by Kátyáyana.

Another and, perhaps, more striking instance is afforded by the Sútra (VII. 3, 69) where Páṇini renders the word *bhojya* by *bhakshya;* for Kátyáyana corrects him in saying that he ought to have rendered *bhojya* by *abhyavahárya.* Now, if we consult the use of these words in the classical language, there can be no doubt that *bhojya* and *abhyavahárya* mean "what is fit for consumption," and apply to solid as well as to liquid substances; that, on the other hand, *bhakshya* means "what is fit to be eaten," and applies to solid food only. Is it likely, however, that Paṇini should have blundered in the application of words which, it would seem, the most ignorant would employ properly? Patanjali, who, as I have already observed, is always disposed to stand by Páṇini, again takes up his defence, and observes, that Páṇini's using the word *bhakshya* instead of *abhyavahárya* need not have been criticised by Kátyáyana, for there are expressions like *ab-bhaksha*, "one who eats water," or *váyu-bhaksha*, "one who eats air," which show that the radical *bhaksh* is used also in reference to other than solid food.[148]

---

[147] VI. I, 147: **आश्चर्यमनित्ये**.—Várttika (misedited in the Calc. ed.): **आश्चर्यमद्भुत इति वक्तव्यम्**.—Bháshya: **इहापि यथा स्यात्। आश्चर्यमुच्चता वृक्षस्य। आश्चर्यं नीला द्यौः। आश्चर्यमन्तरिक्षेऽबन्धनानि नक्षत्राणि न पतन्तीति। तत्तर्हि वक्तव्यम्। न वक्तव्यम्। अनित्य इत्येव सिद्धम्। इह तावदाश्चर्यमुच्चता वृक्षस्येति। आश्चर्यग्रहणेन न वृक्षोऽभिसंबध्यते किं तर्ह्युच्चता सा चानित्या। आश्चर्यं नीला द्यौरिति नाश्चर्यग्रहणेन द्यौरभिसंबध्यते किं तर्हि नीलता सा चानित्या। आश्चर्यमन्तरिक्षेऽबन्धनानि नक्षत्राणि न पतन्तीति नाश्चर्यग्रहणेन नक्षत्राण्यभिसंबध्यन्ते किं तर्हि पतनक्रिया सा चानित्या। तच्चानित्य इत्येव सिद्धम्**.

[148] VII. 3, 69: **भोज्यं भक्ष्ये**.—Várttika: **भोज्यमभ्यवहार्यमिति वक्तव्यम्** (where the nominative of **अभ्यवहार्य** implies an additional criticism against the locative of **भक्ष्य**; see the foregoing remark, page 126).—Bháshya: **इहापि यथा स्यात्। भोज्यः सूपः। भोज्या यवागूरिति। किं पुनः कारणं न सिध्यति। भक्षिरयं खरविशदे वर्तते तेन द्रवे न प्राप्नोति। नावश्यं भक्षिः खरविशदे वर्तते किं तर्ह्यन्यत्रापि वर्तते। तद्यथा। अब्भक्षो वायुभक्ष इति**.

But both instances alleged by Patanjali are conventional terms; they imply a condition of fasting, and derive their citizenship amongst other *classical* words from a Vaidik expression, as Patanjali himself admits, when, in his introduction to Páṇini, he speaks of *ekapadas*, or words, the sense of which can only be established from the context of a Vaidik passage to which they originally belong;[149] they do not show, therefore, that *bhaksh* is applied also to other phrases of the classical language, so as to refer to liquid food. It seems evident, therefore, that in Páṇini's time, which preceded the classical epoch, *bhakshya* must have been used as a convertible term for *bhojya;* while, at Kátyáyana's period, this rendering became incorrect, and required the substitution of another word.

3. The words and the meanings of words employed by Kátyáyana are such as we meet with in the scientific writers of the classical literature: his expressions would not invite any special attention nor call forth any special remark. This cannot be said of the language of Páṇini. In his Sútras occur a great number of words and meanings of words, which—so far as my own knowledge goes—have become antiquated in the classical literature. I will mention, for instance, *pratyavasána*, eating (I. 4. 52; III. 4. 76); *upasamváda*, making a bargain (III. 4. 8); *ṛishi*, in the sense of Veda, or Vaidik hymn (IV. 4. 96); *utsanjana*, throwing up (I. 3. 36); *vyaya*, application, employment in (I. 3. 36); *upasambhásha*, talking over, reconciling (I. 3. 47); *svakaraṇa*, appropriating, especially a wife, marrying (I. 3. 56); *śálínîkaraṇa*, humbling (I. 3. 70); *mati*, desire (III. 2. 188); *abhresha*, propriety (III. 3. 37); *avaklṛipti*, imagining (III. 3. 145); *abhyádána*, commencement (VIII. 2. 87); *hotrá*, in the sense of *ṛitwij*, priest (V. 1. 135); *upájekṛi* and *anwájekṛi*, to strengthen (I. 4. 73); *nivachanekṛi*, to hold one's speech, to be silent (I. 4. 76); *kaṇehan* and *manohan*, to fulfil one's longing (I. 4. 66), etc. etc.[150]

---

[149] For the quotation from Patanjali's preface to Páṇini (ed. Ballantyne, p. 46) see my Dictionary, s.v. अभ्यवहार्य.

[150] Some of these expressions, or others belonging to the same category, occur also

4. To prove a negative, is, no doubt, the hardest of all problems. There are circumstances, however, which may lessen the danger of drawing the conclusion that an author cannot have possessed such and such knowledge when he wrote. If we take into account the evidence afforded by the author's character and work, the judgment passed on his writings by his countrymen, and the condition of the latter,—these elements put together into the scale of criticism will show whether the scale of the author's proficiency can spare, or not, a certain amount of weight without disturbing the balance required. That Páṇini was an eminent writer, is not only manifest from his Grammar, but acknowledged by the common judgment of his countrymen; and the learning and civilization of ancient India was such that we must admit the fullest competence in those who established his celebrity. But we know, too, that Páṇini was a Brahmanic writer. No amount of scholarship could have ensured to him the position he holds in the ancient literature if he had been a professor of the Buddhistic creed. In forming, then, an opinion on Páṇini we must always bear in mind his learning and his religious faith, and the consequences which follow from both these premises.

After these preliminary remarks I will first advert to the Sútra (IV. 2. 129) in which Páṇini teaches the formation of the word *Áraṇyaka*, and says that it means "a man who lives in a forest." That *Áraṇyaka* has this meaning is unquestionable. It means, too, if we consult the lexicographers, "a forest-road, a forest-elephant, a jackall, etc.;" but above all it is the name of those theosophical works which are the precursors of the Upanishads, and are held in the greatest awe by the Hindu authorities.[151] If a learned Hindu were

---

in the Koshas, and in the artificial poetry, especially the Bhaṭṭi-kávya. This circumstance, however, does not disprove that they are obsolete in the real literature, since the Koshas have borrowed them from Páṇini, whereas the Bhaṭṭi-kávya is expressly written to illustrate the rules of Páṇini, and the artificial poetry bases its chief merits on the strangeness of its style and words.

[151] Manu, IV. 123, for instance, applies the same injunction to the termination of a lecture of an Áraṇyaka as to that of a whole Veda: सामध्वनावृग्यजुषी नाधीयीत कदाचन । वेदस्याधीत्य वाप्यन्तमारण्यकमधीत्य च.

asked the meaning of *Áraṇyaka*, he would certainly first point to the sacred works which bear this name, and then refer to the meaning "forester," just as, I suppose, a European questioned on the sense of the word "Bible," would first say that it means "Testament," and then remember its etymological sense, "book." Yet Páṇini merely speaks of *Áraṇyaka*, "the forester." No wonder that Kátyáyana supplies, in a Várttika of his, the defect which must have struck him if, and since, he was acquainted with this portion of the sacred literature.[152] But is it possible to assume that Páṇini could have known this sense of the word *Áraṇyaka*, when he is altogether silent on it; and if he did not know it, that the works so called could have already existed in his time?

The acquaintance of Páṇini with a Yajurveda is evidenced by several Sútras of his.[153] But in speaking of a Yajurveda, he does not tell us whether he knew the *Black* as well as the *White* version, or only the *Black* version of it. That the former, which is considered as the literary property of the *Tittiri* school, is older in form and contents than the latter, the *Vájasaneyi-Samhitá*, requires no observation of mine, after the conclusive proofs which have been given by previous writers. To decide, however, whether Páṇini had a knowledge of the Vájasaneyi-Samhitá or not,—in other words, whether both versions of

---

[152] Páṇini, IV. 2, 129: अरण्यान्मनुष्ये.—Patanjali: अत्यल्पमिदमुच्यते मनुष्य इति.—Kátyáyana: पथ्यध्यायन्यायविहारमनुष्यहस्तिष्विति वक्तव्यम्.—Patanjali: आरण्यकः पन्थाः। आरण्यको ऽध्यायः। आरण्यको न्यायः। आरण्यको विहारः। आरण्यको मनुष्यः। आरण्यको हस्ती.—Kátyáyana: वा गोमयेषु.—Patanjali: वा गोमयेष्विति वक्तव्यम्। आरण्यका गोमयाः। आरण्या गोमयाः. (Both Várttikas are marked in the Calcutta edition, as if they did only occur in the Siddhanta-kaumudí). Professor Müller has pointed out that Páṇini does not mention the principal meaning of *Áraṇyaka*, but expresses himself thus (page 339): "Whether Pâṇini knew the Âraṇyakas as a branch of sacred literature is uncertain. Although he mentions the word 'âraṇyaka,' he only uses it in the sense of 'living in the forest;' and it is the author of the Vârttikas who first remarks that the same word is also used in the sense of 'read in the forest.'"

[153] For instance, by the Sútras II. 4, 4 (*adhwaryu*); VI. 1. 117; VII. 4, 38; VIII. 3, 104, etc.

this Veda are separated in time or not, by the Grammar of Páṇini, is a matter which touches closely on our present inquiry with regard to the chronological relation between Páṇini and Kátyáyana.

In mustering the facts which bear on the solution of this question, we shall have, first, to observe that the word *Vájasaneyin* does not occur in a Sútra of, but only as a formation in a *Gaṇa* to, Páṇini (IV. 3. 106), while the formation of *Taittiríya*, from the base *Tittiri*, is taught in a Sútra (IV. 3. 102). There is, consequently, a *primâ facie* doubt against Páṇini's acquaintance with the Vájasaneyi-Samhitá.[154] And this doubt is heightened by the circumstance that the sacred personage, also, who is believed to have collected not only the Samhitá, but the Bráhmaṇa of the White Yajurveda, *Yájnavalkya*, is also not mentioned in the Sútras of, but merely in the Gaṇas to, Páṇini.[155]

Since the question, however, whether Páṇini knew the Vájasaneyi-Samhitá, coincides with the question whether he had a knowledge of the Śatapatha-Bráhmaṇa, I will first quote a passage from Professor Müller's work, which, in a correct and lucid manner, describes the relation of Yájnavalkya to both these works:—"A comparison," he says (p. 353), "of the texts of the Taittirîyas and Vâjasaneyins shows that it would be a mistake to call Yâjnavalkya the author, in our sense of the word, of the Vâjasaneyi-sanhitâ and the Śatapatha-brâhmaṇa. But we have no reason to doubt that it was Yâjnavalkya who brought the ancient Mantras and Brâhmaṇas into their present form, and, considering the differences

[154] Professor Weber has already drawn attention to the fact that in the *Gaṇas* to Páṇini only the first word may safely be ascribed to the knowledge of Páṇini, since it is mentioned by himself; and I may add, those words of a Gaṇa, too, which are impliedly referred to by him; for instance, डतर, डतम, इतर, अन्य, अन्यतर, of the Gaṇa to I. 1, 27, adverted to in the Sútra VII. 1, 25, which otherwise would be unintelligible. See also note 55. With these exceptions, we have no real certainty of deciding whether the words of a Gaṇa were those which Páṇini had in view when he wrote; for not only are there considerable differences in the readings of the Gaṇa collections in existence, but it is certain that these lists have been subject, at various periods, to various interpolations, which materially lessen their critical worth.

[155] In the Gaṇas to IV. 1, 105 and 2, 111.

between the old and new text, we must admit that he had a greater right to be called an author than the founders of the Charaṇas of other Vedas whose texts we possess. In this sense, Kâtyâyana says, in his Anukramaṇî, that Yâjnavalkya received the Yajur-veda from the Sun. In the same sense, the Śatapatha-brâhmaṇa ends with the assertion that the White Yajur-veda was proclaimed by Yâjnavalkya Vâjasaneya."

If, then, we turn our attention to the word *Śatapatha*, we have again to state that it occurs only in a Gaṇa to V. 3, 100 (compare also note 105), but is not mentioned authentically in any Sútra of Páṇini. Yet Kátyáyana, I hold, has helped us to untie this knot, which has been drawn still tighter than it was by Professors Müller and Weber, in spite of the excellent counsel which the latter gives, "not to increase, by inattention, the darkness, which is great enough already in the history of Sanskrit literature."[156]

A rule of Páṇini's, which, literally translated, runs thus, "*amongst the Bráhmaṇas and Kalpas which have been proclaimed by an Old one* (*or by the Old*),"[157] teaches, in its connection with preceding rules, that names of Bráhmaṇas and Kalpas are formed by adding the (technical) affix *ṇini* (*i.e.* the real affix *in* with Vṛiddhi in the base), to the proper name of the personage who proclaimed them, provided that such a personage is an *old* authority. Kaiyyaṭa gives as an instance of a Bráhmaṇa so formed, the word *Śáṭyáyanin*, derived from *Śáṭyáyana*, the saint who proclaimed this Bráhmaṇa; and other instances are mentioned by Patanjali in his comment on a previous Sútra. To this rule *Kátyáyana* added a Várttika, which, according to the text in the Calcutta edition, would mean literally: "*In reference to Yájnavalkya and so on* (*there is*) *an exception, on account of the contemporaneous-*

---

[156] Indische Studien, vol. I., p. 483: "We have already darkness enough in the history of Hindu literature; let us abstain at least from increasing it through our own inattention!"

[157] IV. 3, 105: पुराणप्रोक्तेषु ब्राह्मणकल्पेषु, which words are completed by the Sútras IV. 3, 101 and 103.

ness;"[158] and the comment on this additional rule is afforded by Patanjali, in the instance he gives: *Yájnavalkáni Bráhmaṇáni*, where the Bráhmaṇa referred to the authorship of Yájnavalkya, is not formed by means of the (technical) affix *ṇini*, but by the (technical) affix *aṇ* (i.e. *a*, with Vṛiddhi in the base).

The great importance of this additional rule of Kátyáyana is obvious. It has been made the subject of several remarks in the "Indische Studien," where Professor Weber writes (vol. i. p. 57, *note*):—"By the Yâjnavalkâni-brâhmaṇâni [*Yâjnavalkyâni*, as the "Indische Studien" writes it, is probably an error of the press] there [*i.e.* in the commentary of the Calcutta edition to IV. 3, 105], *and also in the Vârtika*, and in IV. 2. 66, there can probably be meant none but the Çatapatha-brâhmaṇa, either the whole of it, or from XI. to XIV., which, therefore, Patanjali even did not consider as purâṇa-proktam [*i.e.* proclaimed by an old authority]." Again (vol. i. p. 146), "A matter of importance is the distinct separation of Brâhmaṇas composed by the *Old* (purâṇa) IV. 3. 105, by which [expression], in contradistinction, the existence also of such as belong to a more recent time (tulyakâlâni, says the Vârtika) is necessarily implied; amongst the latter, recent ones, the Yâjnavalkâni [the repeated error of the press, "*Yâjnavalkyâni*," becomes suspicious] (comp. p. 57, *note*), and the Saulabhâni (otherwise unknown) Brâhmanâṇi are mentioned in the Vârtika; amongst the old ones, the scholiast there, (is it on Patanjali's authority?[159]) names the Bhâllavinaḥ and the Çâṭyâya-

[158] Várttika of the Calcutta edition to IV. 3, 105: याज्ञवल्क्यादिभ्यः प्रतिषेधस्तुल्यकालत्वात्.

[159] For this query of Professor Weber, compare note 139. But I cannot help asking how he reconciles the statement of the note to vol. I. p. 57, just quoted, where he speaks of Patanjali in terms of that assurance which can only proceed from personal knowledge,—with his repeated avowal of not having read the Mahábháshya, and with the text itself of p. 57 to which this note refers, since he is doubtful even there whether the Calcutta editors have taken their instances to IV. 3, 105 from Patanjali or not? As a guess, his attributing the words याज्ञवल्कानि ब्राह्मणानि to Patanjali happens to be quite correct; but it would have been certainly much better to give it distinctly as such, than leave us doubtful now as to the nature of other statements of his.

ninaḥ." And (vol. i. p. 177, *note*):—"Now we have seen (pp. 57 *note*, and 146) that the Yâjnavalkâni-brâhmaṇâni ["Yâjnavalkyâni" again, which now becomes very suspicious], are considered by the author of the Vârttikas as *contemporaneous* with Pâṇini. The question, therefore, is whether by it [*i.e.* the Yájnavalkáni-bráhmaṇáṇi] we have really to understand the Çatapatha-brâhmaṇa itself, or, in general, Brâhmaṇas only, which were *composed* by Yâjnavalkya, or such as merely *treated* of him. In the former case, it would follow, too, from his proved contemporaneousness with Uddâlaka, and from Uddâlaka's preceding Pâṇḍu, that the epoch of Pâṇḍu is later than that of Pâṇini." But (vol. ii. p. 393) he observes: "By the Yâjnavalkâni-brâhmaṇâni[160] we, probably, have not to understand those [Bráhmaṇas] which have been *composed* by Yâjnavalkya himself, but those which merely *treated* of him; and a specimen of these is preserved us in the Yâjnavalkîyam-kâṇḍam of the Vṛihadaraṇyaka (see my Akad. Vorles. p. 125-26); therefore, if this [my] second view is correct, the contemporaneousness of Yâjnavalkya and Uddâlaka with Pâṇini, which is the necessary consequence of my first view, would fall to the ground, together with Pâṇini's preceding Páṇḍu, whose priority in time is again the consequence of such a contemporaneousness."[161]

There is nothing novel or remarkable in the circumstance of

---

[160] Professor Weber again writes "*Yájnavalkyâni.*" Being compelled, therefore, to abandon the hypothesis of an error of the press, the more so as the same "*Yájnavalkyâni-bráhmaṇâni*" make their reappearance, in their *alphabetical place*, in his Index to the first two volumes of the "Indische Studien"—I must refer him for the correct form "*Yájnavalkáni*," to Páṇini VI. 4, 151.—It is needless for me to say that the "*editor*" of Páṇini likewise writes याज्ञवल्क्यानि IV. 2, 66 and 3, 105, intending probably to improve on the Calcutta edition, which IV. 3, 105 writes याज्ञवल्कानि, but IV. 2, 66 याज्ञवल्क्यानि. *Habent sua fata libelli!*

[161] The self-quotation of Professor Weber (Akad. Vorles. p. 125, 126) need not be repeated here, since it merely contains the same conjecture that the *Yájnavalkáni* (correctly written in the Akad. Vorles., but re-quoted from this work "*Yájnavalkyâni*" in the Ind. Stud. vol. II. p. 390) *bráhmaṇáni* are the same as the *Yájnavalkíyam-káṇḍam* which *treats of* Yájnavalkya.—The text of the quotations given above, it is superfluous for me to mention, is in German. To save space I have confined myself to communicating merely a translation of it, which, I trust, no one will find wanting in strictest

Professor Weber's recanting on one page what he maintained with the most specious arguments on another, or of his leaving the bewildered reader between a chaos of what are to him established facts; but however interesting it may be thus to obtain from him an autobiography of his mind, and an insight into the state of maturity in which he presents us with his researches, I must, this time, defend him against himself, and show that, *within the sphere of his own presumptive facts*, there is not the slightest ground for immolating by his last conjecture the statements contained in the first three quotations from his essays.

The exception made by Kátyáyana to the rule of Páṇini (IV. 3, 105) is contained in the word *Yájnavalka*, as we learn from the authentic comment of Patanjali. There is no proof, whatever, that it can extend to any other derivative of Yájnavalkya. Whatever, therefore, be the import of the word *Yájnavalkíya*, the *Yájnavalkíyam káṇḍam* has nothing to do with the *Yájnavalkáni bráhmaṇáni* mentioned by Patanjali in reference to our Várttika. But, in the second instance, the word *pratishedha*, or "exception," used by Kátyáyana necessarily concerns works of the *same category*. As little as an author could, for instance, call geology an exception to astronomy, as little, I hold, could Kátyáyana speak of an "*exception*" to names of Bráhmaṇas when he had in his mind, as Professor Weber thinks, the name of a particular chapter of an Áraṇyaka. And thirdly, this same word 'exception' in the Várttika must likewise concern the *proclaiming* of such a work by the personage who becomes the base of the derivative; for Páṇini uses the word *prokta* "proclaimed," distinctly enough in the Sútra which is criticized by the Várttika. There would be no "*exception*," if the formation alluded to by Kátyáyana, meant a work "*treating of*" the personage who is the base of the derivative. But, when Professor Weber, in his "Akademische Vorlesungen" (pp. 125, 126) crowns his syllogism by the remark that he prefers his last conjecture because it "appears, indeed, extremely ticklish (bedenk-

fairness and literal accuracy. The words between brackets, marked [ ], are my own parenthetical explanations, as the reader will easily see for himself. The italics in the quotation are Professor Weber's own.

lich)" to him "to consider the whole Çatapathabrâhmaṇa or as much as its last books, as bearing distinctly the name of Yâjnavalkya —however much it may contain his system [?]—or as contemporaneous with, or as preceding even by little, Pâṇini's time;" and when he adds, in the fulness of his authority, "but for the Yâjnavalkîyam-kâṇḍam I have not the slightest hesitation in doing the latter" [*Letzteres zu thun*,—what *latter ?*], I fear I should overstep the limits of *scientific* criticism, if I attached a single remark to a passage like this, which treats its readers as if the personal feelings of Professor Weber had all the weight of scientific arguments, and deals with one of the most important problems of Sanskrit literature in such a manner as if it were matter for table talk.

Before I proceed in my observations on the point at issue, I will state the views of Professor Müller on this Várttika. He writes (p. 353): "In the same sense Pâṇini, or rather his editor, says in the first Vârttika to IV. 3, 105, that there were modern Brâhmaṇas proclaimed by Yâjnavalkya, and that their title differed by its formation from the title given to more ancient Brâhmaṇas;" and (p. 363): "It is wrong, for instance, to speak of the Yâjnavalkyâs in the same sense as we speak of the Taittirîyas, and the works promulgated by Yâjnavalkya, although they are Brâhmaṇas, are called Yâjnavalkyâni [*sic*] Brâhmaṇâni. 'And why?' says Kâtyâyana; 'because they are of too recent an origin; that is to say, they are almost contemporaneous with ourselves.'"

Where, I must now ask, does Kátyáyana speak of Bráhmaṇas "*more* ancient" than the Bráhmaṇas proclaimed by Yájnavalkya? and where, I must further ask, does he say that the latter are "*almost*" contemporaneous? Again, what proof has Professor Weber that Kátyáyana meant by contemporaneous, as he says (see above, p. 134), *contemporaneous wi'h Pâṇini?* and what proof has Professor Müller that Kátyáyana implied by this word, *contemporaneous with himself?* Assuredly, all these questions ought to have been settled first, and by very substantial proofs, before an edifice of chronology was allowed to be built on them. Not only does Kátyáyana nowhere indicate a *degree*, either in the relative age of the Bráhmaṇas of Yájnavalkya and those subject to the

Sútra of Páṇini, or in the contemporaneousness of the former with him,—but, in my opinion, the word *pratishedha*, "*exception*," already adverted to, is altogether fatal to the ellipsis supplied by Professors Weber and Müller when they refer to the word *contemporaneous*. This word "*exception*" clearly proves that Kátyáyana could never have held the dialogue with which Müller enlivens the scene of the Várttika. For if the Bráhmaṇas spoken of in the Várttika, were contemporaneous with Páṇini or with Kátyáyana, the Várttika would have made an *addition*, not an *exception* to the rule of Páṇini, since the latter merely treats of such Bráhmaṇas as are *old* from his point of view, and is no wise concerned with any Bráhmaṇas of *his* time.

In short, the Várttika can, on account of the word *exception*, convey no other sense than that Páṇini himself was guilty of an inaccuracy, by omitting to state that the Bráhmaṇas which had been proclaimed by Yájnavalkya (and others) were exempt from his Sútra IV. 3, 105, *these Bráhmaṇas being as old as those which he had in view when he gave this rule.*

Did the words of the Várttika, such as they are printed in the Calcutta edition, admit of the slightest doubt—if interpreted properly,—or had the inferences drawn from them been propounded with less consequence, and did not the discussion I have raised concern a principle, viz. the method of examining the relation of Kátyáyana to Páṇini, the course I should have taken, in refuting the opinion of Professors Weber and Müller would have been a different one. I should have at once stated the fact, that the inadvertence of the Calcutta editors of Páṇini—(need I repeat that Dr. Boehtlingk's reprint is as conscientious in this case as in all analogous instances?)—has skipped *two words* which belong to the Várttika,—words, which, indeed, are not absolutely required for a correct understanding of the Várttika, but the presence of which would have prevented as much as the possibility of a misconception, however inattentive the reader of the Várttika might be. These words are no other than the words of Páṇini's Sútra itself, which Kátyáyana, no doubt with the distinct purpose of obviating the very possibility of a misunderstanding, has embodied again in his Várttika in placing them before his own critical remark. In short, the Várttika runs thus: "Among the Bráhmaṇas and Kalpas, which are proclaimed by an *old* one (or by the *old*), there is an exception in reference to Yájnavalkya, on account of the contemporaneousness," viz., *of these latter Bráhmaṇas with the old Bráhmaṇas spoken of by Páṇini.* In this sense, then, Patanjali remarks, after having named the Bráhmaṇas of Yájnavalkya and Sulabha, "Why (is there an exception to these?) 'On account of the contemporaneousness;' that is to say, because they, *too*, are of the same time;" and Kaiyyaṭa adds: '*because they belong to the same time as the Bráhmaṇas proclaimed by Śáṭyáyana, and so on.*'"[162]

The ground on which we now stand is once more the ground we have occupied before. And when I previously asked whether it is likely that Páṇini could have blundered in conjugating or declining a common word, or whether he was not proficient enough to use the expression "eatable," or whether he could have ignored the meaning of Áraṇyaka,—I must now add the question whether he was likely to give a rule which, by an essential omission, would have vitiated the name of a principal Bráhmaṇa? Could he have ignored that name which stands foremost amongst all the authors

---

[162] Páṇini, IV. 3, 105: पुराणप्रोक्तेषु ब्राह्मणकल्पेषु.—Kátyáyana: पुराणप्रोक्तेषु ब्राह्मणकल्पेषु याज्ञवल्क्यादिभ्यः प्रतिषेधस्तुल्यकालत्वात्.—Patanjali: पुराणप्रोक्तेष्वित्यत्र याज्ञवल्क्यादिभ्यः प्रतिषेधो वक्तव्यः। याज्ञवल्कानि ब्राह्मणानि। सौलभानीति। किं कारणम्। तुल्यकालत्वात्। एतान्यपि तुल्यकालानीति.—Kaiyyaṭa: तुल्यकालत्वादिति। शाट्यायनादिप्रोक्तैर्ब्राह्मणैरेककालत्वादित्यर्थः. For the sake of greater clearness, and in order to anticipate any objection, I will mention, that the Sútra of Páṇini itself precedes the words of the Várttika in the MS. E.I.H. 330, whence this passage is quoted; so that there can be no assumption of a meaningless or careless repetition of the words पुराणप्रोक्तेषु ब्राह्मणकल्पेषु. Moreover, the beginning of Patanjali's commentary on the Várttika, and his method of commenting, as explained above, is sufficient to remove all doubt—if any still existed—that they belong to the Várttika.—Professor Benfey, too, is therefore mistaken, when, in his learned and valuable "*Vollständige Grammatik der Sanskritsprache*" (§ 518) he says, "it has been explicitly stated [viz. by our Várttika] that Yâjnavalkya and some others do not belong to the *old*."

of Bráhmaṇas? So much so, that we have heard only by name of the Bráhmaṇas of Bhallu, Śáṭyáyana, and Sulabha; but are full of the Śatapatha-bráhmaṇa, proclaimed by Yájnavalkya?

In my belief there is but this alternative: either Patanjali, who mentions the Bhállavins, together with other Bráhmaṇas, in his comment on the Várttika 26 to IV. 2, 104, is correct in saying that the Bráhmaṇa of Yájnavalkya is coeval with them, in this case all these Bráhmaṇas must have been unknown to Páṇini, and other Bráhmaṇas must have been before his mind's eye, when he wrote the Sútra IV. 3, 105; or Páṇini *did* know and *meant* to imply in his rule the Bráhmaṇa of Bhallu, and of others named by Patanjali,—then the error must be on Patanjali's side, when he asserts that Yájnavalkya was their contemporary. I say purposely, it must be an error of Patanjali, for there is no evidence to show that Kátyáyana alluded to *Bhallu*, for instance, when he speaks of contemporaries of Yájnavalkya; he may have referred, for aught we know, to proper names belonging to other old authorities—old from Páṇini's point of view; and his error would then have consisted in making Yájnavalkya the contemporary of the personages who were the authors of those old works.

Yet both—the error of Patanjali and the error of Kátyáyana—become explainable on the assumption that there is *such a considerable period of time between Páṇini and Kátyáyana, and much more so between Páṇini and Patanjali* that Kátyáyana even could consider as "old" that which was not only not old, but in all probability did not yet exist in Páṇini's time.

It is curious, though I lay no stress on this circumstance, that the *Káśiká-vṛitti* should *pass over in silence the whole Várttika of Kátyáyana*, but should, in giving the counter-instance, "Yájnavalkáni Bráhmaṇáni," add: "Why does this rule of Páṇini (restrict the formation of Bráhmaṇa-names with the affix *in*) to those Bráhmaṇas proclaimed by the 'old?' Because the Bráhmaṇas of Yájnavalkya, etc., are called Yájnavalkáni Bráhmaṇáni, etc; for, *according to legendary reports, these and similar Bráhmaṇas do not belong to a remote time.*[163] Thus, on traditional grounds—which we should have thanked Jayáditya if he had designated in more precise terms—the Káśiká, too, discards the notion of the *Yájnavalkáni Bráhmaṇáni* being an exception to the much-quoted rule of Páṇini. On the contrary, it looks, as we see, on the derivative *Yájnavalka* as a counter-instance, which confirms the statement of Páṇini; but, I hold that this commentary was wanting in judgment when it passed over in silence the Várttika of Kátyáyana, since the latter, by its very mistaken reproach, affords us a valuable means of judging on the chronological relation between Páṇini and Kátyáyana.

Before I support with further arguments the conclusions I have drawn with regard to this chronological relation between the two grammarians, it will be expedient to take a cursory view of the *principal categories* of *known* ancient writings not already mentioned; acquaintance with which, on the one hand, is shown by Páṇini himself; and the existence of which, on the other, may either be assumed to fall within a period not very distant from the time when Páṇini wrote, or in his time, to be open to doubt, on account of the reasons previously alleged.

Since Páṇini teaches, in the rule I have so often referred to, that all ancient Bráhmaṇas and Kalpa works bear names which end in the (technical) affix *ṇini*, the names of the former, by the common consent of all commentators, ancient and modern, being used in the plural only, we are justified in inferring that none of the works of the category now preserved in manuscript, so far as my knowledge

---

[163] The commentary of the Káśiká on this Sútra which, as in general, is much better and more clearly worded than the comment of the Calcutta Pandits, runs thus (MS. E.I.H. 2440): प्रत्ययार्थविशेषणमेतत् । तृतीयासमर्थात्प्रोक्ते णिनिप्रत्ययो भवति । यत्तत्प्रोक्तं पुराणप्रोक्तं चेत् । ब्राह्मणकल्पास्ते भवन्ति । पुराणेन चिरन्तनेनर्षिणा प्रोक्तं पुराणप्रोक्तम् । ब्राह्मणेषु तावत् । भाल्लविनः । शाण्डायनिनः (should be शाट्यायनिनः) । ऐतरेयिणः ॥ कल्पेषु । पैङ्गी कल्पः । आरुणपराजी ॥ पुराणप्रोक्तेष्विति किम् । याज्ञवल्कानि ब्राह्मणानि । आश्मरथः कल्पः । याज्ञवल्कादयो हि न चिरकाला इत्याख्यानेषु वार्ता. I may add, that the Siddhánta-kaumudí also makes no mention of the Várttika of Kátyáyana, but, in reference to our question, merely contains these words (p. 81 *b*. line 1): पुराणेति किम् । याज्ञवल्कानि (misedited याज्ञवल्क्यानि) ब्राह्मणानि.

goes, are ancient works from Páṇini's point of view. That one of them, at least, the Kalpa work of Kátyáyana, cannot have existed in Páṇini's time, would be the consequence of the foregoing inquiry; but I should not venture to say more than I have said of the other ritual books of the same category.

Again, if the conclusion I drew as to Páṇini's not having been acquainted with the *Áraṇyakas* be correct, it would imply, of necessity, that the *Upanishads* could not have existed when he lived, since they are a further development of this class of works; and this conclusion, again, strengthens the arguments I have adduced for the non-existence, in Páṇini's time, of the Vájasaneyi-Saṁhitá, arranged by Yájnavalkya; for an important Upanishad, the *Íśa-Upanishad*, is the last portion of this version of the Yajurveda.[164]

That Páṇini was conversant, not only with a *Black Yajur-*

---

[164] Páṇini mentions the word *Upanishad* once, viz. I. 4, 79, but not in the sense of a sacred work. It occurs twice in the Gaṇas, viz., to IV. 3, 73 and 4, 12; in the former it has the sense of such a work, but it is doubtful whether it has in the latter also.—In a note at page 325, Professor Müller gives a detailed account of the history of *Anquetil du Perron's Oupnekhat*, "which contains the translation of fifty Upanishads from Persian into Latin." Since his bibliographical sketch cannot fail to be of much interest and use to many of his readers, it will not be superfluous to correct a mistake of his when he states that the *French translation* of Anquetil du Perron was "not published." It was not published *entirely*; but in the well-known work of Tieffenthaler, Anquetil, Rennell, and Bernoulli: "*Description historique et géographique de l'Inde*, etc. *Berlin*; *vol. I. second edition*, 1791; *vol. II.* 1786; *vol. III.* 1788," the second part of the second volume contains his translation "en françois barbare," as the author himself calls it, of the "*Oupnekhat Naraïn* (*tiré*) *de l'Athrban Beid*" (p. 297 ff.); of the "*Oupnekhat tadiv* (*tiré*) *du Djedjr Beid*" (p. 301 ff.); of the "*Oupnekhat Athrbsr* (*tiré*) *de l'Athrban Beid*" (p. 308 ff.) and of the "*Oupnekhat Schat Roudri* (*tiré*) *du Djedjr Beid*" (p. 323 ff.). The same volume also contains an interesting paper of his: "*nouvelles preuves que l'Oupnekhat ne parle nulle part du Kalïougam, ni des trois autres Iougams*" (Table des Articles; p. 548 ff.).—There is another work, published anonymously, which comprises, besides other interesting matter, translations in German of portions of Oriental works; the first volume of this work—the only one that appeared, I believe—bears the title "*Sammlung Asiatischer Original-Schriften.—Indische Schriften.—Zürich*, 1791," and contains, amongst others, a German translation of the first three Upanishads published in the work of Tieffenthaler, Anquetil du Perron, etc. As this volume is curious and of great scarcity, I subjoin a list of its contents, as given by the

veda,[165] but with a *Ṛig*- and and a *Sáma- veda*, is borne out by several Sútras of his. We may expect, too, that he, like every other Hindu, looked upon the Ṛigveda as the principal Veda; and this assumption is confirmed by the circumstance of his calling a *Páda* of the Ṛigveda simply *the* "Páda," without the addition of the word Ṛik.[166] But there is no evidence to show that he knew an *Atharvaveda*. The word *atharvan*, it is true, occurs three times, but only in the Gaṇas to his rules, and there even only as the name of a priest. We may add, also, that the word *átharvaṇika* is found in two Sútras (IV. 3, 133, and VI. 4, 174), where it is ex-

---

author himself: "*Bagawudam. Tewetat. Der Talapoeng Reg. Patimuk. Des Fo Buch. Upnekhat. Mahabarat. Ind.Raschah. Ambertkend. Bedang Schaster. Dirm Schaster. Neadirsen. Götter Verzeichnis. Schastah-Bade. Lords Schaster. Tirunamalei. Ramesuram. Ramesuram Phil. Gespräch. Sastiram.*"—A note appended to the translation of the "Upnekhat Athrbsar," at p. 286 of this work, drew my attention to "*A prayer directed by the Brahmans to be offered up to the Supreme Being; written originally in the Shanscrit language, and translated by C. W. Boughton Rouse, Esq.; from a Persic Version of Dara Shekoo, a son of Jah Jehan, Emperor of Hindostan*"—which prayer is appended to the "*Institutes of Timour,*" by *Joseph White* (Oxford, 1783); for the note in question says that this prayer is a free and abridged version, from the Persian, of the same Upnekhat Athrbsar (or Upanishad Atharvaśiras). But having compared them, I cannot convince myself that such is the case; though the ideas expressed in both compositions have much similarity.—In passing, I may mention, also, that this same prayer attracted the attention of the "Monthly Review of 1783," and, in consequence, that of *August Hennings* in his interesting work, "*Versuch einer Ostindischen Litteratur-Geschichte nebst einer kritischen Beurtheilung der Aechtheit der Zend-Bücher. Hamburg und Kiel*, 1786." This work, which is extremely rare, bears testimony to the extensive scholarship of its author; it gives a critical review—more or less detailed—of 114 works, and has an Appendix, entitled "*Grundlage zu einem vollständigen Verzeichnisse aller Schriften die Ostindien und die damit verbundene Länder betreffen. In alphabetischer Ordnung als ein Anhang zur Litteratur-Geschichte Ostindiens. Hamburg.*" This Appendix contains the titles of not less than 1372 works of the 16th, 17th, and 18th century, referring to the history, "antiquities, nations, languages, religions, and the natural history of India," many of which are unknown not only to me, but to several Oriental scholars, librarians, and bibliographers whom I have consulted about them.

[165] See note 153.

[166] For his knowledge of the *Ṛigveda*, compare VI. 3, 55, 133; VII. 4, 39, etc.; for the occurrence of *páda*, VI. 1, 115; VII. 1, 57; VIII. 1, 18, etc.; for *Sámaveda*, I. 2, 34; IV. 2, 7; V. 2, 59, etc.

plained by Patanjali as meaning "the office and the sacred record of the Atharvan,"—that Patanjali confirms the occurrence of the word *atharvan* in the Gaṇa to the Sútra IV. 2, 63, where it can only mean a literary work; and, besides, that the word *átharvaṇa* occurs twice in the Gaṇas.[167] Yet even the testimony of Patanjali cannot entirely remove the uncertainty which, as we have seen above, must always adhere to the Gaṇas as evidence for or against Páṇini, with the exception of their first word, mentioned by himself, or such of their words as are referred to by other rules of his. Nor does the occurrence of the word *átharvaṇika* in the two Sútras quoted necessarily confirm the interpretation of Patanjali. It may there only mean the office of an Atharvan priest, who, probably, was employed in the performance of sacrificial acts. In short, there is no valid ground for attributing to Páṇini a knowledge of the fourth and least sacred Veda, the Atharvaveda; and this doubt derives some additional weight from the fact that, though the word *Angiras*, one of the reputed Ṛishis of the Atharvaveda, is mentioned in a Sútra (II. 4. 65), neither the compound *Atharvángirasas*, nor its derivative, *Atharvángirasa*, is met with in the Sútras of Páṇini, though the former is the name, as well of the two seers of the Atharvaveda, as especially of the hymns of this Veda itself,—while the latter means the observances connected with the Atharvaveda, and would have deserved a place amongst grammatical rules.

In the last chapter of his learned work, Professor Müller gives instances of hymns which he considers as belonging to the oldest portion of Vaidik literature. It seems difficult to follow his arguments so as to arrive at a settled conviction on this point; for the

[167] For *Atharvan*, see the Gaṇas to IV. 2, 38 and 63; (it occurs, too, in a Várttika to IV. 3, 133). For *Átharvaṇika*, IV. 3, 133; VI. 4, 174 and the Gaṇas to IV. 2, 63 and (in the Káśiká) 60; for *Átharvaṇa* the Gaṇas to IV. 2, 38 and 63 and (in the Káśiká) 60.—On IV. 3, 133, Patanjali remarks, after the words of the Sútra: . . . आथर्वणो धर्मः। आथर्वण आम्नायः। इदमाथर्वणार्थम्। आथर्वणिकार्थं च चतुर्ग्रहणं क्रियते। वसन्तादिष्वथर्वशब्द आथर्वणशब्दस्य (comp. IV. 2, 63) यथा ते षष्ठेऽध्याये (VI. 4, 174) प्रकृतिभावार्थं ग्रहणं क्रियते etc.

reasons he gives in assigning these hymns to the earliest portions of Hindu poetry rest on impressions so individual, that assent or dissent of those who read the Ṛigveda hymns will depend much on their own disposition. I should, for instance, for my part, hesitate very much to assign to a hymn which speaks of thirty-three gods[168] a place amongst the most ancient hymns, since it betrays, in my opinion, a very artificial and developed condition of religiousness, and a considerable deviation from what I hold to be the primitive feeling of the human mind. The impression I derive from another hymn, a poetical version of which Professor Müller gives (p. 564), and a prose translation of which we owed already to Colebrooke (Misc. Ess. I. p. 33), would be to the same effect,—that it belongs, not to the earliest, but to the very latest hymns of the Ṛigveda-Saṁhitá; for it seems to me that a song which begins, "There was no entity, nor non-entity . . . . . death was not, nor was there immortality;" and concludes: "Then who can know whence it proceeded, or whence this varied world arose, or whether it uphold itself, or not? He who, in the highest heaven, is the ruler of this universe, does indeed know, but not another can possess that knowledge"—it seems to me that such a song must be already the result of the greatest struggles of the human heart: the full-grown fruit of a long experience in thought,—in other words, that it marks the end, and not the beginning, of a phase of religious development.

I agree with Müller in one important point, viz. (p. 566): that "the evidence of language is the most decisive for settling the relative age of Vedic hymns," and I should have agreed with him still more if he had said that it is the only safe criterion with a European of the nineteenth century to settle this point. Therefore, when he adds that "the occurrence of such a word as *tadânîm* is more calculated to rouse doubts as to the early date of this [last-named] hymn than the most abstruse metaphysical ideas which may be discovered in it,"—though I do not share the opinion expressed in his latter words,—I hold the adverb he men-

---

[168] Müller's Ancient Sanskrit Literature, p. 531.

tions to be quite sufficient authority for removing this hymn from the earliest portion of Hindu songs.

But setting aside our personal feelings, which, after all, are of no consequence, we cannot be indifferent about learning what Páṇini considered to be the older or the more recent Vaidik hymns. A direct opinion on this point we can scarcely expect to obtain from himself; but indirect evidence of his own impressions, or, more probably, of the tradition current in his time, I believe may be collected from his Sútras; and, however scanty it be, and however much we may think we may be able, without his aid, to arrive at a similar result in regard to the hymns I am going to name, it will not be superfluous to advert to it here. The hymns of the Ṛig-veda—and, consequently, those collected from it for the version of the Sáma-, and the two other Vedas—were "seen," as I have shown above (p. 62), by the Ṛishis, who received them from a divinity. This general belief was, as I there proved, shared in by Páṇini, who, therefore, was not so unshackled by the inspiration-doctrine as Professor Müller represents him to have been in his discussion on old and new Bráhmaṇas.[169] But there is a marked difference in the language he uses when speaking at one time of one category, and, at another, of another category of hymns; and it is this difference which induces me to express a doubt whether he looked upon all Vaidik hymns as *immediate* revelations from above.

In his Sútras IV. 2, 7 to 9, he teaches the formation of words expressing the name of Sámaveda-hymns, and he applies to the latter the word "*seen*," *i.e.*, received by inspiration from the divinity. In the Sútra IV. 3, 101, on the other hand, he heads a chapter, which comprises the next ten rules, with the words, "*proclaimed by him*," which words imply that the Vaidik compositions—the names of which he teaches the student to form in these rules—were *promulgated* by the Ṛishis, whose names are the bases of the several derivatives.[170] That these two different expressions were

[169] **Ancient Sanskrit Liturature, p. 361: "Pâṇini, whose views are not shackled by the inspiration-doctrine which blinded and misled all the followers of the orthodox Mîmânsâ school, broadly states the fact that there are old and new Brâhmaṇas, etc."**

[170] IV. 2, 7: दृष्टं साम.—IV. 3, 101: तेन प्रोक्तम्.—Praudhamanoramá: प्रकर्षेणोक्तं

chosen by Páṇini deliberately, results from the contents of the last-named rules. They contain amongst others (IV. 3, 105), names of Kalpa works, which, at no period of the Hindu religion, were "seen" or ascribed to superhuman authorship. This word "*proclaimed*" has also been noticed especially by Kátyáyana and Patanjali, who judge as follows of its import in these rules:—*Kátyáyana:* "(It might seem that) this word 'proclaimed' is purposeless, since no affix is visible in (certain) derivatives (which imply its sense)."—*Patanjali:* "Why is it purposeless? 'Because,' says Kátyáyana, 'no affix is visible.' That is to say, if 'proclaimed' means that the Vaidik version of the Kalápas or Kaṭhas is *recited* village for village, a derivative implying such a sense has no (special) affix."—*Kátyáyana:* "(It is purposeless, too) if applied to the sense 'book,' for (in this case) an affix is taught (elsewhere)."—*Patanjali:* "There *is* an affix, if the sense 'composed, as a book,' is implied by it; but such an affix is provided for by another rule of Páṇini, viz., IV. 3, 116. Could we, then, consider this word 'proclaimed' (in our rule) as used in reference to the Veda? But again, the Vedas are not made (like a book); they are permanent (or eternal)."—*Kátyáyana:* "If (however, one should assert that this word) concerns the Veda, (he would be correct, provided that he meant to impart to the word 'proclaimed') a *figurative* sense."—*Patanjali* (after repeating these latter words): "Is it not said, however, that 'the Vedas are not made, but that they are permanent (*i.e.*, eternal)?' (Quite so); yet, though their sense is permanent, the order of their letters has not always remained the same; and it is through the difference in the latter respect that we may speak of the versions of the Kaṭhas, Kalápas, Mudakas, Pippaládakas, and so on."[171] Now, whatever opinion we may entertain of

---

प्रोक्तम्। अध्यायनेनार्थव्याख्यानेन वा प्रकाशितमित्यर्थः। प्रकर्षेणेति वचनान्नेह। देवदत्तेनाध्यापितम्. Compare the following note.

[171] Páṇini: तेन प्रोक्तम्.—Kátyáyana: प्रोक्तग्रहणमनर्थकं तच्चादर्शनात्.—Patanjali: प्रोक्तग्रहणमनर्थकम्। किं कारणम्। तच्चादर्शनात्। ग्रामे ग्रामे कालापकं काठकं च

Patanjali's accounting for the various versions of the Vaidik texts, it is evident that Páṇini—who comprises Kalpas under the term "proclaimed"—looked upon the works, the names of which are taught in these rules, not as having been "seen" or received *immediately* from the divinity. They must, in his mind, therefore, belong to a later period than the Sámaveda hymns which he treats

---

प्रोच्यते । न तत्र प्रत्ययो दृश्यते.—Kátyáyana: ग्रन्थे च दर्शनात्.—Patanjali: यत्र च दृश्यते ग्रन्थः स भवति तत्र कृते ग्रन्थ इत्येव सिद्धम् (IV. 3, 116) । छन्दोऽर्थं तर्हीदं वक्तव्यम् । न हि छन्दांसि क्रियन्ते । नित्यानि छन्दांसि.—Kátyáyana: छन्दोऽर्थमिति चेत्तुल्यम्.—Patanjali: छन्दोऽर्थमिति चेत्तुल्यमेतद्भवति । [The MS. contains here a repetition, which is evidently a mistake of the copyist] ननु चोक्तं न हि छन्दांसि क्रियन्ते नित्यानि छन्दांसीति । यद्यप्यर्थो नित्यः । या त्वसौ वर्णानुपूर्वी सानित्या तद्भेदाच्चैतद्भवति काठकं कालापकं मौदकं पैप्पलादकमिति । न तर्हीदानीमिदं वक्तव्यम् । वक्तव्यं च । किं प्रयोजनम् । यत्तेन प्रोक्तं न च तेन कृतम् । माथुरी [cf. Kaiyyaṭa: माधुरी] वृत्तिः । यदि तर्हि (त.स्य निबन्धनमस्ति । इदमेव वक्तव्यम् । तदप्यवश्यं वक्तव्यम् । यत्तेन कृतं न च प्रोक्तं वाररुचं काव्यम् । जालूकाः श्लोकाः.—Kaiyyaṭa: प्रपूर्वो वचिः प्रकाशने ऽध्यायनरूपे वा वर्तते करणे वा । तत्राद्ये ऽर्थे प्रत्ययो न दृश्यते । द्वितीये तु सूत्रान्तरेण (*i.e.* IV. 3, 116) सिद्धमिति मत्वाह । प्रोक्तग्रहणमिति ग्राम इति । सुशर्मादीनां प्रतिग्रामं प्रवक्तृत्वे ऽपि सुशर्मणा प्रोक्तं काठकमसौशर्मणमिति [probably: काठकम् । सौ°] प्रयोगो न दृश्यत इत्यर्थः । नित्यानीति । कर्तुरस्मरणात्तेषामिति भावः । या त्वसाविति । महाप्रलयादिषु वर्णानुपुर्वीविनाशे पुनरुत्पद्य (MS. पुनतत्पद्य) ऋषयः संस्कारातिशयाद्वेदार्थं स्मृत्वा शब्दरचना विदधतीत्यर्थः (MS. विद्दतीत्यर्थः) । तद्भेदादिति । आनुपूर्वीभेदादित्यर्थः । ततश्च कठादयो वेदानुपूर्व्याः कर्तार एव ननु स्थिता एव सुशर्मादिवत्प्रवक्तारः । ततश्च छन्दस्यपि कृते ग्रन्थ इत्येव (IV. 3, 116) सिद्धः प्रत्यय इति भावः । माधुरीति । माधुरेण प्रथमतः प्रकाशितेत्यर्थः । (IV. 3, 108) कलापिनो ऽणित्यण्ग्रहणस्याधिकविधानार्थं छाट्टृद्धादप्यनाश्भवति (MS. °र्थद्याट्टृद्धा°°) । द्विविधं चेह प्रोक्तं गृह्यते परकृतं स्व(कृ)तं वा यत्प्रकाशितं तेन प्रोक्ताधिकार एव कठादिभ्यो वक्ष्यमाणप्रत्ययविधानम्.—Nágojibhaṭṭa: तेन प्रोक्तम् । कालापककाठकयोर्गोत्रचरणाद्वुञ् (IV. 3, 126) धर्माम्नाययोरिति बोध्यम् । प्रपूर्वो वचिरिति । अध्यायनरूपे प्रकाशने वा [both MSS. of the E. I. H., No. 350 and 1209, in the same order] वर्तते करणे वेत्यन्वयः । ननु काठकमित्यादौ प्रत्ययदर्शनान्न प्रत्ययो दृश्यत इत्यनुपपन्नमत आह । सुशर्मादीनामिति । भाष्ये ग्रन्थे चेति तेन कृते ग्रन्थ इत्यर्थः (IV. 3, 116) । ग्रन्थः स इति तेन कृतो ग्रन्थः स इत्यर्थः । अंशेन वेदस्य नित्यत्वं स्वीकृत्यांशेनानित्यत्वमाह । यद्यप्यर्थ इति । अनेन

of in the rules IV. 2. 7-9 as having been "*seen.*" Nor would there be anything remarkable in this view, if it merely referred to the Bráhmaṇa works which also are the subject of his rules; for this class of inspired literature is looked upon by all the authorities as being inferior in degree, and, I hold therefore, less immediate, as an emanation than the hymns of the Saṁhitás. But there

---

वेदत्वं शब्दार्थोभयवृत्तिध्वनितम् (MS. 1209 °त्तितिध्व°; perhaps °त्तिरितिध्व°)। ननु धाता यथा पूर्वमकल्पयदित्यादिश्रुतिबलेनानुपूर्व्यपि सैवेति नव्यपूर्वमीमांसासिद्धान्तात्सा नित्येत्ययुक्तमत आह। महाप्रलयादिष्विति। आनुपूर्व्यास्तत्तत्क्षणघटितत्वेनानित्यत्वमिति भाव इति केचित्। तन्न। यद्यप्यर्थो नित्य इत्यादिवाक्यशेषविरोधात्। अर्थस्यापि ज्योतिष्टोमादेरनित्यत्वात्। प्रवाहाविच्छेदेन नित्यत्वं तूभयोरपि तस्मान्मन्वन्तरभेदेनानुपूर्वी भिन्नैव। प्रतिमन्वन्तरं चैषा श्रुतिरन्या विधीयत इत्युक्तेरित्यन्ये। परे तु। अर्थो नित्य इत्यत्र क्षतकत्वविरोध्यनित्यत्वस्यैवाभ्युपगमः पूर्वपक्षिणा तादृशनित्यत्वस्यैव च्छन्दःसूक्तेः। एवं चार्थशब्देनात्रेश्वरः। मुख्यतया तस्यैव सर्ववेदतात्पर्यविषयत्वात्। वेदैश्च सर्वैरहमेव वेद्य इति गीतोक्तेरित्याहुः (XV. 15)। वर्णानुपूर्व्या अनित्यत्वे मानमाह तद्भेदाच्चेति। अनित्यत्वव्याप्यभेदेन तत्सिद्धिः। भेदोऽत्र नानात्वम्। ईश्वरे तु न नानात्वं (? MSS. नतत्वं?)। भेदे मानं व्यवहारमाह। काठकेत्यादि। अर्थैक्येऽप्यानुपूर्वीभेदादेव काठककालापकादिव्यवहार इति भावः। अत्रानुपूर्व्यनित्येत्युक्तेः पदानि तान्येवेति ध्वनितं तदाह। ततश्च कठादय इत्यधिकं मञ्जूषायां द्रष्टव्यम्। ननु माधुरावृद्धाच्छेन भाव्यमत आह (comp. IV. 2, 114)। कलापिनोऽणिति (IV. 3, 108)। नन्वेवं कठादिभ्यः प्रोक्ताधिकारे प्रत्ययविधानं व्यर्थम्। तन्न। यत्प्रोक्तं न च तेन क्षतमित्यर्थबाधादत आह। द्विविधं चेति प्रोक्ताधिकार एवेति। क्षतग्रहणेन स्वाप्रकाशितस्वक्षतस्यैव ग्रहणादिति भावः. [Obvious mis-spellings in the MSS.—especially in MS. 350, which here is more indifferent than MS. 1209—whence this passage is taken have been left unnoticed by me. The text here given is, in my opinion, as correct as the MSS. in question will allow to edit it.]

I have quoted the full gloss of the three principal commentators on this important Sútra and its Várttikas, because it is of considerable interest in many respects and, at the same time, bears out my statement at page 65. We see Kaiyyaṭa and Nágojibhaṭṭa writhing under the difficulty of reconciling the eternity of the Veda with the differences of its various versions, which nevertheless maintain an equal claim to infallibility. Patanjali makes rather short work of this much vexed question; and unless it be allowed here to render his expression *varṇa* (which means "letter"), "word," it is barely possible even to understand how he can save consistently the eternity or permanence of the "sense" of the Veda. That the modern Mímánsists maintain not only the "eternity of the sense" but also the "permanence of the text," which is tantamount to the exclusive right of one single version, we learn, amongst others, from Nágojibhaṭṭa. But as such a doctrine has its obvious dangers, it is not shared in

occurs in midst of these rules one (IV. 3, 106) which contains the word *Chhandas*, which, being contradistinguished from the word *Bráhmaṇa* in the preceding rule (IV. 3, 105), cannot have there any other sense than that of *Mantra*, as I have shown above; or, if it should be thought that it is contrasted there with Kalpa as well as with Bráhmaṇa in the preceding rule, it would mean Veda in general—Mantra *and* Bráhmaṇa. And, in connection with this word Páṇini writes, "*Śaunaka.*" Śaunaka, however, we know, from Sáyaṇa's commentary on the Ṛigveda and the Anukramaṇí, was the Ṛishi who is supposed to be the author of the second Maṇḍala, as we now possess it, though in a former version it appears to have belonged to the Ṛishi Gṛitsamada.[172]

Should, then, my view of Páṇini's rule be correct, it will follow that Páṇini considered this second Maṇḍala as of a later date than the other Maṇḍalas; and we cannot but admit that even the first hymn of the second Maṇḍala fully confirms this impression, for, by speaking of Hotṛi, Potṛi, Neshtṛi, Agnídhra, Praśástṛi, Adhwaryu, and Bráhman priests, it certainly betrays a very advanced development of sacrificial and artificial rites.

Mímánsá is a word of special grammatical interest, not in so

by the old Mímánsists, nor by Nágoji, as he tells us himself. He and Kaiyyaṭa inform us therefore that, *amongst other* theories, there is one, according to which the order of the letters (or, rather, words) in the Vaidik texts got lost in the several Pralayas or destructions of the worlds; and, since each Manwantara had its own revelation, which differed only in the expression, not in the sense of the Vaidik texts, the various versions known to these commentators represent these successive revelations which were "remembered," through "their excessive accomplishments," by the Ṛishis, who, in this manner, produced, or rather reproduced, the texts current in their time, under the name of the versions of the Kaṭhas, Kalápas, and so on. In this way each version had an equal claim to sanctity. There is a very interesting discussion on the same subject by *Kumárila*, in his *Mímánsá-Várttika* (I. 3, 10). I forbear, however, quoting it on the present occasion on account of its great length, and because I hope to be able to give it in a more appropriate place.

[172] Compare *Sáyaṇa* in the beginning of his commentary on the second Maṇḍala; Professor Wilson's detailed account in his translation, vol. ii., p. 207; and Professor Müller's Ancient Literature, pp. 231, 232; as well as the corresponding passage from Shaḍguruśishya, at p. 237.

far as its affix *á* is concerned—for the latter belongs to a general category of derivatives dealt with by Páṇini in his rule III. 3, 102 —but on account of the irregular formation of its base. It must be admitted that the Sútra I. 3, 62 may be looked upon as including this base also; but whether the instance *mímáns*, given by the commentators, has there the general sense of *considering*, or the special sense of the philosophical reasoning of the Mímánsá, cannot be inferred from the general tenor of this rule. This latter sense is emphatically expressed by two words derived from *mímáns*, viz., *Mímánsá*, the name of the philosophy; and *Mímánsaka*, a Mímánsá philosopher. Neither word occurs in Páṇini.[173] Nor does he mention *Jaimini*, the author of the Mímánsá-Sútra; and it is, perhaps, worthy of our attention, that not even the Gaṇas to Páṇini contain the formation of this word, which is of as much interest as any other word of the Gaṇa *Báhwádi* (IV. 1, 96).[174]

The word *Vedánta* having no remarkable grammatical peculiarities, had no claim to the notice of Páṇini; but had he been aware of the word *Vedántin*, "one who knows the Vedánta," it would certainly have required a special rule of his, since there is no Sútra in his Grammar by which the sense of this derivative could be made out satisfactorily. And as Páṇini notices but *one single word* in which the base is not a proper name, and the affix *in* (technically *ini*) imparts to the

---

[173] Even Kátyáyana gives no Várttika to teach the formation of *mímánsaka*, though this word is of some interest from a grammatical point of view. Amongst those words which designate followers of a doctrine or philosophy, it is the only one formed with a *kṛit*-affix. It occurs, *e.g.* as an instance of Patanjali, to I. 2, 64, v. 17, II. 2, 29, and in a Káriká of the latter to III. 2, 123, where it is rendered by Kaiyyaṭa *vichâraka*; it occurs, too, as an instance, not in the Mahabháshya, but the Kásiká and Siddh.-k. to II. 1, 53, in the compound मीमांसकदुर्दुरूढ; and it is probably the property of the Calcutta Paṇḍits, as an instance to IV. 3, 9.

[174] With regard to Jaimini, I have only to add that the instance जैमिनिकडार or कडारजैमिनि to II. 2, 38 has not yet found a place in the Bháshya or in Kaiyyaṭa's commentary; it occurs in the Kásiká and the Gaṇaratnamahodadhi; but on what authority Jayáditya and Vardhamána give this handsome epithet to the old Jaimini, or whether it is levelled against another Jaimini, I have no means of stating.

derivative the sense of studying or knowing, viz., *anubráhmaṇin*, "one who studies or knows a work like a Bráhmaṇa" (IV. 2, 62), the omission of *Vedántin* acquires increased significance.[175]

Sánkhya is a peculiar form. It comes from *sankhyá*, and designates the philosophy which is based on *synthetic* (sam) *reasoning* (khyá). Its very name shows that it is the counterpart, as it were, of *Nyáya* (ni-áya), or the philosophy founded on "*analytical reasoning.*" For while the former builds up a system of the universe, the latter dissects it into categories, and "enters into" its component parts. Yet a grammatical rule would have had to explain why the name of the former system is not a *kṛit*-formation,—for instance, its very base, *sankhyá*, analogously to the *kṛit*-formation *nyáya*. It has not been noticed by Páṇini. Nor does he teach—as he probably would have done had this philosophy existed in his time—that the same word means, as a masculine, a follower of the Sánkhya philosophy.[176]

The word *Yoga* occurs several times in the Sútras,[177] but never in the sense of a system of philosophy; and the only two derivatives of this word which are taught by Páṇini, viz., *yogya* and *yaugika* (V. 1, 102) are two words which have no

---

[175] In the Sútra IV. 3, 111, the affix *in* (technically, *ini*) has a similar purport, but the base implies a proper name; thus, *Karmandin*, *Kṛiśáświn* mean "one who studies or knows the works of Karmanda, Kṛiśáśwa."

[176] For the various explanations, given by native authorities, of this term, I need now refer to one essay only, since it probably comprises all the literary information—*and not only on this point*—which can be obtained in our days on Sánkhya writers, and certainly more than any one scholar in Europe would have at his command—I mean the learned and excellent preface of *Dr. Hall* to his elaborate edition of the *Sánkhya-Pravachana*. The latter sense of the word *Sánkhya*, "a follower of the Sánkhya philosophy," occurs, *e.g.* in the *Bhagavad-Gítá*, III. 3; or, together with the word *Káṇáda*, "a follower of the Vaiśeshika doctrine," in the commentary of *Śankara* on the *Vedánta Sútra*, II. 3, 51: बहुष्वात्मसु सर्वगतेषु प्रतिशरीरं बाह्याभ्यन्तराविशेषेण संनिहितेषु मनोवाक्कायैर्धर्माधर्मलक्षणमदृष्टमुपार्ज्यते । साङ्ख्यानां तावत्तत् । . . . . . . काणादानामपि etc.

[177] I. 2, 54. 55.—III. 4, 20.—V. 1, 102; 4, 44. 47. 50. 126.—VI. 4, 74. 75.—VIII. 1, 59.

connection whatever with its philosophical meaning. In the sense of "religious austerity," it *seems* to have been known by Páṇini, though he has no rule on the formation of this word, apparently because it offers no other grammatical interest than that which would be satisfied by his general rules III. 3, 18 and VII. 3, 52; for he has a rule on the formation of *yogin* (III. 2, 142). But this word means *a man who practises religious austerities;* it does not mean a follower of the Yoga system of philosophy.

That *Nyáya* was known to Páṇini in the sense of *syllogism* or *logical reasoning*, or perhaps *logical science*, I conclude from the Sútra III. 3, 122,[178] where its affix conveys the sense of instrumentality, *i.e.* that by which analysis (*lit.* entering-into) is effected, for the same form, *nyáya*, is made the subject of another rule (III. 3, 37), where Páṇini gives as its meaning "propriety, good conduct," which would lead to its later meaning, "policy." Unless we drew this distinction between the two Sútras named, the first Sútra would become superfluous. Nor is it probable that a civilization like that which is traceable in Páṇini's rules could have done without a word for syllogistic thought. But between this sense of the word *nyáya*, and its designating the special

---

[178] I regret that I must again animadvert on an error of the Calcutta editors. In their gloss on the Sútra III. 3, 122, they give the following etymology of न्याय, "घीञ् । नीयन्ते ऽनेनेति । न्यायः." According to them, this word would therefore come from नी "to lead," an etymology which, of course, is absolutely impossible. Nor is there any trace of it in any of the commentaries known to me. Patanjali and his commentators have no remark on this easy word. The *Kášiká*, which explains every Sútra, writes नीयते ऽनेनेति न्यायः, but neither allows these words to be preceded by "घीञ्," nor, as this quotation shows, to contain a third person of the *plural* (नीयन्ते). Its gloss obviously means, "because entering is made (नि + ईयते) by it, the derivative is न्याय." The *Siddhánta-kaumudí* (fol. 211 *a*, line 7) has an analogous interpretation: "नियन्ति . . . . . अनेन," etc., which is still more transparent. But what must one think of the proficiency of an "editor" of Páṇini, who has none of the laborious work—which always gives a title to indulgence—of comparing MSS. and compiling a commentary,—who merely reprints the labour of others,—and yet, even in a simple case like this, does not feel induced to consult the Kášiká or Siddhánta-kaumudí, though he *talks* a great deal, even on this occasion, of the Kášiká "A. B. and C," but without mastering its "*a*, *b*, *c*," simply repeats the gross blunder of the editors of his edition of Páṇini!

system of Gautama there is a vast difference. Nay, had Páṇini even written the Gaṇa IV. 2, 60, which implies, in its present version, the formation *naiyáyika*, this latter word would not require us to infer that it means there a follower of Gautama's school; it may only signify a man who studies or knows the laws of syllogism.[179] To substantiate this conclusion, with all the detail it deserves, would be a matter of great interest; for no philosophical school has dealt more largely with grammatical subjects than the *Nyáya* school, and its branch, the *Vaiśeshika*. The nature of "sound" and "word," the question whether word is "eternal or transitory," the "power" or purport of words, the relation of base and affix, and such kindred matters are treated of in a vast literature based on the Sútras of Gautama; and the controversies of the Naiyáyikas with the Vaiyakaraṇas or etymologists need not blush before those of our modern philosophers. I must, however, confine myself on the present occasion, as heretofore, to giving a small amount of proof, that Páṇini could not have known the Sútras of Gautama.

After having refuted the opinion that the sense of a word conveys either the notion of *genus* or that of *species*, or that of *individual*, each taken separately, *Gautama* continues:—"1. The sense of a word conveys (at the same time) as well the notion of *genus* (*játi*), as that of *species* (*ákṛiti*), as that of an *individual* (*vyakti*). 2. An individual (*vyakti*) is a bodily form as a receptacle for the particularization of qualities. 3. Species (*akṛiti*) is called the characteristic mark of genus. 4. Genus (*játi*) is that which has the property of (intellectually) producing (species) of the same kind."[180]

---

179 To arrive at the form नैयायिक it is necessary to combine with the Gaṇa quoted, the Sútra VII. 3, 3. The same word न्याय in the philosophical sense, occurs in the Gaṇa to IV. 3, 73, where a MS. of the Káśiká has even the reading न्यायविद्या; and probably, in the same sense in the Gaṇa to VIII. 1, 27; but even if Páṇini himself had written it there, we should not be justified in giving it a more definite sense than the one stated. In the Sútra IV, 4, 92, and the Gaṇa to IV. 3, 54, it has the sense of "propriety."

180 Nyáya Sútras II. 131—134: जात्याकृतिव्यक्तयस्तु पदार्थः ॥ व्यक्तिर्गुणविशेषाश्रयो

Let us now refer to the terminology of Páṇini, and see how he dealt with similar notions. In the first place, we find that he does not make use of a term *ákṛiti*. We meet, in his Grammar only with the two terms *játi* and *vyakti*. In the rule I. 2, 52, he speaks of (words which express) "qualities as far as a *játi* goes;" and the instance of the *játi*, given by Patanjali, is a tree.[181]

मूर्तिः ॥ आकृतिर्जातिलिङ्गाख्या ॥ समानप्रसवात्मिका जातिः ॥.—The object of Gautama is to show that *individual*, *species*, and *genus* are notions which cannot be conceived, independently of one another, and that a separation of one from the other produces a fallacy. In translating the term *vyakti*, stress must be laid on the word *viśesha*, "particularization;" otherwise there would be but *one* individual. The same consideration induced me to differ, in my translation of *ákṛiti*, from Dr. Ballantyne, who, in his meritorious edition and learned translation of the Nyáya-Sútras, renders this term "*form*," which undoubtedly is its usual sense in *non-philosophical* writings. But when *Viśwanátha*, in his comment on the Sútra II. 124, writes: आकृतिरवयवसंस्थानविशेषः and on II. 133: जातिलिङ्गमित्याख्या यस्या जातेर्गोत्वादेर्हि सास्नादिसंस्थानविशेषो लिङ्गम्,—he intends, in my opinion, to convey the understanding, that *ákṛiti* is "the *particularization* of organisms," and "the characteristic mark of 'cowhood' is the *particularization* of the organism of a cow," which, translated into our philosophical language, would mean that *ákṛiti* is *species*. In my rendering of the fourth Sútra (II. 134), the parenthetical words are borrowed from *Viśwanátha*, who comments on them thus; समानः समानाकारकः प्रसवो बुद्धिजननमात्मा स्वरूपं यस्याः सा तथा च समानाकारबुद्धिजननयोग्यत्वमर्थः There can be no doubt, therefore, that Gautama meant our term *genus*.

[181] I. 2, 52: विशेषणानां चाजातेः.—I must observe here that the Káśiká and, on its authority, the Calcutta edition, are quite at variance with Patanjali, in explaining the last words of this Sútra, as if it had the sense च अजातेः. Patanjali distinctly rejects such an explanation, on the ground that it is impossible to speak of qualities which are not *játis*. He rejects, too, such instances as पञ्चाला जनपदः, सुभिक्षा संपन्नपानीयः, बहुमाल्यफलः, which illustrate his *púrvapaksha*; an instance of his conclusion is बदरी सूक्ष्मकण्टका मधुरा वृक्षः.—Patanjali: कथमिदं विज्ञायते । जातिर्यद्विशेषणमाहोस्विज्जातेर्यानि विशेषणानीति । किं चातः । यदि विज्ञायते जातिर्यद्विशेषणमिति सिद्धं पञ्चाला जनपद इति । सुभिक्षा (MS.°क्षः) संपन्नपानीयः । बहुमाल्यफल इति न सिध्यति । अथ विज्ञायते । जातेर्यानि विशेषणानीति । सिद्धं सुभिक्षा (MS.°क्षः) संपन्नपानीयः । बहुमाल्यफल इति । पञ्चाला जनपद इति न सिध्यति । एवं तर्हि नैवं विज्ञायते जातिर्यद्विशेषणमिति नापि जातेर्यानि विशेषणानीति । कथं तर्हि विशेषणानां युक्तवद्भावो भवति.—Várttika: आ जातेः.—Patanjali: आ जातिप्रयोगात् । किमर्थं पुनरिदमुच्यते.—Várttika: विशेषणानां वचनं जातिनिवृत्त्यर्थम्.—Patanjali: जातिनिवृत्त्यर्थो ऽयमारम्भः । किमुच्यते जातिनिवृत्त्यर्थ इति न पुनर्विशेषणानामपि युक्तवद्भावो यथा

At I. 2, 58, he treats of the optional use of the singular or plural: "if the word expresses a *játi*," (*e.g.* a Bráhmaṇa or the Bráhmaṇas); at V. 2, 133, he applies the term *játi* to the elephant,—at V. 4, 37, to herbs,—at V. 4, 94, to stones and iron, a lake and a cart,—at VI. 1, 143, to the fruit Kustumburu,—at VI. 3, 103, to grass;—and IV. 1, 63, is a rule on "*játi*-words, which are not permanently used in the feminine gender." It is not necessary to multiply these instances, in order to show that Páṇini understands by *játi* the same thing that Gautama understands by *ákṛiti*, viz., *species*;[182] and I may add at once, that he has no word at all for the notion of "*genus*."

As to *vyakti*, it occurs but once in the Sútras, viz., I. 2, 51,

---

स्यादिति.—Várttika: समानाधिकरणत्वात्सिद्धम्.—Patanjali: समानाधिकरणत्वाद्विशेषणानां युक्तवद्भावो भविष्यति। यद्येवं नार्थो ऽनेन लुपो ऽन्यत्रापि जातेर्युक्तवद्भावो न भवति। क्वान्यत्र। बदरी सूक्ष्मकण्टका मधुरा वृक्ष इति। किं पुनः कारणमन्यत्रापि जातेर्युक्तवद्भावो न भवति etc.—Kaiyyaṭa: .... अजातेरित्यसमर्थसमासः। भवति नानञः संबन्धात्। उभयथा चाव्याप्तिः प्रतिषेधस्येति प्रश्नः। आ जातिप्रयोगादिति सूत्र आङः प्रश्लेषः न तु नञः etc.

[182] There is, indeed, a Káriká of Patanjali which explicitly corroborates this comparison which I have made between Páṇini and Gautama, and which, moreover, has an additional import in affording evidence that Gautama is prior to Patanjali. I mean the Káriká to IV. 1, 63, which says: आकृतिग्रहणा जातिर्लिङ्गानां च न सर्वभाक्। सकृदाख्यातनिर्ग्राह्या गोत्रं च चरणैः सह, *i.e.*, "*játi* has (in Páṇini) the sense of *ákṛiti*; it does not possess all the genders, and, once determined, is easily recognized (elsewhere); *but* it is, too, a family with its schools." The following passages from Kaiyyaṭa will bear out my translation: आकृतिर्ग्रहणं यस्याः साकृतिग्रहणावयवसन्निवेशविशेषव्यङ्ग्येत्यर्थः [For these last words compare *Viśwanáthá's* comment on the *Nyáya Sútra* II. 133, in note 180.] । एतेन गोत्वादिजातिर्लक्षिता ब्राह्मणत्वादिस्तु न संगृहीता ब्राह्मणक्षत्रियादीनां संस्थानस्य सदृशत्वादिति तत्संग्रहायाह। लिङ्गानामिति, etc. ...... । सकृदिति। अयं गौरिति सकृदुपदिष्टा जातिर्निर्ग्रहीतुं निश्चेतुं पिण्डान्तरे शक्येत्यर्थः। गोत्रमिति। अपत्यमित्यर्थः। चरणशब्देन शाखाध्यायिनो गृह्यन्ते। गोत्रस्य सर्वलिङ्गत्वात्पृथगुपादानम्। नाडायनं नपुंसकमिति दर्शनात्. And after having explained the Káriká of "another" quoted by Patanjali, on the same subject, Kaiyyaṭa adds, "from this quotation by Patanjali it has been inferred that the former Káriká expresses his own opinion:" पूर्वोक्तमेव लक्षणं भाष्यकारस्य मतम्। अपर आहेत्यभिधानादित्याहुः.—On another occasion Patanjali, in adapting himself to Páṇini's use of the term *játi* (*i.e.* = *ákṛiti*), observes in a somewhat poetical strain (I. 2, 52, after the last words of the quotation from the Bháshya in note 181): आविष्टलिङ्गा

and means there "*linga*" generic mark, which, in grammatical terminology, is *gender*.[183] The notion of individuality is not represented by a special word in the language of Páṇini; the nearest approach to it is his word *adhikaraṇa*, as it is used in the rules II. 4, 13. 15, and V. 3, 43, where it is rendered by the commentators by *dravya* "substance." The term *viśeshya* may be compared to *adhikaraṇa;* but as it signifies "the object to be

---

जातिर्यल्लिङ्गमुपादाय प्रवर्तते। उत्पत्तिप्रभृत्या विनाशात्तल्लिङ्गं न जहाति [Kaiyyaṭa: आविष्टं लिङ्गं यया साविष्टलिङ्गा नियतलिङ्गेत्यर्थः, etc.] *i.e.*, "If *játi* has a fixed gender,—whenever it has taken that gender, from birth to death it does not abandon that gender."—I must also call attention to another passage from the Mahábháshya, which likewise shows that *játi* has, in Páṇini, Gautama's sense of *ákṛiti*, and which at the same time proves that Patanjali not only had a knowledge of the philosophical application of the latter term, but, when speaking in his own name, uses *ákṛiti* in the same manner in which it is used by Gautama. In the passage I am alluding to, he broaches the same problem which is proposed by the Nyáya-Sútras, but as a grammarian, and in reference to Páṇini, who has no term for *genus*, he comprises in his question merely the alternative whether the sense of a word *in Páṇini* implies "species" (*ákṛiti*), or "individuality" (*dravya*). His answer is, that it comprises both, for those who maintain the former alternative are justified in their opinion by the Sútra I. 2, 58, and those who incline towards the latter, by the Sútra I. 2, 64. *Patanjali's Introduction* (ed. Ballantyne, p. 40-42): किं पुनराकृतिः पदार्थ आहोस्विद्द्रव्यम्। उभयमित्याह। कथं ज्ञायते। उभयथा ह्याचार्येण सूत्राणि प्रणीतानि। आकृतिं पदार्थं मत्वा जात्याख्यायामेकस्मिन्बहुवचनमन्यतरस्यामित्युच्यते। द्रव्यं पदार्थं मत्वा सरूपाणामेकशेष आरभ्यते.—Whether *Kátyáyana*, in using the expression असर्वलिङ्गा जातिः (I. 4, 1. v. 3, of the Calcutta edition), merely adapted himself to the manner in which Páṇini uses जाति, or whether he, too, had not yet a knowledge of Gautama's definition would have remained doubtful, had he not availed himself, in another of his Várttikas, of the term *ákṛiti* exactly in the sense in which it is defined by the Nyáya Sútra—viz., in the Várttika 5 (ed. Calc.) to VII. I, 74: न वा समानायामाकृतौ भाषितपुंस्कविज्ञानात्; and though Patanjali observes that this Várttika is superfluous, since its contents are a matter of course, we may, nevertheless, be thankful for its word आकृति, and the conclusions it enables us to draw in our present case.—Patanjali: न वा वक्तव्यम्। किं कारणम्। समानायामाकृतौ भाषितपुंस्कविज्ञानात्। समानायामाकृतौ यद्भाषितपुंस्कम्। आकृत्यन्तरे चैतद्भाषितपुंस्कम्। किं वक्तव्यमेतत्। न हि कथमनुच्यमानं गंस्यते। एतदप्यर्थनिर्देशात्सिद्धम्; and Kaiyyaṭa . . . . तच्च पीलुशब्दो वृक्षाकृतौ पुंलिङ्गः फलाकृतौ नपुंसकलिङ्ग इति पुंवद्भावाप्रसङ्गः.

[183] *Vyakti* is used in the same sense by Kátyáyana in the Várttika 1 (of the Calc. ed.) to I. 2, 52.

qualified," it is not the counterpart of *játi*, but of *viśeshaṇa*, "the quality."[184]

The result of the foregoing comparison between Páṇini and Gautama must remove, I believe, every doubt as to the chronological position of both. The expressions of Páṇini show that he had not even conceived so much as the philosophical problem started and solved by Gautama. The very manner in which Patanjali is compelled to answer the question, whether "the sense of a word" in Páṇini "implies species or individuality"—viz., that at one time it implies the former, and at another, the latter, shows that philosophical investigations into the "sense of the word" had not yet troubled Páṇini's mind. A mere difference of opinion between the grammarian and the Nyáya philosopher would be no proof for the posteriority of the latter; but the absence of the problem itself, in the Sútras of Páṇini, is, I hold, sufficient ground for this inference. A problem of this kind could not have been slighted by Páṇini if he had been aware of it; it would have entered unconsciously, as it were, into his terminology, and into the mode of delivering his rules. There is abundant evidence in Patanjali's Great Commentary, that his training must have been a philosophical one; and it is Kátyáyana's superiority, too, in this respect, which inflicts on Páṇini a quantity of Várttikas finding fault with his empiric and unphilosophical treatment of grammatical facts.

After this conclusion, it seems needless to add that the Sútras ignore the word *vaiśeshika*, which, from a grammatical point of view, would have had as much claim to being noticed by Páṇini as any word comprised in his rules IV. 2, 60 and 63. The formation *vaiśeshika* is taught in the Gaṇa to V. 4, 34, but merely in the sense of *viśesha*.

There is an important class of ancient works the chronological relation of which to Páṇini deserves our peculiar attention here, from the circumstance that their contents are more or less kindred

---

[184] Compare II. 1, 57; also V. 1, 119, v. 5 (ed. Calc.)

with those of Páṇini's work,—I mean the grammatical works known under the name of *Uṇṇádi-Sútras*, *Dhátupâṭha*, *Práti-'ákhyas*, *Phiṭ-Sútras*, and we may add to them the *Nirukta*, the exegetical work of *Yáska*. Each of these works, with *perhaps* the exception of one, if I am not mistaken, is unanimously considered by Sanskrit scholars, as prior to the Grammar of Páṇini.

Before I proceed to examine whether this view can be upheld or not, I will quote Professor Müller's opinion on the age of the *Uṇṇádi-Sútras*. "We do not know," he says, "by whom these Uṇâdi affixes were first collected, nor by whom the Uṇâdi-Sûtras, as we now possess them, were first composed. All we can say is, that, as Pâṇini mentions them, and gives several general rules with regard to them, they must have existed before his time."[185]

On the same subject, Dr. Aufrecht, to whom we are indebted for a careful edition of the *Uṇṇádi-Sútras*, together with a commentary by *Ujjwaladatta*, expresses himself thus[186]:—"We have no direct tradition as to the author of the *sûtras*. They were composed before the time of *Pâṇini*, as they are referred to by him in two different passages of his Grammar. The fact, however, that both *Yâska* and the author of the above-quoted Kârikâ [viz., to III. 3, 1] specify *Çâkaṭâyana* as the grammarian who derived all nouns from verbs, speaks in favour of *Nâgoji's* conjecture, that the authorship is to be attributed to *Çâkaṭâyana*. Nor is this supposition entirely unsupported by the evidence of the *sûtras* themselves. In one place (II. 38) we are told that the people of the north used the word *kârshaka* for 'a husbandman;' in another (IV. 128), that they employed *kâri* in the meaning of 'an artisan.' This distinction refers to a period of the language

---

[185] Ancient Sanskrit Literature, p. 151.

[186] "Ujjvaladatta's Commentary on the Uṇâdi-Sûtras, edited from a Manuscript in the Library of the East India House, by Theodor Aufrecht. Bonn, 1859;" Preface, p. viii.—The Uṇṇádi-Sutras were first published in the Calcutta edition of the Siddhánta-kaumudí, afterwards reprinted—without any further consultation of MSS., but with deteriorations, by—*Dr. Boehtlingk*. Compare note 53.

of which no mention is made by any grammarian after *Pâṇini*. In another rule (III. 144,) we find the name of *Çâkravarmaṇa*, an old grammarian who is only once more quoted, namely, in *Pâṇini*, VI. 1, 130. It is of some importance also, that the author of the *sûtras* considers *açman* (stone) and *bhuvana* (world) as Vaidic, whereas they are treated by *Pâṇini* as words of common occurrence. These facts, even when taken collectively, furnish no decisive evidence as to the authorship of the *sûtras*, but they show, at all events, that they were composed a considerable time before *Pâṇini*."

I have in the first instance, to demur to the correctness of one of these "facts," which, if it were real, would dispense with any further proof of the Uṇṇádi-Sútras having preceded—not, indeed, Páṇini, for such an inference would always remain hazardous—but his grammatical work. It is true that this grammarian speaks twice of *Uṇṇádis*, but he *never* speaks of Uṇṇádi-*Sútras*.[187] The former term merely implies a list of Uṇṇádi affixes, and may imply, according to analogous expressions in Páṇini, a list of words formed with these affixes;[188] but it can never imply a work which treats of these affixes and these formations, like the Uṇṇádi-Sútras which we are speaking of. Between a list of Uṇṇádis—affixes or words—and Uṇṇádi-Sútras, there is all the difference which exists between a lexicographical and a grammatical work. All the conclusions, therefore, which are based on the identity of both, vanish at once.

With the conjecture of Nágojibhaṭṭa I shall deal hereafter; but when Dr. Aufrecht quotes the meaning of *kárshaka*, 'husbandman,' and of *kári*, 'artisan' as proving his conclusion, I candidly confess that I do not understand how the fact of these words having been used by the people of the north, in the sense given, can have the remotest bearing on the point at issue, even if in

---

187 III. 3, 1: उणादयो बहुलम्; and III. 4, 75: ताभ्यामन्यत्रोणादयः.

188 *Vaidyanátha* on the Paribháshá उणादयो ऽव्युत्पन्नानि प्रातिपदिकानि—: उणादयः। तदन्तानि तदन्तत्वेनाभिमतानि वा.

the *whole stretch of the voluminous* grammatical literature subsequent to Páṇini, all of which, of course, is covered by his assertion, no grammarian had made mention of the distinction he is adverting to.[189] The Uṇṇádi Sútras profess to give such information as is not contained in Páṇini's work; he himself informs us of this character of the Uṇṇádi list in the two rules alleged. It is but natural, therefore, that we should find in these two Uṇṇádi rules, as indeed we find in all the rest, much interesting matter of which no trace occurs in the Sútras of Páṇini.

But even assuming that my inability to understand this premiss of Dr. Aufrecht only proves my own incapacity, I might go further and ask—What proof does there exist that these two Sútras, which have nothing characteristic or peculiar in them, were not added to the original Sútras at a later time, since Dr. Aufrecht himself has shown that the genuineness of *sixteen* Sútras was suspected by Ujjwaladatta himself? And I may add—Are there not, for instance, in a valuable commentary on more than 300 of these Uṇṇádi-Sútras, composed by *Nṛisinha*, who lived *Samwat* 1577, or 1520 after Christ, at least in the MS. I have consulted, not only many readings which differ from the text of Ujjwaladatta, as edited by Dr. Aufrecht, but three Sútras the substance of which is now in the Commentary, and three Sútras which are neither met with in the text of Bhaṭṭoji nor in that of Ujjwaladatta?[190] It seems,

---

[189] And has this question—which portion of the grammatical literature is later than Páṇini?—been so finally settled that, *at present*, any one is allowed to speak of it as *a matter of course?*

[190] Between the Sútras III. 60 and 61 we read in the E. I. H. MS. 98 of *Nṛisinha's Swaramanjarí* (on accentuation)—where these Uṇṇádi-Sútras occur—a Sútra which is neither amongst those of Ujjwaladatta, nor in his Commentary, viz.: धारेर्णिक् च ॥ Comm.: धारयतीति धरुणः । दिवो धर्मं धरुणे । धरुण एकविंशः । मध्योदात्तः. Between IV. 2 and 3, it has a Sútra the contents—but not the wording—of which are embodied in Ujjwaladatta's Sútra IV. 2: कृशेः किच्च ॥ Comm.: कृशेरानुप्रत्ययः किच्च । कृशतीति कृशानुः । सम्राडसि कृशानुः. Between IV. 90 and 91: तमेर्वुक् च (its substance occurs in the commentary on Sútra IV. 90); Comm.: तमेरूलप्रत्ययः । वुगागमो दीर्घश्च । ...... (?) । ताम्यति तेनेति तांबूलम्; and शृणातेर्दुग्वृद्धिश्च (embodied also in the Commentary of Ujjwaladatta) ॥ Comm.: शृणातेरूलप्रत्ययः । दुग्वृद्धिश्च । शृणातीति शार्दूलः । गवयः शार्दूलाय राज्ञः. Before V. 28, it mentions a Sútra which is neither

therefore, that with the actual doubts we must entertain as to the originality of several Uṇṇádi-Sútras, it is by no means safe to appeal to two or any such Sútras for chronological evidence, unless they be able to show cause why they should not be ranked amongst the additions of later times.[191]

And again, what possible conclusion as to the chronological relation of the Uṇṇádi-Sútras to Páṇini can be drawn from another quotation made by Dr. Aufrecht? *Chákravarmaṇa*, he says, is once quoted by the Uṇṇádi-Sútras, and "*only once more, namely, in Páṇini.*" I will make no remark on these latter words. That they are quoted by both is undeniable; but since it happens that both Dr. Aufrecht and I have quoted Páṇini, does it follow that either of us lived a "considerable time" before the other, or before any other writer who may also have quoted Páṇini? When, however, Dr. Aufrecht points out that the author of the Uṇṇádi-Sútras "considers *açman* (stone) and *bhuvana* (world) as Vaidic, whereas they are treated by Páṇini as words of common occurrence," I, too, lay much stress on the statement contained in this passage of the Uṇṇádi-Sútras, but by it arrive at the

---

amongst those of Ujjwaladatta nor embodied in his Commentary: शाखा ॥ Comm.: शाखेति निपात्यते ।शो तनूकरणे । शाखाभ्यः स्वाहा etc. Before V. 52 which precedes V. 70, and follows V. 69 and the new Sútra (*i.e.* V. 69—the new Sútra—52. 70): दिवेर्डिंचेडिनच् ॥ Comm.: दीव्यतीति द्यौः । दिवौ । दिवः; this Sútra, too, is neither amongst the Sútras nor in the Commentary of Ujjwaladatta.

[191] Dr. Aufrecht himself observes (p. ix) with perfect accuracy: "the uṇâdisûtras have not been handed down to us in their original form. It was not the intention of the author to give a complete list of all the uṇâdi-words, but merely to collect the most important of them. Hence we frequently meet with the sentence: बहुलमन्यत्रापि 'in various other words, too,' or अन्येभ्यो ऽपि दृश्यंते 'the same suffixes are found in other words, too.'" The former of these expressions, quoted by Dr. Aufrecht, occurs, indeed, five times and the latter once; and Patanjali says in his Káriká to III. 3, 1, and in his comment on it: बाहुलकं प्रकृतेस्तनुदृष्टेः ॥ तन्वीभ्यः प्रकृतिभ्य उणादयो दृश्यन्ते न सर्वाभ्यो दृश्यन्ते ॥ प्रायसमुच्चयनादपि तेषाम् ॥ प्रायेण खल्वपि समुच्चिताः । न सर्वे समुच्चिताः ॥ कार्यसशेषविधेश्च तदुक्तम् ॥ कार्याणि खल्वपि सशेषाणि कृतानि । न सर्वाणि लक्षणेन परिसमाप्तानि. Since, then, the Uṇṇádis are admitted, even by Patanjali, to be an incomplete list, and if there is evidence to prove that at recent periods writers permitted themselves to supply the deficiencies, it will be admitted that my hesitation is not a hypercritical one.

very opposite inference to that which has suggested itself to him. For, if Páṇini treated these words which occur in the Vedas as words of common life, and, on the other hand, the author of the Sútras in question had ceased to use them in his conversational speech, and records the fact that they belong, not only to literary language, but to that of the very oldest literature,—I do not conclude that such facts "show, at all events, that they (the Uṇṇádi-Sutras) were composed a considerable time before Páṇini;" but I conclude that Páṇini lived in that Vaidik age when *aśman* and *bhuvana* were as well Vaidik as common words, and therefore required no distinctive remark of his; that, on the contrary, the author of the *two* Uṇṇádi-Sútras in question belonged to a period when these words had become obsolete in common life,—in short, that Páṇini lived a considerable time before this grammarian.

An inference, however, of such importance as this could not be considered as resting on sufficiently solid ground if there were no other means of establishing it than two Sútras of a work avowedly open to interpolations at various periods of Sanskrit literature.

In order to support it with stronger arguments, I must raise a previous question, which does not concern the Uṇṇádi-Sútras alone—the question, *whether or not Páṇini was the originator of all the technical terms he employs in his work?* Since he adverts, several times, in his rules, to grammarians who preceded him,[192] it would probably—not necessarily—be possible to answer this question if we possessed the works of these grammarians. *Śákaṭáyana's* grammar seems indeed, to have come down to us, but though, in such a case it would be within my reach, it must still remain at present a sealed book to me, and I must treat it like the works of Gárgya, Káśyapa, and the other predecessors of Páṇini who merely survive in name and fame.[193]

[192] See note 97.

[193] The knowledge that Śákaṭáyana's Grammar exists, and is preserved amongst the treasures of the Library of the Home Government for India, we owe, like so much of our knowledge of Sanskrit literature, to the lamented Professor Wilson, who speaks of

There are, in my opinion, two Sútras of Páṇini which may serve as a clue through the intricacies of this problem.

In five important rules of his, Páṇini states that, on principle, he will exclude from his Grammar certain subjects, as they do not fall within his scope. But since he gives reasons for doing so, he at the same time enables us to infer what he considered his duty, as a grammarian, to teach.[194] Amongst these rules, one (I. 2, 53) referring to a subject touched on by him in a previous Sútra, says: "Such matter will not be taught by me, for it falls under the category of conventional terms, which are settled (and

---

it in his *Mackenzie Collection*, vol. I. p. 160. Many years ago I obtained sight of the precious volume; but as it is written on palm leaves in the Hálá Kernáta character, and as I could not attempt to make it out without a magnifying glass, and then only with much difficulty, I was compelled to abandon my desire of mastering its contents. It is to be hoped now that a learned, laborious, and competent Sanskrit scholar will transcribe and publish this awkward MS., and thus relieve Sanskrit studies from a suspense which no one can feel more keenly than I do in writing these lines. I must add, at the same time, that doubts have been lately expressed to me whether this MS. contains really the original work of Śákaṭáyana, or merely a Grammar founded on his.

[194] These rules are I. 2, 53-57. They contain Páṇini's grammatical creed, and are the key-stone of his work. But all that the "editor" of Páṇini has to offer with respect to them is the following attempt at an epigram (vol. II. p. 47): "Páṇini makes an expedition against his predecessors." And thus, in taking up that which is merely incidental, and, compared with the subject itself, quite irrelevant, he completely leads the reader away from the real importance of these rules. The *Káśiká*, it is true, mentions that Páṇini differs in the principles he lays down in these rules from previous grammarians; but it is far from making a joke or concentrating the essence of its comment on so futile a point. It shows, on the contrary, the full bearing of these rules, and, I believe, it would have done still better had it embodied in its gloss the remarks of Patanjali on some of these Sútras. At all events, the commentary of the Káśiká on them was deemed important enough even by Dr. Boehtlingk to be quoted by him on this occasion in its full extent, though his reason for doing so is merely to show the "expedition of Páṇini against his predecessors." "*The whole*," (viz., this expedition) he writes in introducing the Káśiká, "*becomes sufficiently clear through an excellent commentary, I mean the Káśiká-vṛitti, which will make any other remark superfluous.*" As the quotation he then gives from the Káśiká is the *only one, of any extent, in his whole second volume*, and as he assumes all the appearance of treating it with that minute and critical and conscientious circumstantiality which even in an incidental quotation must be extremely welcome,—I mean by giving the various readings of his MSS. ("*A*" = MS. 829; "*B*" = MS. 2440 of the East India House—*wrongly*

therefore do not require any rule of mine; *literally:* for it has the authority of a *sanjná* or conventional term)." To these words *Patanjali* appends the following gloss: "When Pánini speaks of conventional terms which he will not teach, because they are settled, does he mean, by this expression, such technical terms as *ṭi*, *ghu*, *bha*, and the like? No; for *sanjná* is here the

---

described by him at p. liv.), by recording the omissions in either of them, even so far as the omission of a "च" is concerned,—in short, as he gives us in his lengthened and highly valuable extract from the Káśiká a specimen of his *editorial character*, I considered it my duty to make a comparison of his edition of this portion of the Káśiká with the two MSS. named and used by him. For though I was perfectly well acquainted with his so-called Commentary on Páṇini, and though it has been my thorough conviction for very many years that his curtailed reprint of the Calcutta edition—I will not qualify it now otherwise—by suppressing important texts and by propagating errors which, even in a reprint, are not excusable, has been more an impediment to a *conscientious* study of Sanskrit grammar, and of Páṇini in particular, than his very imperfect commentatorial remarks may have done service to beginners,—though my opinion of the literary activity of Dr. Boehtlingk was the result of a careful study of his works, and was by no means founded on occasional errors of his, or formed in disregard of all the difficulties he had to contend with;—in short, though not all the imperfections of his writings—*if they amounted only to such*—would ever have induced me to stint the share of indulgence which I hold ought to be always and largely awarded to *laborious* and *honest* work, whatever be its failings, I have considered it my duty to make this comparison since, within the chain of the peculiar circumstances which weigh on his edition of Páṇini and on some of his other "*editions*," too, the point I wanted to ascertain, once more, did not so much concern a question of scholarship as one of scientific reliability. The result of my comparison was this. Dr. Boehtlingk records at his quotation from the Káśiká to I. 2, 53, the various readings of MS. *A*: निर्दिश्यते (for *B* प्रतिनिर्दिश्यते), कस्मात् (for *B* कुतः), वरणावर (for *B* वरणा), लिङ्गवचनं (for *B* लिङ्गवचनं च), and यथा च (for *B* यथा); but he does not say that *A* reads the last words: आपो दारा गृहाः सिता (*sic*) वर्षा इति.—At I. 2. 54 he mentions that MS. *A* has omitted the word शब्द; but he does not state that *A* reads व्यक्तः instead of *B's* reading वक्तव्यः, nor that *B* has a marginal note on the word अप्रख्यानात् which runs thus: योगजनपदादेः चत्रियादिभिः संबन्धः। तस्याप्रख्यानादनुपलब्धेरित्यर्थः. And he edits on his own authority—without any remark whatever—वृचयोगं नगरे—*which is perfectly meaningless*—while both MSS. read वृचयोगान्नगरे.—At I. 2, 55, he mentions that *A* has omitted यदि and तस्य; moreover that *B* reads: चत्रियसंबन्धं जनपदे पञ्चालशब्दः। ततो°; but he does not say that *A* omits also योगाभावे before तस्य, and adds तच्च before the last words प्रवृत्त इति. And what is much worse, he not only edits तत्रावश्यमभ्युपगन्तव्यम्, while both MSS. read तत्रावश्यमेवाभ्युपगन्तव्यम्, but नायं निमित्तकः—*which is simple nonsense*—while both MSS. have the intelligible reading नायं योगनिमित्तकः.—At I. 2, 56, he observes that इति is omitted in *B* and

same as *sanjnána*, 'understanding' (*i.e. a name which has a real meaning*, that may be traced etymologically)." And *Kaiyyaṭa* enlarges upon these words in the following strain: "The question of Patanjali is suggested by the rule of analogy. His answer is in the negative, because context itself has a greater weight than (mere) analogy. Now, though such terms as *ṭi*, *ghu*, *bha*, and the like, are settled terms, this circumstance would not have been a sufficient reason in an *etymological* work (like that of Páṇini) for leaving them untaught, for they have no etymology.' 'Understanding,' (as Patanjali paraphrases *sanjná*) means mentally entering into, understanding the component parts of a word, [or it means the words which admit of this mental process.]" [195]

तत् in *A*; but he does not mention that instead of *B's* °प्रमाणत्वात् । अन्य, etc., *A* reads: °प्रमाणत्वादित्यन्य, etc.; nor does he mention that *B* reads अर्थसिद्धस्तच किं यत्नेन while *A* reads अर्थः सिद्धः किं तच यत्नेन; but, again, he edits, without any remark whatever, अर्थान्यप्रमाणत्वात्, which is *ungrammatical*, in spite of the concurrent and correct reading of both MSS.: अर्थस्यान्यप्रमाणत्वात् (or *A* °त्वादिति, see before).—His remarks at I. 2, 67, are that *A* omits अशिष्य — भवतः, and that *B* reads हि (for *A* च), परिभाषन्तः (for *A* परिभाषन्ते), and मत्वर्थे (for *A* अन्यपदार्थौ). Yet he does not record the various inaccuracies of *A*, which are essential for those not acquainted with this MS., in order that they may form an opinion on it and on its relation to the readings of *B*. Thus he omits stating that *A* reads the commencing words अशिष्यमिति वर्तते, that it omits इदं स्वः कर्तव्यं, and reads पुनराऊरह उभ° for *B's* more correct reading पुनराऊः । अहरुभ°. But Dr. Boehtlingk likewise does not mention that *B* has a marginal note to the word न्याय्यात्, viz., न्यय्यो (*sic*) यमः; that *A* reads चाशिष्ये ते for *b's* चाशिष्ये (in the commencement); that *B* adds तु after अपरे (last line of his page 48); that *A* reads तथा चोपसर्जन° for *B* तथोपसर्जन° (first line of his page 49), and नैव व्युत्पाद्यन्ते for *B* न चैवं व्युत्पाद्यन्ते. And to crown the edition of this portion of the "excellent commentary, I mean the *Káśiká-vṛitti*, which will make all further explanation superfluous," Dr. Boehtlingk prints, without a single remark (p. 49, line 4), तथोपसर्जनमप्रधानमिति गम्यते; when *A* has the following passage: तथोपसर्जनं वयमच गृहे ग्रामे वा । उपसर्जनमप्रधानमिति गम्ये (*sic.*), whereas *B* gives the complete sentence in this way: तथोपसर्जनं । प्रस्तावादर्थवौचित्याद्देशकालविभागतः । शब्दैरर्थाः प्रतीयंते न शब्दादेव केवलात् । वयमच गृहे ग्रामे वा उपसर्जनमप्रधानमिति गम्यते.—And such is his edition of even an easy text of a commentary to *only five* Sútras of Páṇini,—of a commentary, too, so pompously announced by himself, and laid before the public with so much appearance of care and conscientiousness!

[195] Páṇini, I. 2, 53: तदशिष्यं संज्ञाप्रमाणत्वात्.—Patanjali: किं या एताः कृत्रि-

From this rule of Páṇini and the commentaries alleged we learn therefore—

1. That his Grammar does not treat of those *sanjnás* or conventional names which are known and settled otherwise.

2. That this term *sanjná* must be understood in our rule to concern only such conventional names as have an etymology.

3. That it applies also to grammatical terms which admit of an etymology, but not to those which are merely grammatical symbols.

4. That such terms as *ṭi*, *ghu*, and *bha*, *were known and settled before Páṇini's Grammar*, but that, nevertheless, they are defined by Páṇini because they are not etymological terms.

Having thus obtained, through the comment of Patanjali on the Sútra in question, a means by which to judge of the originality of Páṇini's terms, we must feel induced to test its accuracy before we base our inferences on it; and the opportunity of doing so is afforded not merely by the technical symbols which Patanjali himself names,—we easily ascertain that Páṇini has given a definition of them,—but also by another of these important five Sútras. This Sútra (I. 2, 56) says: "Nor shall I teach the purport of the principal part of a compound (*pradhána*), or that of an affix (*pratyaya*), because they, too, have been settled by others (*i.e.* people know already from other authorities, that in a compound the sense of the word gravitates towards its principal part, and in a derivative towards the affix.)"[196]

Thus we learn here from Páṇini himself that the term *pratyaya* (affix) was employed before he wrote his work; and if Patanjali's interpretation be correct, Páṇini, who also makes use of this term,

---

माष्टिघुभादिसंज्ञाः तत्प्रामाण्यादशिष्यम् । नेत्याह । संज्ञानं संज्ञा.—Kaiyyaṭa: किं या एता इति । प्रत्यासत्तिन्यायाश्रयेण प्रश्नः । नेत्याहेति । प्रत्यासत्तेः सामर्थ्यं बलवत् । न हि टिघुभादिसंज्ञानां प्रमाणत्वं युक्तवज्ञावशास्त्रस्याशिष्यत्वे हेतुरुपपद्यते । संबन्धाभावात् । संज्ञानमिति । अवगमः संप्रत्यय इत्यर्थः.

[196] Páṇini, I. 2, 56: प्रधानप्रत्ययार्थवचनमर्थस्यान्यप्रमाणत्वात्. There is no Bháshya on this rule.

must have left it undefined, since it has an etymology and was "settled" in his time. And such, indeed, is the case. Páṇini uses the word *pratyaya* many times (*e.g.* I. 1, 61. 62. 69; 2, 41. 45; 3, 63. etc. etc.), he heads with it a whole chapter which extends over three books of his work, yet he gives no definition whatever of its sense. Finding, then, that Patanjali's comment is confirmed by Páṇini's own words, we may proceed; and we then obtain the result that the Sútras employ but do not explain such terms, for instance, as *prathamá* (nominative), *dwitíyá* (accusative), *tṛitíyá* (instrumental), *chaturthí* (dative), *panchamí* (ablative), *shashṭhí* (genitive), and *saptamí* (locative). And the commentators apprise us that these words were technical names used by the eastern grammarians, which are refered to by Páṇini in some of his rules.[197] We likewise meet in his work with such terms as *samása* (compound II. 1, 3), *tatpurusha* (II. 1, 22), *avyayíbháva* (II. 1, 5), *bahuvríhi* (II. 2, 23), *kṛit* (III. 1, 93), *taddhita* (IV. 1, 76), etc. etc.: he enumerates all the special compounds or affixes which fall under these heads, but does not give any definition whatever of the meaning of these names. Again, the commentaries, in adverting to them, tell us that the terms expressing compounds, for instance, belong to "older grammarians."

When, on the other hand, we see that he *does* give a definition of *karmadháraya* (I. 2, 42), or of *saṁyoga* (I. 1, 7), or of *anunásika* (I. 1, 8), terms which are conventional and admit of an etymological analysis, we are at once compelled to infer that he was the first who employed these technical names *in the sense stated by him.* And this conclusion would apply with equal force to all other terms of a similar kind which do not merely head an enumeration of rules but are clearly defined by him, *e.g.* to *savarṇa* (I. 1, 9), *pragṛihya* (I. 1, 11), *lopa* (I. 1, 60), *hraswa, dírgha, pluta* (I. 2, 27), *udátta* (I. 2, 29), *anudátta* (I. 2, 30), *swarita* (I. 2, 31), *apṛikta* (I. 2, 41), etc. etc. Nor do I believe that this conclusion becomes invalidated in those instances in which Páṇini gives a definition, while yet there may be a strong presumption that the term defined was already

[197] II. 3, 46. 2. 3. 13. 30. 7 etc.

used in his time, for it seems to me that, in such a case, his definition either imparted an additional sense to the current term, and, in reality, thus created a new term of his own, or had a special bearing on the technical structure of his own work. When, for instance, he defines the term *dwandwa*,[198] though there is a *probability* that this term was used by previous grammarians,[199] his definition may have corrected the current notion on the subject implied by it, as I infer from the lengthened discussion of Patanjali. Or, when he uses the term *upasarjana* in one of those five rules already mentioned, thus allowing us to conclude that it was a current term in his time,[200] and still appears to define it in two other rules,[201] his definition is in reality no definition at all; it merely instructs the pupil how he may recognize an upasarjana-rule in his work.[202]

---

[198] II. 2, 29: चार्थे द्वन्द्वः.

[199] Káśiká (M.S. 829, E.I.H.) on I. 2, 57: तथा च पूर्वाचार्याः परिभाषन्ते। अन्यपदार्थो बहुव्रीहिः। पूर्वपदार्थप्रधानो ऽव्ययीभावः। उत्तरपदार्थप्रधानस्तत्पुरुषः। उभयपदार्थप्रधानो द्वन्द्व इत्येवमादिः. MS. 2140, E.I.H., reads मत्वर्थे instead of अन्यपदार्थो, but both readings are objectionable, as we may infer from the Mahábháshya on II. 1, 20: इह कश्चित्समासः पूर्वपदार्थप्रधानः। कश्चिदुत्तरपदार्थप्रधानः। कश्चिदन्यपदार्थप्रधानः। कश्चिदुभयपदार्थप्रधानः etc.; and these identical words reoccur in the Mahábháshya to II. 1, 49. Neither of the terms *bahuvríhi*, *avyayíbháva*, or *tatpurusha* is explained by Páṇini.—Compare also note 44, and my Dictionary, *s.v.* अन्यपदार्थप्रधान.

[200] I. 2, 57: कालोपसर्जने च तुल्यम्.

[201] I. 2, 43: प्रथमानिर्दिष्टं समास उपसर्जनम्.—I. 2, 44: एकविभक्ति चापूर्वनिपाते.

[202] In the foregoing remarks I have drawn a distinct line between the *definition* which Páṇini gives of a term,—as when he says "*abhyasta* are the two syllables constituting a reduplicated base" (VI. 1, 5), or "*prátipadika* is that which has a sense but is neither a verbal root nor an affix" (I. 2, 45); and the *enumeration* he makes of the matter comprised under a term, as when he says "*dhátu* is called *bhú*, etc." (I. 3. 1), or "*pratyaya* (affix) is that which is treated from the beginning of the third book up to the end of the fifth" (III. 1, 1). For I hold that Páṇini could not, at one time, feel the necessity of defining the linguistic properties of a grammatical category, and at another leave unexplained the notion, for instance, of a verbal root, an affix, a particle, and so on, while using these terms extensively, unless these notions were sufficiently clear at the time he wrote, and his grammatical purposes were attained by stating what application he gave to these terms in his work. An evidence of the plausibility of this view is afforded *e.g.* by the terms *átmanepada* and *parasmaipada*.

To extend this inference to purely grammatical symbols like those mentioned by Patanjali, e.g., *gha*, *shash*, *luk*, *ślu*, *lup*, etc. etc., would be wrong, after the remark of this grammarian; for, as we learn from him, that they are not *sanjnás*, in the sense in which Páṇini uses this word in his rule I. 2, 53, we cannot decide to what extent he may have invented these names, or whether he even invented any of them, since Patanjali distinctly tells us, as we have seen, that *ṭi*, *ghu*, *bha*, were terms already known to Páṇini.

If, then, we apply the test we have obtained to the Uṇṇádi-Sútras, we shall have, in the first place, to observe that the technical, and, at the same time, significant names which would fall under the category of Páṇini's rule (I. 2, 53), and which are not only used in, but are indispensable to, the mechanism of these Sútras are the following: *abhyása*, *avyaya*, *udátta*, *upadhá*, *upasarga*, *dírgha*, *dhátu*, *pada*, *vṛiddhi*, *lopa*, *samprasáraṇa*, *hraswa*.[203] Amongst these, Páṇini gives no definition whatever of *dhátu*; for his explanation is merely an enumeration (I. 3, 1); and the same remark applies to *upasarga* (I. 4, 59), and perhaps to *vṛiddhi* (I. 1, 1) and *avyaya* (I. 1, 37. 38, etc.). It is probable, therefore, that Páṇini did not invent these terms, but referred to them as of current use. On the other hand, he distinctly defines *hraswa*, *dírgha*, *udátta*, *upadhá*, *lopa*, *samprasáraṇa*, and *abhyása*.[204] The term *pada* is also defined by him, but it seems that he merely extended its current application for his own purposes, since the commentaries tell us that "the former grammarians" gave a definition of the terms for compounds, and this definition contains the word *pada*. That the Uṇṇádi-Sútras contain no definition of any technical word requires no confirmation from me.

In rules VI. 3, 7 and 8, Páṇini mentions that these terms are used by "grammarians," which expression can only mean that they were in use before he wrote; and in rules I. 4, 99 and 100 he enumerates the conjugation endings *comprised* under these denominations, *but gives no definition* of the terms themselves.

[203] *E.g.* I. 12. 15. 27. 32. 48.—II. 16. 59. 65.—III. 114.—IV. 55. 136. 144.—V. 19, etc.

[204] I. 2, 27: ऊकालोऽज्झ्रस्वदीर्घप्लुतः.—I. 2, 29: उच्चैरुदात्तः.—I. 1, 65: अलोऽन्त्यात्पूर्व उपधा.—I. 1, 60: अदर्शनं लोपः.—I. 1, 45: इग्यणः संप्रसारणम्.—VI. 1, 4: पूर्वोऽभ्यासः (comp. also note 44).

Now, had Páṇini not written the five Sútras (I. 2, 53-57) in which he explains the method of his Grammar, or had he explained all the technical terms used by him, the absence of a definition of such terms in the Uṇṇádi-Sútras would not justify us in arriving at any conclusion as regards the mutual relation of the two works. But since we know that Páṇini does not define all his terms; and, on the other hand, that a treatise like the Uṇṇádi-Sútras uses those terms which are defined by him, and *exactly in the same sense in which they occur in his work*, the only possible conclusion is that this treatise was written later than the Grammar of Páṇini. And this also must have been the opinion of *Ujjwaladatta* and *Bhaṭṭojidíkshita*, for both grammarians, in their comment on an Uṇṇádi-Sútra, which is an original one, if any be, since it treats of a whole category of Uṇṇádi words, state in the plainest possible language that *this Sútra is given as an exception to a rule of Páṇini.*[205] Nay, we owe to Dr. Aufrecht himself a very interesting passage from *Vimala's Rúpamálá*, which distinctly ascribes the authorship of these Uṇṇádi-Sútras to *Vararuchi*. But as Vararuchi is a name of Kátyáyana also,[206] this work seems to intimate that Kátyáyana completed the Grammar of Páṇini, not only in his Várttikas, but in the important work which concerns us here.[207]

---

[205] Uṇṇádi-Sútra, IV. 226: गतिकारकयोः पूर्वपदप्रकृतिस्वरत्वम्.—Ujjwaladatta: .... गतिकारकोपपदात्कृत् (Páṇini, VI. 2, 139) इत्युत्तरपदप्रकृतिस्वरत्वे सति शेषस्यानुदात्तत्वे प्राप्ते वचनमिदमारभ्यते.—Bhaṭṭojidíkshita (Siddh.-k. p. 204 *b*, l. 6) ... गतिकारकोपपदात्कृदित्युत्तरपदप्रकृतिस्वरत्वे सति शेषस्यानुदात्तत्वे प्राप्ते तदपवादार्थमिदम्.

[206] See also Ancient Sanskrit Literature, p. 240.

[207] I subjoin a literal copy of this extract from the edition of Dr. Aufrecht, p. ix.: "उणादयो बहुलम् ॥ संज्ञाविषये स्युः ॥ ताभ्यामन्यत्रोणादयः ॥ संप्रदानापादानाभ्यामन्यस्मिन्नेवार्थे स्युः । लघ्वानुसरणोन्नेया (MS. लघ्वानुसारिणोन्नेया) अनुबन्धा उणादिषु । बहूलोक्त्या प्रसाध्यानि तेषु कार्यांतराणि च । उणादिस्फुटीकरणाय वररुचिना पृथगेव सूत्राणि प्रणीतानि । तद्यथा । कृवापाजिमिस्वदिसाध्यशूभ्य उण् ॥" He adds to this quotation the following curt rebuke: "This assertion, which makes Vararuci older than *Pâṇini*, has no claim to probability." But I must ask—Is there one single word in this passage which justifies, in the slightest degree, the stricture passed by Dr.

Although it follows from all these premises that the *treatise* on the Uṇṇádi-words, the existing collection of Uṇṇádi-Sútras, is later than the Grammar of Páṇini, there still remains the question: What relation exists between the latter work and a *list* of Uṇṇádi-affixes or words which Páṇini twice quotes in his rules?

Yáska relates, in an interesting discussion on the derivation of nouns, that there were in India two classes of scholars, the one comprising the *Nairuktas*, or etymologists (his commentator *Durga* adds: except *Gárgya*), and the grammarian *Śákaṭáyana*; the other consisting of some of the *Vaiyákaraṇas*, or grammarians, and the etymologist *Gárgya*. The former maintained that all nouns are derived from "verbal roots;" the latter that only those nouns are so derived in which accent and formation are regular, and the sense of which can be traced to the verbal root, which is held to be their origin. They denied, as Yáska tells us, the possibility of assigning an origin to such words as *go*, "cow," *aśwa*, "horse," *purusha*, "man."[208] Now, it is this latter description of words which is the subject of the Uṇṇádi list: they are the Uṇṇádi words. We must ask, therefore, did Páṇini belong, as regards his linguistic notions, to the *Nairuktas* or to the "some of the *Vaiyákaraṇas*?"

Aufrecht on Vimala? The latter says, "To illustrate (or to make clear) the Uṇṇádi affixes, *Vararuchi* composed the (Uṇṇádi) Sútras as a separate work." He draws a distinction therefore, as I have already done, between the Uṇṇádi list and the Sútras on them; but where does he say that Vararuchi is older than Páṇini? Dr. Aufrecht evidently mistook his own conclusions, quoted above, which precede this passage from *Vimala's Rúpamálá*, for the opinion of the latter work. Having first established his conclusions in the manner we have seen, he seems never to have doubted that any writer can differ from his view. Therefore, when meeting with Vimala, who reports that Vararuchi is the author of the Uṇṇádi Sútras, he upbraids this poor grammarian with having made Vararuchi older than Páṇini.

[208] See Roth's Nirukta, I. 12; Müller's Ancient Sanskrit Literature, p. 164; and Aufrecht's Uṇṇádi-Sútras, p. vi. vii. Yáska, according to the present edition, adds to the three instances given the word हस्तिन् also. He can scarcely have meant the word "elephant," which is not a kṛit, but a regular taddhita derivative of *hasta*: nor does this word occur in the Uṇṇádi-Sútras. It seems therefore probable that he said, or at least meant, the real Uṇṇádi word *hasta*, "hand.' But as *Durga*, too, at all events in the MS. at my command, writes हस्तीति, I do not venture upon more than a conjecture that the latter words are to be corrected in the text of the Nirukta: हस्त इति.

Since the former designation is chiefly applied to the exegetes of the Vaidik texts, and the latter is emphatically used by the grammarians, it seems probable that Páṇini, in this question of the derivability of Uṇṇádi words, would stand on the side of these Vaiyákaraṇas. And this unquestionably is the opinion of Patanjali, as may be judged from the following facts:—In the rules VII. 1, 2, Páṇini teaches, amongst other things, that when an affix contain the letters *ḍh*, or *kh*, or *chh*, these letters are merely grammatical symbols, the real values of which are severally *ey*, *ín*, *íy*. To this rule *Kátyáyana* appends the remark that the Uṇṇádi affixes form an *exception*, when Patanjali explains this view of the author of the Várttikas by the instances *śankha*, *śaṇḍha*; for though these words are formed with the affixes *kha* and *ḍha*, the letters *ḍh* and *kh*, in their affixes, are real, not symbolical. "And," continues Kátyáyana, in two subsequent Várttikas, "though Páṇini speaks himself, in Sútra III. 1, 29, of an affix *íyañg* (not *chhañg*, as might be expected according to rule VII. 1, 2), this does not invalidate my exception, for the latter is based on the circumstance that Páṇini treats in his rule VII. 1, 2, not of verbal but of nominal bases." "True," rejoins Patanjali; "but Kátyáyana might have spared this discussion, for "*nominal bases formed with Uṇṇádi affixes are bases which have no grammatical origin.*"[209]

In rule VII. 3, 50, Páṇini teaches that the letter *ṭh* in the affix *ṭha* has the value of *ik*; that *ṭha*, therefore, means in reality *ika*;[210]

---

[209] VII. 1, 2: आयनेयीनीयियः फढखछघां प्रत्ययादीनाम्.—A Várttika: तच्चोणादिप्रतिषेधः.—Patanjali: तच्चोणादीनां प्रतिषेधो वक्तव्यः शङ्खः शण्ढः (comp. Uṇ. S. I. 101. 104).—Várttika: धातोर्वैयङ्वचनात्.—Patanjali: अथवा यदयमृतेरीयङ्गिति (III. 1, 29) धातोरीयङं शास्ति etc.—Várttika: प्रातिपदिकविज्ञानाच्च पाणिनेः सिद्धम्. — Patanjali: प्रातिपदिकविज्ञानाच्च भगवतः पाणिनेराचार्यस्य सिद्धम्। उणादयो ऽव्युत्पन्नानि प्रातिपदिकानि.

[210] VII. 3, 50: ठस्येकः.—A Várttika: संघातग्रहणं चेदुणादिमाथितिकादीनां प्रतिषेधः.—Patanjali: ..... उणादीनां तावत्। कण्ठः पण्ठः शण्ठः (comp. Uṇ. S. I. 105; IV. 104) etc.—Várttika: तस्माद्विशिष्टग्रहणम्.—Patanjali (after a lengthened discussion asks and answers): एवमप्युणादीनां प्रतिषेधो वक्तव्यः। न वक्तव्यः। उणा-

in rule VII. 4, 13, that a long vowel *á*, *í*, *ú*, becomes short before the affix *ka*;[211] in VIII. 2, 78, that the short vowels *i* and *u* become long before a radical consonant *r* and *v*, if these consonants are followed by another consonant;[212] in VIII. 3, 59, that the *s* of an affix is changed under certain conditions to *sh*.[213] To all these rules Kátyáyana takes exception by excluding from them the *Uṇṇádi words*. Thus *kaṇṭha*, *panṭha*, *śanṭha*, are formed with the affix *ṭha* which does not mean *ika*; *ráká* and *dháká* retain their long *á* before the affix *ka*; from *jṛí* is derived *jívri*, not *jívṛi*; *kiri* and *giri* form their dual *kiryos* and *giryos*, not *kíryos* and *gíryos*; and in the words *kṛisara*, *dhúsara*, the *s* has not become *sha*; while, on the other hand, this change has taken place in *varsha* and *tarsha*,[214] though the conditions named by Páṇini in rule VIII.

दयो ऽव्युत्पन्नानि प्रातिपदिकानि । एवमपि कर्मठ इत्यत्र प्राप्नोति (comp. V. 2, 35, where the affix is not a *kṛit*, but a *taddhita*).

[211] VII. 4, 13 : के ऽणः.—Várttika : के ऽणो ह्रस्वत्वे तद्धितग्रहणं कृन्निवृत्त्यर्थम्.—Patanjali : के ऽणो ह्रस्वत्वे तद्धितग्रहणं कर्तव्यम् । किं प्रयोजनम् । कृन्निवृत्त्यर्थम् । कृति मा भूत् । राका धाक (MS. धाका) इति (*cf.* Uṇ. S. III. 40) । तत्तर्हि वक्तव्यम् । न वक्तव्यम् । उणादयो ऽव्युत्पन्नानि प्रातिपदिकानि etc.

[212] VIII. 2, 78 : उपधायां च.—A Várttika : उपधादीर्घत्वे ऽभ्यासजिव्रिचतुर्णां प्रतिषेधः.—Patanjali : उपधादीर्घत्वे ऽभ्यासजिव्रिचतुर्णां प्रतिषेधो वक्तव्यः । रिर्यतुः । रिर्युः । संविव्यतुः । संविव्युः ॥ अभ्यास ॥ जिव्रिः (MS. अभ्यासजिव्रिः) ॥ चतुर्यिता । चतुर्यितुम्.—Várttika : उणादीनां प्रतिषेधश्च.—Patanjali : उणादीनां च प्रतिषेधो वक्तव्यः । किर्योः । गिर्योरिति ..... but after some discussion he concludes : जिव्रिप्रतिषेधश्च न वक्तव्यः (MS. वक्तव्यं) । उणादयो ऽव्युत्पन्नानि प्रातिपदिकानि (*cf.* Uṇ. S. V. 49); and again ...... न सुपो विभक्तिविपरिणामात् । गीर्भ्यां गीर्भिरित्यदोषः । उणादिप्रतिषेधो वक्तव्य इति । परिहृतमेतत् । उणादयो ऽव्युत्पन्नानि प्रातिपदिकानीति (*cf.* Uṇ. S. IV. 142).

[213] VIII. 3, 59 : आदेशप्रत्यययोः.—Várttika : आदेशप्रत्यययोः षत्वे सरकः प्रतिषेधः.—Patanjali : आदेशप्रत्यययोः षत्वे सरकः प्रतिषेधो वक्तव्यः । कृसरः । धूसरः । अत्यल्पमिदमुच्यते सरक इति.—Várttika : सरगादीनामिति वक्तव्यम्.—Patanjali : इहापि यथा स्यात् । वर्षम् । तर्षमिति । तत्तर्हि वक्तव्यम् । न वक्तव्यम् । उणादयो ऽव्युत्पन्नानि प्रातिपदिकानि etc. (*cf.* Uṇ. S. III. 73. 62).

[214] In the E. I. H. MS. of the Mahábháshya and in the Calcutta edition of Páṇini the instances to VIII. 3, 59, v. 2, are वर्स and तर्स (instead of वर्ष and तर्ष); but it is evident that this reading is erroneous; for, in his first Várttika, Kátyáyana intends to show that Páṇini's rule is too wide; and, in the second, that it is too narrow, if applied

3, 59 would not justify it there. But Patanjali, who supplies us with all these instances, in order to establish, first, the sense of the Várttikas, always rejects the criticism of Kátyáyana, and defends Páṇini with the same argument which he used before, viz., in saying that "*nominal bases formed with Uṇṇádi affixes are bases which have no grammatical origin*," and therefore do not concern an etymological work like that of Páṇini.

But if Kátyáyana were really wrong in his censure of Páṇini, can the argument used by Patanjali in defence of Páṇini be right? Let us imagine that there existed amongst us two sets of grammarians, the one contending that the words *red*, *bed*, *shed*, are derived from radicals *re*, *be*, *she*, with an affix *d*; and another refuting these etymologists, and asserting that their derivation is

---

to certain Uṇṇádi words. Compare also the Commentary on the Uṇṇádi-Sútra III. 62.—It is needless to observe once more that in this, as in *all similar instances*, the reprint of Dr. Boehtlingk has simply continued the mistake of the Paṇḍits, though it always assumes the air of having taken its information from the MSS. Thus, in this very Várttika, the Calcutta edition has a misprint सरकप्रतिषेधः, and Dr. Boehtlingk writes—not "the Calcutta edition," but—"*Ein vârtika:* सरकप्रतिषेधः (*sic*)," as if this reading were an original one. But the E. I. H. MS. of the Mahábháshya reads quite correctly: "सरकः प्रतिषेधः"; and Kaiyyaṭa has even a special remark to the effect, that though the Uṇṇádi-Sútra III. 73 (comp. also 70) teaches the affix सरन्, the Várttika and Bháshya write सरक् (of which सरकः is the genitive), because this affix is कित् viz: अशेः सरन्नित्यतः सरन्प्रत्ययः (MS. °यो) क्षधूमदिभ्यः किदित्यचानुवर्तते (Uṇ. S. III. 73) । कित्त्वातिदेशाच्च कित्कार्यलाभाज्ज्ञाप्यवार्त्तिकयोः सरकपठितः. In all these instances, and others too (*e.g.* to VII. 2, 8, v. 1 of the Calc. ed.), the E. I. H. MS. of the Mahábháshya, and the Calcutta edition—as often as it gives this passage—write: उणादयो ऽव्युत्पन्नानि प्रातिपदिकानि (the MS. of the Mahábháshya without the ऽ; the correctness of the reading given, however, does not only result from the commentaries, but from the Paribháshá works; MS. 778 of the Paribháshenduśekhara *e.g.* writes उणादयो ऽव्यु°); when the first word, though literally meaning "the affixes *uṇ*, etc." has the sense, "the words formed with the affixes *uṇ*, etc." (comp. I. 1. 72), in conformity with the use which Páṇini makes of the words कृत् and तद्धित (in the *masculine* gender), *e.g.* I. 1. 38; 2, 46; VI. 2, 155. Compare also *Vaidyanátha's* explanation, in note 188. The reading "उणादीन्यव्युत्पन्नानि प्रातिपदिकानि", which is given by Dr. Aufrecht, p. vi., I have *never* met with, though I have frequently met with the phrase quoted above, not only in the grammatical commentaries, but in all the Paribháshá-works, which give it as a Paribháshá. I, therefore, very much doubt its correctness, *even if it should really be found in any MS.*

absurd; that *red*, *bed*, *shed* are "bases without a grammatical origin." Is it probable, on the same supposition, that a member of the last-named category, in writing a grammar and in dealing with these words, would ascribe to them an affix *d*? Yet, if Patanjali were right, Páṇini would belong to this latter category, and he would have committed such an incongruity. He has not only spoken of an Uṇṇádi affix *u*, but he calls it by its technical name *uṇ*, which means that he bore in mind a distinct form of a radical, the vowel of which would become subject to the Vṛiddhi increase if it is joined to this affix *u*. The Uṇṇádi words must, consequently, have been to Páṇini words in which he perceived a real affix and a real radical,—words, in short, with a distinct etymology. There is other evidence to the same effect besides the two rules of his which contain the word *uṇṇádi*. In rule VII. 2, 9, he mentions the affixes *ti*, *tu*, *tra*, *ta*, *tha*, *si*, *su*, *sara*, *ka*, *sa*; all these are Uṇṇádi affixes, and consequently represent to him as many radicals as are capable of being combined with them for the formation of nominal bases.[215] That there is a flaw in the defence of Patanjali, must have been already perceived by *Kaiyyaṭa*, for this commentator tries to reconcile the fact I have pointed out with the assertion of Patanjali. I will quote his words, but merely to show that it was a desperate case to save Páṇini from the Nairukta school, and to give him the stamp of a pure-bred Vaiyákaraṇa. On the occasion of Patanjali's commenting on the Várttika to VIII. 3, 59, and repeating the remark already mentioned, *Kaiyyaṭa* says: "Though the Uṇṇádi words have been derived for the *enlightenment of the ignorant*, their formation is not subject to the same grammatical influence as it would be if they had an origin;" and, after having endeavoured to prove the correctness of this view through rule VIII. 3, 46, he winds up with the following words: "Therefore . . . . . . in the Uṇṇádi formations, *kṛisara*, etc., *sara* etc. do not fall under the technical category

[215] VII. 2, 9: तितुत्रतथसिसुसरकसेषु च.

of affixes, so that the rule which concerns the change of an affixal *s* to *sh*, would have to be applied in their case."[216]

That Kátyáyana, when he found fault with Páṇini, must have taken my view, is obvious. He must have looked upon Páṇini as judging of the Uṇṇádi words in the same way as Śákaṭáyana did: otherwise his "*pratishedhas*" *exceptions*, or even his *additions* to the rules in question, would have been as irrelevant as if he had increased them with matter taken from medicine or astronomy.

The conclusion, however, at which I have thus been compelled to arrive, viz., that Páṇini shared in the linguistic principles of Śákaṭáyana, is of importance, if we now consider the relation in which he is likely to have stood to the original Uṇṇádi list and to the criticisms of Kátyáyana.

Nágojíbhaṭṭa, who wrote notes on Kaiyyaṭa's gloss on Patanjali, conjectures from the Káriká to III. 3, 1, that the Uṇṇadi *Sútras* were the work of Śákaṭáyana.[217] His conjecture rests on the statement of Yáska, alluded to by Patanjali, that this grammarian con-

---

[216] Patanjali to VIII. 3, 59 (comp. note 213): उणादयो ऽव्युत्पन्नानि प्रातिपदिकानि.—Kaiyyaṭa: उणादय इति। अबुधबोधनाय व्युत्पाद्यमाना अप्युणादयो व्युत्पत्तिनिमित्तं कार्यं न लभन्ते। अतः कृकमिकंसेत्यत्र (VIII. 3, 46) पृथक्कंसग्रहणात्। न वा एतद्विषत्वं व्युत्पत्तिहेतुकमुणादीनामवश्याभ्युपेयम्। सर्पिषा वृत्त इत्यादिसिद्ध्यर्थमित्यर्थः। एवं तर्हीति कृसरादिषु षत्वे कर्तव्ये प्रत्ययसंज्ञा न भवति.—I here subjoin the interesting comment of *Śíradeva*, in his *Paribháshávṛitti* (MS. E.I.H. 593), on this Paribháshá, as it is appealed to by other authors of Paribháshá-works: उणादयो ऽव्युत्पन्नानि प्रातिपदिकानि ॥ अयं चार्थो ऽर्थवत्सूत्रप्रणयनादस्तीत्याहुः। अन्यथा सर्वेषामुणादीनां धातुजत्वे कृदन्तत्वात्प्रातिपदिकसंज्ञासिद्धौ तच्च कुर्यात्। अन्ये त्वतः कृकमीत्यत्र (VIII. 3, 46) कमिग्रहणं कृत्वा कंसग्रहणादेतामाहुः। तेन कृगॄकुटिविदिभ्याश्च (*sic.* comp. Uṇ. S. IV. 142) इः किदितीकारप्रत्ययान्तयोः किरिगिरिशब्दयोरोसि यणादेशे कृते धातुत्वाभावाद्धलि चेति (VIII. 2, 77) दीर्घत्वं न भवति। किर्योः। गिर्योरिति। एतच्च न सम्यक्। अचः परस्मिन्निति (I. 1, 57) स्थानिवत्त्वाद्दीर्घाप्रसङ्गात्। न चास्ति दीर्घविधिं प्रति न स्थानिवदिति। स्वरदीर्घयलोपेषु लोपाजादेश एव न स्थानिवदिति वचनात् (comp. I. 1, 58)। यथा प्रतिदीव्नेति। एवं तर्हि जीर्यतेर्धातोर्जीर्यतेः क्रिन् रश्च व इति (Uṇ. S. V. 49) क्रिन्प्रत्यय इत्वे रपरत्वे च रेफस्य वकारे कृते जिव्रिरिति धातुत्वाभावाद्दीर्घो न भवतीति.

[217] See also Dr. Aufrecht's Preface to the Uṇ. S. p. vii, where the Commentary of Nágojíbhaṭṭa is quoted, and translated by him.

tended for the possibility of deriving all nominal bases from verbal roots. Now, I have shown before, that the opinion of Nágojibhaṭṭa cannot be adopted so far as the *Sútras* are concerned, for they were written *after* Páṇini's work, and Śákaṭáyana wrote before Páṇini.[218] It may, at first sight, however, appear to be consistent with fact, if only the Uṇṇádi *list* were meant, for Śákaṭáyana's views are such as would admit of nominal derivation by means of Uṇṇádi affixes. Yet, since Nágoji's conjecture is purely personal, and is not supported by any evidence, I may be allowed, after the explanation I have given, to assume that the Uṇṇádi list is of Páṇini's authorship. Indeed, how could Kátyáyana take *exception* to the *technical* application or to the *working of a rule of Páṇini's*, and supply this defect by pointing to the Uṇṇádi list, unless he looked upon Páṇini as being the author of both? Had he thought that the Uṇṇádi list was written by Śákaṭáyana, he would have laid himself open to serious reflections, in censuring the *anubandhas* of Páṇini for not fitting the system of Śákaṭáyana. We might make an assumption, it is true, by which we could reconcile Śákaṭáyana's authorship of the Uṇṇádi list with Kátyáyana's strictures on Páṇini,—the assumption that Páṇini's work represented, as it were, besides its own property, that of Śákaṭáyana's too,—that both grammarians owned one set of technical signs, and that perfect unanimity reigned between their works. The *Gaṇaratnamahodadhi* of *Vardhamána* gives numerous quotations from the Grammar of Śákaṭáyana, but as several of them merely give the substance of his rules, it would scarcely be safe to judge of his system on the authority of this valuable Gaṇa work.[219] Unless, therefore, it can be shown that there was no

---

[218] See note 97.

[219] Relative to this work, which is of the greatest importance for the study of Sanskrit grammar, Dr. Boehtlingk gives the following information (vol. II., p. xxxix.—xli.):— "A third work, which contains the *Gaṇas*, is the *Gaṇaratnamahodadhi* (the great Ocean of the Gaṇa-pearls). In London there exist two MS. copies of this work: the one in the Library of the Royal Asiatic Society, the other in that of the East India House. [He adds some remarks on the age of the former MS., and continues]: The work

difference whatever and, much more so, if it can be shown that there *was a difference* between the technical method of both these grammarians, common sense would lean in favour of the conclusion that Kátyáyana, in his Várttikas, hit at but one of his predecessors, and that this predecessor was the author as well of the eight grammatical books as of the Uṇṇádi list,—Páṇini.

---

consists of eight chapters (अध्याय) and about 450 double verses. Its author is *Çrî-Vardhamâna*, a pupil of *Çrî-Govinda*, and, as it is stated in the introductory verses, it owes its origin to the request of his pupils, three of whom he names in the commentary on his work, viz., Kumârapâla, Haripâla, and Munik̦andra. Text and commentary are so corrupt in both Manuscripts, that at the very best only a tolerable text could be made up. Besides, this collection was not intended for the work of Pâṇini, but for some more modern grammar. There occur *Gaṇas* in it which are neither mentioned in the Sûtras nor in the Vârttikas. Then, again, we find two Gaṇas which are separate in our collection [Dr. B. means the Gaṇas edited by him] combined into one, when the derivatives formed according to two different rules, differ from one another only in accent. The various readings of the *Gaṇaratnamahodadhi* (G. R. M.) I have indicated merely at the Gaṇa काण्ड्वादि."—To this statement I have to append the following remarks:—

1. When Dr. Boehtlingk tells the public that there are but two MS. copies of this work in London, his readers will no doubt believe, if they believe him,—indeed, they cannot draw any other inference from his words than—that there are in London only two texts of the Gaṇas collected by Vardhamána in his work, the Gaṇaratnamahodadhi. I cannot suppose that there can be any one who would interpret the meaning of his words in the sense that there are only two catalogued Nos. of this work in the libraries he is speaking of. Yet I am compelled to take this favourable—though very unreasonable—view of his statement, in order not to be compelled to qualify it otherwise. For, the fact is that the bound volume No. 949 of the Library of the E. I. H., which he is speaking of, is, indeed, one volume only, but contains *two distinct copies* of the work in question, written in *different* handwritings, and constituting, therefore, *two separate* MSS. These, added to the copy in the R. A. S., form, therefore, at first sight, *three* MSS., not *two*, as he says. But I should trifle with my readers if I considered this correction as sufficient to illustrate the character of Dr. Boehtlingk's statement. The first MS. of No. 949 contains the text of the Gaṇaratnamahodadhi only, on 30 leaves. The second MS. of the same No. 949, which is a commentary, by the same author, on his work, contains, first the text, and afterwards the comment, which repeats every word of the text, either literally or impliedly, by stating the derivatives from the word or words as they occur in the text. The same method is observed in the MS. belonging to the Royal Asiatic Society. Hence we possess, in London, not *two texts*, nor yet *three*, but in reality *five* texts of this work.

2. The MSS. in question are, no doubt, open to correction, as, indeed, probably every Sanskrit MS. in existence *is*, but I hold that at all events the ancient copy of the R.A.S.

The proof that such a difference existed between Páṇini and Śákatáyana, indeed, between him and all the grammarians who preceded his work, is afforded by a statement of Patanjali, which is so important that it settles definitely, not only the question of the authorship of the Uṇṇádi list, but of all the other works which follow the *anubandha* terminology of Páṇini. In his comment on

---

will, in spite of its inaccuracies, be ranked by every one conversant with MSS., amongst *the best Sanskrit MSS. in existence.* And having considered it incumbent on me to study this book carefully, I have no hesitation in maintaining that even a tolerable Sanskrit scholar would be able to make a perfectly good edition of at least the text of this work, with the aid of these five copies of the text, the two copies of the commentary, and, as a matter of course, with the aid that may be got from Páṇini and his commentaries.

3. As to the nature of this work: I must allow the reader to draw his own conclusions with regard to the credit that may be attached to the information given by Dr. Boehtlingk, when I state that there is not one single Gaṇa in the Gaṇaratnamahodadhi, the contents of which may not be referred either to Páṇini's Sútras or to the Várttikas of Kátyáyana, the Káśiká, etc., and the commentaries on them, or to the Gaṇas connected with these works, though the latter frequently do not contain so much matter as the Gaṇas of Vardhamána, who is later, and, as we may expect, made his own additions to previous lists. The substance of its Gaṇas, increased sometimes in the manner stated, is often contained in several rules of, and in the *commentaries* on, Páṇini and Kátyáyana, which have been brought into Gaṇa shape, while, at other times, several of its Gaṇas, also increased, as the case may be, differ from the Gaṇas to Páṇini merely in so far as the heading word of the one occurs in the middle of the other, and *vice versâ.* Thus the two combined Gaṇas कुण्डा-दिपचादी of the G. R. M. do not occur in the Gaṇas to Páṇini, but give the substance of Páṇini's Sútra, and the commentaries on, IV. 1, 42; its Gaṇa वृन्दारकादि that of the commentaries on II. 1, 62; मतल्लिकादि that of the comm. on II. 1, 66; खसूच्यादि that of the comm. on II. 1, 53; नभ्राडादि that of VI. 3, 75; व्यासादि that of Várttika I. to IV. 1, 97; केदारादि that of IV. 2, 39. 40; अजादि that of the Várttikas to V. 1, 77; ऋगादि that of IV. 3, 72, etc. etc.—On the other hand, the Gaṇa of the G. R. M. उत्थापनादि is equivalent to the Gaṇa to Páṇini अनुप्रवचनादि (V. 1, 111), its Gaṇa देवव्रतादि to अवान्तरदीक्षादि (V. 1, 94. v. 3); धनपत्यादि to अश्वपत्यादि (IV. 1, 84); अश्मादि to आकर्षादि (V. 2, 64); शिशुक्रन्दादि to इन्द्रजननादि (IV. 3, 88); वल्वजादि to कुमुदादि (IV. 2, 80); भिक्षादि to खण्डिकादि (IV. 2, 45), etc. etc.—There are omitted, *on principle*, in the G. R. M., all the Gaṇas (1) which have reference to the enumeration of affixes, *e.g.*, तसिलादि, असादि, etc.; (2) of radicals which are referred to by Páṇini in rules on *conjugation*, such as भ्वादि, अदादि, etc.; द्युतादि, पुषादि, etc.; (3) those which concern Vaidik words; and (4) those apdended to Páṇini's rules on accentuation.—Of other Gaṇas to Páṇini and the Várttikas, mentioned in the Káśiká, Siddhánta-kaumudí, and the Gaṇa lists, which do not fall under

the Sútra VII. 1, 18, which makes use of the technical declension affix *aṅṅg* (= *au*), he shows that the mute letter *ṅg* has none of the properties which inhere in this *anubandha* in the system of Páṇini. After some discussion on the various modes in which this *anubandha* could be dealt with, so as not to interfere with the consistency of the method of Páṇini, he concludes with

---

any of these categories, there are omitted in the G. R. M. the Gaṇas to Páṇini or the Várttikas: आबादि (III. 3, 94. v. 1), इत्वादि (V. 2, 29. v. 5), उपकूलादि ? (IV. 3, 58. v. 1), कमलादि (IV. 2, 51. v. 1), गम्यादि (III. 3, 3), दूर्वादि (IV. 2, 51. v. 2), नावादि (II. 3, 17. v. 2), निष्कादि (V. I, 20), न्यङ्क्वादि (VII. 3, 53), पार्श्वादि (III. 2, 15. v. 1), प्रकृत्यादि (II. 3, 18. v. 1), प्रतिवेशादि (VI. 3, 122. v. 3), प्रादि (I. 4, 58), छगादि (IV. 3, 164), भवदादि (V. 3, 14. v. 1), भीमादि (III. 4, 74), युवादि (VIII. 4, 11. v. 1), यौधेयादि (IV. 1, 178; V. 3, 117), रसादि (V. 2, 95), वरणादि (IV. 2, 82), विल्वकादि (VI. 4, 153), वृषलादि (V. 3, 66. v. 5), शाकपार्थिवादि (II. 1, 69. v. 1), संकलादि (IV. 2, 75), सपत्न्यादि (IV. 1, 35), सवनादि (VIII. 3, 110), सुवास्त्वादि (IV. 2, 77), स्तोकादि (VI. 3, 2), हरीतक्यादि (IV. 3, 167), and perhaps बह्वादि (IV. 1, 45), since only some words of this Gaṇa are included in the Gaṇa of the G. R. M. शोणादि.—These omissions will be excused, if a report, current at Benares, be true, that the author died before he completed his work; but I have no doubt, whether this report be true or not, that they will be looked upon with the *greatest indulgence* by Dr. Boehtlingk, as he himself, in his so-called "Alphabetical Gaṇapâṭha," has omitted *not less than about* 90 *Gaṇas to the Sútras and Várttikas.*

4. That a work so conscientiously described by Dr. Boehtlingk can have no value in his eyes is very obvious. Others, however, may think differently, when they become acquainted with the real character of the *Gaṇaratnamahodadhi.* Its Gaṇas, as I mentioned before, are all based on rules of Páṇini, which very frequently are literally quoted for their authority; while even, when they are not literally quoted, the reference made to their contents plainly shows their close relation to them. The commentary not only enumerates every derivative formed—thus securing in most instances, beyond a doubt, the reading of the text,—but often gives instances from other works—grammatical, lexicographical, and poetical, several not yet published; as, for instance, those of *Gaja, Chandra, Jayáditya, Jinendrabuddhi, Durga, Bhoja, Śákaṭáyana, Haláyudha,* etc. And, above all, it supplies us with the meanings of a considerable portion of such Gaṇa-words as have been hitherto either not understood at all, or understood imperfectly. Of the 12,000 words and upwards, which I have collected from this work for grammatical and lexicographical purposes, there are at least 3,000 which would fall under the latter category; and they have signally avenged themselves on the detractor of this work, as, in his own Dictionary, he is now compelled to leave, in a great many instances, a very telling blank space, which would have been filled up if he had really read the Gaṇaratnamahodadhi, while in other instances he would have obtained additional meanings to those which he assigns to certain words. When I mention, moreover, that this *Gaṇaratnamahodadhi* is the *only known work in existence* which gives a

the following words: "Or this rule belongs to a Sútra of a former grammarian; *but whatever anubandhas occur in a Sútra of a former grammarian, they have no anubandha effect in this work.*"

Hence we learn from Patanjali, who is the very last author that can be suspected of having made such an important assertion without a knowledge of the works anterior to the Grammar of Páṇini, that, though Páṇini adopted from his predecessors such technical symbols as *ṭi*, *ghu*, *bha*, and though he availed himself of other terms of theirs which have a meaning and an etymology (see page 166),—he did not adopt their technical *anubandhas*; and if he avails himself of such an anubandha, as that in rule VII. 1, 18, we must look upon it as a quotation made by him, but not as influencing the rule in which it occurs.[220]

Now, all the Uṇṇádi affixes have *anubandhas*, which are exactly the same, and have the same grammatical effect, as those used by Páṇini. They cannot be later than his work, for it refers to them: they cannot have preceded it, for Patanjali says that "whatever *anubandhas* occur in a Sútra of a former grammarian, they have no *anubandha* effect in Páṇini's work." Consequently the Uṇṇádi list *must be of Páṇini's own authorship.*

---

commentary on the Gaṇas to, or connected with, Páṇini—so obscure in many respects,—comprising also, as I before observed, many Sútras of, and Várttikas to, Páṇini; and when, thus, it becomes evident that a conscientious editor of Páṇini ought to have *eagerly* availed himself of the instruction afforded him by this unique work, it will, perhaps, be intelligible why a certain Nemesis has induced Dr. Boehtlingk to divert the attention of the scientific public from the MSS. of this work, by describing their condition and contents as he has done. As a matter of curiosity, I may, in conclusion, add, that the only Gaṇa of the G. R. M., the various readings and meanings of which he has registered in his "Alphabetical Gaṇapâṭha"—the Gaṇa काष्ठादि—occurs *very near the end* of the whole work, viz., at fol. 28, in the text of MS. 949 of the E. I. H., which ends on fol. 30; and at fol. 119 of the combined text and commentary of the same MS., which ends on fol. 121. In the palm-leaf MS. of the R. A. S., which ends on fol. 178, this Gaṇa stands at fol. 168. The title of a Sanskrit book, I need not mention, is always given at the *end* of a manuscript.

[220] VII. I, 18: औङ आपः.—Patanjali (towards the end of his discussion): अथवा पूर्वसूत्रनिर्देशो ऽयम्। पूर्वसूत्रे च ये ऽनुबन्धाः। न तैरिहेत्कार्याणि क्रियन्ते.—Kaiyyaṭa: अथवेति पूर्वाचार्यैरिदं अपि द्विवचने ङिती पठिते न चेह क्वचिदप्यौङ्प्रत्ययो ङिदस्ति सामान्यग्रहणार्थं च पूर्वसूत्रनिर्देशः etc.—For पूर्वसूत्र, compare also note 46.

Having settled this point, we may now ask, whether the criticisms of Kátyáyana do not lead to a further inference? When Kátyáyana finds fault with Páṇini for having overlooked the fact that the vowel *á* remains long in *ráka*, *dháka*, or for having given an inadequate rule for such derivations as *kṛisara* and *dhúsara*, *varsha* and *tarsha*, such criticism applies to omissions which may occur in the case of an author, even a Páṇini. But when he reproaches him with having spoiled the consistency of his *anubandhas*—so dear to a Hindu grammarian—this blemish seems to me so important, and would probably appear so much more important to a Hindu Pandit, that it compels my conclusions to take another course. For it was obviously so easy for him to modify his rules VII. 1, 2, and VII. 3, 50, in order to meet the objections raised by Kátyáyana,—to do, in other words, that which he has done in an analogous case;[221] and the matter he is reproached with in the Várttikas must have been so deeply impressed on his mind that it seems almost impossible not to draw another result from the strictures of Kátyáyana. And this result is no other than that either the words which are alluded to by the author of the Várttikas in these criticisms did not yet exist when Páṇini wrote, or that they had in his time another etymology than that stated by Kátyáyana. And if this view be correct, it would also add another fact to those I have advanced in favour of the argument that Páṇini and Kátyáyana cannot have been contemporaries.

The passage just now quoted from Patanjali's Great Commentary, and the conclusions which had to be drawn from it, enable us at once to see that Páṇini must also have been the author of the Dhátupáṭha frequently referred to in his rules. This list makes

---

[221] Nominal bases derived with the *kṛit* affixes तृच् or तृन् have certain properties of declension which are taught by Páṇini. The Uṇṇádi say (II. 96) that some of the bases नप्तृ, नेष्टृ, त्वष्टृ, होतृ, पोतृ, भ्रातृ, जामातृ, मातृ, पितृ, दुहितृ are derivatives formed with तृच् and others with तृन्. But since all of them do not share in the declension properties of the तृच् and तृन् bases, Páṇini gives a rule, VI. 4, 11, which obviates an objection that might have been made, like that brought forward by Kátyáyana in his Várttikas to VII. 1, 2 and VII. 3, 50.

use of the same mute letters which are the *anubandhas* of Páṇini's Grammar, and their grammatical value is exactly the same in both works. According to Patanjali's statement, therefore, the Dhátupáṭha of Páṇini cannot have been arranged by any one else than Páṇini.[222] Whether another Dhátupáṭha existed previously to Páṇini does not concern us here, since it is not known to us; nor does it belong to my present purpose to examine whether the Dhátupáṭha which has reached us has received additions from those who wrote, and commented on, it, *and if so, to what extent.* There is the same probability for such additions having been made to the original list as in the case of all other Gaṇas; and we may fairly, therefore, ascribe the present Dhátupáṭhas to various authors, who also, perhaps, added meanings to the list composed by Páṇini, since there is no *direct* evidence to show that Páṇini did more than arrange this list with the *anubandhas* attached to the radicals. All these questions, however, are foreign to the present subject. It is quite enough for the settlement of this question that the groundwork of the only Dhátupáṭha we now possess, is, like the groundwork of the Uṇṇádi list, the work of Páṇini.

The problem which concerns the chronological relation between Páṇini and the *Prátiśákhyas*, more especially those of the *Ṛigveda* and the *Vájasaneyi-Saṁhitá*, has a still greater claim to our attention than that discussed in the foregoing remarks.[223] The

---

[222] Compare my previous observations at page 54 and the following pages.

[223] I can here only speak of those two Prátiśákhyas which have become generally accessible—the Ṛik P. through the valuable and learned edition of Mr. Regnier, and the Vájasaneyi P. through that of Professor Weber—because I am not sufficiently acquainted with the two others, which are not yet published, and are not met with in the libraries of London, so as to feel justified in uttering opinions which I could not fully substantiate. But as I have no ground for doubting the *matter-of-fact* statements concerning these two latter works, for which we are indebted to the industry of Professor Weber in his preface to his edition of the Vájasaneyi P., I should infer from them that the Átharvaveda P. must be more recent than the Ṛik P., and that, in all probability, the Taittiríya P. also is posterior to the same Prátiśákhya. So far, therefore, as this latter inference—but this latter inference only—is concerned, and with

immediate connection of these grammatical writings with the collections of Vaidik hymns, gives to them an appearance of importance which some may deny to the *Dhátupáṭha* and the *Uṇṇádi* list. Besides, the speculations to which they have been subjected by several authors show that in spite of the seeming unanimity of their results, there is no work of Hindu antiquity which has caused more uncertainty, as respects the question of date, than these Prátiśákhya works.

There are, I conceive, two ways in which the solution of the problem of which I am here speaking, may be attempted, the one *literary*, the other *historical*. But before I offer from the evidence at my disposal such facts as may enable us to arrive at a settled conclusion on this point, it is my duty to state the prevalent opinion as to the relation of these works to Páṇini, and the reasons with which this opinion has hitherto been supported. I take for this purpose the works of those authors who have dealt more comprehensively than others with subjects which concern the Vaidik literature, and whose conclusions express, I believe, on this point, the creed of actual Sanskrit philologers.

Professor Müller writes in his History of Ancient Sanskrit Literature (p. 120), as follows: "The real object of the Prâtiśâkhyas, as shown before, was not to teach the grammar of the old sacred language, to lay down the rules of declension and conjugation, or the principles of the formation of words. This is a doctrine which, though it could not have been unknown during the Vedic period, has not been embodied, as far as we know, in any ancient work. The Prâtiśâkhyas are never called Vyâkaraṇas, grammars, and it is only incidentally that they allude to strictly grammatical questions. The perfect phonetic system on which Pâṇini's Grammar is built is no doubt taken from the Prâtiśâkhyas; but the sources of Pâṇini's strictly grammatical doctrines must be looked for elsewhere."

---

all the reservation which is implied by the source whence my information has been obtained, I shall feel free to speak of *all* the Prátiśákhyas. Otherwise I shall merely treat of the two former.

Thus, according to this author, all the Prátiśákhyas "*no doubt*" preceded Páṇini's Grammar; and we must infer, too, from Professor Müller's words, that he meant by Prátiśákhyas those either edited or preserved in MSS., since his conclusions cannot *consistently* have been founded on any imaginary Prátiśákhya which may or may not have preceded those that we now possess,—which may or may not have dealt with the same subjects in the same manner as the works we are here alluding to. Nor can it have been his object merely to state what is sufficiently known, that there were other grammarians, though not authors of Prátiśákhyas, before Páṇini who gave rules on Vaidik words, since Páṇini himself makes mention of them.

Professor Roth, whom we have to thank for an edition of Yáska's Nirukta, states his view to the same effect in the following words:[224] "Grammar, therefore, took the same natural course of developement as we find it has taken elsewhere. It did not proceed from the foundation of the living language, but owed its origin to the observation of that difference which exists between certain forms of language in the actual intercourse of life and those of written works; and, at first, it confined itself to pointing out chiefly these differences. Then, again, it comprised, not the whole mass of literature, but only single books, especially important to certain classes of society (*einzelne in den betreffenden Kreisen besonders wichtige Bücher*). Thus the path was opened to a general grammar treating as well of written as of spoken language; we meet this first in Páṇini, and from this time all those special grammars gradually disappear from general use."

There is but one thing wanting to this very interesting statement of Professor Roth's, viz., that he should inform us whence he obtained this invaluable historical account of the rise and progress of Sanskrit grammar. No doubt he has some voucher of high authority for the important fact that grammar began and proceeded in India in the manner he describes; and that these special gram-

[224] In the Preface to his editition of the Nirukta, p. xliii.—The original text of this quotation, it is superfluous to mention, is in German, and in *very good* German, too.

mars, the Prátiśákhyas, which he enumerates immediately afterwards, were the pioneers of Páṇini's work. But as he has forgotten to give us the name of his authority, we must, for the present at least, be permitted to look upon this graphic narration of his as a contribution to Vaidik poetry.

Professor Weber, with a caution that almost startles one in so bold a writer, who, as we have seen above (p. 77), has witnessed the progress of the Arians in their conquest of India 1500 B.C., does not sweep over *all* the Prátiśákhyas with his chronological brush, but merely records his views of the relation of Páṇini to one of them, the Prátiśákhya of Kátyáyana, or that of the Vájasaneyi-Sanhitá.

"We now come to Pâṇini himself," he says in his preface to his edition of this work, "that is to say ("*resp.*"), to the description of the relations which exist between him and the Vâjas. Prât. These relations are, on the one hand, very close,—since a great number of the rules contained in it re-occur, individually, either literally or nearly literally in Pâṇini, and since the Vâj. Pr., like Pâṇini, now and then makes use of an algebraic terminology; but, on the other hand, there is again a vast gulf between them, since this algebraic terminology does not entirely correspond, like that of the Ath. Pr., with that of Pâṇini, but, on the contrary, partly thoroughly (*zum Theil ganz*) differs from it. The particulars on this point are the following:—There correspond with Pâṇini—tiṅ I, 27, âṅ VI, 24 (MS. *A*, however, reads merely â), luk III, 12, lup I, 114 (✓ lup —"*resp.*"—lopa occur several times, but already, too, in the Ṛik Pr. and Taitt. Pr.); the use of t in et and ot, I, 114, IV, 58, may likewise be added, and, amongst other expressions which are not algebraic, upapadam VI, 14. 23; yadvṛittam VI, 14 (compare Pán. VIII. 1, 48, kiṁvṛitta); anudeça I, 143; dhâtu, verbal root, V, 10; anyataratas V, 15 (Páṇ. anyatarasyâm); linga, gender, IV, 170 (only in *BE.*); samjnâ IV, 96.—But there belong exclusively to the Vâj. Pr., and there have been nowhere shown to exist the algebraic terms: sim I, 44, IV, 50, for the eight simple vowels; jit I, 50. 167. III, 12. IV, 118, for the tenues inclusive of the sibilants (except h); mud I, 52. III, 8. 12. IV, 119 for ç, sh, s; dhi I, 53. IV, 35. 37. 117, for the sonant sounds; and to these may be added—bhâvin I, 46. III, 21. 55. IV, 33. 45. VII, 9, for the designation of all vowels except ă; rit=riphita IV, 33. VI, 9, and samkrama III, 148. IV, 77. 165. 194; for they, too, are peculiar to the Vâj. Pr. alone.

"If thus, then, the independence of this Pr. of Pâṇini be vouched for with a tolerable amount of certainty (*mit ziemlicher Sicherheit*), we shall be able to look upon the numerous literal coincidences between both, either as [the result of their] having drawn [them] from a common source, or of Pâṇini having borrowed [them] from the Vâj. Prât., just as we have the same choice in the case of the rules which are common to the Kâtîya-çrauta-sûtra I. 8, 19. 20, and Pâṇ. I. 2, 33. 34. In the latter case the former conjecture may be preferable (compare also Vâj. Pr. I. 130); but in our present case I should myself, indeed, rather (*in der That eher*) prefer deciding for Pâṇini's having borrowed [them] immediately [from the Vájasaneyi-Prátiśákhya], on account of the great speciality of some of these rules. For, a certain posteriority (*eine gewisse Posteriorität*) of the latter—independently of [his] having much more developed the algebraic terminology—seems to me to result with a tolerable amount of certainty (*mit ziemlicher Sicherheit*), from the circumstance also, that the pronunciation of the short *a* was in his time already so much (*bereits so sehr*) *saṁvṛita*, covered, that he does not make this vowel, but *u*, the type of the remaining vowels, whereas the Vâj. Pr. (and likewise the Ath. Pr.), it is true, agree with him in the samvṛitatâ of the vowel a, but still retain it as the purest vowel; compare the note to I. 72. But it is true that local differences might have been the cause of this, since Pâṇini seems to belong to the North-West, but the Vâj. Pr. to the East, of India.

"For the posteriority of the Vâj. Pr. to Pâṇini (*für eine Posteriorität des Vâj. Pr. nach Pâṇini*) it might be alleged, at the very utmost (*höchstens*), that the author of the Vârttikas to Pâṇini bears the same name as the author of the Vâj. Pr. There are, indeed, between both some direct points of contact,—comp. III. 13. 41. 46,—but then again there are also direct differences; comp. (III. 85) IV. 119. In general, sameness of names, like that of

Kâtyâyana, can never prove the identity of persons [who bore them]; there is nothing proved by it, except that both belonged to the same family, or ("*resp.*") were followers of the same school,—the Katâs.

"Amongst the Sûtras which are identical in the Vâj. Pr. and in Pâṇini, we must now point out, first, some general rules which are of the greatest importance for the economy of the whole arrangement of both texts, and which, indeed, are of so special a nature that they seem to claim with a tolerable amount of force (*mit ziemlicher Entschiedenheit*) [the assumption of the one] having borrowed from the other. They are the three following (called paribháshá by the scholiast to Pâṇini): tasminn iti nirdishṭe pûrvasya, Vâj. Pr. I, 134. Pân. 1, 66;—tasmâd ity uttarasyâdeḥ, Vâj. Pr. I. 135. Pâṇ. I. 1, 67 (without âdeḥ, but see 54);—shashṭhî sthâneyogâ, Vâj. Pr. I, 136. Pâṇ. I. 1, 49.—There are very remarkable also: saṁkhyâtânâm ânudeço yathâsaṁkhyam, Vaj. Pr. I, 143, compared with Pâṇ. I. 3, 10 yathâsaṁkhyam anudeçah samânâm; and vipratishedha uttaram balavad alope, I, 159, compared with vipratishedhe paraṁ kâryam, Pâṇ. I. 4, 2. But both [passages] do not require [the supposition of] *such* a special relation (*beidc bedingen indess nicht ein so specielles Verhältniss*), for they might be brought home to a common source in the general grammatical tradition (*sondern könnten auf gemeinsame Quelle in der allgemeinen grammatischen Tradition zurückgeführt werden*) (the sâmânyam of the Ath. Pr. I, 3, evam iheti ca vibhâshâprâptaṁ sâmânye). Likewise, varṇasyâdarçanaṁ lopah, I, 141, Pâṇ. I. 1, 60 (without varṇasya);—uccair udâttaḥ—nîcair anudâttaḥ—ubhayavân svaritaḥ I, 108-110; Pâṇ. I. 2, 29-31 (where samâhâraḥ stands for ubh.);—tasyâdita udâtta° svarârdhamâtram, I, 126, Pâṇ. I. 2, 32 (where ardhahraswam);—udâttâc cânudâtta° svaritam—nodâttasvaritodayam IV, 134. 140, udâttad anudâttasya svaritaḥ—nodâttasvaritodayam, Pâṇ. VIII. 4, 66. 67;—samânasthânakaraṇâsyaprayatnaḥ savarṇah, I. 43, tulyâsyaprayatnaṁ savarṇam, Pâṇ. I. 1, 9;—âsî3d iti cottaraṁ vicâre, II, 53, upari svid âsîd iti ca, Pâṇ. VIII. 2, 102 (97);—nuç câmreḍite, IV, 8, kân âmreḍite, Pâṇ. VIII. 3, 12.—There are besides these a very great number (*eine sehr grosse Zahl*) of coincidences [between them]; for instance,

IV, 49 (Pâṇ. VI. 1, 84), VI, 19-23 (Pâṇ. VIII. 1, 58-63), which, however, may be accounted for simply (*einfach*) by the similarity of their subject. In some of these instances the Vâj. Pr. is decidedly inferior (*steht entschieden zurück*) to Pâṇini (comp. the note to II, 19. 20). Its grammatical terminology does not appear to have attained the survey and systematic perfection represented in Pâṇini;[225] but compare also my former general statement on the want of skill or ("*resp.*") probably want of practice of the author (*vgl. indess auch das bereits im Eingange*—p. 68—*über die Ungeschicklichkeit resp. wohl Ungeübtheit des Vfs. im Allgemeinen Bemerkte*). In most instances, however, from being restricted to the one text of the Vâjas. Saṁhitâ, he is in a better position than Pâṇini, who has to deal with the whole linguistic stock; and therefore he is enabled to give rules with a certain safety and precision, when Pâṇini either wavers in indecision (bahulam) or decides in an erroneous and one-sided way (comp. the notes to II, 30. 55. III, 27. 95. IV, 58)."[226]

Two distinct reasons have induced me to give a full hearing to Professor Weber on this important question. I do so, in the first

---

[225] The words of the text are: "Die grammatische Fixirung scheint eben daselbst noch nicht zu der in Pâṇini repraesentirten Uebersicht und systematischen Vollkommenheit gelangt gewesen zu sein." I confess my utter inability to guarantee the correctness of the translation of this passage. What is the "grammatical fixing?" and of what? I have assumed that these words may have been intended for "terminology;" but for aught I know they may mean anything else. And what "survey" is represented in Páṇini?

[226] Indische Studien, vol. IV. pp. 83—86. Once more, and considering the possibility of a reproach which may be made to my translation of his words, I must express the conviction that I have not only brought the original before the English reader literally and faithfully, but even favourably. Professor Weber's mode of composition, in all his writings, is not only grammatically incorrect and illogically elliptical, but devoid of the very smallest amount of that care which every reader is entitled to expect in his author. I could have wished that he, not I, had been compelled to undergo the agony of rendering his original into English, with a view of combining the consideration due to my readers with a scrupulous faithfulness, in the version of his words and thoughts. The words between [ ] have been added by me in order to make something like sense of some of his sentences.

place, because the lengthened passage I have quoted from his Preface to the Vájasaneyi-Prátiśákhya—*in my opinion, his most important literary work*—is a thorough specimen of the manner and of the critical method—of the scholarship also, as I shall show hereafter—in which he deals with, and which he brings to bear on, all his learned investigations; in the second place, because to give him a hearing at all—and his great industry and his merit of having touched, with no inconsiderable damage to himself, upon all the *burning* questions of ancient Sanskrit literature, entitles him to one—was to give him a *full* hearing, in the fullness of all his words. For, though it be possible to perceive the qualities of a clear spring by taking a draught from it, however small, a whirlpool can only be appreciated by seeing it entire and in the condition in which it happens to exist.

If I had attempted, for instance, to maintain that Professor Weber looks upon the algebraic terminology of Kátyáyana's Prátiśákhya and Páṇini's Grammar, "on the one hand as very close to, and on the other hand as thoroughly differing from, one another" (p. 186, lines 15-21), he would have justly upbraided me with not representing him faithfully, for he really says: the one differs "partly thoroughly" from the other. Again, should I have ventured upon the statement that he considers Páṇini's work as later than this Prátiśákhya, because he says that it has borrowed a good deal from it; he would have pointed at p. 187, line 18, where he speaks of a "certain posteriority" of Páṇini, which kind of posteriority is just as intelligible to my mind as the answer which some one, whom I asked about his travels, gave me, viz., that he had been, but not exactly, on the Continent. Or, if I had said that his chief argument for this "certain posteriority" is the difference in the pronunciation of the short *ă*, between Páṇini and Kátyáyana, since this difference led to his conclusion with "a tolerable amount of certainty" (p. 187, line 20), he would reply: "You are mistaken. I stated that this difference may have been caused by local reasons (line 27); it has, therefore, not the slightest conclusiveness." Or, if I gave his opinion on the relative proficiency of both authors to this effect, that he considers the Vájasaneyi-

Prátiśákhya as being "*decidedly* inferior" (p. 189, line 4) in this regard to Páṇini's work, he would have pointed to line 15, in showing me how much I erred in attributing to him the idea of such "a decided inferiority;" for it is the Prátiśákhya, on the contrary, which, "in most instances, gives the rules with a certain amount of safety and precision, when Páṇini either wavers in indecision, or decides in an erroneous and one-sided way."

We must, therefore, leave the whirlpool, such as it is; and in doing so we cannot but appreciate the immense advantage which an author enjoys, when he is impartial enough to arrive at his conclusions unbiassed by a knowledge of the subject of which he is speaking. Professor Weber has made up his mind that the Vájasaneyi-Prátiśákhya *must* be anterior to Páṇini, probably because it "appears extremely ticklish" to him to decide otherwise; hence he is not troubled with any of those cares which are likely to disturb the minds of scholars who would first endeavour to study both works before they drew their inferences from them. He meets with an overwhelming amount of identical passages in the two works: he finds that their terminology is likewise identical to a certain degree,—hence he concludes: either Páṇini has borrowed these passages and this terminology from Kátyáyana, or both authors have borrowed them from a common source. For, as to a third alternative,—that Kátyáyana may have borrowed such passages from Páṇini, it is dispatched by him "with a tolerable amount of certainty," as ranging amongst things impossible, because Páṇini is later than the Vájasaneyi-Prátiśákhya; and this posteriority, again, he chiefly bases on the argument that the pronunciation of the short *ă* was, in the time of Páṇini, "already so much covered," that he had to take the vowel *u* for his type of a vowel sound, whereas Kátyáyana could still make use of the vowel *a* as the typical vowel in his Vaidik rules. Now, though I have already mentioned that this great argument is strangled by him as soon as it is born, I must nevertheless take the liberty of asking for the authority which supplied him with the circumstantial account of this phonetic history of the vowel *ă?* Páṇini and Kátyáyana both state and imply, as he himself admits, that the vowel *ă* is pronounced ***saṁvṛita***, or with the contraction of the throat; they do not say one single word more on the pronunciation of this sound; nor is there any grammarian known to me who does so much as allude to the fantastical story narrated by Professor Weber relative to this vowel *ă*. An ordinary critic, then, would content himself with the authentic information supplied him by both grammarians; and if he perceived that Páṇini, in his rule I. 2, 27, gives the vowel *ŭ* as a *specimen* vowel, and not as a type, while Kátyáyana chooses the vowel *ă* for such a *specimen*, he would conclude that, even should there be a real scientific motive for this difference, it cannot be founded on a different pronunciation of the vowel *ă*, since it is repudiated by both grammarians. But a critic like Professor Weber, who looks upon facts as worsted if they do not agree with his theories, concludes that this vowel *ă* was "*already so much* saṁvṛita" in the time of Páṇini, that he must needs throw it overboard, and receive *ŭ* into the ark of his grammatical terminology.

And here I may, in passing, advert once more to a practice sometimes met with in literary arguments. It consists in quietly introducing into the premises some such innocent words as "more," or "almost," or "already," or "so much," or similar adverbs of small size, which have not the slightest claim to any such hospitality; and then, suddenly, these little interlopers grow into mastership, and sway the discussion into which they had stealthily crept. Thus, Páṇini and Kátyáyana, as I have just said, speak of the vowel *ă* simply as *saṁvṛita;* and upon these words Professor Weber reports that "*ă* in the time of Páṇini was *already so much* saṁvṛita"—that important secrets may be extracted from this grand discovery.

The foregoing illustration of Professor Weber's critical remarks does not embrace the arguments in which he splits into two, Kátyáyana, the author of our Prátiśákhya, and Kátyáyana who wrote the Várttikas to Páṇini; for I shall first quote the observations of Professor Müller on this treatment of Kátyáyana. In speaking of the Vájasaneyi-Prátiśákhya he expresses himself thus:[227] "It was composed by Kâtyâyana, and shows a considerable advance in grammatical technicalities [viz., in comparison with the Prátiśákhya of the Black Yajurveda]. There is nothing in its style that could be used as a tenable argument why Kâtyâyana, the author of the Prâtiśâkhya, should not be the same as Kâtyâyana, the contemporary and critic of Pâṇini. It is true that Pâṇini's rules are intended for a language which was no longer the pure Sanskrit of the Vedas. The Vedic idiom is treated by him as an exception, whereas Kâtyâyana's Prâtiśâkhya seems to belong to a period when there existed but one recognised literature, that of the Ṛishis. This, however, is not quite the case. Kâtyâyana himself alludes to the fact that there were at least two languages. 'There are two words,' he says (I. 17), '*om* and *atha*, both used in the beginning of a chapter; but *om* is used in the Vedas, *atha* in the Bhâshyas.' As Kâtyâyana himself writes in the Bhâshya, or the common language, there is no reason why he should not have composed rules on the grammar of the profane Sanskrit, as well as on the pronunciation of the Vedic idiom."

In other words, Professor Müller sees that in no *grammatical* work known to him—and I may safely add to anyone else—mention is made of two Kátyáyanas; he sees, no doubt, too—though he does not state the fact adverted to by Professor Weber himself—that several Várttikas to Páṇini correspond in substance with the Sútras of the Vájasaneyi-Prátiśákhya; he deducts, moreover, from very correct and plausible premises, that there is nothing in either work to discountenance the possibility of the author of the Várttikas having also written a work on the pronunciation of Vaidik words; and since he doubtless coincides with me in the opinion that even Sanskrit philology can neither gain in strength nor in esteem by freeing itself from the fetters of common sense,—he arrives at the result that the hypercritical splitting of the one Kátyáyana into two, as proposed by Professor Weber, is utterly *fantastical*. I shall support his view with stronger proof than may be gathered from the quotations I have made; but in leaving for a while the

[227] Ancient Sanskrit Literature, p. 138.

whirlpool of the Indische Studien, I must now take up Professor Müller's own theory.

After the words just given, he continues as follows: "Some of Kâtyâyana's Sûtras are now found repeated *ipsissimis verbis* in Pâṇini's Grammar. This might seem strange; but we know that not all the Sûtras now incorporated in his grammar came from Pâṇini himself, and it is most likely that Kâtyâyana, in writing his supplementary notes to Pâṇini, simply repeated some of his Prâtiśâkhya-sûtras, and that, at a later time, some of these so-called Vârttikas became part of the text of Pâṇini."

Thus, in order to establish the theory that Páṇini's work is later than the Prátiśákhya of Kátyáyana, whom Müller, as we know, conceives to be a contemporary of Páṇini, he presents us with this very plausible sequence and chain of works:—1. The Prátiśákhya of Kátyáyana. 2. The Grammar of Páṇini. 3. The Várttikas of Kátyáyana. And since some rules of the second work are identical with some of the first, he assumes that such rules marched from the first into the third, and they then gradually invaded the second work. Now even supposing that such a migration of rules could be supported by a particle of evidence, what becomes of those stubborn Prátiśákhya-Sútras and Várttikas of Kátyáyana which are identical in their contents—as I shall hereafter show—and which have not ventured to walk into the Sútras of Páṇini? They become the stumbling-block of the whole theory; for since Páṇini, and especially Páṇini the contemporary of Kátyáyana, could not have written rules of which the defects must have been apparent to him, if he had seen rules so much better in a work written before his own, the substance of these Sútras of Kátyáyana could not have simultaneously preceded and followed the Grammar of Páṇini. But I need not go further in showing the weakness of this theory, for I have already explained (p. 29, etc.) that out of the 3996 Sútras which form the present bulk of Páṇini's Grammar, only three, or perhaps four, may be ascribed to Kátyáyana, on *critical* and *tenable* grounds. A mere supposition, unsupported by any *proof*, that the Vájasaneyi-Prátiśákhya is older than Páṇini's work, can certainly not justify the sweeping doubt which is levelled by Professor Müller against the whole work of Páṇini, and which is not even substantiated—as we might have expected it to have been—by a distinct enumeration of all or any of those Sútras which he would propose to restore to their rightful owner, Kátyáyana.

In now proceeding to state the reasons which induce me to look upon all Prátiśákhya-Sútras, not only as posterior to Páṇini's Grammar, but to Páṇini himself, and separated from him by at least several generations, I must, in the first place, point out the general fallacy which has led to the assumption that these works are anterior to Páṇini. It consists in applying the standard of the notion of *grammar* to both categories of works, and having done this, in translating the result obtained, which is less favourable to the Prátiśákhyas than to Páṇini's work, into categories of time—priority and posteriority. An analogous fallacy would be too apparent to require any remark, if it premised conclusions concerning the chronological relation of works of a totally different nature and character. It may assume however, as it has done, a certain degree of plausibility if it be applied to works of a similar category.

I must observe, therefore, in adverting to Professor Müller's own words, as before quoted, that the term *vyákaraṇa*, grammar, though constantly and *emphatically* given to Páṇini's work, has not been applied by any author within my knowledge to a *Prátiśákhya* work.[228] This circumstance, however, implies an important fact which must not be overlooked. Tradition, from immemorial times, as every one knows, connects with the Veda a class of works which stand in the most intimate relation to it—the *Vedánga* works. One of them is the *Vyákaraṇa*. The *Prátiśákhyas* do not belong to them. Thus, tradition even in India,—and on this kind of tradition probably the most squeamish

---

[228] I may here observe that the full title of Patanjali's Great Commentary is not simply *Mahábháshya*, but *Vyákaraṇa-Mahábháshya*. The end, for instance, of a chapter in the sixth book of the Great Commentary runs thus: इति श्रीमद्भगवत्पतञ्जलिविरचिते व्याकरणमहाभाष्ये षष्ठाध्यायस्य द्वितीयपादे प्रथमाह्निकम्.

critic will permit me to lay some stress,—does not rank amongst the most immediate offsprings of the Vaidik literature, those works which *apparently* stand in the closest relation to it,—which have no other object than that of treating of the Vaidik texts of the Saṁhitás;—but it has canonized Páṇini's Vyákaraṇa, which, on the contrary, would seem to be more concerned with the language of common life than with that of the sacred hymns. Is it probable, let me ask, even at this early stage, that tradition would have taken this course if it had looked upon these Prátiśákhyas as prior to the work of Páṇini?

But this question will receive a more direct answer if we compare the aim and the contents of both these classes of works. *Vyákaraṇa* means "*un-doing*," *i.e.*, analysis, and Páṇini's Grammar is intended to be a linguistic analysis: it *un-does* words and *un-does* sentences which consist of words; it examines the component parts of a word, and therefore teaches us the properties of base and affix, and all the linguistic phenomena connected with both; it examines the relation, in sentences, of one word to another, and likewise unfolds all the linguistic phenomena which are inseparable from the meeting of words.

The *Prátiśákhyas* have no such aim, and their contents consequently differ materially from those of the *Vyákaraṇa*. Their object is merely the ready-made word, or base, in the condition in which it is fit to enter into a sentence, or into composition with another base, and more especially the ready-made word or base as part of a Vaidik hymn. These works are no wise concerned in analyzing or explaining the nature of a word or base; they take them, such as they occur in the Pada text, and teach the changes which they undergo when they become part of the spoken sentence, *i.e.*, of the spoken hymn. And the consequence implied by these latter words entails, moreover, on the Prátiśákhyas the duty of paying especial attention to all the phenomena which accompany the *spoken* words; hence they deal largely with the facts of pronunciation, accent, and the particular mode of sounding a syllable or word in connection with ritual acts.

This brief comparison will already have hinted at the point

of contact which exists between Páṇini and the authors of these Prátiśákhya works. Leaving aside the wider range of the domain of the former, and the narrower field of the Vaidik pursuits of the latter, we may at once infer that both will meet on the ground of phonetic rules, of accentuation, and of the properties of sound; but we shall likewise infer that any other comparison between both would be as irrelevant as if we compared Páṇini with Suśruta, or the Prátiśákhyas with the Jyotisha.

The aim of both categories of works being entirely different, there is neither a logical nor an historical necessity, nor does there exist a fact or a circumstance which would enable us to conclude, from the absence in these Prátiśákhyas of certain grammatical matter, that their authors were not as much conversant with it as Páṇini, who treats of it, because it is his object, and therefore his duty, to treat of it.

These facts being beyond the reach of doubt, we may again raise an *a-priori* question whether it is more probable that the *plan* of Páṇini's work preceded in time the *plan* of a Prátiśákhya work, or the reverse?

Throughout a great portion of his admirable Introduction to Páṇini, Patanjali endeavours to impress on the reader the great importance of grammatical study for promoting the objects of religion and holiness. He shows that a knowledge of language is necessary to a proper understanding of the sacred texts; that no priest is safe in the practice of rites without a thorough comprehension of the grammatical laws which define the nature of sounds and words,—in short, that nothing less than eternal bliss depends very much on the proper and correct use made of words, and, as a consequence, on the study of Páṇini.

Here, then, we have a distinct definition of the relation of Páṇini to the Vaidik texts,—a distinct statement of the causes which have produced the *Vyákaraṇa*. And what do they show else, than that Páṇini must have stood in the midst of a *living* religion, of a creed which understood itself, or at least had still the vigour to try to understand itself?

In Páṇini there is organism and life. In the Prátiśákhyas there is mechanism and death. They do not care for the sense of a word. A word *antaḥ*, for instance, is to them merely a combination of five sounds, nothing else; for whether it represent the nominative of *anta*, "end," or the adverb *antar*, "between," is perfectly indifferent to them. The rule of Kátyáyana's Prátiśákhya on this word (II. 26), is, therefore, as dreary as a grammatical rule could ever be imagined to be, and the critical remarks which Professor Weber has attached to this rule merely prove that, on this occasion, also he beats the air.

It does not follow, as I have before observed, that, because linguistic death reigns in these Sútras, Kátyáyana or their other authors must have been as ignorant of grammar as it would seem if these works made any claim to be grammars at all. It merely follows that, in the period in which they were written, there existed a class of priests who had to be drilled into a proper recital of the sacred texts; and it may follow, too, that this set of men had none of the spirit, learning, and intelligence, which Patanjali would wish to find in a man who practices religious rites.

In other words, it seems to me that between Páṇini's living grammar and these dead Prátiśákhyas, there lies a space of time sufficient to create a want, of which a very insignificant trace is perhaps perceptible in some of Páṇini's Vaidik rules, but which must have been irresistible at the period of the Prátiśákhya works.

In substantiating with material proofs the priority of Páṇini's work, I may dispense with giving evidence that Páṇini meant, in his eight grammatical books, to concern himself with Vaidik language as well as the language of common life. For I should have simply to quote hundreds of his rules which are entirely devoted to Vaidik texts, and I should have to carry the reader through the whole Introduction of Patanjali, which proves, as I have already mentioned, that one of the chief objects of grammar is the correct apprehension of the hymns. I will merely therefore compare, first some matter treated by Páṇini with some matter treated by the Ṛik-Prátiśákhya,—such matter, of course, as admits of a point of contact between both, and therefore of a comparison at all.

The fifth chapter of the latter work treats of the cases in which the consonant *s* becomes *sh*; the same subject is comprised in the latter part of the third chapter of Páṇini's eighth book; but this book does not contain the smallest number of the cases mentioned in the Ṛik-Prátiśákhya. The same work enumerates in the same chapter the words and classes of words in which *n* becomes *ṇ*, and very few only of these instances are taught by Páṇini in the last chapter of his work. A similar remark applies with still greater force to a comparison of Páṇini's rules on the prolongation of vowels with those given by the Ṛik-Prátiśákhya in its seventh, eighth, and ninth chapters. In short, there is not a single chapter in this work which, whenever it allows of a comparison between its contents and the contents of analogous chapters of Páṇini's Grammar, must not at once be declared to be infinitely more complete than the rules on them delivered by Páṇini.

In addressing myself for a like purpose to the Vájasaneyi-Prátisákhya, I might seem to do that which is superfluous. For, as I have shown before that Páṇini was not acquainted with a Vájasaneyi-Saṁhitá, it would require no further proof that he must have preceded a work which is entirely devoted to this collection of hymns. But as such a comparison, being extended also to the Várttikas, would involve at the same time the question whether the author of the Várttikas and the author of the Prátiśákhya is the same person or not; and as it would, too, bear on the very appreciation of the character of this Vaidik work, I will enter into it with greater detail than was required for the conclusions which follow from a comparison between the Ṛik-Prátiśákhya and Páṇini.

It is a remarkable feature in the explanatory gloss which Professor Weber has attached to his edition of the Vája-saneyi-Prátiśákhya, that he evinces much pleasure in schooling Kátyáyana for introducing irrelevant matter into his work; now upbraiding him for his remarks on the common dialect, which ought not to have concerned him in a Sútra of this kind; then finding fault with him for treating of words which do not occur in the Vájasneyi-Saṁhitá, and which, likewise, ought not to have troubled him. Professor Weber has given us too, in the beginning of his preface, a valuable collection of instances, which in his opinion prove either that Kátyáyana must have had before him a different version of the White Yajurveda than the one known to us, or that he has botched on to his Prátiśákhya a number of rules which, for his purpose, were out of place; or, to sum up in the words of the *Indische Studien*, already referred to, that Kátyáyana shows neither skill nor practice in his treatment of the matter edited and commented upon by Professor Weber. But what would the latter think if Kátyáyana applied this very reproach to him? if he told Professor Weber that he did not even understand the character of the Prátiśákhya which he was editing and subjecting to all this learned criticism?

Let me, then, take the place of Kátyáyana, and maintain for him, that he is not only the very same Kátyáyana who wrote the Várttikas to Páṇini, but that his Vájasaneyi-Prátiśákhya has the double aim of being a Vaidik treatise as well as of containing *criticisms on Páṇini.* And let me, therefore, tell Professor Weber that since there is abundant proof of this view in Kátyáyana's Vaidik work, all his handsome epithets are put out of court. And this, I hold, will also settle the question why we meet with so many Sútras in Kátyáyana which are identical with those of Páṇini; for we shall presently see that this identity is merely an apparent one, and, in reality, no identity at all.

I will take this point up first, and show that Kátyáyana merely repeated the words of Páṇini in order to attach his critical notes to them, just as I sometimes literally repeated the words of Professor Weber himself, merely for the purpose of improving on him.

Páṇini says (I. 1, 60) *adarśanaṁ lopaḥ.* "This is not distinct enough," I hear *Kátyáyana* say; hence he writes (I. 141) *varṇasyádarśanaṁ lopaḥ.—Páṇini* gives the definition: (I. 2, 29. 30) *uchchair udáttaḥ* and *níchair anudáttaḥ.* "So far so good," I suppose Kátyáyana to say; "but you give the necessary complement of these two rules in the words (I. 2, 31) '*samáháraḥ swaritaḥ'*; I object to this definition, for the swarita would better have been defined thus," *ubhayavân swaritaḥ* (K. I. 108–110).—P. I. 2, 32: *tasyádita udáttam ardhahraswam;* but K. I. 126: *tasyádita udáttaṁ swarárdhamátram.*—P. VIII. 4, 67, 66: *nodáttaswaritodayam* (with the quotation of a dissent on the part of Gárgya, Káśyapa, and Gálava); *udáttád anudáttasya swaritaḥ.* The former rule is approved of by Kátyáyana, who repeats it literally, but the latter he words thus: *udáttách chánudáttaṁ swaritam* (IV. 140, 134).—P. I. 1, 8: *mukhanásikávachaṇo 'nunásikaḥ;* but K. I. 75: *mukhánunásikákaraṇo 'nunásikaḥ.*—P. 1. 1, 9: *tulyásyaprayatnaṁ savarṇam.* "Would it not be clearer," we hear Kátyáyana say, "to give this definition thus: (K. I. 43) *samánasthánakaraṇásya-prayatnaḥ savarṇaḥ.*"—P. VI. 1, 84: *ekaḥ púrvaparayoḥ;* but K. IV. 49: *athaikam uttarach cha.*—P. I. 1, 66: *tasminn iti nirdishṭe púrvasya.* "This rule I adopt," Kátyáyana probably thought, (I. 134) "but for your next rule (I. 1, 67), *tasmád ity uttarasya,* I prefer the clearer wording" (I. 135) *tasmád ity uttarasyádeḥ,* "and your *shashṭhí stháneyogá* (1. 1, 49), evidently a rule which you ought to have put with those two preceding Paribháshá rules which are its complement, instead of separating it from them by seventeen other rules, I place it, therefore, immediately after these" (I. 136).

I will not add more instances of the same kind; they have all been carefully collected by Professor Weber; but he is far from perceiving that the identity between the language of both authors is merely an apparent one, and that the additional words of Kátyáyana, either in the same Sútra or in one immediately following, but intimately connected with it, are so many criticisms on Páṇini, which are even made more prominent by the repetition of a certain amount of Páṇini's words. For to assume, even without any of the further proofs which I shall adduce, that Kátyáyana first delivered his clearer and better Sútras, and that Páṇini hobbled after him with his imperfect ones, is not very probable.

The following synopsis of rules is an extract from those I have collected for the purpose of determining whether it could be a matter of accident that the Prátiśákhya Sútras of Kátyáyana are, to a considerable extent, nothing but Várttikas to Páṇini.

Páṇini writes (VIII. 2, 87), "*om abhyádáne*," which rule proves that in his time *om* was not confined to Vaidik use only; but Kátyáyana writes (I. 18 and 19), "*omkáram̃ vedeshu*" and "*athakáram bháshyeshu*." No doubt if Kátyáyana had not written with a direct glance at Páṇini, this latter rule would be out of place, but in this combination its origin becomes intelligible. P. says (VIII. 1, 46), "*ehi manye prahàse lṛiṭ*." Though this rule does not treat of the accent of *manye*, it nevertheless would follow from other rules of Páṇini, that *manye* is ádyudátta in its combination with *ehi*. This inference is emphatically corrected by K. 2, 15: *manye padapúrvam̃ sarvatra*. Professor Weber, it is true, says that this word *sarvatra*—which embodies the *emphasis* of the censure of Kátyáyana—is meaningless: once more, no doubt, Kátyáyana has bungled through "want of practice and skill." How much Páṇini's rules VIII. 1, 19 and 72, *ámantritasya cha*, and *ámantritam púrvam avidyamánavat*, are the torment of commentators, may be seen from many instances in Sáyaṇa's Commentary on the Ṛigveda. K. improves them considerably by II. 17 and 18: *padapúrvam ámantritam anánárthe 'pádádau* and *tenánantará shashty ekapadavat*.—K. writes II. 22: *bhútir ádyudáttam*: this rule again rouses the critical indignation of Professor Weber. "Why," he exclaims, "is this word singled out (by Kátyáyana)? Assuredly, it is not the single *ktin* formation in the V. S." My answer is, because Kátyáyana had studied Páṇini, and Professor Weber, it is clear, has not; for Páṇini says, III. 3, 96, that *bhúti* is *antodátta* in the Veda; and Kátyáyana therefore singled this word out with the decided intention of stating that in the Vájasaneyi-Sam̃hitá Páṇini's rule would be erroneous. This instance, I hold, moreover, is one of those which add some weight to the proof I have already given, that Páṇini did not know, and therefore preceded, the Vájasaneyi-Sam̃hitá.—K. says, II. 48, *devatádwandwáni chánámantritáni*; and his words are a distinct criticism on P. VI. 2, 141, *devatádwandwe cha*.—In rule VIII. 3, 36, Páṇini teaches that Visarjaníya may remain such (or, as the Sútra expresses itself, on account of previous Sútras, may *become* Visarjaníya), before sibilants, or may become assimilated to the following sibilant. But he committed the venial offence of not stating that this latter alternative rests on the authority of Śákaṭáyana, and the former on that of Śákalya. Could Kátyáyana, therefore, forego the opportunity of writing (III. 8): "*pratyaya-savarṇam mudi Śákaṭáyanah,*" and (III. 9), "*avikáraṁ Śákalyaḥ śashaseshu*" ?—In VI. 1, 134, Páṇini gives a comprehensive rule on the elision of the final *s* in regard to the Vaidik use of the nominative of *tad.* "No," says Kátyáyana (III. 14), "in the V. S. this elision occurs before vowels only in two instances: *sa oshadhímayoḥ.*"—K. (III. 22) says *ávir nir iḍa iḍáyá vasatir varivaḥ*, and thus criticises the imperfection of P.'s rule VIII. 3, 54, *iḍáyá vá.*—In III. 27, *adhvano rajaso rishaḥ spṛiças pátau*, he shows the clumsiness of P.'s rule VIII. 3, 52, *pátau cha bahulam;* in III. 30, *paráv avasáne*, the imperfection of P.'s VIII. 3, 51, *panchamyáḥ paráv adhyarthe;* in III. 55, *bhávibhyaḥ saḥ shaṁ samánapaḍe*, that of P.'s VIII. 3, 59, *ádeśapratyayayoḥ.*—In the Sútras III. 56 and 57, Kátyáyana teaches that the intervention of *anuswára*, *k* and *r* do not prevent *s* from becoming *sh*, if this change would have to take place otherwise. "These rules," says Professor Weber, "have no business here, for Saṁhitâ and Pada-text agree in this respect, and these rules are quite general grammatical rules;" and in support of this argument he quotes Uvaṭa, who also points out the superfluity. The latter consoles us for it, it is true, by the remark that a man should not complain if he found honey though he intended only to fetch fuel, or a fish though his object were to fetch water, or fruits though he went out merely to pluck flowers. But as Professor Weber is not so easily consoled, and not so leniently disposed towards Kátyáyana as Uvaṭa is, I may tell him that these rules are levelled against Páṇini's rules VIII. 3, 57 and 58, which omit to include *r*. At II. 55, *dwandwaṁ çendrasomapúrvam púshágniváyushu*, Professor Weber discharges a witticism. "None of the compounds" (referred to in the Sútra), he says, "occur in the V. S. or the Śat. Br. . . . . How is that to be explained? Did our Homer nod when he composed this rule? or did he have before him passages of the V. S. which it no longer contains [Professor Weber probably meant to say, '*which was not the V. S. we now possess*']? or is the text of our Sútra corrupt, and have we to read another word for *soma?*" I will try to relieve his anxiety by expressing the belief that this Sútra and the next, II. 56, are criticisms on Páṇini's general rule VI. 2, 141, and on his special rule VI. 2, 142.—The rule of Páṇini VIII. 3, 107, *suñaḥ*, is criticised in three Sútras of Kátyáyana III. 59, 60. 61, *okárát su; och chápṛiktát*, and *abheś cha.*

The Várttika 3 to III. 3, 108 says *varṇát káraḥ;* K. I. 37, *káreṇa cha;* both are identical in their contents, and complete Páṇini's rule III. 3, 108. The same remark applies to the Várttika 4 to P. III. 3, 108, *rád iphaḥ*, and to K. I. 40, *ra ephena cha*, in reference to the same rule of Páṇini.—K. III. 38, *aharpatau repham*, points out an omission in P. VIII. 2, 70: the same criticism is conveyed by the Várttika 2 to this Sútra of Páṇini, *aharádínám patyádishu.*—K. III. 12, *luñg mudi jitpare* fills up a blank in P. VIII. 3, 36, *vá śari*; and likewise a Várttika on this Sútra to the same effect, *vá śarprakaraṇe kharpare lopaḥ.*—P.'s rule VI. 3, 109, *pṛishodarádíni yathopadishṭam*, is criticised by K. III. 41 and 42, *ukáram dur de* and *náśe cha*, as well as by a Várttika to the former rule, which has the same contents: *duro dáśanáśadabhadhyeshútvam̃ vaktavyam uttarapadádeś cha shṭutvam.*—A Várttika to the same rule of P., *shasha utvam̃ datṛidaśasúttarapadádeḥ shṭutvam̃ cha*, is identical in contents with K. III. 46, *shaḍ daśadantayoḥ sam̃khyávayorthayoś cha:* both are criticisms on P. VI. 3, 109.—The first Várttika to III. 2, 49 (improperly marked, like the two others, in the Calcutta edition, as if these Várttikas did not occur in the Mahábháshya), *dáráv áhano 'ṇṇantyasya cha ṭaḥ sanjnáyám*, is similar in contents with K. III. 47, *ta ághád anáḍambarát:* both complete P. III. 2, 49, *áśishi hanaḥ.*—The important omission in P.'s Sútra VIII. 4, 1, *rashábhyán no ṇaḥ samánapade*, is, with almost a literal reference to these words, criticised by K.'s III. 83, *ṛisharebhyo nakáro ṇakáram̃ samánapade*, and by his Várttika to the former rule, *rasbábhyám̃ ṇatva ṛikáragrahaṇam.*

I need not increase the foregoing quotations by a comparison of the contents of whole chapters of the Vájasaneyi-Prátiśákhya with the analogous contents of whole chapters in Páṇini. For, though the result would be exactly the same as it has been in the case of our comparison between the *Ṛik-Prátiśákhya* and Páṇini's work, even the isolated Sútras which I have contrasted in these quotations sufficiently show that Páṇini could never have laid his Grammar open to such numerous criticisms as he has done, if the work of Kátyáyana had been composed before his own. My synopsis, moreover, shows that many rules of Kátyáyana become utterly inexplicable in his Prátiśákhya work *unless they be judged in their intimate connection with the Grammar of Páṇini.* And, as it is simply ridiculous to assume that "Homer constantly nodded" in writing an elaborate work, which evidences considerable skill and practice in the art of arranging the matter of which he treats, there is no other conclusion left than that the Prátiśákhya of Kátyáyana had the twofold aim which I have indicated above.

There might, however, remain a doubt as to whether Kátyáyana first wrote his Prátiśákhyas or his Várttikas to Páṇini. Two reasons induce me to think that his Prátiśákhya preceded his Várttikas. In the first place, because the contrary assumption would lead to the very improbable inference that a scholar like Kátyáyana, who has given such abundant proof of his thorough knowledge of Sanskrit grammar, left a considerable number of Páṇini's rules without those emendations which, as we must now admit, are embodied in his Prátiśákhya work. If we made a supposition of this kind, we should imply by it that he belongs to that class of authors who present their writings in a hurried and immature state, and, upon an after thought, make their apology in an appendix or an additional book. If we assume, on the other hand, that he first wrote his Prátiśákhya Sútras, which neither imposed upon him the task, nor gave him an opportunity, of making a thorough review of Páṇini, we can understand that they might have seduced him now and then into allowing himself to be carried away by the critical tendency which he afterwards fully developed in his Várttikas; and we can then, too, understand why these Várttikas treat merely of those Sútras of Páṇini which were not included in his former work.

My second reason for this view is derived from a comparison between such of his Sútras and such of his Várttikas as are closely related to one another. For if we examine the contents and the wording of either we cannot fail to perceive that some of Kátyáyana's Várttikas show an improvement on some of his Sútras, and we may infer that they were given on account of this very improvement. Thus the Várttika to VIII. 3, 36, quoted before, contains the word *vá*, which is not in the Sútra III. 12; the Várttika *duro*, &c., to VI. 3, 109 embraces more formations than the Sútras III. 41 and 42; the Várttikas 1-3 to III. 2, 49 do not contain, it is true, the word *áḍambara* alluded to in III. 47—perhaps because it was already contained in this Sútra—but increase considerably the contents of this rule; the Várttika 2 to VIII. 2, 70 treats of a whole Gaṇa, while the Sútra III. 38 merely names its heading word; and so on. Nor could we forego such a comparison on the ground that there is a difference of purpose in the Sútras which are attached to the Vájasaneyi-Saṁhitá, and in the Várttikas, which are connected with Páṇini,—that, consequently, an improvement of the Várttikas on the Prátiśákhya need not tell on the chronological relation between both. For we have seen that Kátyáyana's Prátiśákhya does *not* strictly confine itself to the language of his Saṁhitá or even to that of the Vedas in general. Already the instances given before would suffice to bear out this fact, in the appreciation of which I so entirely differ from Professor Weber's views; and a striking instance of this kind is afforded by Kátyáyana's Sútra III. 42, quoted before. It treats of a case entirely irrelevant for the Vájasaneyi-Saṁhitá; this case is taken up again and enlarged upon in a Várttika to VI. 3, 109, and there is no reason why the additions made in this Várttika might not have been entitled with equal right to a place amongst Kátyáyana's Sútras, as Sútra III. 42 itself. Their not standing there shows to my mind that this Várttika is later than this rule of the Prátiśákhya work.

It will readily be seen that I have arrived at the result of the priority of Páṇini's work to the Prátiśákhya of Kátyáyana, in entire independence of all the assistance which I might have derived from my previous arguments. I have hitherto abstained from availing myself of their aid, because an inference must gain in strength if it be able to show that two entirely distinct lines of argument necessarily lead to the same goal. Such is the case with the question before us. For if we now appeal, once more, to the important information which Patanjali supplied, viz., that the "*anubandhas* of former grammarians have no grammatical effect in the work of Páṇini:" in other words, that if a grammarian uses *anubandhas* employed by Páṇini in the same manner as he did, his work must have been written after Páṇini's work,—we need only point to the pratáyhára *tiṅg*, in Kátyáyana's Sútra I. 27, in order to be relieved from any doubt that Páṇini's grammar is prior to the Sútra of Kátyáyana. That Kátyáyana added in his Sútras other technical terms to those of Páṇini, cannot be a matter of surprise; indeed, it is even less remarkable than it would be under ordinary circumstances if we consider that he made—either as inventor or as borrowing from older grammarians—such additions to the terminology of Páṇini in his very Várttikas, where one would think there was the least necessity for them,—where, for instance, he might have easily done without such new terms as *sit*, *pit*, *jit*, *jhit*, *ghu*, in the sense in which he uses them.[229]

Thus far my *literary* argument on the chronological relation between Páṇini and the Prátiśákhya works. The *historical* proof, that not only the work of Páṇini, but *Páṇini himself, preceded, by at least two generations, the author of the oldest Prátiśákhya*, requires, in the first place, the remark that by the latter designation I mean the Prátiśákhya of the Ṛigveda hymns.

Since Professor Weber, in his introduction to his edition of the Vájasaneyi-Prátiśákhya has given proofs that this work as well

[229] Várttika 1 to Páṇini I. 1, 68: सित्तद्विशेषाणां वृक्षाद्यर्थम्; Várttika 2: पित्पर्यायवचनस्य च स्वाद्यर्थम्; Várttika 3: जित्पर्यायवचनस्यैव राजाद्यर्थम्; Várttika 4: झित्तस्य च तद्विशेषाणां च मत्स्याद्यर्थम्.—In his Káriká to VII. 1, 21 (compare note 114) Kátyáyana uses the term घु in the sense of उत्तरपद, as results from the commentary of Patanjali.—Káriká: औशघौ etc.—Patanjali: औशघाविति वक्तव्यम्। किमिदमघाविति। अनुत्तरपद इति etc.—The same term घु occurs in Patanjali's Káriká to VI. 4, 149 (see note 121): . . . घौ लोपो ऽन्तिषद्वित्यत्र etc., when Kaiyyaṭa observes: घुशब्देनोत्तरपदं पूर्वाचार्यप्रसिद्धोच्यते.

as the Atharvaveda-Prátiśákhya—and I infer too, that of the Taittiríya-Saṁhitá—are more recent than the Ṛik-Prátiśákhya, and since these reasons are conclusive to my mind, I need not, by the addition of other proof to that which he has afforded us on this point, weaken the great pleasure I feel, in being able, for once in a way, to coincide with him in his views.

It is necessary, however, that I should first touch in a few words on the question of the authorship of this Ṛik-Prátiśákhya. It is adverted to in the first verse of this work, in a passage which contains all the information we possess on this point. The passage in question runs thus: "After having adored Brahma, Śaunaka expressed the characteristic feature of the Ṛig-veda verses."

Now, as it is not unusual in Sanskrit writings for the author to introduce himself in the commencement of his work by giving his name, and speaking of himself in the third person, this verse alone would not justify us in looking upon the words quoted as *necessarily* containing a mere report of Śaunaka's having delivered certain rules which another later author brought into the shape of the Ṛik-Prátiśákhya as we now find it. But it must be admitted, also, that it does not absolutely compel us to ascribe this work to Śaunaka himself. It leaves us free to interpret its sense according to the conclusions which must be derived from the contents of the work itself.

These contents have already required us to establish the priority of Páṇini's Grammar to this Prátiśákhya work. If, then, we find that Páṇini speaks of Śaunaka as of an ancient authority,[230] while there is no evidence to show that the Śaunaka named in both works is not the same personage, there is from the point of view of my former '*literary*' argument, a certainty that Śaunaka was *not* the author of the Prátiśákhya here named.[231]

---

[230] IV. 3, 105: पुराणप्रोक्तेषु ब्राह्मणकल्पेषु; 106: शौनकादिभ्यश्छन्दसि. Compare also page 149.

[231] This is the view, too, of *Uvaṭa*, the commentator on this Prátiśákhya. He says that Śaunaka's name is mentioned for the sake of remembering him: नामग्रहणं स्मरणार्थम्. See Mr. Regnier's edition of the Ṛik-P. in the Journal Asiatique, vol. VII. (1856), p. 183.

This inference, however, it must be admitted, is only entitled to be mentioned thus at the beginning of the *historical* argument, in so far as it may *afterwards* strengthen and corroborate it, but not, if it had to be used in order to premise the conclusions which will have to be drawn.

Another preliminary remark, also, must be devoted to the sweeping assertion of Professor Weber, already quoted, which is to this effect, that "sameness of names can never prove the identity of the persons" who bear these names. It is true he qualifies this *dictum* by adding after "names," "like Kátyáyana;" but, even with this restriction, I cannot convince myself that literary criticism gains in strength by carrying Pyrrhonism beyond the confines of common sense. If great celebrity attaches to a name in certain portions of Sanskrit literature; and if the same name re-occurs in other and *kindred* portions of this same literature, I believe we are not only free, but compelled, to infer that the personage bearing this name in both such places is the same personage, unless there be particular and *good* reasons which would induce us to arrive at a contrary conclusion. I thus hold that a critic has no right to obtrude his doubts upon us until he has given good and substantial reasons for them.

After this expression of dissent from the critical principles of Professor Weber, I may now recall the fact I have mentioned on a previous occasion (p. 80), that there is a grammatical work, in a hundred thousand Ślokas, called *Sangraha*, whose author is *Vyáḍi* or *Vyáḷi*. I know of no other grammatical work bearing this name *Sangraha*, nor of any other celebrated grammarian named *Vyáḍi*. Both names, however, are not unfrequently met with in the grammatical literature. *Vyáḍi* is quoted several times in the *Ṛik-Prátiśákhya*,[232] and there is no valid reason for doubting that he is there the same person as the author of the *Sangraha*. This same work and its author are sometimes alluded to in the illustrations which the commentators give of the Sútras to Páṇini or the

[232] Ṛik-P. III, 14. 17; VI, 12; XIII, 12. 15. See Mr. Regnier's *Index des noms propres* to his edition of the Ṛik-Prátiśákhya, *s.v.* Vyâḷi.

Várttikas of Kátyáyana;[233] and both, indeed, as I shall show hereafter, appear to have stood in a close relation to the Mahábháshya of Patanjali. We are, however, only concerned here with one instance with which Patanjali illustrates the second Várttika of Páṇini's rule II. 3, 66.

It is this: "*beautiful indeed is Dákshάyaṇa's creation of the Sangraha.*"[234]

From it we learn, then, in connection with the information we already possess of the proper name of the author of the Sangraha, that Vyáḍi and Dákshάyaṇa are one and the same grammatical authority. Dákshάyana, however, is not only a descendant of *Daksha*, but of *Dákshi* also,[235] and of the latter, at least in the third generation, while he may possibly have held a far more distant place in the lineage of this personage who is so often named in the ancient literature. For Páṇini, who defines the term *yuvan* as the son of a grandson or of a more remote degree in the lineage of a family chief,[236] gives a rule in reference to this term, which the principal commentators illustrate by the name of *Dákshάyaṇa*.[237]

---

[233] Patanjali's commentary on v. 6 (of the Calcutta edition) to IV. 2, 60 gives the instances: सर्ववेदः। सर्वतन्त्रः। सवार्त्तिकः। ससंग्रहः; or the Káśiká to VI. 3, 79: ससंग्रहं व्याकरणमधीते.

[234] This instance follows another which says: "beautiful indeed is Páṇini's creation of (his) Sútra."—Várttika 2 to II. 3, 66: शेषे विभाषा.—Patanjali: शोभना खलु पाणिनेः सूत्रस्य कृतिः। शोभना खलु पाणिनिना सूत्रस्य कृतिः। शोभना खलु दाक्षायणस्य संग्रहस्य कृतिः। शोभना खलु दाक्षायणेन संग्रहस्य कृतिः.

[235] Páṇini, IV. 1, 95: अत इञ्.—Kátyáyana: इञो वृद्धावृद्धाभ्यां फिञ्फिनौ विप्रतिषेधेन.—Patanjali: इञो वृद्धावृद्धाभ्यां फिञ्फिनौ भवतः विप्रतिषेधेन। इञो ऽवकाशः। दाक्षिः etc.—Káśiká: दक्षस्यापत्यं दाक्षिः.

[236] Páṇini, IV. 1, 162: अपत्यं पौत्रप्रभृति गोत्रम्; 163: जीवति तु वंश्ये युवा; 164: भ्रातरि च ज्यायसि; 165: वान्यस्मिन्सपिण्डे स्थविरतरे जीवति.

[237] IV. 1, 101: यञिञोश्च. This Sútra has no direct commentary by Patanjali, and I shall therefore first quote the Káśiká on it: यञन्तादिञन्ताच्चापत्ये फक्प्रत्ययो भवति। गार्ग्यायणः। वात्स्यायनः॥ इञन्तात्। दाक्षायणः। प्लाक्षायणः। द्वीपादनुसमुद्रं यञ् (IV. 3, 10) । (IV. 2, 80) सुतंगमादिभ्य इञित्यतो न भवति॥ गोत्रग्रहणेन यञिञौ विशेष्येते। तदन्ताद्यून्येवायं प्रत्ययः (comp. IV. 1, 94).—But there is no occasion for doubt-

If we now turn to Páṇini himself, we have it on the authority of Patanjali that his mother bore the name of *Dákshí*.[238] And *Dákshí*, again, is, on the faith of all commentators on a rule of Páṇini, the female family head of the progeny of Daksha, standing in the same relationship to Daksha as the male family chief Dákshi; she is, in other words, the oldest sister (*vṛiddhá*) of the latter personage.[239] Vyáḍi, therefore, was a *near relative of Páṇini*, and Páṇini must have preceded him by *at least two generations*.

---

ing the genuineness of this Sútra on account of there being no Bháshya to it (compare note 139), for Patanjali refers to it in his comment on the fifth Paribháshá (in the Calc. ed.) to I. 1, 72 and has also, amongst others, the instance दाक्षायण; viz. (ed. Ballantyne, p. 795); Paribháshá: प्रत्ययग्रहणं चापञ्चम्याः । प्रत्ययग्रहणं च अपञ्चम्याः प्रयोजनम् । यञिञोः फग्भवति । गार्ग्यायणः । वात्स्यायनः । परमगार्ग्यायणः परमवात्स्यायनः । दाक्षायणः । परमदाक्षायणः etc.—That Dákshāyaṇa is the *yuvan*, not the *son* of Dákshi is sufficiently clear from the Káśiká itself, since it refers to IV. 1, 94. For this reason it also gives as an instance of a *yuvan* to I. 2, 66, besides गार्ग्यायणः and वात्स्यायन (omitted in the Calc. ed.), the word दाक्षायणः—Patanjali contents himself with the instance गार्ग्यायणः; but it commences its counter-instance to II. 4, 58 in this way: अञिञोरिति किम् । दाक्षेरपत्यं युवा दाक्षायणः. We must, consequently, consider it an inaccuracy when the same Káśiká gives its counter-instance to II. 4, 60 in these words: प्राचामिति किम् । दाक्षिः पिता । दाक्षायणः पुत्रः. The Calcutta edition continues it, and Dr. Boehtlingk, of course, reprints it without a single remark. In short, whenever we open his discreditable reprint, we understand perfectly well why he writes in his preface, p. xxxviii.: "The Calcutta edition is very correct, so much so that only on the very rarest occasions have I had an opportunity of preferring the readings of the Manuscripts."

[238] Káriká to I. 1, 20: सर्वे सर्वपदादेशा दाक्षीपुत्रस्य पाणिनेः etc.

[239] Páṇini, VI. 4, 148: यस्येति च.—Patanjali: इवर्णान्तस्येति किमुदाहरणं हे दाक्ष्या दाक्षेयः । हे दाक्षि इति यदि लोपो न स्यात् etc.—Kaiyyaṭa: इवर्णान्तस्येति । हे दाक्षीति । दाक्षिशब्दादितो मनुष्यजातेरिति (MS. हे दाक्षेनिर्दिक्षिश॰॰) (IV. 1, 65) ङीषि कृते तस्य संबुद्धौ ह्रस्वे कृते etc.—IV. 1, 65: इतो मनुष्यजातेः.—Káśiká .... दाक्षी ....—IV. 1, 94: गोत्राद्यून्यस्त्रियाम्.—Káśiká ... अस्त्रियामिति किम् । दाक्षी ...—I. 2, 66: स्त्री पुंवच्च (where स्त्री implies in reference to the preceding Sútra वृद्धा स्त्री, *i.e.* the eldest daughter of a grandson, or a further descendant, considered as the female head of the family).—Káśiká: वृद्धो यूनेति (I. 2, 65) च सर्वम् । स्त्री वृद्धा यूना सह वचने शिष्यते । तल्लक्षणश्चेदेव विशेषो भवति । पुंस इवास्याः (thus MS. 829; MS. 2440 एवास्याः) कार्यं भवति । स्त्र्यर्थः पुमर्थवद्भवति । गार्गी च गार्ग्यायणश्च गार्ग्यौ । वात्सी च वात्स्यायनश्च वात्स्यौ । दाक्षी च दाक्षायणश्च दाक्ष्यौ (thus MS. 2440; MS. 829 दाक्षी).

Now since the Ṛik-Prátiśákhya quotes Vyáḍi, as we have seen, on several occasions, and since the Prátiśákhya of Kátyáyana is more recent than this work, I must leave it to the reader to determine how many generations must, in all probability, have separated Páṇini from the author of the Ṛik-Prátiśákhya on the one hand, and from the author of the Vájasaneyi-Prátiśákhya and the Várttikas on the other.

After this statement, which, I fear, is entirely fatal to a great many chronological assumptions which have hitherto been regarded as fully established, *and to the critical and linguistic results which have been built on these assumptions*, it is not necessary—but it will nevertheless be interesting—to see that modern and ancient grammatical authorities contain additional testimony to the conclusion I have here arrived at.

When explaining the uncritical condition of the Paribháshá collections, I pointed out that if they were looked upon as an indivisible whole, there could be no doubt that they must be later than Páṇini,—since one of them uses the word *Páṇiníya*. I pointed out, too, that the compilers of these collections, Vaidyanátha, for instance, must have taken this view of their chronological relation to Páṇini. Now at the end of the *Laghuparibháshávṛitti* we read that "some ascribe the composition of all the Paribháshás to the Muni *Vyáḍi*."[240] They must consequently have considered him as posterior to Páṇini.

I will at once, however, ascend to the author of the Great Commentary. In illustrating the first Várttika to Páṇini's rule VI. 2, 36, Patanjali writes down the following compound: Ápiśala-Páṇiníya-Vyáḍíya-Gautamíyáḥ.[241] It tells its own tale: it names first the disciples of *Ápiśali*—of whom we know, through Páṇini himself, that he preceded him,—then those of *Páṇini*,

[240] Laghuparibháshávṛitti: इदं भर्तृहरिवचनम् । केचित्तु व्याख्यानत (the first Paribháshá) इत्यादिपरिभाषा व्याडिमुनिविरचिता इत्याहुः.

[241] Páṇini, VI. 2, 36: आचार्योपसर्जनश्चान्तेवासी.—Kátyáyana: आचार्योपसर्जने ऽनेकस्यापि पूर्वपदत्वात्संदेहः.—Patanjali; आचार्योपसर्जने ऽनेकस्यापि पदस्य पूर्वपदत्वात्संदेहो भवति । आपिशलपाणिनीयव्याडीयगौतमीयाः.

afterwards those of *Vyáḍi*, and ultimately those of *Gautama*. There can be no doubt that we have here a sequence of grammarians who wrote one after the other; but, if any doubt still existed, it would be dispelled by the grammatical properties of the compound itself; for a Várttika to II. 2, 34, teaches that—unless there be reasons to prevent it—the name of the more important part must come first in a Dwandwa compound; and for a similar reason other Várttikas teach that, for instance, in forming such a compound of the names of seasons, the name of the earliest season in the year must precede that of a subsequent one; or in compounding the names of castes, they must follow one another in their natural order; or in making a Dwandwa of the names of two brothers, the name of the older has precedence of the name of the younger.[242] But as none of the grammatical reasons taught by Páṇini in previous rules would compel the component parts of the compound alleged to assume another order than that which they have, we can only interpret their sequence in the manner I have stated.[243]

The descent from the height of the Prátiśákhyas to the level plain of the Phiṭsútras would almost seem to require an explanation. Before I give it, however, I will refer to Professor Müller's Ancient Sanskrit Literature, and state its opinion on the rela-

---

[242] Páṇini, II. 2, 34: अल्पाच्तरम्.—Várttika 3 (of the Calc. ed.) अभ्यर्हितं च.—Patanjali: अभ्यर्हितं पूर्वं निपततीति वक्तव्यम्। मातापितरौ श्रद्धामेधे.—Várttika 2 (of the Calc. ed.) ऋतुनक्षत्राणामानुपूर्व्येण समानाक्षराणाम्.—Patanjali; ऋतुनक्षत्राणामानुपूर्व्येण समानाक्षराणां पूर्वनिपातो वक्तव्यः। शिशिरवसन्तौ.—Várttika 5 (of the Calc. ed.) वर्णानामानुपूर्व्येण.—Patanjali: वर्णानां चानुपूर्व्येण पूर्वनिपातो भवतीति वक्तव्यम्। ब्राह्मणक्षत्रियविट्शूद्राः.—Várttika 6 (of the Calc. ed) भ्रातुश्च ज्यायसः.—Patanjali: भ्रातुश्च ज्यायसः पूर्वनिपातो भवतीति वक्तव्यम्। युधिष्ठिरार्जुनौ.

[243] Such a reason would be, for instance, if one part of the compound belonged to the words technically called घि (I. 4, 7—9); for in such a case the base घि would have precedence of a base ending in अ (compare II. 2, 32). On this account the names of the three grammarians, Śákalya, Gárgya and Vyáḍi, form in the Ṛik-Prátiśákya, XIII. 12, the dwandwa: व्याळिशाकल्यगार्ग्याः.

tion of these Sútras to Páṇini. It is contained in the following words:[244]

"As to Śântana's Phiṭsûtras, we know with less certainty to what period they belong. A knowledge of them is not presupposed by Pâṇini, and the grammatical terms used by Śântana are different from those employed by Pâṇini,—a fact from which Professor Boehtlingk has ingeniously concluded that Śântana must have belonged to the eastern school of grammarians. As, however, these Sûtras treat only of the accent, and the accent is used in the Vedic language only, the subject of Śântana's work would lead us to suppose that he was anterior to Pâṇini, though it would be unsafe to draw any further conclusion from this."

Once more I am unable to assent to the arguments of my learned predecessor on this subject. If the knowledge of a work, as he admits, is not presupposed by Páṇini, it would seem to follow that such a work is not anterior but posterior to him, since it is scarcely probable that he could have ignored the information it contains. Nor has Professor Müller given any evidence to show that the contents of the Phiṭsútras are restricted to the Vaidik language only. On the contrary, the great bulk of the words treated of in these Sútras belongs with equal right, and, in some respect, with much greater right, to the classical language, in preference to that of the Vaidik hymns or Bráhmaṇas. And as no word can be pronounced without an accent, it is not intelligible why such a treatise should not be of as great importance for the student who recites the Mahábhárata as for the priest who reads the Ṛigveda poetry. Páṇini himself has, indeed, embraced in his rules on accentuation a great number of words no trace of which occurs in the Saṁhitás. But even if the statement made by Professor Müller were unobjectionable, why should it follow that an author who—and because he—writes on a Vaidik subject, must, or is even likely to, be anterior to an author who treats of the classical literature? And Páṇini moreover treated of both.

As little as I can adopt, on these premises, the conclusions Prof.

[244] Ancient Sanskrit Literature, p. 152.

Müller draws, so little can I join in the compliments he pays to the ingenuity of Dr. Boehtlingk.[245] For since Páṇini himself, as I have shown before, makes use of the terms *prathamá*, *dwitíyá*, *tṛitíyá*, *chaturthí*, etc., and of *auṅg*, *áṅg* (in the sense of an instrumental in the singular),[246] all of which are terms of the eastern grammarians, and, as everyone knows that Páṇini did not belong to them, I can see no ingenuity in assigning Śántana to this school on the sole ground of his having used terms which differ from those of Páṇini; especially when these terms have no grammatical influence whatever, like the anubandhas of Páṇini, and are not distinctly defined in the commentary as terms of the eastern grammarians.[247]

[245] As in the case of the Calcutta edition of Páṇini, and of the Uṇṇádi-Sútras, the edition of the Phiṭsútras also was entrusted by Dr. Boehtlingk to his compositor, who reprinted the text of these Sútras from the Calcutta edition of the Siddhánta-kaumudí.—The difficulties offered by these Sútras are not inconsiderable, and might have yielded good materials for many remarks. Dr. Boehtlingk's Commentary on them consists of 32 lines, which contain the substance of about 12, nearly all of which are insignificant. Even his very small Index to the Sútras is imperfect; for it omits the Sútra यथेति पादान्ते which he mistook for a part of the commentary on IV. 15, and the Sútra उपसर्गाश्चाभिवर्जं which also he has reprinted as if it were a portion of the commentary on IV. 12, though he himself is doubtful as to its proper position there. He professes, too, to have given an Index of the contents, "for those who mean to pursue the subject." But as one of the latter, I had to make a thorough Index of all the technical symbols in the Sútras, and also of a good number of real words which occur in the commentary and text, but which, in accordance with his notion of an Index, or through his usual inaccuracy, are omitted in his Index; *e.g.* अंशुक II. 13; अदिति IV. 15; अभि IV. 13; अम्बा I. 2; आन्त I. 4; आथर्वण IV. 11; इष्टका III. 19; ऋतु II. 22; छकलास II. 22; छत्तिका I. 21; छचिम II. 8, and very many more. Of compounds he has never enabled the reader to find the latter part; and such general terms as उदात्त, स्वरित, अनुदात्त, अचर etc., which are as indispensable for a student as the individual words themselves, are of course, also omitted. And all these remarks are suggested by the *edition* of a text which comprises no more than 88 Sútras. It is, of course, needless for me to add that the trouble of consulting or using a very valuable commentary on these Sútras, the *Phiṭsútra-vṛitti*, does not enter into the plan of an editor whose activity in editing grammatical Sanskrit texts only consists in putting the printed Calcutta works into different type.

[246] See notes 197, 220, and Páṇini, VII. 3, 105.

[247] Dr. Boehtlingk enumerates the terms which induced him to draw the inference alluded to by Müller, that Śántana belonged to the eastern grammarians; and he adds also the Sútras where they occur, viz. अष् II. 4, 19, 26; नप् II. 3; फिष् I. 1; यमन्वन्

The real reasons for this assumption, which I share in, must, in my opinion, be sought for elsewhere; and as they are connected with the question of the chronological relation of the Phiṭsútras to Páṇini, I will first explain why I speak of them after the Prátiśákhya works.

It is because they stand on the same linguistic ground as the latter writings, and because it was safer to survey this ground in the wider field of the Prátiśákhya literature than in the narrow precincts of the Sútras of Śántana. This having been done, we need now merely recall the results obtained.

We have seen that the Prátiśákhyas represent the mechanic treatment of the language, unlike Páṇini's method, which is organic and shows the growth and life of the language he spoke. The same is the case in these Phiṭsútras. Whereas Páṇini endeavours to explain the accent of words by connecting it with the properties of the word,—whereas he seeks for organic *laws* in the accents of uncompounded or compounded words and, only reluctanctly, as it were, abandons this path whenever he is unable to assign a general reason for his rules,—the Phiṭsútras, like the Prátiśákhyas, deal merely with the ready-made word,[248] and attach to it those mechanical rules which bewilder and confuse, but must have been well adapted for an intellectual condition fitted for admiring the Prátiśákhya works. They belong, in my opinion, like the Prátiśákhyas, not to the flourishing times of Hindu antiquity, but to its decadence.

II. 18; शिट् II. 6; स्फिक् II. 16; हय् II. 25. Amongst these, स्फिक् does not occur in the text of the Sútras of Bhaṭṭoji, but is a *various reading* mentioned by him in his commentary, which reports on *this various reading* that it is a term of the eastern grammarians. The text of his Sútras has लुप् instead of स्फिक्. As to the other quotations given by Dr. Boehtlingk, *not one* tells us that these terms are terms of the eastern grammarians. There was, consequently, not a particle of evidence to draw from *them* that inference which he so positively draws. It is a mere guess, the probable correctness of which is corroborated, but by such evidence as never occurred to him.

[248] Phiṭsútra, I. 1: फिषो ऽन्त उदात्तः.—Phiṭsútravṛitti: .... अर्थवदधातुरप्रत्ययः (comp. Páṇ. I. 2, 45) फिट्। कृत्तद्धितसमासाश्चेति (comp. Páṇ. I. 2. 46).—Compare also the end of note 255.

In the second place, we have seen that on the ground which is common to both, the Prátiśákhyas possess a far greater amount of linguistic material than Páṇini does; and we had to conclude that Páṇini could on no account have ignored the knowledge they conveyed, had they existed before his time. Precisely the same remark applies to the little treatise of Śántana; for, brief as it is, it is richer in many respects than the *analogous* chapter which Páṇini devoted to the same subject; and it would be inconceivable that Páṇini should bring forward his rules, so much more incomplete in *substance* than the Phiṭsútras, had they been the precursor of his work.

But, thirdly, we were compelled to admit that, at least, one of the Prátiśákhyas, that of Kátyáyana, was written with the direct intention of completing and criticising Páṇini; and I may here observe, that Professor Weber has, with very good reasons, assigned to this grammarian a place within the Eastern school. These features, too, characterise the tract of Śántana.

Some of his rules are delivered with the evident purpose of criticising Páṇini, and we meet on one occasion with the remark of the commentator that the *eastern grammarians* point out the difference between a rule of Páṇini and one of Śántana, when the context in which this passage occurs leaves no doubt that they meant a criticism on Páṇini. And from this remark alone I should conclude that Śántana was one of their school, while, from all these reasons combined, I draw the inference that he must have written after Páṇini.

I will give some proof to substantiate this view, and to show, moreover, that there are grammatical authorities in India who expressly imply the view here taken of the posteriority of these Sútras to Páṇini.

According to Páṇini's rule, VI. 1, 213, a word *ibhya* would have the *udátta* on the first syllable; Bhaṭṭojidíkshita, in his comment on the *Phiṭsútras*, quotes this rule in order to show that Śántana gave his Sútra I. 5, with a view of stating that Páṇini's

28

rule would not apply to this word.[249] He quotes the same rule of Páṇini for a similar purpose when he comments on I. 18,[250] for, according to this rule, *arya* is not udátta on the first, but on the last syllable; and also in his comment on IV. 8, for, according to this Sútra, the words *tilya*, *śikhya* (*martya*), *dhánya* and *kanyá*, are not udátta on the first, but swarita on the last syllable.[251] On the rule I. 7, Bhaṭṭoji reports that, in the opinion of certain grammarians, Śántana gave it in order to "*kill*" Páṇini's rule VI. 2, 2.[252] Śántana's rule I. 23, Bhaṭṭoji says, contravenes Páṇini's rule VI. 1, 197.[253] And it is the same grammarian who, when explaining that *saha*, as a part of Śántana's rule IV. 13, is udátta on the last syllable, reports: "The eastern grammarians inform us that *saha* in PÁṆINI's rule VI. 3, 78, is udátta on the first syllable;" and he adds the advice: "*think on that.*"[254] But I find no evidence in the arguments of Dr. Boehtlingk, as regards the relation of Śántana

---

[249] Páṇini, VI. 1, 213: यतो ऽनाव:.—Phiṭsútra, I, 5: ध्यपूर्वस्य स्त्रीविषयस्य.—Bhaṭṭojid.: .... विषयग्रहणं किम्। इभ्या ..... यतो ऽनाव इत्याद्युदात्त इभ्यशब्द:.

[250] Phiṭsútra, I. 18: अर्यस्य स्वाम्याख्या चेत्.—Bhaṭṭojid.: यान्तस्यान्त्यात्पूर्वमिति (III. 13)। यतो ऽनाव इति वाद्युदात्ते प्राप्ते वचनम् (where the word प्राप्ते sufficiently indicates Bhaṭṭoji's view of the chronological relation between Śántana and Páṇini. The same rule is given by Kátyáyana in his Várttika to Paṇini, III. 1, 103).

[251] Phiṭsútra, IV. 8: तिल्यशिक्यकाश्मर्यधान्यकन्याराजन्यमनुष्याणामन्त:.—Bhaṭṭojid.: स्वरित: स्यात्। तिलानां भवनं चेत्रं तिल्यम्। यतो ऽनाव इति प्राप्ते.—The Phiṭsútra-vṛitti reads this Sútra: तिल्यशिक्यमर्त्यकाश्मर्यधान्य०० .

[252] Phiṭsútra, I. 7: हिष्ठवत्सरतिशत्थान्तानाम्.—Bhaṭṭojid.: .... संवत्सर:। अव्ययपूर्वपदप्रकृतिस्वरो (comp. Páṇ. VI. 2, 2) ऽनेन बाध्यत इत्याहु:.

[253] Phiṭsútra, I. 23: ज्येष्ठकनिष्ठयोर्वयसि.—Bhaṭṭojid.: अन्त उदात्त: स्यात्। ज्येष्ठ आह चमसा ....। इह नित्त्वाद्युदात्त एव (comp. Páṇ. VI. 1, 197).

[254] Phiṭsútra, IV. 14 (not 13): एवादीनामन्त:.—Bhaṭṭojid.: एवमादीनामिति पाठान्तरम्। एव। एवम्। नूनम्। सह। ते पुत्तसूरिभि: सह। षष्ठस्य तृतीये सहस्य स इति (Páṇ. VI. 3, 78) प्रकरणे सहशब्द आद्युदात्त इति प्राञ्च:। तच्चिन्त्यम्.—The statement of the Pránchas mentioned by Bhaṭṭojidíkshita, is that of Patanjali in his comment on VI. 3, 78, v. 1, viz.: आद्युदात्तनिपातनं करिष्यते; and Kaiyyaṭa in referring to Phiṭsútra IV. 12, observes: निपाता आद्युदात्ता इति सहशब्द आद्युदात्त:. But this reference of Kaiyyaṭa by no means admits of the conclusion that he looked upon Páṇini's rule as more recent than this Phiṭsútra; for this rule is not concerned with the accent of सह; it is Patanjali who alludes to it; and Kaiyyaṭa comments, in the words alleged, on Patanjali, not on Páṇini.

to the eastern grammarians, of his having followed the advice of Bhaṭṭojidíkshita.

Of equal importance with these observations of Bhaṭṭoji, is a passage in the notes of Nágojibhaṭṭa on Kaiyyaṭa, when the latter accompanies the gloss of Patanjali to Kátyáyana's Várttika 6, to Páṇini VI. 1, 158, with his own remarks. For Nágojibhaṭṭa, after having observed that a rule of Páṇini would contain a fault when compared with the standard of the Phiṭsútras, pointedly winds up with the following words: "But, on the other hand, *these Phiṭsútras, when considered in reference to Páṇini, are as if they were made to-day.*"[255]

It is clear, therefore, that the best Hindu grammarians, too,

---

[255] Várttika 6 (of the Calc. ed.) to VI. 1, 158: प्रकृतिप्रत्यययोः स्वरस्य सावकाशत्वादप्रसिद्धिः.—Patanjali: प्रकृतिप्रत्यययोः स्वरस्य सावकाशत्वादप्रसिद्धिः स्यात्। प्रकृतिस्वरस्यावकाशः। यत्रानुदात्तप्रत्ययः। पचति। पठति॥ प्रत्ययस्वरस्यावकाशः। यत्रानुदात्ता प्रकृतिः सम त्वम्। सिम त्वम्। इहोभयं प्राप्नोति। कर्तव्यम्। तैत्तिरीयम्। विप्रतिषेधात्प्रत्ययस्वरो भविष्यति। नैवं विप्रतिषेधे परमित्युच्यते (I. 4, 2)। न परः प्रत्ययस्वरः। नैष दोषः। इष्टवाची परशब्दः। विप्रतिषेधे परं यदिष्टं तद्भवतीति.—Várttika 7 (of the Calc. ed.): विप्रतिषेधात्प्रत्ययस्वर इति चेत्काम्यायादिषु चित्कारणम्.—Patanjali: विप्रतिषेधात्प्रत्ययस्वर इति चेत्काम्यायादयश्चितः कर्तव्याः। पुत्रकाम्यति। गोपायति। ऋतीयते। नैष दोषः। प्रकृतिस्वरोऽत्र बाधको भविष्यति। प्रकृतिस्वरे प्रत्ययस्वराभावः। कर्तव्यम्। तैत्तिरीयम्—Kaiyyaṭa, on the preceding passages: . . . . . विप्रतिषेधादिति। पूर्वविप्रतिषेधादित्यर्थः। काम्यादय इति। काम्यचश्चित्करणं प्रत्याख्यातं तत्कर्तव्यमेव . . . . . .—Nágojibhaṭṭa: सम त्वमित्यत्र त्वत्त्वसमसिमेत्यनुच्चानीति (Phiṭsútra, IV. 10) प्रकृतिरनुदात्ता। तित्तिरिः शकुनीनां च लघुपूर्वमिति (Phiṭsútra, II. 21) मध्योदात्तः. . . . .। फिट्स्वरोऽपि षाष्ठ एवेति तैत्तिरीयेऽपि दोषः। यद्वा फिट्सूत्राणि पाणिन्यपेक्षया आधुनिककर्तृकाणीति परत्वं बोध्यम्.—The Phiṭsútra II. 21, referred to by Nágojibhaṭṭa, is read differently in Bhaṭṭoji's text from that of the Vṛitti. I subjoin both readings with their commentary, in order to illustrate at the same time the nature of the latter commentary as compared with that of Bhaṭṭoji. The latter reads शकुनीनां च लघुपूर्वम्, and comments: पूर्वं लघूदात्तं स्यात्। कुक्कुटः। तित्तिरिः.—The Phiṭsútravṛitti reads शकुनीनां च लघुपूर्वाणाम्, and comments लघुपूर्वौ येषां शकुनिवाचिनां लघावन्ते द्वयोश्च बह्वषो गुरुरुदात्तो भवति। कृकवाकुः। कृकलासः। कपोतः॥ शकुनीनामिति किम्। वराहः॥ लघुपूर्वाणामिति किम्। कुक्कुटः। तित्तिरिः। खञ्जरीटः.—I may quote here a passage from Sáyaṇa's Commentary on Ṛigveda I. 1, 1, in order to obviate a misunderstanding of it.

looked upon these Sútras not only as not anterior to Páṇini, but as quite recent, when compared with his work.

On *Yáska*, Professor Müller expresses himself thus:[256]

"There are some discussions in the beginning of the Nirukta which are of the highest interest with regard to etymology. While in Greece the notions of one of her greatest thinkers, as expressed in the Cratylus, represent the very infancy of etymological science, the Brahmans of India had treated some of the vital problems of etymology with the utmost sobriety. In the Prâtiśâkhya of Kâtyâyana we find, besides the philosophical division of speech into nouns, verbs, prepositions, and particles, another division of a purely grammatical nature and expressed in the most strictly technical language. '*Verbs* with their conjugational terminations; *Nouns*, derived from verbs by means of Krit-suffixes; *Nouns*, derived from nouns by means of taddhita-suffixes, and four kinds of compounds,—these constitute language' [Vájas. Prát. I. 27.]

"In the Nirukta this division is no longer considered sufficient. A new problem has been started, one of the most important problems in the philosophy of language, whether all nouns are derived from verbs? No one would deny that certain nouns, or the majority of nouns, were derived from verbs. The early grammarians of India were fully agreed that *kartṛi*, a doer, was derived from *kṛi*, to do; *pâchaka*, a cook, from *pach*, to cook. But

---

With regard to the accent of the word अग्नि he writes: गार्ग्यस्य मतेऽग्निशब्दस्याखण्डप्रातिपदिकत्वात्फिषो ऽन्त उदात्त इत्यन्तोदात्तत्वम्. These words need not mean that Gárgya, the predecessor of Páṇini, deducts from Phiṭsútra I. 1, the accent of अग्नि, but they may—and, I conclude, *do*—mean: "since, according to the opinion of Gárgya, *agni* is an indivisible base (*i.e.* a base which must not be analysed; compare note 248), its accent is the *udátta* on the last syllable, agreeably to Phiṭsútra I. 1.—The last reference, therefore, would belong to Sáyaṇa, not to Gárgya; and the only inference we might be allowed to draw from the words of Sáyaṇa would be, that Gárgya looked upon *agni* as an Uṇṇádi-formation (compare p. 171), and, perhaps—but not necessarily,—that already in his time there existed a rule on accentuation similar in *purport* to that of the Phiṭsútra alleged. It is not admissible, therefore, to adduce this passage in proof that, in Sáyaṇa's opinion, the Phiṭsútras were known to Gárgya.

256 Ancient Sanskrit Literature, p. 163.

did the same apply to all words? Śâkaṭâyana, an ancient grammarian and philosopher, answered the question boldly in the affirmative, and he became the founder of a large school, called the *Nairuktas* (or Etymologists), who made the verbal origin of all words the leading principle of all their researches."[257]

It is sufficiently clear from the preceding words that Professor Müller considers Yáska as more recent than Kátyáyana, and since he himself admits (see above p. 193) "that there is nothing in the style of the Prâtiśâkhya composed by Kâtyâyana that could be used as a tenable argument why Kâtyâyana, the author of the Prâtiśâkhya, should not be the same as Kâtyâyana, the contemporary and critic of Pâṇini," he must also consider the author of the Nirukta as subsequent to Páṇini.

To refute his view on the relative position of Kátyáyana and Yáska, we need now merely point to the facts with which we are already familiar. Müller's reason for Yáska's posteriority to Kátyáyana is founded, as we see, on the assumption that the problem of the derivability or non-derivability of *all* nouns from verbs had not yet been proposed in the time of Kátyáyana. But whence does he know this? The Prátiśákhya of Kátyáyana is no sufficient testimony for establishing this theory. When Kátyáyana there says that nouns are either nouns derived from verbs, or nouns derived from nouns,—either kṛit or taddhita derivatives,—he has already said too much in a work of this kind, which has nothing to do with the origin of words, and which alludes to this and other matter, foreign to a Prátiśákhya itself, only *because*, and *in so far as*, it concerns its *other purpose*, viz. that of criticizing Páṇini. Whether or not therefore it dealt with a problem such as that of which Müller is speaking, is merely a matter of chance.

But this problem itself, as we have seen, is epitomized in the term *uṇṇádi*. A grammarian who uses this term shows at the same time that he is cognizant of that division between the old grammarians which Yáska describes. For whichever side he

[257] In the continuation of this passage Professor Müller gives the statement similar to that which is contained above, on page 171.

espouse, he has expressed by the term *uṇṇádi*, that there are kṛit-derivatives which are of an exceptional kind and which are looked upon by some as being, strictly speaking, no derivatives at all. Now, I have quoted several instances which prove that Kátyáyana dealt with the question of Uṇṇádi words. Hence he *was* aware of that problem discussed in the Nirukta; it was *not* "a new problem" to him; and all the inferences that may or may not be built on its absence in the Vájasaneyi-Prátiśákhya become invalidated at once.

But the knowledge possessed by Páṇini, of this problem itself would, of course, not prove anything as to his priority or posteriority to Yáska, who speaks of it. It leaves this question just where we find it, and we must seek for other evidence to settle it.

Such, I hold, is afforded by the fact that Páṇini knows the name of Yáska, for he teaches the formation of this word and heads a Gaṇa with it.[258] And as we know at present of but one real Yáska in the whole ancient literature, a doubt as to the identity of the author of the Nirukta and the family chief adduced by Páṇini, would have first to be supported with plausible arguments before it could be assented to.

A second and equally strong reason is, in my belief, afforded by the test I have established above, on the ground of the grammatical *sanjnás* which occur in Páṇini's work.

Amongst these terms there is one especially which allows us to judge of the relative position of Yáska and Páṇini, viz., the term *upasarga*, prefix or preposition. Páṇini employs it in many Sútras; he does not define it; it must consequently have been in use before he wrote. *Yáska*, however, enters fully into the notion expressed by it, as we may conclude from the following words of his Nirukta:—[259]

---

[258] Páṇini, II. 4, 63: यास्कादिभ्यो गोत्रे.

[259] Nirukta, I. 3 (according to the edition of Professor Roth): न निर्बद्धा उपसर्गा अर्थान्निराहुरिति शाकटायनो नामाख्यातयोस्तु कर्मोपसंयोगद्योतका भवन्त्युच्चावचाः पदार्था भवन्तीति गार्ग्यस्तद्य एषु पदार्थः प्राहुरिमे तं नामाख्यातयोरर्थविकरणम्।

"Śákaṭáyana says that 'the prepositions when detached (from noun or verb) do not distinctly express a sense;' but Gárgya maintains that 'they illustrate the action which is the sense expressed by a noun or verb (in modifying it); and that their sense is various (even when they are detached from a noun or verb).' Now they express (even in their isolated condition) that sense

---

आ इत्यर्वागर्थे प्र परेत्येतस्य प्रातिलोम्यमभीत्याभिमुख्यं प्रतीत्येतस्य प्रातिलोम्यमति सु इत्यभिपूजितार्थे निर्दुरित्येतयोः प्रातिलोम्यं न्यवेति विनिग्रहार्थीया उदित्येतयोः प्रातिलोम्यं समित्येकीभावं व्यपेत्येतस्य प्रातिलोम्यमन्विति सादृश्यापरभावमपीति संसर्गमुपेत्युपजनं परीति सर्वतोभावमधीत्युपरिभावमैश्वर्यं वैवमुच्चावचानर्थान्प्राहुस्त उपेक्षितव्याः.—Of the commentary of Durga on this passage I subjoin here only those passages which are required for a justification of my translation, and of the instances added to the text of Yáska (MS. E.I.H., 206): नामा॰ । तुशब्दो ऽवधारणार्थः । नामाख्यातयोरेव यो ऽर्थः कर्म तत्रैव विशेषं कंचिदुपसंयुज्य द्योतयन्ति । स एष नामाख्यातयोरेवार्थविशेष उपसर्गसंयोगे सति व्यज्यते ॥ . . . उच्चा भवन्तीति । वच्चाः (*sic*) पदार्था भवन्तीति गार्ग्यः । उच्चाश्च । वच्चाश्च (*sic*) । उच्चावचाः । बहुप्रकारा इत्यर्थः । एषामुपसर्गपदानामर्थाः पदार्था भवन्ति । वियुक्तानामपि नामाख्याताभ्यामिति गार्ग्यः । आचार्यो मन्यत इति वाक्यशेषः । एकैको ह्येषां प्रादीनां नामाख्यातवियोगे ऽप्यनेकार्थ इत्यभिप्रायः ॥ . . . . ॥ तद्य एषु पदार्थः प्राहुरिमे तम् । तदेतदुपपन्नं भवति । य एषूपसर्गेष्वनेकप्रकारो ऽर्थ इति प्राहुरेव तमिम उपसर्गपदविशेषाः पृथगपि सन्तः कः पुनरसावित्युच्यते । नामाख्यातयोरर्थविकरणम् ॥ . . . ॥ आ इत्यर्वागर्थे । तद्यथा । आ पर्वतादिति । अर्वागिति गम्यते ॥ . . . . प्र परेत्येतस्य प्रातिलोम्यम् । प्रपरावित्येतावुपसर्गावेतस्यैवाङो ऽर्थस्य प्रातिलोम्यमाहतुः । प्रगतः । परागतः ॥ अभीत्याभिमुख्यमाह । अभिगतः ॥ प्रतीत्येतस्यैवाभेः प्रातिलोम्यमाह । प्रतिगत इति ॥ अति सु इत्येतावभिपूजितार्थे वर्तेते । अतिधनः । सुब्राह्मण इति ॥ निर्दुरित्येतयोः प्रातिलोम्यम् । निर्धनः । दुर्ब्राह्मण इति ॥ न्यवेति विनिग्रहार्थीयौ । निगृह्णात्यवगृह्णाति ॥ उदित्ययमेक एव द्वयोः प्रातिलोम्यमाह। उद्गृह्णातीति ॥ समित्येकीभावमर्थमाह । संगृह्णातीति ॥ व्यपेत्येतस्य प्रातिलोम्यमाहतुः । विगृह्णात्यपगृह्णातीति ॥ अन्विति सादृश्यापरभावमाह । अनुरूपमस्येति सादृश्यम् । अनुगच्छतीत्यपरभावम् ॥ अपीति संसर्गमाह । सर्पिषो ऽपि स्यात् । मधुनो ऽपि स्यात् ॥ उपेत्युपजनम् । उपजनमाधिक्यम् । उपजायते ॥ परीति सर्वतोभावमाह । परिधापयतीति ॥ अधीत्युपरिभावमाह । ऐश्वर्यं वा । अधितिष्ठति । अधिपतिरिति । आह । नामाख्यातयोस्तु कर्मोपसंयोगद्योतका भवन्तीत्युक्तम् । अत्र नाम्नः कर्मोपसंयोगद्योतका भवन्तीति । एवं न गृह्यन्ते । उपसर्गाः क्रियायोग इति (Páṇ. I. 1, 59) प्रसिद्धो ह्युपसर्गाणां क्रियापदेन योगो न नाम्न उपसर्गा हि क्रियाङ्गत्वेनैव नामान्यास्कन्दन्तीति.

which inheres in them; it is this sense which modifies the sense of a noun or verb. The preposition *á* expresses the sense of limit (e.g. *up to* the mountain); *pra* and *pará* express the reverse of *á* (*e.g.* gone *forth* or *away*); *abhi*, the sense of towards (*e.g.* gone *towards*—in a friendly sense); *prati*, the reverse of *abhi* (*e.g.* gone *against*); *ati* and *su*, excellence (*e.g.* having *much* wealth, an *excellent* Bráhmaṇa); *nir* and *dur*, the reverse of these two (*e.g.* having *no* wealth, a *bad* Bráhmaṇa); *ni* and *ava*, downwardness (*e.g.* he takes *down*); *ud*, the reverse of these two (*e.g.* he takes *up*); *sam*, junction (*e.g.* he takes *together*); *vi* and *apa*, the reverse of *sam* (*e.g.* he takes *away*); *anu*, similarity or being after (*e.g.* having a *similar* appearance, he goes *after*); *api*, co-existence (*e.g.* let it be a *drop* of butter, a *drop* of honey);[260] *upa*, excess (*e.g.* he is born *again*); *pari*, surrounding (*e.g.* he puts *round*); *adhi*, being above and superiority (*e.g.* he stands *over*, a *supreme* lord). In this manner they express various senses, and these have to be considered."

This passage records, as we see, besides the definition of Yáska, the opinions of Śákaṭáyana and of Gárgya; it is silent on Páṇini. Yet how much more complete and scientific is *his* treatment of the prepositions! Durga, the commentator of Yáska, feels this defect in Yáska, for at the end of his gloss he says: "*upasargas* can only be joined to a verb, not to a noun; it is therefore only through the mediation of the former that they can ascend also to the latter" (viz. in so far as nouns are derived from verbal roots).

Páṇini teaches that the first and general category to which prepositions belong, is that of *nipátas* or particles: he then continues, that they are *upasargas* when they are joined to "verbal action" (*i.e.* to a verb); *gatis*, if the verbal roots to which they are attached become developed into a noun; and that they are *karmapravachaníyas* if they are detached and govern a noun.[261] Of such

---

[260] It seems to me doubtful whether संसर्ग implies the sense which is illustrated by the instance of Durga; without his words, which clearly refer to Patanjali's comment on Páṇini, I. 4, 96, I should have rendered संसर्ग by *union*, and thought of an instance like अपिनह्यति.

[261] Páṇini, I. 4, 58: प्रादयः; 59: उपसर्गाः क्रियायोगे; 60: गतिश्च; 83: कर्मप्रवचनीयाः.

a distinction there is no trace in the Nirukta, which stops, as we see, at the speculations of Śákaṭáyana and Gárgya, both predecessors of Páṇini. Nor can the meanings which Yáska assigns to the prepositions, so far as completeness is concerned, be compared to those we meet with in the rules of Páṇini. *Abhi*, for instance, has with him not only the sense mentioned by Yáska, but that of "towards, by (severally), with regard to;" *ati*, that of "excellence and transgression;" *apa*, that of "exception;" *anu*, that of "in consequence of, connected with, less than, towards, by (severally), with regard to, to the share of;" *prati*, the sense of "towards, by (severally), with regard to, to the share of, instead of, in return of;" *pari*, the sense of *prati*, except in the two last meanings, and that of an "expletive;" *adhi*, that of "superiority and of an expletive."[262]

It seems impossible, therefore, to assume that Yáska could have known the classes of *upasarga* as defined by Páṇini, and their meanings as enumerated by him when he wrote the words before quoted. But not knowing the grammar of Páṇini, is, in the case of Yáska, tantamount to having preceded it.

Though Yáska be older than Páṇini, and Páṇini older than Kátyáyana, there still remains the mystery as to the era of Páṇini. No work of the ancient literature, within my knowledge, gives us the means of penetrating it. But as the remotest date of Hindu antiquity, which may be called a real date, is that of *Buddha's* death, it must be of interest to know whether Páṇini is likely to have lived before or after this event.

Not only is the name of *Śákyamuni*, or Śákya, never adverted to in the Sútras of Páṇini,[263] but there is another fact connected with this name which is still more remarkable.

---

[262] Compare I. 4, 84—97.

[263] The formation शाक्य occurs in three Gaṇas; as a derivative from शक with यञ् in the Gaṇa to IV. 1, 105; with ञ्य to IV. 3, 92, but there it becomes doubtful, through the difference in the readings of the MSS.; and as a derivation from शाक with ण्य in the Gaṇa to IV. 1, 151.

The great schism which divided ancient India into two hostile creeds, centres in the notion which each entertained of the nature of eternal bliss. The Brahmanic Hindus hope that their soul will ultimately become united with the universal spirit; which, in the language of the Upanishads, is the neuter Brahman; and, in that of the sects, the supreme deity, who takes the place of this philosophical and impersonal god. And however indefinite this god Brahman may be, it is nevertheless, to the mind of the Brahmanic Hindu, an *entity*. The final salvation of a Buddhist is entire *non-entity*. This difference between the goal of both created that deep and irreconcileable antagonism which allowed of none of the compromise which was possible between all the shades and degrees of the Brahmanic faith, from the most enlightened to the most degenerate. The various expressions for eternal bliss in the Brahmanic creed, like *apavarga*, *moksha*, *mukti*, *niḥśreyasa*, all mean either "liberation from this earthly career" or the "absolute good;" they therefore imply a condition of hope. The absolute end of a Buddhist is without hope; it is *nirváṇa* or extinction. This word means literally "*blown out;*" but there is this difference, if I am not mistaken, between its use in the Brahmanic and in the Buddhistic literature,—that, in the former, it is employed, like other past participles, in any of the three genders, whereas in the latter it occurs only in the neuter gender, and there, too, only in the sense of an abstract noun, in that of *extinction*, *i.e.*, absolute annihilation of the soul. I have no instance at my command in which *nirváṇa*, when used in the classical literature, implies any other sense than the sense "*blown out*," or a sense immediately connected with it. Thus Patanjali, when illustrating the use of this past participle, gives the instances: "the fire is *blown out* by the wind, the lamp is *blown out* by the wind;" and Kaiyyaṭa who, on the same occasion, observes that a phrase, "the wind has ceased to blow," would not be expressed by "*nirváṇo* vátaḥ, but by *nirváto* vátaḥ," corroborates the instances of Patanjali with one of his own: "blowing out (has been effected) by the wind." But Páṇini, who teaches the formation of this participle in rule VIII. 2, 50, which has indirectly called forth all these instances, says:

"(the past participle of *vá* with prefix *nir* is) *nirváṇa* (if the word means) '*free from wind*,' (or, 'not blowing, as wind')."[264]

This is the natural interpretation of Páṇini's rule. *Kátyáyana*, it is true, gives a Várttika which corrects the word *aváte* into *avátábhidháne* "(if it have) not the sense of wind (or of blowing);" yet it is very remarkable that Patanjali, in commenting on this Várttika, does not interpret its words in his usual manner, but merely adds to them the instances I have just named; it is remarkable, too, that he introduces them with the observation: "(this Várttika is given in order to show) that (nirváṇa) is *also* or is emphatically used in the following instances." Still he has no instance whatever for the sense stated by *Páṇini*, and his word "*also*" or "emphatically" does not appear to be justified by the criticism of Kátyáyana, which simply corrects the word *aváte* into *avátábhidháne* without any additional remark.

In short, my opinion on this Várttika is analogous to that which I have expressed in previous instances. The sense of *nirváṇa*, "free from wind (or not blowing)," had become obsolete in the time of Kátyáyana, who merely knew that sense of it which found its ulterior and special application in the *nirváṇa* of the Buddhistic faith. But since there is no logical link between this latter word and the *nirváṇa*, "wind-still," of Páṇini; and since it is not probable that he would have passed over in silence that sense of the word which finally became its only sense, I hold that this sense did not yet exist in his time; in other words, that his silence affords a strong probability of his having preceded the origin of the Buddhistic creed.

The task I had proposed to myself would now seem to have

[264] VIII. 2, 50: निर्वाणो ऽवाते.—Kátyáyana: अवाताभिधाने.—Patanjali: अवाताभिधान इति वक्तव्यम् (these words have been mistaken for the Várttika itself, in the Calcutta edition) । इहापि यथा स्यात् । निर्वाणो ऽग्निर्वातेन । निर्वाणः प्रदीपो वातेनेति—Kaiyyaṭa: अवाताभिधान इति । तेन निर्वातो वात इत्यत्रैव नत्वनिषेधो न तु भावे निष्ठायामिति निर्वाणं वातेनेति भाव्यमिति वार्त्तिककारस्य दर्शनम् । अन्ये तु वातकर्तृके धात्वर्थे सर्वत्र निषेधमिच्छन्ति । निर्वातो वातः । निर्वातं वातेनेति । निर्वाणः प्रदीपो वातेनेत्यत्र तु वातः करणमिति प्रतिषेधाभावः.

reached its natural close for the present; yet if, after this brief and imperfect attempt to do justice to one of the most difficult questions of Sanskrit literature, I were now to take leave of Páṇini, even temporarily, without devoting a special word to Patanjali, I should fail in gratitude to this great teacher, who has supplied us with nearly all the materials for this discussion and its results.

"At what time," says Professor Müller,[265] "the Mahâbhâshya was first composed, it is impossible to say. Patanjali, the author of the Great Commentary, is sometimes identified with Pingala; and on this view, as Pingala is called the younger brother, or at least the descendant of Pâṇini, it might be supposed that the original composition of the Mahâbhâshya belonged to the third century. But the identity of Pingala and Patanjali is far from probable, and it would be rash to use it as a foundation for other calculations."

This is the only date, the fixing of which is called "*impossible*," in Müller's Ancient Sanskrit Literature; and as it has hitherto been my fate to differ from this work in all its chronological views, I seem merely to follow a predestined necessity in looking upon the date of Patanjali as the only one which I should venture to determine with anything like certainty.

I do so, because Patanjali, as if foreseeing the conjectural date which some future Pandit would attach to his life, or the doubt that might lift him out of all historical reach, once took the opportunity of stating a period before which we must not imagine him to have lived, while on another occasion he mentions the time when he actually did live.

"If a thing," says Páṇini, "serves for a livelihood, but is not for sale" (it has not the affix *ka*). This rule Patanjali illustrates with the words "Śiva, Skanda, Viśákha," meaning the idols that represent these divinities and at the same time give a living to the men who possess them,—while they are not for sale. And, "why?" he asks. "The *Mauryas* wanted gold, and therefore established religious festivities. Good; (Páṇini's rule) may apply to such (idols, as *they* sold); but as to idols which are hawked

---

[265] Ancient Sanskrit Literature, p. 244.

about (by common people) for the sake of such worship as brings an immediate profit, their names will have the affix *ka*." [266]

Whether or not this interesting bit of history was given by Patanjali ironically, to show that even affixes are the obedient servants of kings, and must vanish before the idols which *they* sell, because they do not take the money at the same time that the bargain is made—as poor people do,—I know not. But, at all events, he tells us distinctly by these words that he did not live before the first king of the Maurya dynasty who was Chandragupta, and who lived 315 B.C. And I believe, too, if we are to give a natural interpretation to his words, that he tells us, on the contrary, that he lived *after the last king* of this dynasty, or in other words later than 180 before Christ. But he has even been good enough to relieve us from a possibility of this doubt when commenting on another rule of Páṇini, or rather on a criticism attached to it by Kátyáyana.

In Sútra III. 2, 111, Páṇini teaches that the imperfect must be used, when the speaker relates a past fact belonging to a time which precedes the present day. Kátyáyana improves on this rule by observing that it is used, too, when the fact related is *out of sight, notorious, but could be seen by the person who uses the verb.* And Patanjali again appends to this Várttika the following instances and remark: "*The Yavana besieged* (imperfect) *Ayodhyá; the*

---

[266] V. 3, 99: जीविकार्थे चापण्ये.—Patanjali: अपण्य इत्युच्यते तत्रेदं न सिध्यति। शिवः स्कन्दो विशाख इति। किं कारणम्। मौर्यैर्हिरण्यार्थिभिरर्चाः प्रकल्पिताः। भवेत्। तासु न स्यात्। यास्त्वेताः संप्रतिपूजार्थाः। तासु भविष्यति.—Kaiyyaṭa: यास्त्वेता इति। याः परिगृह्य गृहाद्गृहमटन्ति तास्वित्यर्थः। यास्तु विक्रीयन्ते तासु न भवति। शिवकान्विक्रीणीत इति.—Nágojibhaṭṭa: मौर्या विक्रेतुं प्रतिमाशिल्पवन्तस्तैरर्चाः कल्पिताः (MS. 351: मौर्यौः विक्रीतुं प्रतिमाशित्पवंतस्तै°° *sic.*; MS. 1209: मौर्याः विक्रेतुं प्रतिमां शिल्पवांतस्तै°° *sic.*)। विक्रेतुमिति शेषो ऽतस्तासां पण्यत्वात्तत्र प्रत्ययश्रवणप्रसङ्ग इति भावः। तत्र प्रत्ययश्रवणमिष्टमेवेति वदन्सूत्रस्योदाहरणं दर्शयति। भवेदित्यादि। यास्त्वेता इति च। संप्रतिपूजार्थाः। संप्रतिस्तनिर्माणसमकालमेव फलजनिका याः पूजा जीविकाप्रदत्वेन तदर्था इत्यर्थस्तदाह। याः परिगृह्येति। यास्तु गृहे पूज्यन्ते शिष्टैस्तासु शिवाभेदबुद्धेः सत्त्वेन सादृश्यबुद्ध्यभावेन प्रत्ययस्यैवाभावः। एवं चित्रेष्वपि द्रष्टव्यम्.

Yavana besieged (imperfect) *the Mádhyamikas.* Why does Kátyáyana say, '*out of sight?*' (because in such an instance as) 'the sun rose' (the verb must be in the aorist). Why '*notorious?*' (because in such an instance as) 'Devadatta made a mat' (the verb must be in the preterit). Why does he say: '*but when the fact could be seen by the person who uses the verb?*' (because in such an instance as) 'According to a legend Vásudeva killed Kansa' (the verb must likewise be in the preterit).[267]

Hence he plainly informs us, and this is acknowledged also by Nágojibhaṭṭa, that he lived at the time—though he was not on the spot— when "*the Yavana besieged Ayodhyá,*" and at the time when "*the Yavana besieged the Mádhyamikas.*" For the very contrast which he marks between these and the other instances proves that he intended practically to impress his contemporaries with a proper use of the imperfect tense.

Now the *Mádhyamikas* are the well-known Buddhistic sect which was founded by *Nágárjuna.*[268] But here, it would seem,

---

[267] III. 2, 111: अनद्यतने लङ्.—Kátyáyana: परोक्षे च लोकविज्ञाते प्रयोक्तुर्दर्शनविषये.—Patanjali: परोक्षे च लोकविज्ञाते प्रयोक्तुर्दर्शनविषये लङ् वक्तव्यः। अरुणद्यवनः साकेतम्। अरुणद्यवनो माध्यमिकान्॥ परोक्ष इति किमर्थम्। उदगादादित्यः। लोकविज्ञात इति किमर्थम्। चकार कटं देवदत्तः॥ प्रयोक्तुर्दर्शनविषय इति किमर्थम्। जघान कंसं किल वासुदेवः.—Kaiyyaṭa: परोक्षे चेति। अननुभूतत्वात्परोक्षो ऽपि प्रत्यक्षयोग्यतामात्राश्रयेण दर्शनविषय इति विरोधाभावः.—Nágojibhaṭṭa on these instances of Patanjali: भाष्ये जघानेति किम्। स बधो हि नेदानीन्तनप्रयोक्तुर्दर्शनयोग्यो ऽपीत्यर्थः। अरुणदित्युदाहरणे तु तुल्यकालः प्रव(र्त)त(इ)ति बोध्यम्—That these instances concern the moment at which Patanjali wrote them, is therefore certain, beyond all doubt. But we obtain at the same time an insight into the critical condition of the later commentaries on Páṇini, when we find, for instance, that the Káśiká copies these instances, but without saying that they belong to Patanjali. The same is the case in the present edition of Páṇini. On account of the importance of this passage of the Mahábháshya, I will remind the reader that it is contained in the MS. E.I.H. No, 330, the only one I could consult. The two MSS. of the Káśiká in the library of the E.I.H. have instead of माध्यमिकान्, a word मध्यमिकाम्; but since the latter is not only meaningless, but grammatically wrong, there can be no doubt that the reading of the MS. 330 is the only correct one.

[268] See Burnouf's Introduction à l'histoire du Buddhism Indien, vol. I., p. 359: Lassen's Indische Alterthumskunde, vol. II. p. 1163 and the quotations there.

that at this early stage we are already at a chronological standstill. For the Northern Buddhists say that Nágárjuna lived 400, and the Southern Buddhists that he lived 500, years after Buddha's death. And again, while we believed that the researches of that admirable work of Professor Lassen had finally settled this latter date, and "for a last time,"—while we believed, in other words that it was 543 before Christ, Professor Müller seizes and shakes it once more and makes Buddha die 477 before Christ. Were I to agree with the opinion which he has elsewhere expressed,[269] that "in the history of Indian literature, dates are mostly so precarious, that a confirmation, even within a century or two, is not to be despised," I should be out of all my difficulties. For since the difference stated as regards the life of Nágárjuna would not amount to more than 166 years, it would fall within the alloted space. But I am not so easily satisfied. Dates in Sanskrit literature, as anywhere else, are either no dates at all—and then they are not so much as precarious—or they are dates, and then we must look closely at them.

The doubts which Prof. Müller has expressed in reference to the assumed date of Buddha's death, viz., 543 B.C., are by no means mere vague and personal doubts. On the contrary, they are embodied in an elaborate discussion, which not only proves a conscientious research, but is extremely valuable on account of the opportunity it gives of surveying the real difficulties of the question, and of forming one's own opinion, with greater safety and ease: and, whether dissenting from him or not, one is happy to deal with his arguments.

My objection to them may be summed up in the commencing and the closing words of his own investigation.

"It has been usual," he says in his Ancient Sanskrit Literature (p. 264), "to prefer the chronology of Ceylon, which places Buddha's death in 543 B.C. But the principal argument in favour of this date is extremely weak. It is said that the fact of the Ceylonese era being used as an era for practical purposes speaks in favour of its correctness. This may be true with regard to the

[269] Ancient Sanskrit Liturature, p. 243.

times after the reign of Aśoka. In historical times, any era, however fabulous its beginning, will be practically useful; but no conclusion can be drawn from this, its later use, as to the correctness of its beginning. As a conventional era, that of Ceylon may be retained, but until new evidence can be brought forward to substantiate the authenticity of the early history of Buddhism, as told by the Ceylonese priests, it would be rash to use the dates of the Southern Buddhists as a corrective standard for those of the Northern Buddhists or of the Brahmans."

And, towards the close of his inquiry, he expresses himself thus (p. 298):—"At the time of Aśoka's inauguration, 218 years had elapsed since the conventional date of the death of Buddha. Hence if we translate the language of Buddhist chronology into that of Greek chronology, Buddha was really supposed to have died 477 B.C. and not 543 B.C. Again, at the time of Chandragupta's accession, 162 years were believed to have elapsed since the conventional date of Buddha's death. Hence Buddha was supposed to have died 315 + 162 = 477 B.C."

In quoting these two passages, I show at once that Professor Müller attaches no faith to the tradition which concerns the date of Buddha's death, but that he attaches faith to that which places Aśoka 218, and Chandragupta 162, years after that event. But if tradition is to be believed in one portion of the history connected with the rise and progress of the Buddhist faith, why not in another, and in all? The arguments which are good for the one case will equally apply to the other; and if tradition be wrong in fixing Buddha's death at 543 B.C., we must also reject it when giving the dates 162 and 218, and the sum total will then have no quantities out of which it can be produced. And this objection would seem to derive additional force from the very words of Professor Müller just quoted; for he says himself that the argument in favour of the date 543 B.C., so far as it is founded on the practical use made of this date, "may be true with regard to the times after the reign of Aśoka." But 218 after Buddha's death, is the date of Aśoka himself, and 162 that of Chandragupta, who preceded that king. Both, consequently, would, in Professor Müller's opinion, deserve the same amount of belief as the date of Buddha's death itself.

The grounds on which Professor Müller differs from Professor Lassen have been fully discussed by him, as already observed; but as the essentials of this discussion lie in a nutshell, they admit of being here stated in reference to the question which actually concerns us.

Both scholars assume—and so long as Greek chronology deserves any credit at all, they do so, I hold, without the possibility of a contradiction—that Chandragupta, who is Sandrocottus, reigned 315 B.C. Buddhistic tradition, however, says that he lived 162 years after Buddha's death, which means that if this event took place 543 B.C., he reigned 381 B.C. But since 315 must be right, and 381 must be wrong, either Buddha's death occurred 477 B.C., or Chandragupta lived 66 years later than Hindu traditions allows him to live, viz., 228 years after 543 B.C. Lassen decides in favour of the latter alternative, no doubt, by saying to himself that since there is an error of 66 years, it was more likely committed by tradition in remembering the duration of the reign of kings who preceded Chandragupta, than in recording an event that was engrossing the national mind, and much more important to the national feeling and interest than an exact chronicle of by-gone, and some of them insignificant, kings. Müller prefers the precise tradition of 162 years, and therefore arrives at 477 B.C. as the date of Buddha's death.

Let us return, after this statement, to the events which Patanjali tells us occurred in his time, and confront them with the opinions of the two scholars named.

If Nágárjuna lived 400 years after Buddha's death, his date, according to Professor Lassen's conclusions, would be 143,—or, if he lived 500 years after this event, 43 years B.C. Again, his date, according to Professor Müller's conclusions, would be 77 B.C., or 23 after Christ. But I must mention, too, that Professor Lassen, on the ground occupied by him, supposes a further mistake of 66 years in the tradition which places Nágárjuna 500 years after Buddha's death, and that he thus also advocates the date of the founder of the Mádhyamikas as 23 years after Christ.[270] Now, since the sect which was founded by Nágárjuna existed not only simultaneously with, but after, him, that event which was contemporaneous with Patanjali and the Mádhyamikas, "*the siege of Ayodhyá by the Yavana*" must have occurred within or *below* the circle of these dates. The latter alternative, however, is again checked by the date of Abhimanyu, who reigned about 60 years after Christ; for we know from the chronicle of Kashmir that he introduced into his country the Commentary of Patanjali, which must consequently have been in existence during his reign.

In other words, the extreme points within which this historical event must have fallen, are the years 143 before, and 60 after Christ; and as in the time of Abhimanyu the Great Commentary had already suffered much, according to the report of Rájataranginí, it is necessary to limit even the latter date by, at least, several years.

Yet the word "*Yavana*" carries with it another corrective of this uncertainty. According to the researches of Professor Lassen it is impossible to doubt that *within this period*, viz., between 143 before and 60 after Christ, this word Yavana can only apply to the Græco-Indian kings, nine of whom reigned from 160 to 85 B.C.[271] And if we examine the exploits of these kings, we find that there is but one of whom it can be assumed that he, in his conquests of Indian territory, came as far as Ayodhyá. It is *Menandros*, of whom so early a writer as Strabo reports that he extended his conquests as far as the Jumna river, and of whom one coin has actually been found at Mathurá. He reigned, according to Lassen's researches, more than twenty years, from about 144 B.C.[272]

If then this inference be correct, Patanjali must have *written his commentary* on the Várttika to Páṇini III. 2, 111, between 140 and 120 B.C.; and this is the only date in the *ancient* literature of India which, in my belief, rests on more than mere hypothesis.

---

[270] Indische Alterthumskunde, vol. II. p. 412, 413.

[271] Ibid. vol. II., p. 322.

[272] Ibid. vol. II. p. 328.

But it has also the merit of giving that "new evidence" which Professor Müller requires for a corroboration of the chronology of Ceylon. For none of the fluctuating dates I have mentioned will allow us to look upon Menandros and the Mádhyamikas as contemporaries, except the date 143, which was the extreme limit of the date of Nágárjuna's life. And since, on the basis of tradition, this date again becomes impossible,—unless we claim amongst those alleged, 543 for the time of Buddha's death, and 400 years for the succession of Nágárjuna,—Patanjali's Great Commentary becomes invaluable also in this respect, and more especially to those who are concerned in Buddhist chronology.

Of the lineage of Patanjali all the knowledge I possess is that the name of his mother was *Goṇiká*.[273] It occurs in the last words of Patanjali on a Káriká to Páṇini. Of more importance, however, is the information he gives us of his having resided temporarily in *Kashmir*,[274] for this circumstance throws some light on the interest which certain kings of this country took in the preservation of the Great Commentary.

His birthplace must have been situated in the East of India, for he calls himself *Gonardíya*;[275] and this word is given by the Káśiká in order to exemplify names of places in the East. Patan-

---

[273] Patanjali, after quoting the Kárikás to I. 4, 51 gives *his own opinion*, and concludes with these words (MS. E.I.H. No. 171), उभयथा गोणिकापुत्रः .—Nágojibhaṭṭa: गोणिकापुत्रो भाष्यकार इत्याहुः (thus MS. E.I.H. 349; the MS. 1208 गौणिकापु॰).

[274] III.2, 114: विभाषा साकाङ्क्षे.—Patanjali: किमुदाहरणम्। अभिजानासि देवदत्त कश्मीरेषु वत्स्यामः। तत्र सक्तून्पास्यामः। अभिजानासि देवदत्त कश्मीरानगच्छाम। तत्र सक्तूनपिबाम। भवेत्। पूर्वं परमाकाङ्क्षतीति साकाङ्क्षं स्यात्। परं तु कथं साकाङ्क्षम्। परमपि साकाङ्क्षम्। अस्त्यस्मिन्नाकाङ्क्षेत्यतः साकाङ्क्षम्.—Kátyáyana: विभाषा साकाङ्क्षे सर्वत्र.—Patanjali: विभाषा साकाङ्क्षे सर्वत्रेति वक्तव्यम्। क्व सर्वत्र। यदि चायदि च॥ यदि तावत्। अभिजानासि देवदत्त यत्कश्मीरान्गमिष्यामः। यत्कश्मीरानगच्छाम। यत्तत्रौदनं भोक्ष्यामहे। यत्तत्रौदनमभुञ्ज्महि॥ अयदि। अभिजानासि देवदत्त कश्मीरान्गमिष्यामः। कश्मीरानगच्छाम। तत्रौदनं भोक्ष्यामहे। तत्रौदनमभुञ्ज्महि॥

[275] Patanjali to I. 1, 21, v. 2 (of the Calcutta edition; p. 412 ed. Ballantyne): गोनर्दीयस्त्वाह etc.—Kaiyyaṭa: भाष्यकारस्त्वाह etc.—Nágojibhaṭṭa: गोनर्दीयपदं व्याचष्टे। भाष्यकार इति.—It is on this authority that the word *Gonardíya* has found a place amongst the epithets of Patanjali in Hemachandra's Glossary.

jali's birthplace had therefore the name of *Gonarda*.[276] But that he is one of the eastern grammarians is borne out also by other evidence. Kaiyyaṭa calls him on several occasions *Áchárya-déśíya*.[277] If we interpreted this word according to Páṇini's rules V. 3, 67 and 68, it would mean "an unaccomplished teacher;" but as there is not the slightest reason for assuming that Kaiyyaṭa intended any irony or blame when he applied this epithet to Patanjali, it is necessary to render the word by the teacher "who belongs to the country of the Áchárya." Now, since Kaiyyaṭa also distinctly contrasts *áchárya*, as the author of the Várttikas, with *áchâryadéśíya*, the latter epithet can only imply that Patanjali was a countryman of Kátyáyana. Kátyáyana, however, as Professor Weber has shown by very good arguments, is one of the eastern school; Kaiyyaṭa, therefore, must have looked upon Patanjali also as belonging to it.

Another proof is afforded by a passage in the comment of Bhaṭṭo-

---

[276] The Káśiká to I. 1, 75: एङ् प्राचां देशे, gives the instances: एणीपचनीयः। गोनर्दीयः। भोजकटीयः। गोनरीयः (thus MS. E.I.H. 2440; the MS. 829, which is generally more incorrect than the former, has the plurals instead of the singulars: °°याः). Professor Lassen (Indische Alterthumskunde, vol. II., p. 484) assumes a connection between Gonardíya and Gonarda, the name of a king of Kashmir; but I believe that my explanation is supported by the whole evidence combined.

[277] For instance, Patanjali to VI. 1, 158, v. 1 (of the Calcutta edition) writes: ...... यदि पुनरयमधिकारो विज्ञायेत etc.; and Kaiyyaṭa introduces his comment on these words with: आचार्यदेशीय आह यदि पुनरिति and so on, in a similar manner, on other occasions. An instance, however, which will better bear out my conclusion, is afforded by the combined Várttika-Káriká of Kátyáyana (see note 114), and the commentaries to V. 2, 39. After the words of the Sútra, Patanjali says: किमर्थं परिमाण इत्युच्यते। न प्रमाण इति वर्तते। एवं तर्हि सिद्धे सति यत्परिमाणग्रहणं करोति तज्ज्ञापयत्याचार्यः। अन्यत्प्रमाणमन्यत्परिमाणमिति; then follows the first Várttika (or first portion of the Káriká of Kátyáyana): डावतावर्थवैशेष्यान्निर्देशः पृथगुच्यते, which again is followed by the further comment of Patanjali. In reference to this passage, Kaiyyaṭa expresses himself in this way: किमर्थमिति। प्रमाणपरिमाणशब्दयोरेकार्थत्वं मत्वा प्रश्नः। न प्रमाण इति वर्तत इति। काक्वा नञः प्रयोगाद्वर्तत एवेत्यर्थः। अथवानेकार्थत्वान्निपातनानां ननुशब्दस्यार्थे नशब्दो वर्तते। आचार्यदेशीय आह। एवं तर्हीति। आचार्य आह डाताविति etc. He therefore contrasts *áchárya*, who is the author of the Várttika डातावर्थ°, with *ácháryadeśíya*, who is Patanjali

jidíkshita on the Phiṭsútras which I have quoted above.[278] For when this grammarian tells us that the *eastern* grammarians attribute the accent in question of *saha* to Páṇini's rule VI. 3, 78, we find that it is *Patanjali* himself who gives us this information and without any intimation of his having obtained it from other authorities.

I conclude these few remarks on our great teacher with an account which *Bhartṛihari* gives of the early history of the Mahábháshya. It is of considerable interest, inasmuch as we learn from it that there was a party of grammarians who preferred to it the Sangraha (of Vyáḍi), and still more so, as it informs us, that Patanjali's Commentary was founded on this great grammatical work of the relative of Páṇini. The passage in question occurs at the end of the second chapter of *Bhartṛihari's Vákyapadíya*, and, in reference to the word *Bháshya*, which immediately precedes it, makes the following statement: [279]

"After Patanjali had obtained the aid of [*or* had come to] grammarians who had mastered the new sciences more or less [*literally*: in their full extent and in their abridged form], and after he had

---

[278] See page 218.

[279] The text of this passage belongs to the MS. No. 954 in the Library of the Home Government for India, which in a few days will have ceased to be the Library of the East India House. It bears on its outer leaf the corrupt title वाक्यपदीव्याकरण, but at the end of its three chapters the words: इति श्रीभर्तृहरिकृते वाक्यप्रदीपे....... प्रथममकांडः (*sic.*); ...... द्वितीयं कांडम्; ..... तृतीयः कांडः.—I call it Vákyapadíya, because, the MS. in question being very incorrect, I cannot give its reading any preference to the reading वाक्यपदीय by which this work is several times quoted in the portion of the Mahábháshya edited by Dr. Ballantyne. For, the identity of both results from a comparison I have made between the passages quoted in this highly valuable edition and the MS. before me. It is right, however, to mention that the second chapter of the work concludes in this MS. in the following manner: भर्तृहरिकृते वाक्यप्रदीपे द्वितीयं काण्डम्। समाप्ता वाक्यपरदीपका, where the reading वाक्यपरदीपका, when corrected to °पिका, admits of a sense, but suggests also the conjecture that it may be a corruption of वाक्यप्रदीपिका. I now transcribe the passage in question literally, in order to show the condition of the MS., and also to enable the reader to supply better conjectures than I may have made; but some conjectures I have been compelled to make in order to impart a meaning to a few very desperate lines. These conjectures are added in [ ]. After the words एकशेषेण निर्देशो भाष्य एव प्रदर्शितः, which are

acquired the *Sangraha* [of Vyáḍi], he, the Guru, well versed in the sacred sciences, connected all the original nyáyas in the Mahábháshya. But when it was discovered that this Commentary could not be fathomed on account of its depth, and that the minds of those who were not quite accomplished floated, as it were, on the surface, in consequence of their levity, those grammarians who liked dry reasoning, Vaiji, Saubhava, and Haryaksha, who were partisans of the Sangraha, cut in pieces the book of the Ṛishi [Patanjali]. That grammatical document [*or* manuscript of the Mahábháshya], which was obtained from the pupils of Patanjali, then remained for some time preserved in one copy only amongst the inhabitants of the Dekhan. Chandra, again, and other grammarians, who went after the original of the Bháshya, obtained this document from Parvata, and converted it into many books [*that is to say*, took many copies of it], and my Guru, who thoroughly knew the ways of logical discussion and his own Darśana, taught me the compendium of this grammatical work."[280]

---

connected with the subject treated of in the second chapter, *Bhartṛihari* continues : प्रायेण संचेपतुचीनच्यविद्यापरिग्रहान् [प्रायेण संचेपतस्य नव्यविद्यापरिग्रहान्] । संप्राप्य वैयाकरणान् संग्रहे सुपागते [संप्राप्य वैयाकरणान्संग्रहे समुपागते] । क्षते थ पातंजलिना गुरुणा तीर्थदर्शिना [क्षते ऽथ पतञ्जलिना°°] । सर्व्वेषां न्यायवीजानां महाभाष्ये निबंधने [निबन्धने] । अलब्धगाधे गांभार्यौदुत्तान इव मौष्ठवान् [अलब्धगाधे गाम्भीर्यादुत्तान इव सौष्ठवात्] । तस्मिन्नक्षतबुद्धीनां नैवावास्थितनिश्चयः [. . . . नैवावस्थि°] । वैजिसौभवहर्यचैः [°चैः] शुष्कतर्कानुसारिभिः । आर्षे निलाविते ग्रंथे [ग्रन्थे] संग्रहप्रतिकंचुकैः [°कैः] । यः पातंजलिशिष्येभ्यो भ्रष्टो व्याकरणागमः [यः पतञ्जलिशिष्येभ्यो ऽभ्यष्टो°°] । कालेन दाचिणात्येषु ग्रंथमात्रे [ग्रन्थ°] व्यवस्थितः । पर्वतादागमं लब्ध्वा भाष्यवीजानुसारिभिः । स नीतो बहुशाखत्वं चंद्राचार्यादिभिः [चन्द्रा°°] पुनः । न्यायप्रस्थानमार्गांस्तानभ्यस्य ष्वं [स्वं] च दर्शनम् । प्रणीतो गुरुणास्माकंमयमागमसंग्रहः [प्रणीतो गुरुणास्माकमय°°]. The subsequent words, which conclude the second chapter, concern the subject-matter of the work, not the history of the Mahábháshya.

280 This passage will now aid us also in a correct understanding of the interesting verse from the Rájataranginí, which has been quoted, but blighted, by Dr. Boehtlingk in the version he gives of it (vol. II. p. xv and xvi). This verse reads in the Calcutta edition of the latter work (I. 176): चन्द्राचार्यादिभिर्लब्धादेशं तस्मात्तदागमम् । प्रवर्तितं महाभाष्यं स्वं च व्याकरणं कृतम् . Mr. Troyer, in his edition, substitutes for the latter words

A perusal of the foregoing pages will probably have raised the question in the reader's mind, why I have attached an investigation of the place which Páṇini holds in Sanskrit literature to the text of the present ritual work?

I will answer this question without reserve. It is because I hold that an inquiry like this was greatly needed in *the present critical position of Sanskrit philology;* and that no ancient text, whatever its nature, should remain any longer,—much less should come for a first time,—before the public without pre-supposing in its readers a full knowledge of the literary problems I have here been dealing with. For whether my views meet with approval or not, I have, I believe, at least shown that the mode in which these problems have hitherto been discussed, is neither adequate to the difficulties with which they are beset, nor to their bearings on the scientific treatment of the Sanskrit language itself.

No one, indeed, can be more alive than I am myself to the conviction of how much may be added, in the way of detail, to the facts I have adduced; for, however imperfect my present attempt and my own knowledge may be, I still could have largely increased the foregoing inquiry with materials taken from the

---

चन्द्रव्याकरणं कृतम्. Both readings are alike good, for they convey the same sense; and the correction लब्ध्वादेशं for लब्धादेशं, as proposed by Dr. Boehtlingk, is no doubt also good. But the double mistake he has committed in this single verse consists first in giving to आगम the sense of 'coming,' whereas the passage from the *Vákyapadíya* proves that it must there have the sense of "a written document or *manuscript;*" and secondly, in arbitrarily assigning to the causal of प्रवृत् the sense of "*introducing*" in its European figurative sense, which the causal of प्रवृत् never has. The verse in question would therefore not mean, as Dr. Boehtlingk translates it: "After the teacher Chandra and others had received from him (the King Abhimanyu) the order to come there (or to him), they introduced the Mahábháshya and composed a grammar of their own"—but: "After Chandra and the other grammarians had received from him (the King Abhimanyu) the order, *they established a text of the Mahábháshya, such as it could be established by means of his MS. of this work* (*literally:* they established a Mahábháshya which possessed his—the King's—grammatical document, *or*, after they had received from him *the order and his M.S., they established the text of the Mahábháshya*) and composed their own grammars." For we know now that Chandra and the other grammarians of King Abhimanyu obtained such an *ágama* or manuscript of the Mahábháshya from Parvata, and according to the corresponding verse of the Rájataranginí, it becomes probable that this MS. came into possession of Abhimanyu.

Bráhmana-, Upanishad-, and the philosophical literature. I have not done more than allude to the contents of Páṇini's Grammar and I have scarcely hinted at the linguistic results which may be derived from a comparison between Kátyáyana and Patanjali, on the one side, and the recent grammatical literature (which is represented by the Káśiká, the Siddhánta-kaumudí with its Prauḍhamanoramá, and the commentators on the Dhátupáṭha and the artificial poetry), on the other. For my present object was merely to convey a sense of the inherent difficulties of the questions I have been speaking of, and while tracing the outlines of my own results, to offer so much evidence as was strictly necessary for supporting them with substantial proof.

Before, however, I add some words on the *practical object* I had in view in entering upon this investigation, both justice and fairness require me to avow that the immediate *impulse* which led to the present attempt was due to Max Müller's Ancient Sanskrit Literature. So great is my reluctance to the public discussion of literary questions, if such a discussion requires a considerable amount of controversy, and so averse am I to raising an edifice of my own, if, in order to do so, I am compelled to damage structures already in existence, that this feeling would in all probability have prevented me now, as it has done hitherto, from giving public expression to my views, had it not been for the importance I attach to Müller's work. This work reached me, as already mentioned, when the first pages of this Preface were completed; and it was the new material it brought to light, and the systematic and finished form by which its author imparted to his theories a high degree of plausibility, which induced me to oppose to it the facts I have here made known and the results I have drawn from them.

And, as everyone has his own way of paying compliments, this avowal is the compliment which *I* pay to Professor Müller's work. For as I myself care but little for blame, and much less for praise, so long as I consider that I have fulfilled my duty, I could not but assume that he, too, would much prefer, to uninstructive panegyrics which anyone could inflict on him, such dissent as I have here expressed, as it can only lead either to confirmation of the opinions he has advanced, or, by correcting them, to an attainment of that scientific truth for which both of us are earnestly labouring.[281]

And now I shall speak my mind as to the necessity I felt for writing these pages in view of *the present critical position of Sanskrit philology.*

The study of Sanskrit commenced, not with the beginning but with the end of Sanskrit literature. It could not have done otherwise, since it had to discover, as it were, the rudiments of the language itself, and even the most necessary meanings of the most necessary words. We have all been thankful—and our gratitude will never suffer through forgetfulness—for the great advantage we have derived from an insight into the Mahábhárata, the Rámáyaṇa, the Hitopadeśa, the Sakuntalá, through the labours of those great scholars, Sir William Jones, Schlegel, Bopp, and others, who are before the mind's eye of every Sanskritist. But the time of pleasure had to give way to a time of more serious research. The plays and fables are delightful in themselves, but they do not satisfy the great interests of Sanskrit philology. Our attention is now engrossed, and rightly so, by the study of grammar, of philosophy, and, above all, of that literature of ancient India, which—very vaguely and, in some respects, wrongly, but at all events conveniently—goes by the name of the Vaidik literature. With the commencement of that study we always associate in our minds such great names as those of a Colebrooke, a Wilson, a Burnouf, a Lassen, the courageous and ingenious pioneers who opened the path on which we are now travelling with greater safety and ease.

But whence was it that they were able to unfold to us the first secrets of ancient Hindu religion, of ancient Hindu philosophy and

---

[281] Almost simultaneously with the last proof sheets I received the second edition of Professor Müller's "History of Sanskrit Literature." As both editions entirely correspond in their typographical arrangement, and I believe, in their contents also, the quotations here made from the first edition, will be found on the same pages of the second.

scientific research? It was through the aid of the commentaries, in the first rank of which stands that of Patanjali; in the second the works of those master minds, the most prominent of whom are Śankara and Mádhava-Sáyaṇa. Without the vast information these commentators have disclosed to us,—without their method of explaining the obscurest texts,—in one word, without their scholarship, we should still stand at the outer doors of Hindu antiquity.

But to understand the value of these great commentators and exegetes, we must bear in mind the two essentials which have given them the vast influence which they have acquired. The first is the *traditional*, and the second the *grammatical*, element that pervades their works.

The whole religious life of ancient India is based on tradition. *Śruti*, or Veda, was revealed to the Ṛishis of the Vaidik hymns. Next to it comes *Smṛiti*, or tradition, which is based on the revealed texts, and which is authoritative only in so far as it is in accordance with them. Hence a commentator like *Mádhava-Sáyaṇa*, for instance, considered it as incumbent on him to prove that he had not merely mastered the Vaidik texts, but the Mímánsá also, one portion of which is devoted to this question of the relation between Śruti- and Smṛiti- works. It is known that he is one of the principal writers on the Mímánsá philosophy. Without tradition, the whole religious development of India would be a shadow without reality, a phantom too vague to be grasped by the mind. Tradition tells us through the voice of the commentators, who re-echo the voice of their ancestors, how the nation, from immemorial times, understood the sacred texts, what inferences they drew from them, what influence they allowed them to exercise on their religious, philosophical, ethical,—in a word, on their national, development. And this is the real, the practical, and therefore the truly scientific interest they have for us; for all other interest is founded on theories devoid of substance and proof, is *imaginary* and *phantastical*.

But it would be utterly erroneous to assume that a scholar like Sáyaṇa, or even a copy of him, like Mahídhara, contented himself with being the mouth-piece of his predecessors or ancestors. They not only record the sense of the Vaidik texts and the sense of the words of which these texts consist, but they endeavour to show that the interpretations which they give are *consistent with the grammatical requirements of the language itself.* And this proof, which they give whenever there is the slightest necessity for it—and in the beginning of their exegesis, even when there is no apparent necessity for it, merely in order to impress on the reader the basis on which they stand,—this proof is the great grammatical element in these commentatorial works.

In short, these great Hindu commentators do not merely explain the meanings of words, but they justify them, or endeavour to justify them, on the ground of *the grammar of* PÁṆINI, *the Várttikas of* KÁTYÁYANA, *and the Mahábháshya of* PATANJALI.

Let us recall, then, the position we have vindicated for Páṇini and Kátyáyana in the ancient literature, and consider how far this ground is solid ground, and how far, and when, we may feel justified in attaching a doubt to the decisions of so great a scholar as Sáyana.

We have seen that within the whole range of Sanskrit literature, so far as it is known to us, only the Saṁhitás of the Ṛig- Sáma- and Black- Yajurveda, and among individual authors, only the exegete Yáska preceded *Páṇini,*—that the whole bulk of the remaining known literature is posterior to his eight grammatical books. We have seen, moreover, that *Kátyáyana* knew the Vájasaneyi-Saṁhitá and the Śátápaṭha-bráhmaṇa, and that, in consequence, we may assign to him, without fear of contradiction, a knowledge of the principal other Bráhmaṇas known to us, and probably of the Atharvaveda also.

Such being the case, we must then conclude that Sáyaṇa was right in assenting to Patanjali, who, throughout his Introduction to Páṇini, shows that Páṇini's Grammar was written in strict reference to the Vaidik Saṁhitás, which, as I may now contend, were the three principal Saṁhitás. He is right, too, in appealing, wherever there is need, to the Várttikas of Kátyáyana; for the latter endorses the rules of Páṇini when he does not criticise them, and completes them wherever he thinks that Páṇini has omitted to notice a fact. And since we have found that the Ṛik-Prátiśákhya fulfils the same object as these Várttikas, viz. that of completing the rules of Páṇini, and that Kátyáyana's Prátiśákhya, which is later than that attributed to Śaunaka, preceded his own Várttikas, we must grant, too, that he was right in availing himself of the assistance of those works, all of which are prior to the Várttikas of Kátyáyana.

That analogous conclusions apply to the Ishṭis of Pantanjali and to the Phiṭsútras of Śántana is obvious.

But it is from *the chronological position* in which these works stand to one another that we may feel justified in occasionally criticising the decisions of Sáyaṇa. Without a knowledge of it, or at least without a serious and conscientious attempt at obtaining it, all criticisms on Sáyaṇa lay themselves open to the reproach of mere arbitrariness and superficiality.

For, if the results here maintained be adopted, good and substantial reasons—which, however, would first have to be proved—might allow us to doubt the correctness of a decision of Sáyaṇa: if, for instance, he rejected an interpretation of a word that would follow from a rule of Páṇini, on the sole ground that Kátyáyana did not agree with Páṇini; or, if he interpreted a word merely on the basis of a Várttika of Kátyáyana, we might fairly question his decision, if we saw reason to apply to the case a rule of Páṇini, perhaps not criticised by Kátyáyana. Again, if we had substantial reasons for doing so, we might oppose our views to those of Sáyaṇa when he justified a meaning by the aid of the Phiṭsútras alone, though these Sútras may be at variance with Páṇini, for we should say that these Sútras, "when compared to Páṇini, are as if they were made to-day."

In short, the greater the distance becomes between a Veda and the grammarian who appended to it his notes, the more we shall have a plausible ground for looking forward, in preference to him, to that grammarian who stood nearer to the fountain head. Even Páṇini would cease to be our ultimate refuge, if we found Yáska opposed to him; and Gárgya, Śákalya, Śákaṭáyana, or the other predecessors of Páṇini, would deserve more serious consideration than himself, if we were able to see that they maintained a sense of a Vaidik word which is differently rendered by him.

This is the critical process to which I hold that the commentaries of Sáyaṇa may be subjected, should it be deemed necessary to differ from them.

These remarks apply, of course, only to the Saṁhitás which preceded Páṇini; for, as to the literature which was posterior to him, Kátyáyana becomes necessarily our first exegetic authority, and after him comes Patanjali. I need not go further, for I have sufficiently explained the method I advocate, and the exception I take to that dogmatical schooling of these ancient authorities, which, so far from taking the trouble of conscientiously ascertaining their *relative chronological position in the literature* merely exhibits, at every step, its own want of scholarship.

I must now, though reluctantly, take a glance at the manner in which the Vaidik texts, more especially their groundwork, the Saṁhitás, nay, how the whole Sanskrit literature itself, is dealt with by those who profess to be our teachers and our authorities. And still more reluctantly must I advert to one work especially, which, above all others, has set itself up as our teacher and authority—the great Sanskrit Dictionary published by the Russian Imperial Academy.

The principles on which this work deals with the Vaidik texts is expressed by Professor Roth in his preface to it, in the following words:[282] "Therefore we do not believe, as H. H. Wilson does,[283] that Sâjaṇa better understood the expressions of the Veda than any European exegete, and that we have nothing to do but repeat what he says; on the contrary, we believe that a conscientious European exegete may understand the Veda much more correctly and better than Sâjaṇa. We do not consider it the [our] immediate purpose to obtain that understanding of the Veda which was current in

---

[282] "Sanskrit-Wörterbuch herausgegeben von der Kaiserlichen Akademie der Wissenschaften, bearbeitet von Otto Boehtlingk und Rudolph Roth." Preface, p. v.

[283] Note of Professor Roth; "Ṛig-Veda-Sanhitá. A collection of ancient Hindu hymns, etc. Translated from the original Sanskrit. By H. H. Wilson. London, 1850. I. p. 25."

India some centuries ago,[284] but we search for the meaning which the poets themselves gave to their songs and phrases. We consequently hold that the writings of Sâjaṇa and of the other commentators must not be au authority to the exegete, but merely one of the means of which he has to avail himself in the accomplishment of his task, which certainly is difficult, and not to be effected at a first attempt, nor by a single individual. On this account we have much regretted that tho meritorious edition of the commentary on the Ṛigveda, by Müller, is not yet more advanced.[285]

"We have, therefore, endeavoured to take the road which is prescribed by philology: to elicit the sense of the toxts by putting together all the passages which are kindred either in regard to their words or their sense; a road which is slow and tedious, and which, indeed, has not been trodden before, either by the commentators or the translators. Our double lot has, therefore, been that of exegetes as well as lexicographers. The purely etymological proceeding, as it must be followed up by those who endeavour to guess the sense of a word, without having before them the ten or twenty other passages in which the same word recurs, cannot possibly lead to a correct result."[286]

It would be but common fairness to allow these words of

---

[284] Note of Professor Roth: "Wilson, a.a. O. II. p. xxiii." But the page quoted by Professor Roth does not contain one single word in reference to the passage which it apparently intends to bear out.

[285] The first part of the Dictionary of Professor Roth and Dr. Boehtlingk was issued in 1852; the first volume, which is prefaced by the words quoted, in 1855; the first and second part of the second volume in 1856; the third part of the same volume in 1857. Professor Müller's first volume of the Ṛigveda appeared in 1849, the second in 1854, the third in 1856.

[286] In reference to this view of Professor Roth, of the relation of the Hindu commentators to the Vaidik hymns, Professor Weber says in the "Zeitschrift der Deutschen morgenländischen Gesellschaft," vol. X. p. 575: "Allem was darüber gesagt ist schliessen wir uns auf das Unbedingteste and Entschiedenste an;" *i.e.* "To all that has been said on it [on this relation, in the Preface of the Wörterbuch] we (*sic.*, does Professor Weber speak in his own name or in that of the whole Dictionary-company?) assent in the most unconditional and in the most peremptory manner."

Professor Roth to be followed by the entire preface which the lamented Professor Wilson has prefixed to the second volume of his invaluable translation of the Ṛigveda: the more so, as his views have been unscrupulously distorted in the statement here quoted; for though his views are supposed to be refuted by this passage, they could not shine brighter, in genuine modesty, in true scholarship, and in thorough common sense, than when placed by the side of this passage, which I will not qualify but analyze. But as I could not easily quote some twenty pages from Professor Wilson's excellent work, and as I should scarcely do justice to the manes of that distinguished man if I did not allow him to give his full answer, I must leave it to the reader to obtain for himself that contrast to which I here advert.

If, then, we analyze the ideas and principles presented in the passage just quoted, they come before us to the following effect:—

(1) Sáyaṇa gives us only that sense of the Veda which was current in India some centuries ago.

(2) Professor Roth is far more able than Sáyaṇa and other commentators to give us the correct sense of the Veda.

(3) For, he can put together some ten or twenty passages referring to the same word, whereas Sáyaṇa and other commentators could not do this, but had to guess its sense.

(4) He is above confining himself to the purely etymological process, which is that of these commentators.

(5) His object is not to understand the sense of the Veda which was current in India a few centuries back, but to know the meaning which the authors of the hymns themselves gave to their songs and phrases.

(6) Professor Roth is a conscientious European exegete.

Before I give my Várttikas to these six Sútras, which define the exegetical position of the Sanskrit Wörterbuch, I must observe that I am compelled, by the very nature of this Preface, to leave them in a similar position to that occupied by the Preface of Professor Roth itself. His Dictionary is the test of the assertions he makes. The test of my remarks would be a critical review of his

Dictionary. *I hereby promise him that my earliest leisure will be devoted to this review, especially as my materials for it are not only collected and ready, but so abundant as to give me a difficulty of choice.* But my present answer must, of necessity, deal with his generalities only in general terms.

(1) Sáyaṇa or the other commentators give us, he intimates, only that sense of the Veda which was current in India some centuries ago.

A bolder statement I defy any scholar to have met with in any book. Sáyaṇa incessantly refers to Yáska. All his explanations show that he stands on the ground of the *oldest legends and traditions*—of such traditions, moreover, as have no connection whatever with the creed of those sects which represent the degenerated Hindu faith in his time; yet Professor Roth ventures to tell the public at large, authoritatively and *without a particle of evidence*, that these legends and his version of the Ṛigveda are but some centuries old. I believe, and every learned Hindu will hold with me, that Sáyaṇa would have been hooted out of the country where he lived, had he dared to commit the imposition implied in this charge, on King Bukka, his lord, or on his countrymen. I hope, however, that Professor Roth will free himself from the reproach expressed by these words, by showing on what authority he gives such a piece of information, which is either all important for Europe as well as for India, or places him in the most ridiculous position that is conceivable.

(2) When an author tells us that he is able to do that which another author cannot do, we are entitled to infer that he is, at all events, thoroughly acquainted with all that this author has done. I am well aware,—I may add through the pleasure of personal remembrances,—that Professor Roth passed some time at Paris, and some little time in London also, when collecting his valuable materials for his edition of Yáska's Nirukta. Only in London and at Oxford, and, in some small measure, at Paris also, are the materials requisite for studying the Vaidik commentaries of Sáyaṇa obtainable in Europe. Does Professor Roth intimate by the statement above quoted, that his stay in these cities enabled him to

study and copy, for his lexicographical purposes—then not thought of—all the works of Sáyaṇa, or that he, at Tübingen, is in possession of all those materials, the knowledge of which alone could entitle him to claim credit for a statement like that which he has ventured to make? But I need not pause for his reply. He regrets, as we have read, that "the meritorious edition by Müller, of Sáyaṇa's Commentary was not further advanced" when he closed the first volume of his Dictionary. Thus, when he began his "exegetical" work, he was only acquainted with the Commentary of Sáyaṇa as far as the first Ashṭaka; and when he wrote these lines, he may *perhaps* have known its continuation up to a portion of the third Ashṭaka—in other words, no more than a third of Sáyaṇa's whole Commentary on the Ṛigveda; and yet he ventures to speak of the whole Commentary of Sáyaṇa, and to say that he can do what Sáyaṇa was unable to perform? But we almost forget that the words of Professor Roth are by no means restricted to the Ṛigveda Commentary alone; it embraces the commentaries to *all the Saṁhitás*. And here I am once more compelled to ask—Does he assert that he knew, when he wrote these words, Sáyaṇa's Commentary on the Sámaveda and the Taittiríya-Saṁhitá, or even Sáyaṇa's Commentary on the Śatapatha-Bráhmaṇa? For surely he would not think of calling that Sáyaṇa's Commentary to this Bráhmaṇa, which has been presented to us extracted and mangled in Professor Weber's edition of the Śatapatha-Bráhmaṇa. And yet he has the courage to pass this sweeping condemnation on all these gigantic labours of the Hindu mind, while ignorant of all but the merest fraction of them?

(3) Professor Roth no doubt enjoys a great advantage when he can put together some ten or twenty passages for examining the sense of a word which occurs in them; but I beg to submit that there are many instances in which a Vaidik word does not occur twenty or ten, nor yet five or four times, in the Saṁhitás. How does he, then, muster his ten or twenty passages, when, nevertheless, he rejects the interpretation of Sáyaṇa? For it would seem that in such a case the "guessing" of Sáyaṇa, as he calls it, stands on as good ground as his own. But the assurance with

which he implies that Sáyaṇa was not capable of mustering ten or twenty passages which are at the command of Professor Roth, presupposes, indeed, in his readers a degree of imbecile credulity which is, no doubt, a happy condition of mind for those who rejoice in it, and perhaps that best fitted for reading assertions like these, but which may not be quite so universal as he seems to assume. Mádhava-Sáyaṇa, one of the profoundest scholars of India, the exegete of all the three Vedas, as he tells us himself,—of the most important Bráhmaṇas and a Kalpa work,—Mádhava, the renowned Mímánsist—he, the great grammarian, who wrote the learned commentary on the Sanskrit radicals, who shows at every step that he has Páṇini and Kátyáyana at his fingers' ends,—Mádhava, who, on account of his gigantic learning and his deep sense of religion, lives in the legends of India as an incarnation of Śiva,—in short, the great Mádhava, we are told, had not the proficiency of combining in his mind or otherwise those ten or twenty passages of *his own Veda*, which Professor Roth has the powerful advantage of bringing together by means of his little memoranda!

(4) "The purely etymological proceeding," he says, "as it must be followed up by those who endeavour to guess the sense of a word, cannot possibly lead to a correct result."

By these words he compels us to infer, in the first instance, that the meanings which Sáyaṇa gives to Vaidik words are purely etymological; for when he illustrates his statement in a subsequent passage, by alleging such instances as "power, sacrifice, food, wisdom, to go, to move," it is clear that his sweeping assertion cannot be considered as merely embracing these six words, which, in his opinion, sometimes admit of a modification of sense. Just as he cancels the whole spirit of Sáyaṇa's commentary, he tells us with the utmost assurance that the whole commentary of Sáyaṇa is purely etymological. There is, I admit, an advantage in boldness; for if you tell a man while gazing on the noon-day sun that he is actually in the darkness of mid-night, he may probably prefer to doubt the evidence of his senses rather than venture to reject the extraordinary news you bring him. I open at random the three quartos of Max Müller; I look at every page once, twice, many times. No doubt Professor Roth must be quite correct, for my eyes are blind. But, since I suffer under this sudden disability, I may at least be permitted to quote that very page from Wilson's preface to the second volume of his translation which Professor Roth quotes above, as if it bore out his statement concerning the "some centuries."

"As many instances of this elliptical construction," we read there, "have been given in the notes of both this and the former volume, a few additional instances will here be sufficient:—thus (p. 301, v. 9) we have the 'grandson of the waters has ascended above the crooked ——;' 'the broad and golden —— spread around.' What would the European scholar do here without the Scholiast? He might, perhaps, suspect that the term crooked, curved, or bent, or, as here explained, crooked-going, tortuous, might apply *to the clouds*; but he would hesitate as to what he should attach the other epithets to, and the original author alone could say with confidence that he meant '*rivers*,' which thenceforward became the traditional and admitted explanation, and is, accordingly, so supplied by the Scholiast."

Thus, has Sáyaṇa stopped at the etymological sense of "crooked-going," or of "gold-coloured?"

But, in the second instance, though Professor Roth, of course, possesses all the knowledge which these ignorant Hindu commentators were wanting in, he implies by his words, that the meanings he creates in overstepping the purely etymological process, nevertheless rest on it. Since my reply on this point would have to enter into detail, and since I have promised to give *much* detail in the review which will be the commentary on my present remarks, I will merely here state that I know of no work which has come before the public with such unmeasured pretensions of scholarship and critical ingenuity as this Wörterbuch, and which has, at the same time, laid itself open to such serious reproaches of the *profoundest grammatical ignorance*. And, as an etymological proceeding without a thorough knowledge of grammar is etymological thimblerig, I may at least here prepare the reader who takes an interest in such plays, for a performance on the most magnificent scale. Or to speak in plain prose, I shall prove to Professor Roth by means of those same authorities which I have so often impressed on the reader's mind, that his Dictionary has created many meanings without the slightest regard to the grammatical properties of the word, and, in consequence, that his Vaidik exegesis in all these numerous and important instances has just that worth which a Veda revealed by Professor Roth has in comparison with the Veda of India.

(5) The object of Professor Roth is "not to understand the Veda such as it was current in India a few centuries back, but to know the meaning which the poets themselves gave to their songs and phrases."

This is unquestionably most important intelligence. Sáyaṇa gives us the sense of the Veda, such as it was handed down to him —not indeed a few centuries ago, but from generation to generation immemorial—yet within this Kaliyuga, I suppose. Nágojibhaṭṭa, again, we have seen,[287] tells us that in the various destructions of the world, the Ṛishis received new revelations from the divinity, which did not affect the eternal sense of the Veda, but merely the order of its words. But now we learn, for the first time, that Professor Roth has received a revelation at Tübingen, which as yet has neither reached the banks of the Thames nor those of the Ganges. He is going to tell us the sense which the original Ṛishis gave to their songs and phrases, at a period of Hindu antiquity, which is as much within scientific reach as the commencement of the world itself. Who will not hail this revelation which dispenses with grammar and all that sort of thing, and who will not believe in it?

And yet I have one word more to add in regard to Professor Roth's "direct communication with the Hindu divinities." He does not attach any importance, as he tells us, and abundantly proves, to that Veda which is the foundation of the religious

[287] See note 171.

development of India; for that Veda is the Veda of Sáyaṇa, and that Veda, too, which alone concerns us uninspired mortals. But even Professor Roth himself professes, in another part of his Preface, the greatest respect for the native commentaries on theological and ritual books. There he emphatically exclaims (p. iv.): "Indeed, for one of the two portions of the Vaidik literature, for the works on theology and the rites, we cannot wish for any better guides than these commentators, accurate in every respect, who follow their texts word for word, who are untiring in repeating everywhere that which they have already said whenever there could arise even the appearance of a misunderstanding, and who sometimes seem rather to have written for us foreigners than for their priestly pupils grown up under these ideas and impressions." How far his work has embodied the conviction expressed in these words which could not have been expressed with greater truth, I shall have to examine in my review. But I fear that these eloquent words must have escaped his memory in the midst of all the revelations he received. On the Ṛigveda we have already exchanged our views; but not yet on the other Vedas. These are avowedly extracted, or "milked," as the Hindus say, from the Ṛik. That the Sámaveda is entirely taken from it, we have proof,[283] and that the metrical part of the Yajus likewise rests on a version of it, no one will dispute. But both these Vedas are professedly not poetical anthologies. They are purely and simply ritual Vedas, and therefore belong—not only from a Hindu, but from an European point of view also—to the ritual literature. At the Jyotishṭoma, for instance, the priest chants, not the Ṛig-, but the Sáma- veda hymns, though the verses are apparently the same in both. At the Aśwamedha he mutters, not the Ṛig-, but the Yajur- veda hymns. This means that, whatever may have been the "original sense" of such Ṛigveda verses, in their Sáma- or Yajur- veda arrangement which, in numerous instances, has brought Ṛigveda verses of different hymns or books, into a new hymn,—the Sámaveda hymns and the Yajurveda hymns have only a value so far as their immediate

[283] See note 75.

object, the sacrifice, is concerned. Hence even the most transcendental and the most inspired critic has nothing to do in these two Vedas with "the sense which the poets themselves gave to their songs and phrases," he has simply to deal with that sense which religion or superstition imparted to these verses, in order to adapt them to the imaginary effects of the sacrifice. As little as it would be our immediate object, when assisting at the horse-sacrifice, to ask what is the etymology of horse? or as little as it would be seasonable to trace the linguistic origin of a cannon-ball when it whistles past our ears, just so little have we to impart "the original sense"—I mean that sense revealed to Professor Roth—to the verses of the Sáma- and Yajur- veda, even when we are "both exegetes and lexicographers." And yet I shall give abundant proof that, even on these two Vedas, Professor Roth has had revelations of a most astounding character.

(6) "We believe that a conscientious European exegete might understand much more correctly and thoroughly the sense of the Veda than Sáyaṇa." I should encroach on the judgment of the reader, if I ventured upon any remarks on this latter statement after what I have already said.

In now adverting to the treatment which the scientific and classical literature has received in the Sanskrit Wörterbuch, I need only say that this department is in the hands of Dr. Boehtlingk. In saying this, I have said everything. After such an expression of opinion, it will, of course, be my duty to show, at the earliest opportunity, that Dr. Boehtlingk is incapable of understanding even easy rules of Páṇini, much less those of Kátyáyana, and still less is he capable of making use of them in the understanding of classical texts. The errors in his department of the Dictionary are so numerous and of so *peculiar* a kind—yet, on the whole, so thoroughly in accordance with the specimens I have adduced from his Commentary on Páṇini, that it will fill every serious Sanskritist with dismay, when he calculates the mischievous influence which they must exercise on the study of Sanskrit philology.

On the present occasion, I must confine myself to these preliminary remarks, or at best content myself with adverting to one other passage in the Preface to the Wörterbuch. It runs thus (p. vii.): "In order to facilitate the finding (of the words) for those who will make use of our Dictionary, we have to make the following observation. We have banished completely from the verbal roots the vowels *ṛi*, *ṛí*, and *ḷṛi*, as well as the diphthongs at their end; for *ṛi* at the end of nominal bases we have substituted *ar*."

Thus the Wörterbuch does not give, like the Hindu grammarians, a radical *kṛi*, but it gives *kar*; not *klṛip*, but *kalp*; not *jṛí*, but *jar*; not *pitṛi*, but *pitar*; not *dátṛi*, but *dátar*, etc. Now, this Dictionary professes to be a Dictionary of the Sanskrit language, not of some imaginary idiom which may be current at Tübingen or St. Petersburg. One would therefore have supposed that the public was entitled to expect some reason for these changes,—to know by what scientific considerations the authors of this work were guided, when they took upon themselves the responsibility of thus *abolishing the radicals and nominal bases taught by Páṇini and subsequent grammarians.* But, in the fullness of its authority, this work does not condescend to meet any such demand: it simply cancels whole categories of grammatical forms, and those of the greatest importance and comprehensiveness. Whether I am right or not in inferring the arguments which were in the minds of its writers when they presumed thus dictatorially to impose their theories on Sanskrit philology, may be a matter of doubt, but my supposition is that this innovation is founded on researches belonging to comparative philology. It cannot rest on mere Sanskritic ground, since all the forms they have cancelled really occur as thematic forms in the Sanskrit language itself. Thus, to use the same instances: *kṛi* occurs in *kṛi-ta*, *klṛip* in *klṛip-ta*, *pitṛi* in *pitṛi-bhis*, *dátṛi* in *dátṛi-bhis*; and as to *jṛí*,—*jírṇa* can only follow from *jṛí*, not from *jar*. Their reasons, founded on comparative grammar, must then be these: that some bases in *ṛi* are represented in Latin by *er* and *or*, and in Greek by ερ, ηρ, and ορ; *pitṛi-*, for instance corresponds with Latin *pater-*, Greek πατερ-, *dátṛi* with *datôr-* and δοτηρ, etc.

Now even supposing that such an argument had any weight at all in a dictionary of the Sanskrit language, the application made of it would be incongruous. For though *pitar-* corresponds with *pater-*, *dátăr-* does not correspond with *datôr-*; its representative would have had to assume the form *dátár-*. The whole theory therefore, on the supposition I have made, would practically break down, and the innovation would be inconsistent with itself as well as at variance with comparative results.

But can such an argument be at all admissible? If a Sanskrit Dictionary were concerned, like Professor Bopp's Comparative Grammar, with eliciting from the forms of sister languages the forms of that parental language whence they may be supposed to have derived their origin, it would be defensible to give the forms of that parental language itself. But a Sanskrit Dictionary can have no such aim. Its immediate object is the actual language which it has to deal with. It must take it such as it is, in its very deviations from the germ whence it has sprung. Its function is not to *correct* the real historical language, but to record its facts; and in doing so, to collect the materials which are to be used as well by the special as by the comparative philologer. And in so far as its direct purpose is concerned, this is all it has to do. Any observations it may choose to attach to the real historical facts may of course be given; but it shows an utter want of judgment, to say nothing else, when it presumes to alter the very forms of the language itself.

I may venture also to add a few other observations on the forms thus cancelled in this "conscientious" Sanskrit Wörterbuch. It is known that many Sanskrit bases, and amongst them the bases in *ṛi*, undergo various changes in their declension and otherwise. *Pitṛi*, for instance, becomes *pitar*, in the accusative *pitar-am*, while it remains as it is, in the instrumental *pitṛi-bhis; dadhi* remains so in *dadhi-bhis*, but its base is *dadhan*, with the loss of *a*, in *dadhn-á; asthi* forms *asthi-bhis*, but *asthn-á*. Now there exists a paper of Dr. Boehtlingk on the Sanskrit declension; but whoever reads it must fancy that the language either played dice with these and similar forms, or is undergoing some remarkable cure. He talks of bases "which are strengthened as well as weakened," of bases "which are only strengthened," and of bases "which are only weakened." Why language should nurse and physic its bases, as we learn from him, no one will understand. But a sadder spectacle of the treatment of a language or of linguistic facts than is presented in that paper, it is not possible to imagine. The *reasoning* there is exactly on the same level as the reasoning in the "*edition*" of Páṇini, of which so many specimens have now become familiar to the reader of this Preface. Exactly the same game at dice or the same vagaries of disease reign in this Dictionary: thus, though the declension phenomena of *akshi*, *asthi*, *dadhi*, are identical, and acknowledged to be so by Dr. Boehtlingk himself in his paper on Declension (§ 69), in his Dictionary he discourses on the first noun under *akshan*, and again under *akshi*, while, on the contrary, if we look to *asthi*, he refers us to *asthan*; and if under his guidance we now go to *dadhan*, he requests us to seek for information under *dadhi*.

But since the linguistic hospital, which is opened in the works of Dr. Boehtlingk, is fortunately not the place in which the Sanskrit language lies,—for this language has had a sound and rational development—it will be obvious to everyone who happens not to be placed under Dr. Boehtlingk's treatment, that there must be reasons for this variety of thematic forms which constitute the declension of the same base. And as there are such reasons, the immediate consequence is that we cannot decide, *a priori*, whether *kartar* be the "strengthened" form of the original base *kartṛi*, or "*kartṛi*" the "weakened" form of the original base *kartar*. Such a decision can only be taken after a thorough investigation of the influences which cause this change, of the nature of these influences themselves, and of the manner in which they work. And as language does not sit down like a school-boy, first to master the declensions, then the conjugations, and so on,—but as the influences I am speaking of are influences which are traceable in the whole organism of language itself, it is obvious, too, that such an investigation would not restrict itself to the phenomena of declension merely, but extend over the whole area of the linguistic development.

When I myself assumed the responsibility of writing a Sanskrit

Dictionary, I considered it incumbent on me to devote a most serious research to those little facts which, as we have seen, are despatched in five lines by our modern "exegetes and lexicographers." Six years have elapsed since I laid my first results, so far as lexicographical purposes are concerned, before the London Philological Society, and it is only the desire of giving them in their full bearing and extent that has hitherto delayed their presentation through the press. Now, it is questions like these—questions which, in my mind, ought to be decided with the very utmost circumspection, and which cannot be decided without very laborious research,—it is questions like these which have been trifled with in this Wörterbuch in the most unwarranted manner. It does not show that it even understands the important problem which lies in its path; it briefly informs the reader that it has cancelled all the bases in *ṛi*, *ṛí*, *lṛi*, etc. and bids him—good-bye.

Patanjali,—let us for a moment repose after this dreary journey through the Wörterbuch,—Patanjali on one occasion thus speaks to us: "When a man is in want of a pot, he goes to the house of a potter and says: (potter), make me a pot, for I have occasion for it. But (surely) a man who wants to employ words will not go, like the other, to the house of a grammarian and say: (grammarian) make me some words, I have occasion for them."[289] Happy Patanjali! blessed in thy ignorance! Here we have potters who can fabricate—and not simply meanings of words, but the very words themselves, and words, too, which you laboured so earnestly, so learnedly, so conscientiously, to save from the pottering of all future "exegetes and lexicographers." Nay, we have, too, men who can repair to these potters, and call for, and admire, their linguistic wares!

When in the presence of these extraordinary facts, which, unhappily, must silence the expression of all the acknowledgment—

[289] Mahábháshya Introduction (p. 52 ed. Ballantyne): घटेन कार्यं करिष्यन्कुम्भकारकुलं गत्वाह कुरु घटं कार्यमनेन करिष्यामीति । न तद्वच्छब्दान्प्रयुयुक्षमाणो वैयाकरणकुलं गत्वाह कुरु शब्दान्प्रयोक्ष्य इति

nay, of *all the admiration I really entertain for the immense industry* displayed in this Wörterbuch,—when with that deep sense which I entertain of the *duties* and of the *influence* of a Dictionary, and, in the actual condition of Sanskrit philology, more especially of a Sanskrit Dictionary,—when with these convictions, the earnestness of which, I believe, is proved throughout the whole of this investigation,—when—I will not conceal it—under the indignation and grief I felt in seeing a magnificent opportunity thrown away —as I shall abundantly prove that it has been thrown away in the case of the Sanskrit Wörterbuch,—when under these impressions I uttered a warning, five years ago, in the "Westminster Review," a warning contained in three pages, there ensued a spectacle which, during my literary experience, stands without a parallel.

Professor Kuhn,—not indeed a proficient in Sanskrit, nor having ever obtained any position amongst those who are earnestly engaged in Sanskrit philology, but—as a contributor of quotations to the Wörterbuch, launched against me the grossest personal invectives which ever disgraced the pages of a scientific journal. As sound, literary argument was beyond his range, he indemnified himself, and gratified his employers, by calling me names. Unfortunately for him his abuse could produce no effect upon me, for the following reason. Amongst the few critical remarks for which I had room, in the "Westminster Review," there was one which illustrated the manner in which Professor Roth had translated a ritual text. This remark was expressly written for Professor Kuhn's amusement as well as that of Professor Weber. For, at a small Sanskritic party which used to meet every fortnight at Berlin during the years 1847 and 1848, I had shown them the Commentary of Mádhava on a Mímánsá work, the editing of which I had then commenced, this Commentary being the proof of the assertion I had made in 1855 in the "Westminster Review." Professor Kuhn heartily enjoyed, at one of these meetings, the precious translation of the passage in question from the Aitareya-Bráhmaṇa, given by Professor Roth, in the preface (pp. xxxviii-xli) to his edition of the Nirukta. Nay more, so anxious was he to possess its substance, before it was published, that in my presence he took notes from the Commentary I am speaking of,—viz., that of the Jaiminíya-nyáya-málá-vistara. And in the invectives to which I am alluding, he does not deny the existence, nor yet the value, of my evidence, but he words his defence of Professor Roth in so studied and so ambiguous a manner as to create in the minds of his readers a suspicion as to the reliability of the statement I had made, though its truth was perfectly familiar to him.[290]

Now, a writer who has recourse to such weapons as these has laid aside those qualities which are necessary to retain a man within the pale of a gentlemanly consideration, and his language, however

---

[290] In possession of the information I am speaking of he writes as follows: "Der letzteren stellt der verfasser eine bedeutend abweichende des commentators gegenüber, da er aber nur the commentator und nicht all the commentators oder almost all the commentators sagt, so ist stark zu vermuthen, dass noch andere commentare existiren, welche den text wahrscheinlich in der Rothschen weise erklären werden; dabei nehme ich natürlich den Fall als ganz unmöglich an dass der verfasser (der nichts als die übersetzung giebt) etwa selber den commentar missverstanden haben sollte" *i.e.* "In opposition to the latter [viz. the version of Professor Roth of the passage in question] the reviewer gives another of the commentator which is considerably different from it; but as he merely says the commentator, and not all the commentators or almost all the commentators, there is a strong probability (*sic!*) that there are other commentators who probably (*sic!*) explain the text in the manner of Professor Roth. *With these words I assume it, as a matter of course, to be plainly impossible that the reviewer who gives nothing but the translation, should have misunderstood the commentary.*"—That Professor Kuhn had not the slightest doubt as to who was the author of the review in question, even he will not venture to deny; for he has stated the fact in letters and in conversation. But even if he had any such doubt, he knew that I *was* in possession of the commentary, for he had taken notes from it. If, then, the ascertainment of truth alone had been the object of his remark, as the public might expect of an author, and if his notes were not complete enough—which, however, I do not admit—the time required for a letter to me and an answer back, that is to say, five days, would have sufficed to give him all the information he could wish for. It requires, however, no statement from me that his object was not to inform his readers of the *true* state of the facts; it better suited his purpose to insinuate a doubt as to the correctness of the translation I had given. Indeed, Professor Weber,—who, as I have mentioned, possessed the same knowledge and had obtained it in the same manner, as Professor Kuhn, settles the point. Though he did not remain behind his colleague in scurrilous abuse, and though, in speaking of my translation, he shows his usual levity, he, nevertheless, plainly and openly acknowledges the full reliability of the translation I had given, on the ground of the Mímánsá work. He says: "er kennt nämlich offenbar nur die systematisirende Erklärung der Mîmânsâschule, etc.;" *i.e.* "the reviewer obviously knows only the sys-

gross, and adapted to his own character, can not touch one who does not stand on the same level with him.

A similar exhibition took place, I am grieved to say, in a journal of high standing and respectability, in the "Zeitschrift der Deutschen morgenländischen Gesellschaft." It is a salutary practice in the journals of all learned societies, not to admit into their pages scurrilous or libellous attacks against individuals; and this practice has been rigidly adhered to in the journal to which I am adverting, with the single exception of my own case. Professor Weber, who is also in the service of the Wörterbuch, suddenly attacked me in this journal,—not, indeed, with anything that deserves the name of argument, but with personal abuse of the coarsest kind. Five years have passed by, and at last a sense of justice, which does credit to himself, has re-entered the mind of Professor Weber; and in the last number of the "Zeitschrift," which reached me when this Preface was nearly completed in print, he has fully and honestly retracted all his former calumnies; still, however, combining with the compliments he now pays to my Dictionary, the remark that my views of the Wörterbuch show a perfect derangement of my mental faculties, since I do not reject the authority of the greatest Hindu scholars as freely and easily as the work he so assiduously praises.

I am certainly in no humour to find fault with the opinion which he entertains of my mental condition, for it will always give me a sense of safety and satisfaction when I find him bearing testimony to the vast distance which separates our respective modes of studying, and judging of, Hindu antiquity. But, as he has chosen to connect his opinion of me with a piece of scientific advice, this seems a fitting opportunity for illustrating, *once more*, his competence for passing a judgment on matters of Sanskrit philology.

He says: "Another, third, essential difference [between the Wörterbuch and my Dictionary;—I, myself, trust and hope that

tematizing explanation of the Mímánsá school, etc." Thus, whatever be his opinion of this explanation, he speaks of it from *personal knowledge*, and admits that my account of it was correct and not liable of doubt.

attentive readers will find many more *essential* differences than three between the two works] consists . . . . . . in [my] not marking the accent of the words."

In his opinion, therefore, the Wörterbuch *does* mark the accent. Now, setting aside the very considerable quantity of words which are not marked with any accent in this work, the instances in which it is marked there seem to satisfy the scientific requirements of Professor Weber. I ought, then, to mention, in the first place, that in all such cases the accent is put there over the word without any further explanatory remark. But I have shown that there are *periods* in the known Sanskrit *grammatical* literature;—that the first period is that of Páṇini, the second that of the Ṛik-Prátiśákhya, the third (perhaps fourth) that of Kátyáyana, the fourth (or perhaps fifth) that of the Phiṭsútras; and that, as we continue our descent, we have the period of the Káśiká, Kaumudí, etc. Thus, marking an accent without saying to what period such an accent belongs, *and up to what period it remains in force*, is giving evidence of the greatest superficiality,—it is showing, too, that the difficulties of the question we are speaking of, were not at all understood. As regards myself, I believe I might have entered into such detail, since I have considered it my duty to turn my researches into this channel also; and if the scientific and liberal disposition of my publishers could have disregarded all material considerations in the case—and could have added still more to the great concessions of space which they have already made me, to their own material detriment, since the publication of the third part of my Dictionary,—I should have been able not only to give quotations *historically*, which the Wörterbuch, notwithstanding Professor Weber's bold assertion—I will not attach to it another epithet—does not give, and to discuss the matters of accent,—but even to re-edit, little by little, the Commentary to the Śatapatha-bráhmaṇa, as I have already done on several occasions, in order to prove the meanings I give, and which meanings no one could gather from the text as edited by Professor Weber. No doubt I might have done all this had I been perfectly independent of material considerations. But, at all events, had I, in marking the accents, contented myself with that which satisfies completely

Professor Weber's scientific wants, my Dictionary would have become as superficial as the book which he has qualified as a work of the "most scrupulous conscientiousness."[291]

In adverting to Professor Weber's advice, I may as well quote one more instance from his impartial illustration of the difference between the two Dictionaries. It concerns the meanings of words in both. But as I have adverted to this subject before, I need now only say, that he describes the Wörterbuch in the following manner.

"It represents," he writes in the 'Zeitschrift' "the principle of reality in contrast with the historical proceeding of interpretation [which he says, is mine], by allowing the words to interpret themselves through the chronological order (*sic. ! !*) of the quotations added to them, and through these quotations themselves, the authors always quoting the native exegesis also, but merely as a secondary means."[292] And of myself he says, that my "orthodox faith in the authority of native exegetes and grammarians" is something perfectly bewildering; indeed, it presupposes the "derangement of my mental faculties."[293]

It requires all the levity, on the one hand, and all the hardihood, on the other, which are the mixed essentials of Professor

---

[291] In his libel he says; "dieses Werk des bewundernswerthesten Fleisses und der sorgsamsten Gewissenhaftigkeit."

[292] "Zeitschrift der Deutschen morgenländischen Geselschaft," vol. XIV. p. 755: Die Haupttendenz, die er [*i.e*, myself] hiebei verfolgt, besteht eben—und dies markirt einen ferneren Haupt-Unterschied von *Boehtlingk-Roth*—darin, dass er es sich zur Aufgabe macht, die Ansichten der einheimischen Erklärer und Sprachforscher zur prägnanten Geltun gzu bringen, während *Boehtlingk-Roth* diesem historischen Erklärungsverfahren gegenüber das sachliche Princip vertreten, die Wörter nämlich durch zeitliche Ordnung der betreffenden Stellen und durch eben diese Stellen selbst sich uumittelbar erklären zu lassen, wobei sie die einheimische Exegese zwar auch stets anführen, aber doch nur als sekundäres Hülfsmittel betrachten."

[293] *Ibid.* p. 756: "Persönliche Beziehungen haben uns seitdem überzengt, dass der Verfasser bei Abfassung jenes, für uns allerdings immer noch geradezu unbegreiflichen, Angriffes auf das Petersburger Wörterbuch dennoch wirklich im völligen Rechte zu sein glaubte. Es setzt dies freilich nach unserer Ansicht eine Art Verirrung des Denkvermögens voraus, wie sie auf sonstigen Gebieten nicht selten ist, hier aber in der That be-

Weber's literary productions, to allow an author to come before the public with statements like these. As for myself, any one may see that there are various instances in my Dictionary where *I plainly state that I differ from the etymologies or meanings given by the native authorities.* These cases of dissent are certainly not frequent, because a serious investigation of the native grammarians led me in most instances to appreciate their scholarship and the correctness of its results; nor have I the presumption to supersede them with mere vague and vapouring doubts; but that I have ground sometimes to differ even from the views of a Kátyáyana or a Patanjali, Professor Weber will have probably learned now from the foregoing pages, though he might have learned it already from my Sanskrit Dictionary, which he is good enough to favour with his advice. His statement, therefore, concerning my blind belief in all that the Hindu scholars say, is founded on that same overweening superficiality which, as we have seen, leads him to assume the responsibility of schooling Kátyáyana, whom he does not even understand.

But as to his description of the Wörterbuch, I know not how to qualify it without using language which could only be used by a Professor Kuhn. It is one of my most serious reproaches against the Sanskrit Wörterbuch, that it not only creates its own meanings, and by applying them to the most important documents of the literature, *practically falsifies antiquity itself*, but deliberately, and nearly constantly, *suppresses* all the information we may derive from the native commentaries. I have intimated that the great injury they have thus done to the due appreciation of Hindu antiquity, would have been lessened had they at least, as common sense would suggest, given by the side of their own inventions the meanings of Sáyaṇa or Mahídhara or of other authorities, and thus enabled the student to judge for himself. Yet while the reader may peruse their Dictionary page after page,

---

fremdet, eine orthodoxe Hingabe nämlich an die Auktorität der indischen Exegeten und Grammatiker, wie sie uns gegenüber diesen Haarspaltern, die bei aller Spitzfindigkeit denn doch gar oft jenen verblendeten Leitern gleichen, die da Mücken seigen und Kameele verschlucken, sehr wenig am Platze scheint."

sheet after sheet, without discovering a trace of these celebrated Vaidik commentaries, while the exceptions to this rule are so rare as to become almost equal to zero, Professor Weber dares to speculate on the credulity of the public in telling it that this Dictionary ALWAYS *quotes the native exegesis !*

When a cause has sunk so low as to have such defenders and require such means of defence as these, when its own contributors and its noisiest bards have no other praise to chant than such as this, it seems almost cruel to aggravate its agony by exposure or reproach.

But the spectacle exhibited on the appearance of my remarks in the "Westminster Review" does not end here, and its epilogue is perhaps even more remarkable than the play itself. In the same "Zeitschrift der Deutschen Morgenländischen Gesellschaft" there followed another act, which is so characteristic of the system pursued in these attacks, that it deserves a special word, merely for the sake of curiosity. An individual whose sole connection with Sanskrit studies consists in handing Sanskrit books to those who can read them, a literary naught, wholly unknown, but assuming the airs of a quantity, because it has figures before it that prompt it on,—this personage who, as his own friends informed me, is perfectly ignorant of Sanskrit, he, too, was allowed to give *his* opinion on the Wörterbuch. I need not say that, in the absence of all knowledge of the subject itself, it merely vented itself in the most grandiloquent praise; but, to complete its mission, there was added to this fustian, language, in reference to me, such as certainly was never heard, or admitted, before in a respectable journal of any society. He need not tremble lest I should drag him into notoriety. Nature has not fitted him for estimating the ridicule to which he exposed himself in becoming the mouthpiece and the puppet of his instigators. If he deserve anything, it is not chastisement, but pity, and the mercy of a charitable concealment of his name.

And all this outrage, not only against the interests of science and truth, but against the commonest rules of decency, was committed in a series of planned attacks, because I had warned the Sanskrit Wörterbuch of the danger of its career, and had not expressed any admiration for Dr. Boehtlingk's competence or scholarship.

It was then, and on the ground of observations I had made in regard to his want of proficiency, that I was called upon by one of his men, not only to have respect for the "editor of Páṇini," but even for the *hidden* reasons he might have had in foisting on the public his blunders of every kind. The "editor of Páṇini" was held before me as a symbol of scientific accomplishment; his "edition of Páṇini" was the great thunderbolt which was hurled at my head by one of these little Jupiters.[294]

For eighteen years I have been thoroughly acquainted with the value and the character of this "*edition*" of Páṇini; and yet, from a natural disinclination to antagonize with those who have similar pursuits to my own, I have refrained from apprizing the public of the knowledge I possessed in regard to it. Twelve years have passed since I explained my views on this book personally and

---

[294] Prof. Kuhn writes in his "Zeitschrift" the following words: "Wo der alten grammatiker nicht erwähnung gethan ist, geschah es nur deshalb nicht, weil ihre etymologie mit der der verfasser übereinstimmte; stellten dieselben aber ohne jene zu erwähnen eigne etymologieen auf, so liess sich doch wohl voraussetzen, dass der herausgeber des Pâṇini, des Vopadeva u. s. w. dazu seine wohlerwogenen gründe gehabt haben mochte;" *i.e.*, "where no mention was made [in the Wörterbuch] of the old grammarians, this was done because their etymology agreed with that of the authors of the Wörterbuch; but when the latter made their own etymologies without naming the former, it was but natural to suppose that the editor of Pâṇini, of Vopadeva, etc. had his own well-weighed reasons for doing so." The real nature of this statement of Professor Kuhn will become apparent from the review which I shall give of the Wörterbuch. But his information, as it is, is not without great interest. Thus, according to this quotationer of the Wörterbuch, its authors pass over in silence the labours of the Hindu grammarians—not because they see reason to adopt the results of the latter—but because these labours have the honour to meet with the approval of Dr. Boehtlingk and Company. Under any circumstances, however, it was but natural and rational to pass them over in silence and *to suppress the information they give,*—for, either they have the honour of being approved of by Dr. Boehtlingk, or "the editor of Páṇini" had probably his well-weighed reasons for not agreeing with them; and, in the latter case, there was of course not the slightest necessity that he should give or even allude to these important reasons. The passage quoted would alone quite suffice to illustrate the character of the fulsome adulation and of the puffing advertisements—written, of course, exclusively by the employed scribes of the Wörterbuch—which for some years have made their appearance in some literary journals of Germany, and have not only misled, but imposed upon, the public unacquainted or imperfectly acquainted with Sanskrit philology.

privately, at our Sanksritic parties, to Professors Weber and Kuhn; and the longer the interval passed over, the less I felt disposed to speak of it in print. At present, after twenty years' time, I should have considered it almost unfair to rake up the past; for a sense of charity would have told me that the moral and intellectual condition of a man may undergo considerable changes during so considerable a period of his life. But in spite of my strongest desire to combine the defence of literary interests with a regard for all the circumstances connected with the author himself, I am not allowed to remain silent, in consequence of the insolent provocations which I receive. Not only does Dr. Boehtlingk quote *his* "edition" of Páṇini, in his Wörterbuch,—not only does he thus force it, as it were, on us by the references he makes to it, and acknowledge it to this day as his legitimate child,—but one of his own scribes, well acquainted with the judgment I should pass on it, has the hardihood to defy me publicly, by bidding me have respect for the "editor of Páṇini."

Well, then, I have taken up this impertinent challenge. In so far as my present subject permitted, I have illustrated the nature of this immaculate book; and it will not be my fault if I am compelled to recur to it again.

Still a provocation of this kind alone would have as little induced me to take up my pen now as it did heretofore; but when I see the public told authoritatively, yet without any proof, that Sáyaṇa teaches that understanding of the Veda which was current in India no longer than a few centuries ago;—when I see that the most distinguished and the most learned Hindu scholars and divines—the most valuable, and sometimes the only, source of all our knowledge of ancient India—are scorned in theory, mutilated in print, and, as a consequence, set aside in the interpretation of Vaidik texts;—when I see that the most ancient records of Hindu antiquity are interpreted to the European public in such a manner as to cease to be that which they are;—when a clique of Sanskritists of this description vapours about giving us the sense of the Veda as it existed at the commencement of Hindu antiquity;—when I see that the very forms of the language are falsified, and that it is made a principle to slur the grammar of Páṇini, and to ridicule those who lay stress on it;—when I see that one of the highest grammatical authorities of India is schooled for a "want of practice and skill," while this censure is passed without even an understanding of the work to which it refers;—when I see that they who emphatically claim the epithet of "veracious,"[295] make statements which are the very reverse of truth;—and when I consider that this method of studying Sanskrit philology is pursued by those whose words apparently derive weight and influence from the professorial position they hold;—and when, moreover, departing from rule and precedent, I see the journal of a distinguished Society—I fully hope through an oversight of its editor, though a Professor of Sanskrit himself—permanently made the channel for propagating such statements as I have described and qualified, together with these scandalous personal attacks and calumnies,—then I hold that it would be a want of courage and a dereliction of duty, if I did not make a stand against these SATURNALIA OF SANSKRIT PHILOLOGY.

On this ground I have raised my voice, however feeble and solitary for the moment, and have endeavoured to examine the competence of those who set themselves up as our masters and authorities. On this ground I have endeavoured to vindicate for Páṇini the position he holds in Sanskrit literature, and the position he ought to hold amongst honest Sanskrit philologers.

---

[295] Professor Weber in his libel: "einen um so peinlicheren Eindruck muss es auf jeden wahrheitsliebenden Forscher machen, etc.;" *i.e.* "the more painful is the impression which must be produced on every veracious scholar" [viz., if he reads my opinion on the Wörterbuch, which opinion,—I must add, so far from having changed, is even more emphatic now than it was when I wrote the review which has so much displeased him].

STEPHEN AUSTIN, PRINTER, HERTFORD.